R for
Everyone

R for Everyone

Advanced Analytics
and Graphics

Jared P. Lander

✦Addison-Wesley

Upper Saddle River, NJ • Boston • Indianapolis • San Francisco
New York • Toronto • Montreal • London • Munich • Paris • Madrid
Capetown • Sydney • Tokyo • Singapore • Mexico City

For information about buying this title in bulk quantities, or for special sales opportunities (which may include electronic versions; custom cover designs; and content particular to your business, training goals, marketing focus, or branding interests), please contact our corporate sales department at corpsales@pearsoned.com or (800) 382-3419.

For government sales inquiries, please contact governmentsales@pearsoned.com.

For questions about sales outside the U.S., please contact international@pearsoned.com.

Visit us on the Web: informit.com/aw

Library of Congress Cataloging-in-Publication Data

Lander, Jared P.
  R for everyone / Jared P. Lander.
     pages   cm
Includes bibliographical references.
ISBN-13: 978-0-321-88803-7 (alk. paper)
ISBN-10: 0-321-88803-0 (alk. paper)
 1. R (Computer program language) 2. Scripting languages (Computer science) 3. Statistics—Data processing. 4. Statistics—Graphic methods—Data processing. 5. Computer simulation. I. Title.
  QA76.73.R3L36 2014
  005.13–dc23   2013027407

ISBN-13: 978-0-321-88803-7
ISBN-10: 0-321-88803-0
Text printed in the United States on recycled paper at RR Donnelley in Crawfordsville, Indiana.
Fourth printing, January 2015

❖

To my mother and father

❖

Contents

Foreword

R has had tremendous growth in popularity over the last three years. Based on that, you'd think that it was a new, up-and-coming language. But surprisingly, R has been around since 1993. Why the sudden uptick in popularity? The somewhat obvious answer seems to be the emergence of data science as a career and a field of study. But the underpinnings of data science have been around for many decades. Statistics, linear algebra, operations research, artificial intelligence, and machine learning all contribute parts to the tools that a modern data scientist uses. R, more than most languages, has been built to make most of these tools only a single function call away.

That's why I'm very excited to have this book as one of the first in the Addison-Wesley Data and Analytics Series. R is indispensable for many data science tasks. Many algorithms useful for prediction and analysis can be accessed through only a few lines of code, which makes it a great fit for solving modern data challenges. Data science as a field isn't just about math and statistics, and it isn't just about programming and infrastructure. This book provides a well-balanced introduction to the power and expressiveness of R and is aimed at a general audience.

I can't think of a better author to provide an introduction to R than Jared Lander. Jared and I first met through the New York City machine learning community in late 2009. Back then, the New York City data community was small enough to fit in a single conference room, and many of the other data meetups had yet to be formed. Over the last four years, Jared has been at the forefront of the emerging data science profession.

Through running the Open Statistical Programming Meetup, speaking at events, and teaching a course at Columbia on R, Jared has helped grow the community by educating programmers, data scientists, journalists, and statisticians alike. But Jared's expertise isn't limited to teaching. As an everyday practitioner, he puts these tools to use while consulting for clients big and small.

This book provides an introduction both to programming in R and to the various statistical methods and tools an everyday R programmer uses. Examples use publicly available datasets that Jared has helpfully cleaned and made accessible through his Web site. By using real data and setting up interesting problems, this book stays engaging to the end.

—*Paul Dix, Series Editor*

Preface

With the increasing prevalence of data in our daily lives, new and better tools are needed to analyze the deluge. Traditionally there have been two ends of the spectrum: lightweight, individual analysis using tools like Excel or SPSS and heavy duty, high-performance analysis built with C++ and the like. With the increasing strength of personal computers grew a middle ground that was both interactive and robust. Analysis done by an individual on his or her own computer in an exploratory fashion could quickly be transformed into something destined for a server, underpinning advanced business processes. This area is the domain of R, Python, and other scripted languages.

R, invented by Robert Gentleman and Ross Ihaka of the University of Auckland in 1993, grew out of S, which was invented by John Chambers at Bell Labs. It is a high-level language that was originally intended to be run interactively where the user runs a command, gets a result, and then runs another command. It has since evolved into a language that can also be embedded in systems and tackle complex problems.

In addition to transforming and analyzing data, R can produce amazing graphics and reports with ease. It is now being used as a full stack for data analysis, extracting and transforming data, fitting models, drawing inferences and making predictions, plotting and reporting results.

R's popularity has skyrocketed since the late 2000s, as it has stepped out of academia and into banking, marketing, pharmaceuticals, politics, genomics and many other fields. Its new users are often shifting from low-level, compiled languages like C++, other statistical packages such as SAS or SPSS, and from the 800-pound gorilla, Excel. This time period also saw a rapid surge in the number of add-on packages—libraries of prewritten code that extend R's functionality.

While R can sometimes be intimidating to beginners, especially for those without programming experience, I find that programming analysis, instead of pointing and clicking, soon becomes much easier, more convenient and more reliable. It is my goal to make that learning process easier and quicker.

This book lays out information in a way I wish I were taught when learning R in graduate school. Coming full circle, the content of this book was developed in conjuction with the data science course I teach at Columbia University. It is not meant to cover every minute detail of R, but rather the 20% of functionality needed to accomplish 80% of the work. The content is organized into self-contained chapters as follows.

Chapter 1, Getting R: Where to download R and how to install it. This deals with the varying operating systems and 32-bit versus 64-bit versions. It also gives advice on where to install R.

Chapter 2, The R Environment: An overview of using R, particularly from within RStudio. RStudio projects and Git integration are covered as is customizing and navigating RStudio.

Chapter 3, Packages: How to locate, install and load R packages.

Chapter 4, Basics of R: Using R for math. Variable types such as `numeric`, `character` and `Date` are detailed as are `vectors`. There is a brief introduction to calling functions and finding documentation on functions.

Chapter 5, Advanced Data Structures: The most powerful and commonly used data structure, `data.frames`, along with `matrices` and `lists`, are introduced.

Chapter 6, Reading Data into R: Before data can be analyzed it must be read into R. There are numerous ways to ingest data, including reading from CSVs and databases.

Chapter 7, Statistical Graphics: Graphics are a crucial part of preliminary data analysis and communicating results. R can make beautiful plots using its powerful plotting utilities. Base graphics and `ggplot2` are introduced and detailed here.

Chapter 8, Writing R Functions: Repeatable analysis is often made easier with user-defined functions. The structure, arguments and return rules are discussed.

Chapter 9, Control Statements: Controlling the flow of programs using `if`, `ifelse` and complex checks.

Chapter 10, Loops, the Un-R Way to Iterate: Iterating using `for` and `while` loops. While these are generally discouraged they are important to know.

Chapter 11, Group Manipulation: A better alternative to loops, vectorization does not quite iterate through data so much as operate on all elements at once. This is more efficient and is primarily performed with the `apply` functions and `plyr` package.

Chapter 12, Data Reshaping: Combining multiple datasets, whether by stacking or joining, is commonly necessary as is changing the shape of data. The `plyr` and `reshape2` packages offer good functions for accomplishing this in addition to base tools such as `rbind`, `cbind` and `merge`.

Chapter 13, Manipulating Strings: Most people do not associate character data with statistics but it is an important form of data. R provides numerous facilities for working with strings, including combining them and extracting information from within. Regular expressions are also detailed.

Chapter 14, Probability Distributions: A thorough look at the normal, binomial and Poisson distributions. The formulas and functions for many distributions are noted.

Chapter 15, Basic Statistics: These are the first statistics most people are taught, such as mean, standard deviation and t-tests.

Chapter 16, Linear Models: The most powerful and common tool in statistics, linear models are extensively detailed.

Chapter 17, Generalized Linear Models: Linear models are extended to include logistic and Poisson regression. Survival analysis is also covered.

Chapter 18, Model Diagnostics: Determining the quality of models and variable selection using residuals, AIC, cross-validation, the bootstrap and stepwise variable selection.

Chapter 19, Regularization and Shrinkage: Preventing overfitting using the Elastic Net and Bayesian methods.

Chapter 20, Nonlinear Models: When linear models are inappropriate, nonlinear models are a good solution. Nonlinear least squares, splines, generalized additive models, decision trees and random forests are discussed.

Chapter 21, Time Series and Autocorrelation: Methods for the analysis of univariate and multivariate time series data.

Chapter 22, Clustering: Clustering, the grouping of data, is accomplished by various methods such as K-means and hierarchical clustering.

Chapter 23, Reproducibility, Reports and Slide Shows with knitr: Generating reports, slide shows and Web pages from within R is made easy with knitr, LaTeX and Markdown.

Chapter 24, Building R Packages: R packages are great for portable, reusable code. Building these packages has been made incredibly easy with the advent of devtools and Rcpp.

Appendix A, Real-Life Resources: A listing of our favorite resources for learning more about R and interacting with the community.

Appendix B, Glossary: A glossary of terms used throughout this book.

A good deal of the text in this book is either R code or the results of running code. Code and results are most often in a separate block of text and set in a distinctive font, as shown in the following example. The different parts of code also have different colors. Lines of code start with >, and if code is continued from one line to another the continued line begins with +.

```
> # this is a comment
>
> # now basic math
> 10 * 10

[1] 100

>
> # calling a function
> sqrt(4)

[1] 2
```

Certain Kindle devices do not display color so the digital edition of this book will be viewed in greyscale on those devices.

There are occasions where code is shown inline and looks like sqrt(4).

In the few places where math is necessary, the equations are indented from the margin and are numbered.

$$e^{i\pi} + 1 = 0 \tag{1}$$

Within equations, normal variables appear as italic text (x), vectors are bold lowercase letters ($\mathbf{x}$) and matrices are bold uppercase letters ($\mathbf{X}$). Greek letters, such as α and β, follow the same convention.

Function names will be written as `join` and package names as `plyr`. Objects generated in code that are referenced in text are written as `object1`.

Learning R is a gratifying experience that makes life so much easier for so many tasks. I hope you enjoy learning with me.

Acknowledgments

To start, I must thank my mother, Gail Lander, for encouraging me to become a math major. Without that I would never have followed the path that led me to statistics and data science. In a similar vein, I have to thank my father, Howard Lander, for paying all those tuition bills. He has been a valuable source of advice and guidance throughout my life and someone I have aspired to emulate in many ways. While they both insist they do not understand what I do, they love that I do it and have helped me all along the way. Staying with family, I should thank my sister and brother-in-law, Aimee and Eric Schechterman, for letting me teach math to Noah, their five-year-old son.

There are many teachers who have helped shape me over the years. The first is Rochelle Lecke, who tutored me in middle school math even when my teacher told me I did not have worthwhile math skills.

Then there is Beth Edmondson, my precalc teacher at Princeton Day School. After I wasted the first half of high school as a mediocre student, she told me I had "some nerve signing up for next year's AP Calc" given my grades. She agreed to let me take AP Calc if I went from a C to an A+ in her class, never thinking I stood a chance. Three months later, she was in shock as I not only earned the A+, but turned around my entire academic career. She changed my life and without her, I do not know where I would be today. I am forever grateful that she was my teacher.

For the first two years at Muhlenberg College, I was determined to be a business and communications major, but took math classes because they came naturally to me. My professors, Dr. Penny Dunham, Dr. Bill Dunham, and Dr. Linda McGuire, all convinced me to become a math major, a decision that has greatly shaped my life. Dr. Greg Cicconetti gave me my first glimpse of rigorous statistics, my first research opportunity and planted the idea in my head that I should go to grad school for statistics.

While earning my M.A. at Columbia University, I was surrounded by brilliant minds in statistics and programming. Dr. David Madigan opened my eyes to modern machine learning, and Dr. Bodhi Sen got me thinking about statistical programming. I had the privilege to do research with Dr. Andrew Gelman, whose insights have been immeasurably important to me. Dr. Richard Garfield showed me how to use statistics to help people in disaster and war zones when he sent me on my first assignment to Myanmar. His advice and friendship over the years have been dear to me. Dr. Jingchen Liu allowed and encouraged me to write my thesis on New York City pizza, which has brought me an inordinate amount of attention.[1]

While at Columbia, I also met my good friend—and one time TA— Dr. Ivor Cribben who filled in so many gaps in my knowledge. Through him, I met Dr. Rachel Schutt, a source of great advice, and who I am now honored to teach alongside at Columbia.

Grad school might never have happened without the encouragement and support of Shanna Lee. She helped maintain my sanity while I was incredibly overcommited to two jobs, classes and Columbia's hockey team. I am not sure I would have made it through without her.

Steve Czetty gave me my first job in analytics at Sky IT Group and taught me about databases, while letting me experiment with off-the-wall programming. This sparked my interest in statistics and data. Joe DeSiena, Philip du Plessis, and Ed Bobrin at the Bardess Group are some of the finest people I have ever had the pleasure to work with, and I am proud to be working with them to this day. Mike Minelli, Rich Kittler, Mark Barry, David Smith, Joseph Rickert, Dr. Norman Nie, James Peruvankal, Neera Talbert and Dave Rich at Revolution Analytics let me do one of the best jobs I could possibly imagine: explaining to people in business why they should be using R. Kirk Mettler, Richard Schultz, Dr. Bryan Lewis and Jim Winfield at Big Computing encouraged me to have fun, tackling interesting problems in R. Vincent Saulys, John Weir, and Dr. Saar Golde at Goldman Sachs made my time there both enjoyable and educational.

Throughout the course of writing this book, many people helped me with the process. First and foremost is Yin Cheung, who saw all the stress I constantly felt and supported me through many ruined nights and days.

My editor, Debra Williams, knew just how to encourage me and her guiding hand has been invaluable. Paul Dix, the series editor and a good friend, was the person who suggested I write this book, so none of this would have happened without him. Thanks to Caroline Senay and Andrea Fox for being great copy editors. Without them, this book would not be nearly as well put together. Robert Mauriello's technical review was incredibly useful in honing the book's presentation.

The folks at RStudio, particularly JJ Allaire and Josh Paulson, make an amazing product, which made the writing process far easier than it would have been otherwise. Yihui Xie, the author of the `knitr` package, provided numerous feature changes that I needed to write this book. His software, and his speed at implementing my requests, is greatly appreciated.

Numerous people have provided valuable feedback as I produced this book, including Chris Bethel, Dr. Dirk Eddelbuettel, Dr. Ramnath Vaidyanathan, Dr. Eran Bellin,

---

1. `http://slice.seriouseats.com/archives/2010/03/the-moneyball-of-pizza-statistician-uses-statistics-to-find-nyc-best-pizza.html`

Avi Fisher, Brian Ezra, Paul Puglia, Nicholas Galasinao, Aaron Schumaker, Adam Hogan, Jeffrey Arnold, and John Houston.

Last fall was my first time teaching, and I am thankful to the students from the Fall 2012 Introduction to Data Science class at Columbia University for being the guinea pigs for the material that ultimately ended up in this book.

Thank you to everyone who helped along the way.

About the Author

Jared P. Lander is the founder and CEO of Lander Analytics, a data science consulting firm based in New York City, the organizer of the New York Open Statistical Programming Meetup, and an adjunct professor of statistics at Columbia University. He is also a tour guide for Scott's Pizza Tours and an advisor to Brewla Bars, a gourmet ice pop start-up. With an M.A. from Columbia University in statistics and a B.A. from Muhlenberg College in mathematics, he has experience in both academic research and industry. His work for both large and small organizations spans politics, tech start-ups, fund-raising, music, finance, healthcare and humanitarian relief efforts.

He specializes in data management, multilevel models, machine learning, generalized linear models, visualization, data management and statistical computing.

Chapter 1

Getting R

R is a wonderful tool for statistical analysis, visualization and reporting. Its usefulness is best seen in the wide variety of fields where it is used. We alone have used R for projects with banks, political campaigns, tech startups, food startups, international development and aid organizations, hospitals and real estate developers. Other areas where we have seen it used are online advertising, insurance, ecology, genetics and pharmaceuticals. R is used by statisticians with advanced machine learning training and by programmers familiar with other languages, and also by people who are not necessarily trained in advanced data analysis but are tired of using Excel.

Before it can be used it needs to be downloaded and installed, a process that is no more complicated than installing any other program.

1.1 Downloading R

The first step in using R is getting it on the computer. Unlike with languages such as C++, R must be installed in order to run.[1] The program is easily obtainable from the Comprehensive R Archive Network (CRAN), the maintainer of R, at http://cran .r-project.org/. At the top of the page are links to download R for Windows, Mac OS X and Linux.

There are prebuilt installations available for Windows and Mac OS X while those for Linux usually compile from source. Installing R on any of these platforms is just like installing any other program.

Windows users should click the link Download R for Windows, then base and then Download R 3.x.x for Windows; the x's indicate the version of R. This changes periodically as improvements are made.

Similarly, Mac users should click Download R for (Mac) OS X and then R-3.x.x.pkg; again, the x's indicate the current version of R. This will also install both 32- and 64-bit versions.

---

1. Technically C++ cannot be set up on its own without a compiler, so something would still need to be installed anyway.

Linux users should download R using their standard distribution mechanism whether that is apt-get (Ubuntu and Debian), zypper (SUSE) or another source. This will also build and install R.

1.2   R Version

As of this writing, R is at version 3.0.2, which is a big jump from the previous version, 2.15.3. CRAN follows a one-year release cycle where each major version change increases the middle of the three numbers in the version. For instance, version 3.0.0 was released in 2013. In 2014 the version will be incremented to 3.1.0 with 3.2.0 coming in 2015. The last number in the version is for minor updates to the current major version.

Most R functionality is usually backward compatible with previous versions.

1.3   32-bit versus 64-bit

The choice between using 32-bit and using 64-bit comes down to whether the computer supports 64-bit—most new machines do—and the size of the data to be worked with. The 64-bit versions can address arbitrarily large amounts of memory (or RAM) so it might as well be used.

This is especially important starting with version 3.0.0, as that adds support for 64-bit integers, meaning far greater amounts of data can be stored in R objects.

In the past, certain packages required the 32-bit version of R but that is exceedingly rare these days. The only reason for installing the 32-bit version now is to support some legacy analysis or for use on a machine with a 32-bit processor such as Intel's low-power Atom chip.

1.4   Installing

Installing R on Windows and Mac is just like installing any other program.

1.4.1   Installing on Windows

Find the appropriate installer where it was downloaded. For Windows users it will look like Figure 1.1.

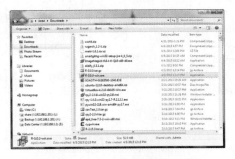

Figure 1.1   Location of R installer.

R should be installed using administrator privileges. This means right-clicking the installer and then selecting Run as Administrator. This brings up a prompt where the administrator password should be entered.

The first dialog, shown in Figure 1.2, offers a choice of language, defaulted at English. Choose the appropriate language and click OK.

Figure 1.2 Language selection.

Next, the caution shown in Figure 1.3 recommends that all other programs be closed. This advice is rarely followed or necessary anymore, so clicking Next is appropriate.

Figure 1.3 With modern versions of Windows, this suggestion can be safely ignored.

The software license is then displayed, as in Figure 1.4. R cannot be used without agreeing to this (important) license, so the only recourse is to click Next.

Figure 1.4 The license agreement must be acknowledged to use R.

The installer then asks for a destination location. Even though the official advice from CRAN is that R should be installed in a directory with no spaces in the name, half the time the default installation directory is Program Files\R, which causes trouble if we try to build packages that require compiled code such as C++ for FORTRAN. Figure 1.5 shows this dialog.

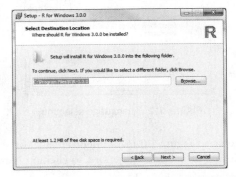

Figure 1.5   It is important to choose a destination folder with no spaces in the name.

If that is the case, click the Browse button to bring up folder options like the ones shown in Figure 1.6.

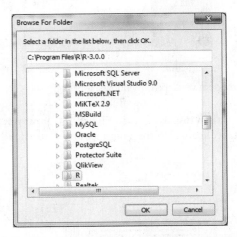

Figure 1.6   This dialog is used to choose the destination folder.

It is best to choose a destination folder that is on the C: drive (or another hard disk drive) or inside My Documents, which despite that user-friendly name is actually located at C:\Users\UserName\Documents, which contains no spaces. Figure 1.7 shows a proper destination for the installation.

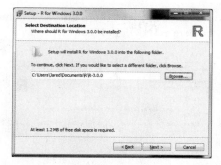

Figure 1.7   This is a proper destination, with no spaces in the name.

Next, Figure 1.8, shows a list of components to install. Unless there is a specific need for 32-bit files, that option can be unchecked. Everything else should be selected.

Figure 1.8   It is best to select everything except 32-bit components.

The startup options should be left at the default, No, as in Figure 1.9, because there are not a lot of options and we recommend using RStudio as the front end anyway.

Figure 1.9   Accept the default startup options, as we recommend using RStudio as the front end and these will not be important.

Next, choose where to put the start menu shortcuts. We recommend simply using R and putting every version in there as shown in Figure 1.10.

Figure 1.10   Choose the Start Menu folder where the shortcuts will be installed.

We have many versions of R, all inside the same Start Menu folder, which allows code to be tested in different versions. This is illustrated in Figure 1.11.

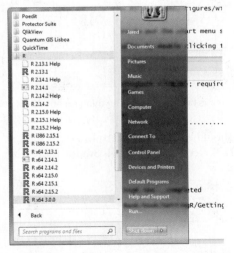

Figure 1.11   We have multiple versions of R installed to allow development and testing with different versions.

The last option is choosing whether to complete some additional tasks such as creating a desktop icon (not too useful if using RStudio). We highly recommend saving the version number in the registry and associating R with RData files. These options are shown in Figure 1.12.

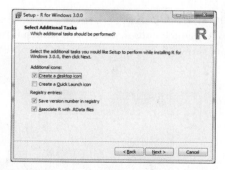

Figure 1.12   We recommend saving the version number in the registry and associating R with RData files.

Clicking Next begins installation and displays a progress bar, as shown in Figure 1.13.

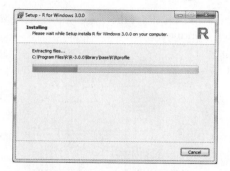

Figure 1.13   A progress bar is displayed during installation.

The last step, shown in Figure 1.14, is to click Finish and the installation is complete.

Figure 1.14   Confirmation that installation is complete.

1.4.2   Installing on Mac OS X

Find the appropriate installer, which ends in .pkg, and launch it by double-clicking. This brings up the introduction, shown in Figure 1.15. Click Continue to begin the installation process.

Figure 1.15   Introductory screen for installation on a Mac.

This brings up some information about the version of R being installed. There is nothing to do except click Continue, as shown in Figure 1.16.

Figure 1.16   Version selection.

Then the license information is displayed, as in Figure 1.17. Click Continue to proceed, the only viable option in order to use R.

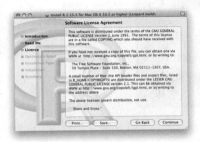

Figure 1.17   The license agreement, which must be acknowledged to use R.

Click Agree to confirm that the license is agreed to, which is mandatory to use R as is evidenced in Figure 1.18.

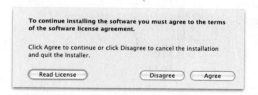

Figure 1.18   The license agreement must also be agreed to.

To install R for all users, click Install; otherwise, click Change Install Location to pick a different location. This is shown in Figure 1.19.

Figure 1.19   By default R is installed for all users, although there is the option to choose a specific location.

If prompted, enter the necessary password as shown in Figure 1.20.

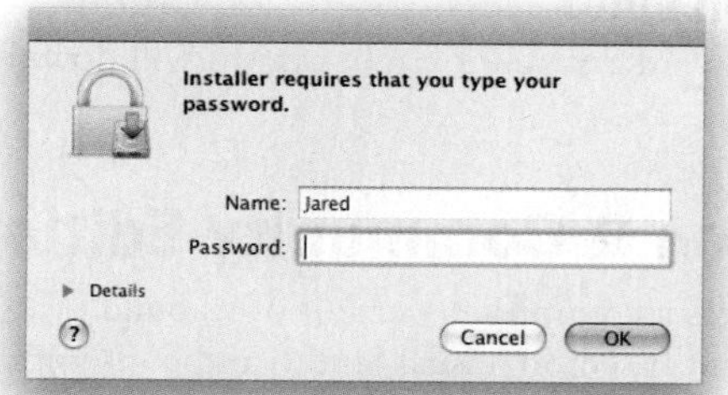

Figure 1.20   The administrator password might be required for installation.

This starts the installation process, which displays a progress bar as shown in Figure 1.21.

Figure 1.21   A progress bar is displayed during installation.

When done, the installer signals success as Figure 1.22 shows. Click Close to finish the installation.

Figure 1.22   This signals a successful installation.

1.4.3   Installing on Linux

Retrieving R from its standard distribution mechanism will download, build and install R in one step.

1.5   Revolution R Community Edition

Revolution Analytics offers a community version of its build of R featuring an Integrated Development Environment based on Visual Studio and built with the Intel Matrix Kernel Library (MKL), allowing for much faster matrix computations. It is available for free at http://www.revolutionanalytics.com/products/revolution-r.php. They also offer a paid version that provides specialized algorithms to work on very large data. More information is available at `http://www.revolutionanalytics.com/products/revolution-enterprise.php`.

1.6 Conclusion

At this point R is fully usable and comes with a crude GUI. However, it is best to install RStudio and use its interface, which is detailed in Section 2.2. The process involves downloading and launching an installer, just as with any other program.

Chapter 2

The R Environment

Now that R is downloaded and installed, it is time to get familiar with how to use R. The basic R interface on Windows is fairly Spartan as seen in Figure 2.1. The Mac interface (Figure 2.2) has some extra features and Linux has far fewer, being just a terminal.

Unlike other languages, R is very interactive. That is, results can be seen one command at a time. Languages such as C++ require that an entire section of code be written, compiled and run in order to see results. The state of objects and results can be seen at any point in R. This interactivity is one of the most amazing aspects of working with R.

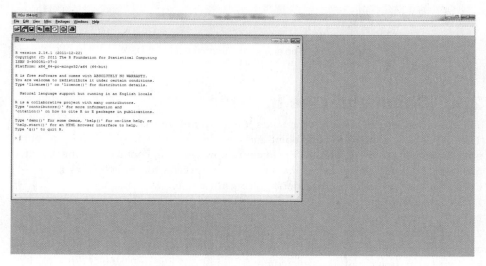

Figure 2.1   The standard R interface in Windows.

There have been numerous Integrated Development Environments (IDEs) built for R. For the purposes of this book we will assume that RStudio is being used, which is discussed in Section 2.2.

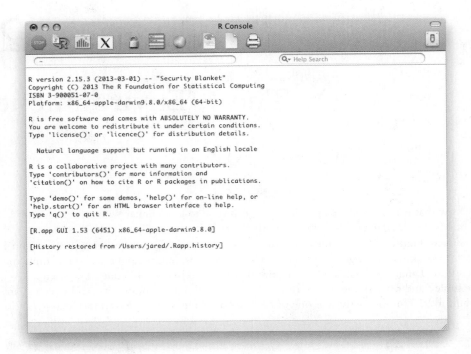

Figure 2.2   The standard R interface on Mac OS X.

2.1   Command Line Interface

The command line interface is what makes R so powerful, and also frustrating to learn. There have been attempts to build point-and-click interfaces for R, such as Rcmdr, but none have truly taken off. This is a testament to how typing in commands is much better than using a mouse. That might be hard to believe, especially for those coming from Excel, but over time it becomes easier and less error prone.

For instance, fitting a regression in Excel takes at least seven mouse clicks, often more: Data >> Data Analysis >> Regression >> OK >> Input Y Range >> Input X Range >> OK. Then it may need to be done all over again to make one little tweak or because there are new data. Even harder is walking a colleague through those steps via email. In contrast, the same command is just one line in R, which can easily be repeated and copied and pasted. This may be hard to believe initially, but after some time the command line makes life much easier.

To run a command in R, type it into the console next to the > symbol and press the Enter key. Entries can be as simple as the number 2 or complex functions, such as those seen in Chapter 8.

To repeat a line of code, simply press the Up Arrow key and hit Enter again. All previous commands are saved and can be accessed by repeatedly using the Up and Down Arrow keys to cycle through them.

Interrupting a command is done with `Esc` in Windows and Mac and `Ctrl-C` in Linux.

Often when working on a large analysis it is good to have a file of the code used. Until recently, the most common way to handle this was to use a text editor[1] such as TextPad or UltraEdit to write code and then copy and paste it into the R console. While this worked, it was sloppy and led to a lot of switching between programs.

2.2 RStudio

While there are a number of IDEs available, the best right now is RStudio, created by a team led by JJ Allaire whose previous products include ColdFusion and Windows Live Writer. It is available for Windows, Mac and Linux and looks identical in all of them. Even more impressive is the RStudio server, which runs an R instance on a Linux server and allows the user to run commands through the standard RStudio interface in a Web browser. It works with any version of R (greater than 2.11.1) including Revolution R from Revolution Analytics. RStudio has so many options that it can be a bit overwhelming. We will cover some of the most useful or frequently used features.

RStudio is highly customizable but the basic interface looks roughly like Figure 2.3. In this case the lower left pane is the R console, which can be used just like the standard R console. The upper left pane takes the place of a text editor but is far more powerful. The upper right pane holds information about the workspace, command history, files in the current folder and Git version control. The lower right pane displays plots, package information and help files.

There are a number of ways to send and execute commands from the editor to the console. To send one line place the cursor at the desired line and press `Ctrl+Enter` (Command+Enter on Mac). To insert a selection, simply highlight the selection and press `Ctrl+Enter`. To run an entire file of code, press `Ctrl+Shift+S`.

When typing code, such as an object name or function name, hitting `Tab` will autocomplete the code. If more than one object or function matches the letters typed so far, a dialog will pop up giving the matching options as shown in Figure 2.4.

Typing `Ctrl+1` moves the cursor to the text editor area and `Ctrl+2` moves it to the console. To move to the previous tab in the text editor, press `Ctrl+Alt+Left` in Windows, `Ctrl+PageUp` in Linux and `Ctrl+Option+Left` on Mac. To move to the next tab in the text editor, press `Ctrl+Alt+Right` in Windows, `Ctrl+PageDown` in Linux and `Ctrl+Option+Right` on Mac. For a complete list of shortcuts click `Help >> Keyboard Shortcuts`.

---

1. This means a programming text editor as opposed to a word processor such as Microsoft Word. A text editor preserves the structure of the text whereas word processors may add formatting that makes it unsuitable for insertion into the console.

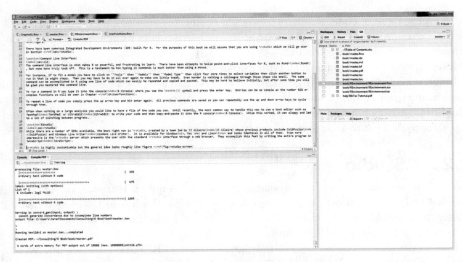

Figure 2.3   The general layout of RStudio.

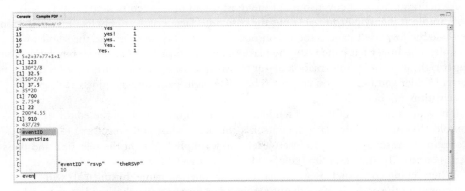

Figure 2.4   Object Name Autocomplete in RStudio.

2.2.1 RStudio Projects

A primary feature of RStudio is projects. A project is a collection of files—and possibly data, results and graphs—that are all related to each other.[2] Each package even has its own working directory. This is a great way to keep organized.

The simplest way to start a new project is to click `File >> New Project` as in Figure 2.5.

---

2. This is different from an R session, which is all the objects and work done in R and kept in memory for the current usage period, which usually resets upon restarting R.

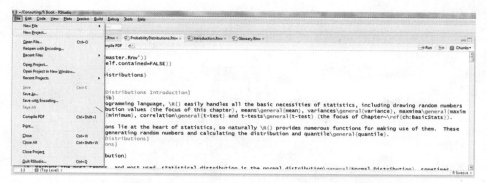

Figure 2.5   Clicking `File >> New Project` begins the project creation process.

Three options are available, shown in Figure 2.6: starting a new project in a new directory, associating a project with an existing directory or checking out a project from a version control repository such as Git or SVN. In all three cases a `.Rproj` file is put into the resulting directory and keeps track of the project.

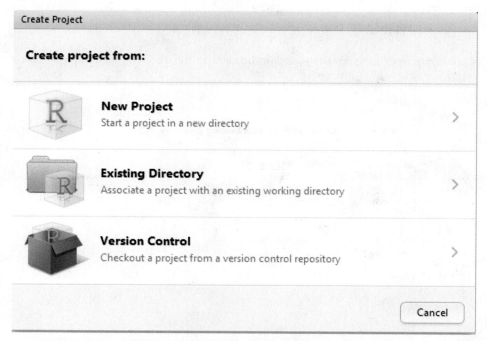

Figure 2.6   Three options are available to start a new project: a new directory, associating a project with an existing directory or checking out a project from a version control repository.

Choosing to create a new directory brings up a dialog, shown in Figure 2.7, that requests a project name and where to create a new directory.

Figure 2.7   Dialog to choose the location of a new project directory.

Choosing an existing directory asks for the name of the directory, seen in Figure 2.8.

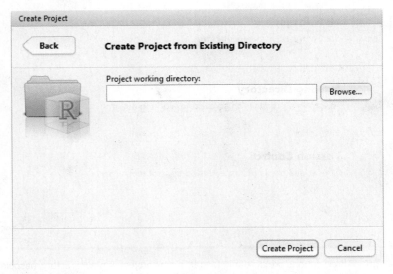

Figure 2.8   Dialog to choose an existing directory in which to start a project.

Choosing to use version control (we prefer Git) firsts asks whether to use Git or SVN as in Figure 2.9.

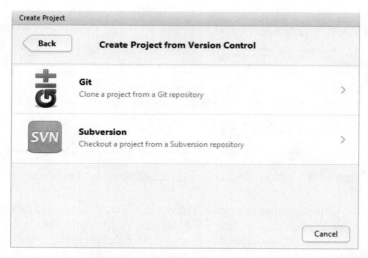

Figure 2.9   Here is the option to choose which type of repository to start a new project from.

Selecting Git asks for a repository URL, such as `git@github.com:jaredlander/coefplot.git`, which will then fill in the project directory name, as shown in Figure 2.10. As with creating a new directory, this will ask where to put this new directory.

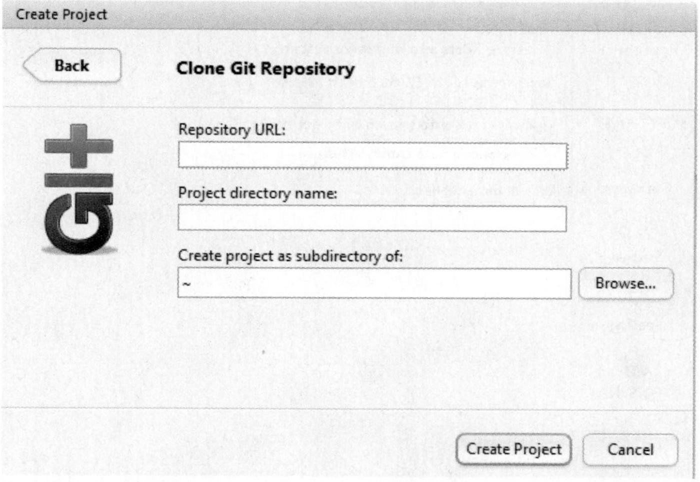

Figure 2.10   Enter the URL for a Git repository, as well as the folder where this should be cloned to.

2.2.2   RStudio Tools

RStudio is highly customizable with a lot of options. Most are contained in the Options dialog accessed by clicking `Tools >> Options`, as seen in Figure 2.11.

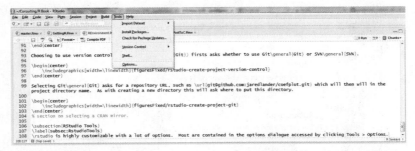

Figure 2.11   Clicking `Tools >> Options` brings up RStudio options.

First are the General options, shown in Figure 2.12. There is a control for selecting which version of R to use. This is a powerful tool when a computer has a number of versions of R. However, RStudio must be restarted after changing the R version. In the

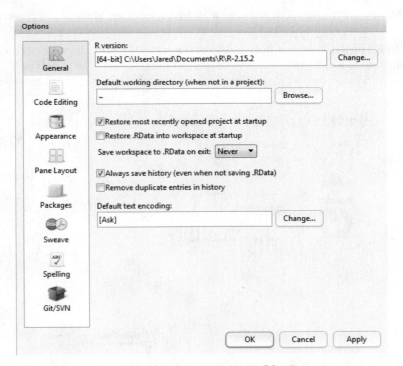

Figure 2.12   General options in RStudio.

future, RStudio is slated to offer the ability to set different versions of R for each project. It is also a good idea to not restore or save .RData files on startup and exiting.[3]

The Code Editing options, shown in Figure 2.13, control the way code is entered and displayed in the text editor. It is generally considered good practice to replace tabs with spaces, either two or four. Some hard-core programmers will appreciate vim mode. As of now there is no Emacs mode.

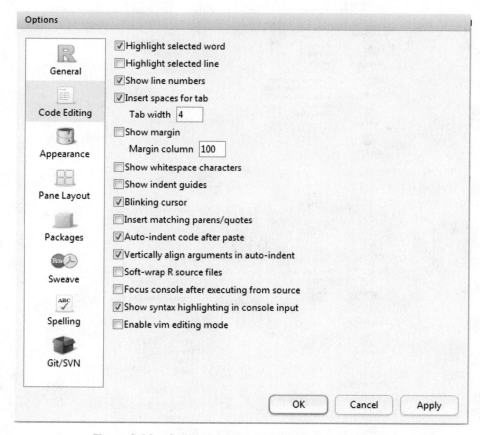

Figure 2.13   Options for customizing the code editing pane.

Appearance options, shown in Figure 2.14, change the way code looks, aesthetically. The font, size and color of the background and text can all be customized here.

The Pane Layout options, shown in Figure 2.15, simply rearrange the panes that make up RStudio.

---

3. RData files are a convenient way of saving and sharing R objects and are discussed in Section 6.5.

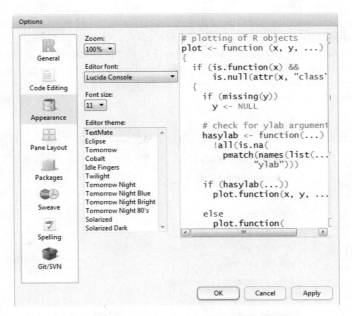

Figure 2.14   Options for code appearance.

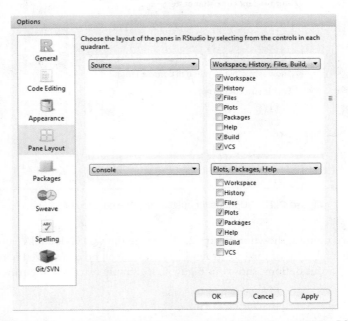

Figure 2.15   These options control the placement of the various panes in RStudio.

The Packages options, shown in Figure 2.16, set options regarding packages, although the most important is the CRAN mirror. While this is changeable from the console, this is the default setting. It is best to pick the mirror that is geographically the closest.

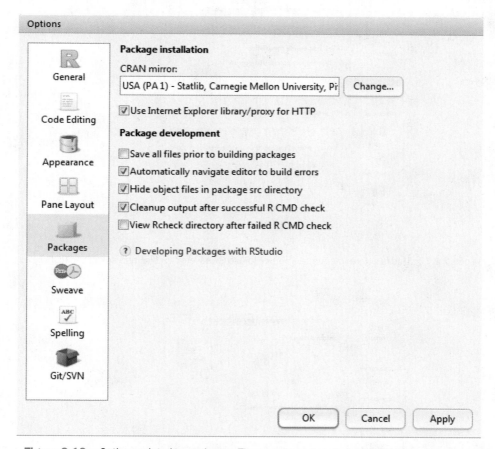

Figure 2.16   Options related to packages. The most important is the CRAN mirror selection.

Sweave, Figure 2.17, may be a bit misnamed, as this is where to choose between using Sweave or knitr. Both are used for the generation of PDF documents with knitr also enabling the creation of HTML documents. knitr, detailed in Chapter 23, is by far the better option, although it must be installed first, which is explained in Section 3.1. This is also where the PDF viewer is selected.

RStudio contains a spelling checker for writing LaTeX and Markdown documents (using knitr, preferably), which is controlled from the Spelling options, Figure 2.18. Not much needs to be set here.

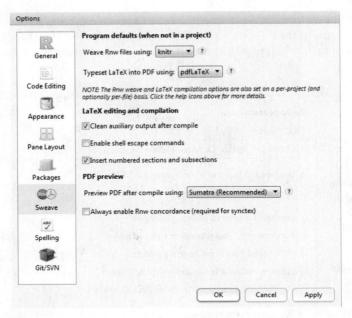

Figure 2.17   This is where to choose whether to use Sweave or `knitr` and select the PDF viewer.

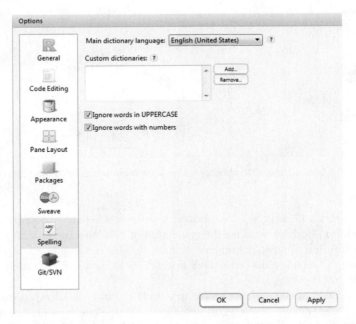

Figure 2.18   These are the options for the spelling check dictionary, which allows language selection and the custom dictionaries.

The last option, Git/SVN, Figure 2.19, indicates where the executables for Git and SVN exist. This needs to be set only once but is necessary for version control.

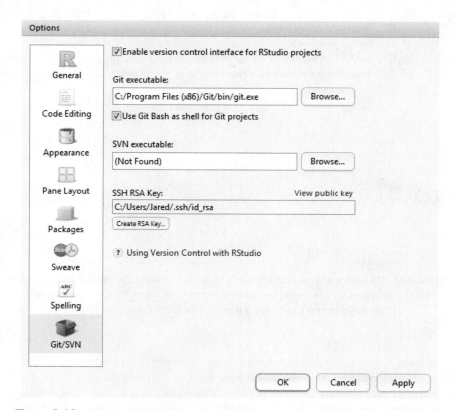

Figure 2.19   This is where to set the location of Git and SVN executables so they can be used by RStudio.

2.2.3 Git Integration

Using version control is a great idea for many reasons. First and foremost it provides snapshots of code at different points in time and can easily revert to those snapshots. Ancillary benefits include having a backup of the code and the ability to easily transfer the code between computers with little effort.

While SVN used to be the gold standard in version control it has since been superseded by Git, so that will be our focus. After associating a project with a Git repository[4] RStudio has a pane for Git like the one shown in Figure 2.20.

---

4. A Git account should be set up with either GitHub (`https://github.com/`) or Bitbucket (`https://bitbucket.org/`) beforehand.

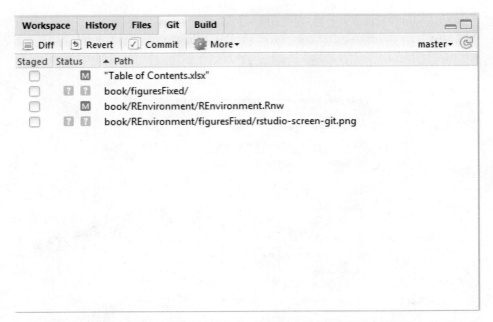

Figure 2.20   The Git pane shows the Git status of files under version control. A blue square with a white M indicates a file has been changed and needs to be committed. A yellow square with a white question mark indicates a new file that is not being tracked by Git.

The main functionality is committing changes, pushing them to the server and pulling changes made by other users. Clicking the Commit button brings up a dialog, Figure 2.21, which displays files that have been modified, or new files. Clicking on one of these files displays the changes; deletions are colored pink and additions are colored green. There is also a space to write a message describing the commit.

Clicking Commit will stage the changes and clicking Push will send them to the server.

2.3   Revolution Analytics RPE

Revolution Analytics provides an IDE based on Visual Studio called the R Productivity Environment (RPE). The greatest benefit of the RPE is the visual debugger. If this feature is not needed,[5] we recommend using Revolution with RStudio as the front-end, which can be set in the General options detailed in Section 2.2.2.

---

5. The latest version of RStudio now also offers a visual debugger.

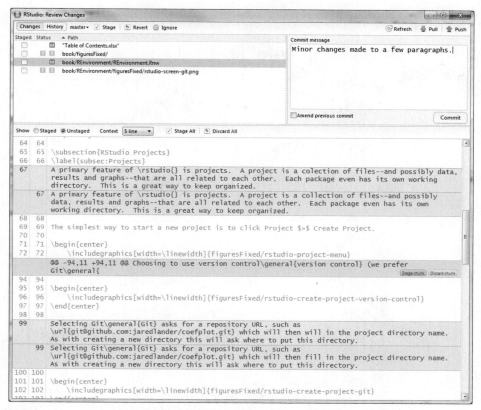

Figure 2.21 This displays files and the changes made to the files, with green being additions and pink being deletions. The upper right contains a space for writing commit messages.

2.4 Conclusion

R's usability has greatly improved over the past few years, mainly thanks to Revolution Analytics' RPE and RStudio. Using an IDE can greatly improve proficiency, and change working with R from merely tolerable to actually enjoyable.[6] RStudio's code completion, text editor, Git integration and projects are indispensable for a good programming work flow.

---

6. One of our students relayed that he preferred Matlab to R until he used RStudio.

Chapter 3

R Packages

Perhaps the biggest reason for R's phenomenally ascendant popularity is its collection of user-contributed packages. As of mid-September 2013, there were 4,845 packages available on CRAN[1], written by an estimated 2,000 different people. Odds are good that if a statistical technique exists, it has been written in R and contributed to CRAN. Not only are there an incredibly large number of packages, many are written by the authorities in the field such as Andrew Gelman, Trevor Hastie, Dirk Eddelbuettel and Hadley Wickham.

A package is essentially a library of prewritten code designed to accomplish some task or a collection of tasks. The `survival` package is used for survival analysis, `ggplot2` is used for plotting and `sp` is for dealing with spatial data.

It is important to remember that not all packages are of the same quality. Some are built to be very robust and are well-maintained, while others are built with good intentions but can fail with unforeseen errors and others still are just plain poor. Even with the best packages, it is important to remember that most were written by statisticians for statisticians, so they may differ from what a computer engineer would expect.

This book will not attempt to provide an exhaustive list of good packages to use because that is constantly changing. However, there are some packages that are so pervasive that they will be used in this book as if they were part of base R. Some of these are `ggplot2`, `reshape2` and `plyr` by Hadley Wickham; `glmnet` by Trevor Hastie, Robert Tibshirani and Jerome Friedman; `Rcpp` by Dirk Eddelbuettel; and `knitr` by Yihui Xie. We have written a package on CRAN, `coefplot`, with more to follow.

3.1 Installing Packages

As with many tasks in R, there are multiple ways to install packages. The simplest is to install them using the GUI provided by RStudio and shown in Figure 3.1. Access the Packages pane shown in this figure either by clicking its tab or by pressing `Ctrl+7` on the keyboard.

---

1. http://cran.r-project.org/web/packages/

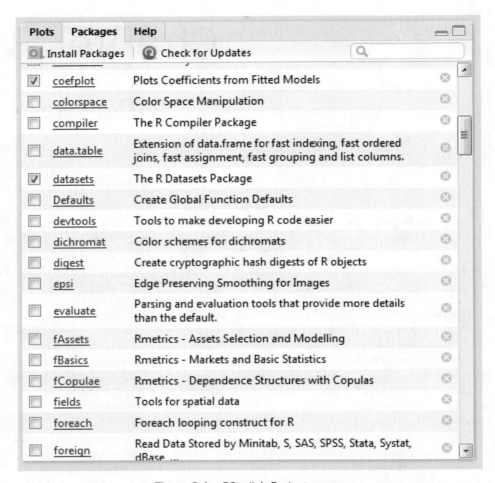

Figure 3.1   RStudio's Packages pane.

In the upper-left corner, click the Install Packages button to bring up the dialog in Figure 3.2.

From here simply type the name of a package (RStudio has a nice autocomplete feature for this) and click Install. Multiple packages can be specified, separated by commas. This downloads and installs the desired package, which is then available for use. Selecting the Install dependencies checkbox will automatically download and install all packages that the desired package requires to work. For example, our `coefplot` package depends on `ggplot2`, `plyr`, `useful`, `stringr` and `reshape2`, and each of those may have further dependencies.

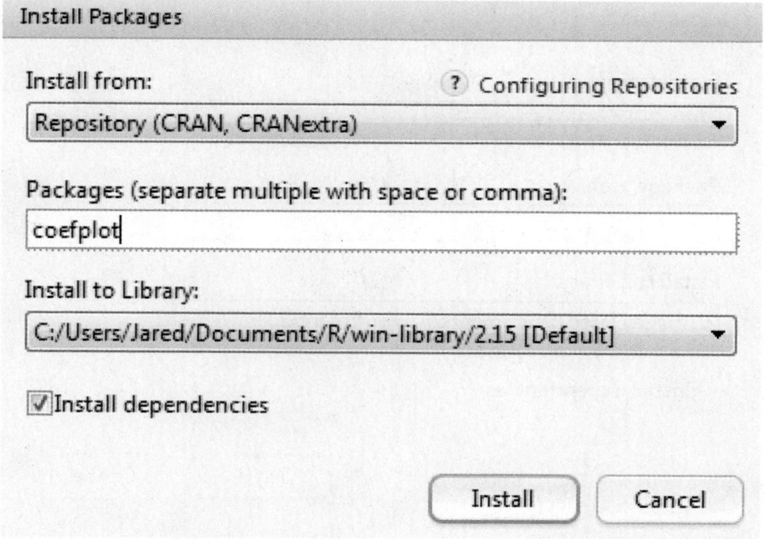

Figure 3.2 RStudio's package installation dialog.

An alternative is to type a very simple command into the console:

```
> install.packages("coefplot")
```

This will accomplish the same thing as working in the GUI.

There has been a movement recently to install packages directly from GitHub or BitBucket repositories, especially to get the development versions of packages. This can be accomplished using devtools.

```
> require(devtools)
> install_github(repo = "coefplot", username = "jaredlander")
```

If the package being installed from a repository contains source code for a compiled language—generally C++ or FORTRAN—then the proper compilers must be installed. More information is in Section 24.6.

Sometimes there is a need to install a package from a local file, either a zip of a prebuilt package or a tar.gz of package code. This can be done using the installation dialog mentioned before but switching the Install from: option to Package Archive File as shown in Figure 3.3. Then browse to the file and install. Note that this will not install dependencies, and if they are not present the installation will fail. Be sure to install dependencies first.

Similarly to before, this can be accomplished using install.packages.

```
> install.packages("coefplot_1.1.7.zip")
```

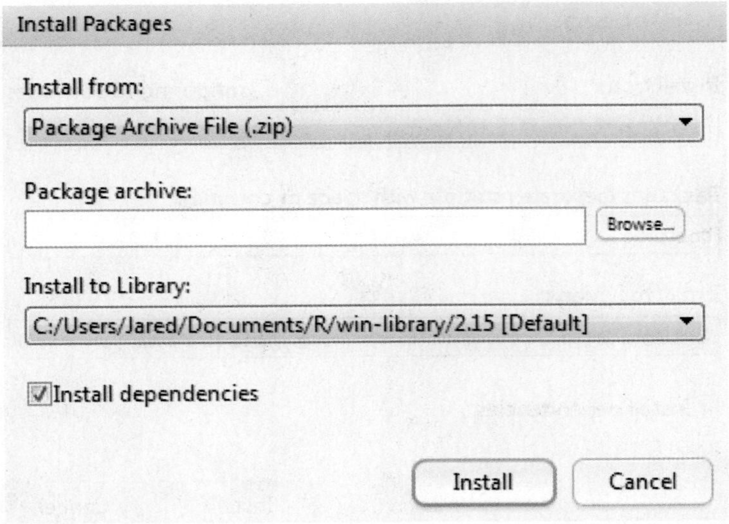

Figure 3.3   RStudio's package installation dialog to install from an archive file.

3.1.1   Uninstalling Packages

In the rare instance when a package needs to be uninstalled, it is easiest to click the white X inside a grey circle on the right of the package description in RStudio's Packages pane shown in Figure 3.1. Alternatively, this can be done with `remove.packages` where the first argument is a `character vector` naming the packages to be removed.

3.2   Loading Packages

Now that packages are installed they are almost ready to use and just need to be loaded first. There are two commands that can be used, either `library` or `require`. They both accomplish the same thing—loading the package—but `require` will return TRUE if it succeeds and FALSE with a warning if it cannot find the package. This returned value is useful when loading a package from within a function, a practice considered acceptable to some, improper to others. In general usage there is not much of a difference, so it comes down to personal preference. The argument to either function is the name of the desired package, with or without quotes. So loading the `coefplot` package would look like:

```
> require(coefplot)

Loading required package: coefplot
Loading required package: ggplot2
```

It prints out the dependent packages that get loaded as well. This can be suppressed by setting the argument `quietly` to TRUE.

```
> require(coefplot, quietly = TRUE)
```

A package only needs to be loaded when starting a new R session. Once loaded, it remains available until either R is restarted or the package is unloaded, as described in Section 3.2.1.

An alternative to loading a package through code is to select the checkbox next to the package name in RStudio's Packages pane, seen on the left of Figure 3.1. This will load the package by running the code just shown.

3.2.1 Unloading Packages

Sometimes a package needs to be unloaded. This is simple enough either by clearing the checkbox in RStudio's Packages pane or by using the `detach` function. The function takes the package name preceded by `package:` all in quotes.

```
> detach("package:coefplot")
```

It is not uncommon for functions in different packages to have the same name. For example, `coefplot` is in both `arm` (by Andrew Gelman) and `coefplot`.[2] If both packages are loaded, the function in the package loaded last will be invoked when calling that function. A way around this is to precede the function with the name of the package, separated by two colons (::).

```
> arm::coefplot(object)
> coefplot::coefplot(object)
```

Not only does this call the appropriate function, it also allows the function to be called without even loading the package beforehand.

3.3 Building a Package

Building a package is one of the more rewarding parts of working with R, especially sharing that package with the community through CRAN. Chapter 24 discusses this process in detail.

3.4 Conclusion

Packages make up the backbone of the R community and experience. They are often considered what makes working with R so desirable. This is how the community makes its work, and so many of the statistical techniques, available to the world. With such a large number of packages, finding the right one can be overwhelming. CRAN Task Views (http://cran.r-project.org/web/views/) offers a curated listing of packages for different needs. However, the best way to find a new package might just be to ask the community. Appendix A gives some resources for doing just that.

---

2. This particular instance is because we built `coefplot` as an improvement on the one available in `arm`. There are other instances where the names have nothing in common.

Chapter 4

Basics of R

R is a powerful tool for all manner of calculations, data manipulation and scientific computations. Before getting to the complex operations possible in R we must start with the basics. Like most languages R has its share of mathematical capability, variables, functions and data types.

4.1 Basic Math

Being a statistical programming language, R can certainly be used to do basic math and that is where we will start.

We begin with the "Hello, World!" of basic math: $1 + 1$. In the console there is a right angle bracket (>) where code should be entered. Simply test R by running

```
> 1 + 1

[1] 2
```

If this returns 2, then everything is great; if not, then something is very, very wrong. Assuming it worked, let's look at some slightly more complicated expressions:

```
> 1 + 2 + 3

[1] 6

> 3 * 7 * 2

[1] 42

> 4/2

[1] 2

> 4/3

[1] 1.333
```

These follow the basic order of operations: Parenthesis, Exponents, Multiplication, Division, Addition and Subtraction (PEMDAS). This means operations inside parentheses take priority over other operations. Next on the priority list is exponentiation. After that multiplication and division are performed, followed by addition and subtraction.

This is why the first two lines in the following code have the same result while the third is different.

```
> 4 * 6 + 5

[1] 29

> (4 * 6) + 5

[1] 29

> 4 * (6 + 5)

[1] 44
```

So far we have put white space in between each operator such as * and /. This is not necessary but is encouraged as good coding practice.

4.2 Variables

Variables are an integral part of any programming language and R offers a great deal of flexibility. Unlike statically typed languages such as C++, R does not require variable types to be declared. A variable can take on any available data type as described in Section 4.3. It can also hold any R object such as a function, the result of an analysis or a plot. A single variable can at one point hold a number, then later hold a character and then later a number again.

4.2.1 Variable Assignment

There are a number of ways to assign a value to a variable, and again, this does not depend on the type of value being assigned.

The valid assignment operators are <- and = with the first being preferred.

For example, let's save 2 to the variable x and 5 to the variable y.

```
> x <- 2
> x

[1] 2

> y = 5
> y

[1] 5
```

The arrow operator can also point in the other direction.

```
> 3 <- z
> z

[1]  3
```

The assignment operation can be used successively to assign a value to multiple variables simultaneously.

```
> a <- b <- 7
> a

[1] 7

> b

[1] 7
```

A more laborious, though sometimes necessary, way to assign variables is to use the `assign` function.

```
> assign("j", 4)
> j

[1] 4
```

Variable names can contain any combination of alphanumeric characters along with periods (.) and underscores (_). However, they cannot *start* with a number or an underscore.

The most common form of assignment in the R community is the left arrow (<-), which may seem awkward to use at first but eventually becomes second nature. It even seems to make sense, as the variable is sort of pointing to its value. There is also a particularly nice benefit for people coming from languages like SQL, where a single equal sign (=) tests for equality.

It is generally considered best practice to use actual names, usually nouns, for variables instead of single letters. This provides more information to the person reading the code. This is seen throughout this book.

4.2.2 Removing Variables

For various reasons a variable may need to be removed. This is easily done using `remove` or its shortcut `rm`.

```
> j

[1]  4
```

```
> rm(j)
> # now it is gone
> j
```

```
Error: object 'j' not found
```

This frees up memory so that R can store more objects, although it does not necessarily free up memory for the operating system. To guarantee that, use gc, which performs garbage collection, releasing unused memory to the operating system. R automatically does garbage collection periodically, so this function is not essential.

Variable names are case sensitive, which can trip up people coming from a language like SQL or Visual Basic.

```
> theVariable <- 17
> theVariable
```

```
[1] 17
```

```
> THEVARIABLE
```

```
Error: object 'THEVARIABLE' not found
```

4.3 Data Types

There are numerous data types in R that store various kinds of data. The four main types of data most likely to be used are numeric, character (string), Date/POSIXct (time-based) and logical (TRUE/FALSE).

The type of data contained in a variable is checked with the class function.

```
> class(x)
```

```
[1] "numeric"
```

4.3.1 Numeric Data

As expected, R excels at running numbers, so numeric data is the most common type in R. The most commonly used numeric data is numeric. This is similar to a float or double in other languages. It handles integers and decimals, both positive and negative, and, of course, zero. A numeric value stored in a variable is automatically assumed to be numeric. Testing whether a variable is numeric is done with the function is.numeric.

```
> is.numeric(x)
```

```
[1] TRUE
```

Another important, if less frequently used, type is integer. As the name implies this is for whole numbers only, no decimals. To set an integer to a variable it is necessary to append the value with an L. As with checking for a numeric, the is.integer function is used.

```
> i <- 5L
> i
```

```
[1] 5
```

```
> is.integer(i)
```

```
[1] TRUE
```

Do note that, even though i is an integer, it will also pass a numeric check.

```
> is.numeric(i)
```

```
[1] TRUE
```

R nicely promotes integers to numeric when needed. This is obvious when multiplying an integer by a numeric, but importantly it works when dividing an integer by another integer, resulting in a decimal number.

```
> class(4L)
```

```
[1] "integer"
```

```
> class(2.8)
```

```
[1] "numeric"
```

```
> 4L * 2.8
```

```
[1] 11.2
```

```
> class(4L * 2.8)
```

```
[1] "numeric"
```

```
>
> class(5L)
```

```
[1] "integer"
```

```
> class(2L)
```

```
[1] "integer"
```

```
> 5L/2L
```

```
[1] 2.5
```

```
> class(5L/2L)
```

```
[1] "numeric"
```

4.3.2 Character Data

Even though it is not explicitly mathematical, the character (string) data type is very common in statistical analysis and must be handled with care. R has two primary ways of handling character data: `character` and `factor`. While they may seem similar on the surface, they are treated quite differently.

```
> x <- "data"
> x

[1] "data"

> y <- factor("data")
> y

[1] data
Levels: data
```

Notice that x contains the word "data" encapsulated in quotes, while y has the word "data" without quotes and a second line of information about the `levels` of y. That is explained further in Section 4.4.2 about `vectors`.

`Characters` are case sensitive, so "Data" is different from "data" or "DATA."

To find the length of a `character` (or `numeric`) use the `nchar` function.

```
> nchar(x)

[1] 4

> nchar("hello")

[1] 5

> nchar(3)

[1] 1

> nchar(452)

[1] 3
```

This will not work for `factor` data.

```
> nchar(y)

Error: 'nchar()' requires a character vector
```

4.3.3 Dates

Dealing with dates and times can be difficult in any language, and to further complicate matters R has numerous different types of dates. The most useful are `Date` and `POSIXct`. `Date` stores just a date while `POSIXct` stores a date and time. Both objects are actually represented as the number of days (`Date`) or seconds (`POSIXct`) since January 1, 1970.

```
> date1 <- as.Date("2012-06-28")
> date1

[1] "2012-06-28"

> class(date1)

[1] "Date"

> as.numeric(date1)

[1] 15519

>
> date2 <- as.POSIXct("2012-06-28 17:42")
> date2

[1] "2012-06-28 17:42:00 EDT"

> class(date2)

[1] "POSIXct" "POSIXt"

> as.numeric(date2)

[1] 1340919720
```

Easier manipulation of date and time objects can be accomplished using the lubridate and chron packages.

Using functions such as as.numeric or as.Date does not merely change the formatting of an object but actually changes the underlying type.

```
> class(date1)

[1] "Date"

> class(as.numeric(date1))

[1] "numeric"
```

4.3.4 Logical

logicals are a way of representing data that can be either TRUE or FALSE. Numerically, TRUE is the same as 1 and FALSE is the same as 0. So TRUE * 5 equals 5 while FALSE * 5 equals 0.

```
> TRUE * 5

[1] 5
```

```
> FALSE * 5
```

```
[1] 0
```

Similar to other types, logicals have their own test, using the is.logical function.

```
> k <- TRUE
> class(k)
```

```
[1] "logical"
```

```
> is.logical(k)
```

```
[1] TRUE
```

R provides T and F as shortcuts for TRUE and FALSE, respectively, but it is best practice not to use them, as they are simply variables storing the values TRUE and FALSE and can be overwritten, which can cause a great deal of frustration as seen in the following example.

```
> TRUE
```

```
[1] TRUE
```

```
> T
```

```
[1] TRUE
```

```
> class(T)
```

```
[1] "logical"
```

```
> T <- 7
> T
```

```
[1] 7
```

```
> class(T)
```

```
[1] "numeric"
```

logicals can result from comparing two numbers, or characters.

```
> # does 2 equal 3?
> 2 == 3
```

```
[1] FALSE
```

```
> # does 2 not equal three?
> 2 != 3
```

```
[1]  TRUE

> # is two less than three?
> 2 < 3

[1]  TRUE

> # is two less than or equal to three?
> 2 <= 3

[1]  TRUE

> # is two greater than three?
> 2 > 3

[1]  FALSE

> # is two greater than or equal to three?
> 2 >= 3

[1]  FALSE

> # is 'data' equal to 'stats'?
> "data" == "stats"

[1]  FALSE

> # is 'data' less than 'stats'?
> "data" < "stats"

[1]  TRUE
```

4.4 Vectors

A vector is a collection of elements, all of the same type. For instance, `c(1, 3, 2, 1, 5)` is a vector consisting of the numbers 1, 3, 2, 1, 5, in that order. Similarly, `c("R", "Excel", "SAS", "Excel")` is a vector of the character elements "R," "Excel," "SAS" and "Excel." A vector cannot be of mixed type.

vectors play a crucial, and helpful, role in R. More than being simple containers, vectors in R are special in that R is a vectorized language. That means operations are applied to each element of the vector automatically, without the need to loop through the vector. This is a powerful concept that may seem foreign to people coming from other languages, but it is one of the greatest things about R.

vectors do not have a dimension, meaning there is no such thing as a column vector or row vector. These vectors are not like the mathematical vector where there is a difference between row and column orientation.[1]

---

1. Column or row vectors can be represented as one-dimensional matrices, which are discussed in Section 5.3.

The most common way to create a `vector` is with c. The "c" stands for combine because multiple elements are being combined into a `vector`.

```
> x <- c(1, 2, 3, 4, 5, 6, 7, 8, 9, 10)
> x

 [1]  1  2  3  4  5  6  7  8  9 10
```

4.4.1 Vector Operations

Now that we have a `vector` of the first ten numbers, we might want to multiply each element by 3. In R this is a simple operation using just the multiplication operator ($*$).

```
> x * 3

 [1]  3  6  9 12 15 18 21 24 27 30
```

No loops are necessary. Addition, subtraction and division are just as easy. This also works for any number of operations.

```
> x + 2

 [1]  3  4  5  6  7  8  9 10 11 12

> x - 3

 [1] -2 -1  0  1  2  3  4  5  6  7

> x/4

 [1] 0.25 0.50 0.75 1.00 1.25 1.50 1.75 2.00 2.25 2.50

> x^2

 [1]   1   4   9  16  25  36  49  64  81 100

> sqrt(x)

 [1] 1.000 1.414 1.732 2.000 2.236 2.449 2.646 2.828 3.000 3.162
```

Earlier we created a `vector` of the first ten numbers using the c function, which creates a `vector`. A shortcut is the : operator, which generates a sequence of consecutive numbers, in either direction.

```
> 1:10

 [1]  1  2  3  4  5  6  7  8  9 10
```

```
> 10:1

 [1] 10  9  8  7  6  5  4  3  2  1

> -2:3

[1] -2 -1  0  1  2  3

> 5:-7

 [1]  5  4  3  2  1  0 -1 -2 -3 -4 -5 -6 -7
```

Vector operations can be extended even further. Let's say we have two vectors of equal length. Each of the corresponding elements can be operated on together.

```
> # create two vectors of equal length
> x <- 1:10
> y <- -5:4
> # add them
> x + y

 [1] -4 -2  0  2  4  6  8 10 12 14

> # subtract them
> x - y

 [1] 6 6 6 6 6 6 6 6 6 6

> # multiply them
> x * y

 [1] -5 -8 -9 -8 -5  0  7 16 27 40

> # divide them--notice division by 0 results in Inf
> x/y

 [1] -0.2 -0.5 -1.0 -2.0 -5.0  Inf  7.0  4.0  3.0  2.5

> # raise one to the power of the other
> x^y

 [1] 1.000e+00 6.250e-02 3.704e-02 6.250e-02 2.000e-01 1.000e+00
 [7] 7.000e+00 6.400e+01 7.290e+02 1.000e+04

> # check the length of each
> length(x)

[1] 10
```

```
> length(y)

[1] 10

> # the length of them added together should be the same
> length(x + y)

[1] 10
```

In the preceding code block, notice the hash # symbol. This is used for comments. Anything following the hash, on the same line, will be commented out and not run.

Things get a little more complicated when operating on two vectors of unequal length. The shorter vector gets recycled, that is, its elements are repeated, in order, until they have been matched up with every element of the longer vector. If the longer one is not a multiple of the shorter one, a warning is given.

```
> x + c(1, 2)

 [1]  2  4  4  6  6  8  8 10 10 12

> x + c(1, 2, 3)

Warning: longer object length is not a multiple of shorter object
length

 [1]  2  4  6  5  7  9  8 10 12 11
```

Comparisons also work on vectors. Here the result is a vector of the same length containing TRUE or FALSE for each element.

```
> x <= 5

 [1]  TRUE  TRUE  TRUE  TRUE  TRUE FALSE FALSE FALSE FALSE FALSE

> x > y

 [1] TRUE TRUE TRUE TRUE TRUE TRUE TRUE TRUE TRUE TRUE

> x < y

 [1] FALSE FALSE FALSE FALSE FALSE FALSE FALSE FALSE FALSE FALSE
```

To test whether all the resulting elements are TRUE, use the all function. Similarly, the any function checks whether any element is TRUE.

```
> x <- 10:1
> y <- -4:5
> any(x < y)
```

```
[1] TRUE

> all(x < y)

[1] FALSE
```

The nchar function also acts on each element of a vector.

```
> q <- c("Hockey", "Football", "Baseball", "Curling", "Rugby",
+        "Lacrosse", "Basketball", "Tennis", "Cricket", "Soccer")
> nchar(q)

 [1]  6  8  8  7  5  8 10  6  7  6

> nchar(y)

 [1] 2 2 2 2 1 1 1 1 1 1
```

Accessing individual elements of a vector is done using square brackets ([ ]). The first element of x is retrieved by typing x[1], the first two elements by x[1:2] and nonconsecutive elements by x[c(1, 4)].

```
> x[1]

[1] 10

> x[1:2]

[1] 10  9

> x[c(1, 4)]

[1] 10  7
```

This works for all types of vectors whether they are numeric, logical, character and so forth.

It is possible to give names to a vector either during creation or after the fact.

```
> # provide a name for each element of an array using a name-value pair
> c(One = "a", Two = "y", Last = "r")

 One  Two Last
 "a"  "y"  "r"

>
> # create a vector
> w <- 1:3
> # name the elements
```

```
> names(w) <- c("a", "b", "c")
> w

a b c
1 2 3
```

4.4.2 Factor Vectors

factors are an important concept in R, especially when building models. Let's create a simple vector of text data that has a few repeats. We will start with the vector q we created earlier and add some elements to it.

```
> q2 <- c(q, "Hockey", "Lacrosse", "Hockey", "Water Polo",
+          "Hockey", "Lacrosse")
```

Converting this to a factor is easy with as.factor.

```
> q2Factor <- as.factor(q2)
> q2Factor

 [1] Hockey      Football   Baseball   Curling   Rugby    Lacrosse
 [7] Basketball  Tennis     Cricket    Soccer    Hockey   Lacrosse
[13] Hockey      Water Polo Hockey     Lacrosse
11 Levels: Baseball Basketball Cricket Curling Football ... Water Polo
```

Notice that after printing out every element of q2Factor, R also prints the levels of q2Factor. The levels of a factor are the unique values of that factor variable. Technically, R is giving each unique value of a factor a unique integer tying it back to the character representation. This can be seen with as.numeric.

```
> as.numeric(q2Factor)

 [1]  6  5  1  4  8  7  2 10  3  9  6  7  6 11  6  7
```

In ordinary factors the order of the levels does not matter and one level is no different from another. Sometimes, however, it is important to understand the order of a factor, such as when coding education levels. Setting the ordered argument to TRUE creates an ordered factor with the order given in the levels argument.

```
> factor(x=c("High School", "College", "Masters", "Doctorate"),
+         levels=c("High School", "College", "Masters", "Doctorate"),
+         ordered=TRUE)

[1] High School College    Masters    Doctorate
Levels: High School < College < Masters < Doctorate
```

factors can drastically reduce the size of the variable because they are storing only the unique values, but they can cause headaches if not used properly. This will be discussed further throughout the book.

4.5   Calling Functions

Earlier we briefly used a few basic functions like nchar, length and as.Date to illustrate some concepts. Functions are very important and helpful in any language because they make code easily repeatable. Almost every step taken in R involves using functions, so it is best to learn the proper way to call them. R function calling is filled with a good deal of nuance, so we are going to focus on the gist of what is needed to know. Of course, throughout the book there will be many examples of calling functions.

Let's start with the simple mean function, which computes the average of a set of numbers. In its simplest form it takes a vector as an argument.

```
> mean(x)
```

```
[1]  5.5
```

More complicated functions have multiple arguments that can be either specified by the order they are entered or by using their name with an equal sign. We will see further use of this throughout the book.

R provides an easy way for users to build their own functions, which we will cover in more detail in Chapter 8.

4.6   Function Documentation

Any function provided in R has accompanying documentation, of varying quality of course. The easiest way to access that documentation is to place a question mark in front of the function name, like this: ?mean.

To get help on binary operators like +, * or == surround them with back ticks (`).

```
> ?`+`
> ?`*`
> ?`==`
```

There are occasions when we have only a sense of the function we want to use. In that case we can look up the function by using part of the name with apropos.

```
> apropos("mea")
```

```
 [1]  ".cache/mean-simple_ce29515dafe58a90a771568646d73aae"
 [2]  ".colMeans"
 [3]  ".rowMeans"
 [4]  "colMeans"
 [5]  "influence.measures"
 [6]  "kmeans"
 [7]  "mean"
 [8]  "mean.Date"
 [9]  "mean.default"
[10]  "mean.difftime"
```

```
[11]  "mean.POSIXct"
[12]  "mean.POSIXlt"
[13]  "mean_cl_boot"
[14]  "mean_cl_normal"
[15]  "mean_sdl"
[16]  "mean_se"
[17]  "rowMeans"
[18]  "weighted.mean"
```

4.7 Missing Data

Missing data plays a critical role in both statistics and computing, and R has two types of missing data, NA and NULL. While they are similar, they behave differently and that difference needs attention.

4.7.1 NA

Often we will have data that has missing values for any number of reasons. Statistical programs use varying techniques to represent missing data such as a dash, a period or even the number 99. R uses NA. NA will often be seen as just another element of a vector. is.na tests each element of a vector for missingness.

```
> z <- c(1, 2, NA, 8, 3, NA, 3)
> z

[1]  1  2 NA  8  3 NA  3

> is.na(z)

[1] FALSE FALSE  TRUE FALSE FALSE  TRUE FALSE
```

NA is entered simply by typing the letters "N" and "A" as if they were normal text. This works for any kind of vector.

```
> zChar <- c("Hockey", NA, "Lacrosse")
> zChar

[1] "Hockey"    NA          "Lacrosse"

> is.na(zChar)

[1] FALSE  TRUE FALSE
```

Handling missing data is an important part of statistical analysis. There are many techniques depending on field and preference. One popular technique is multiple imputation, which is discussed in detail in Chapter 25 of Andrew Gelman and Jennifer Hill's book *Data Analysis Using Regression and Multilevel/Hierarchical Models*, and is implemented in the mi, mice and Amelia packages.

4.7.2   NULL

NULL is the absence of anything. It is not exactly missingness, it is nothingness. Functions can sometimes return NULL and their arguments can be NULL. An important difference between NA and NULL is that NULL is atomical and cannot exist within a vector. If used inside a vector it simply disappears.

```
> z <- c(1, NULL, 3)
> z

[1] 1 3
```

Even though it was entered into the vector z, it did not get stored in z. In fact, z is only two elements long.

The test for a NULL value is is.null.

```
> d <- NULL
> is.null(d)

[1] TRUE

> is.null(7)

[1] FALSE
```

Since NULL cannot be a part of a vector, is.null is appropriately not vectorized.

4.8   Conclusion

Data come in many types, and R is well equipped to handle them. In addition to basic calculations, R can handle numeric, character and time-based data. One of the nicer parts of working with R, although one that requires a different way of thinking about programming, is vectorization. This allows operating on multiple elements in a vector simultaneously, which leads to faster and more mathematical code.

Chapter 5

Advanced Data Structures

Sometimes data requires more complex storage than simple `vectors` and thankfully R provides a host of data structures. The most common are the `data.frame`, `matrix` and `list` followed by the `array`. Of these, the `data.frame` will be most familiar to anyone who has used a spreadsheet, the `matrix` to people familiar with matrix math and the `list` to programmers.

5.1 data.frames

Perhaps one of the most useful features of R is the `data.frame`. It is one of the most often cited reasons for R's ease of use.

On the surface a `data.frame` is just like an Excel spreadsheet in that it has columns and rows. In statistical terms, each column is a variable and each row is an observation.

In terms of how R organizes `data.frames`, each column is actually a `vector`, each of which has the same length. That is very important because it lets each column hold a different type of data (see Section 4.3). This also implies that within a column each element must be of the same type, just like with `vectors`.

There are numerous ways to construct a `data.frame`, the simplest being to use the `data.frame` function. Let's create a basic `data.frame` using some of the `vectors` we have already introduced, namely x, y and q.

```
> x <- 10:1
> y <- -4:5
> q <- c("Hockey", "Football", "Baseball", "Curling", "Rugby",
+        "Lacrosse", "Basketball", "Tennis", "Cricket", "Soccer")
> theDF <- data.frame(x, y, q)
> theDF

  x  y        q
1 10 -4   Hockey
2  9 -3 Football
3  8 -2 Baseball
```

```
4    7 -1    Curling
5    6  0      Rugby
6    5  1   Lacrosse
7    4  2 Basketball
8    3  3     Tennis
9    2  4    Cricket
10   1  5     Soccer
```

This creates a 10x3 data.frame consisting of those three vectors. Notice the names of theDF are simply the variables. We could have assigned names during the creation process, which is generally a good idea.

```
> theDF <- data.frame(First = x, Second = y, Sport = q)
> theDF

   First Second       Sport
1     10     -4      Hockey
2      9     -3    Football
3      8     -2    Baseball
4      7     -1     Curling
5      6      0       Rugby
6      5      1    Lacrosse
7      4      2  Basketball
8      3      3      Tennis
9      2      4     Cricket
10     1      5      Soccer
```

data.frames are complex objects with many attributes. The most frequently checked attributes are the number of rows and columns. Of course there are functions to do this for us: nrow and ncol. And in case both are wanted at the same time there is the dim function.

```
> nrow(theDF)

[1] 10

> ncol(theDF)

[1] 3

> dim(theDF)

[1] 10  3
```

Checking the column names of a data.frame is as simple as using the names function. This returns a character vector listing the columns. Since it is a vector we can access individual elements of it just like any other vector.

```
> names(theDF)
```

```
[1] "First"  "Second" "Sport"
```

```
> names(theDF)[3]
```

```
[1] "Sport"
```

We can also check and assign the row names of a data.frame.

```
> rownames(theDF)
```

```
 [1] "1"  "2"  "3"  "4"  "5"  "6"  "7"  "8"  "9"  "10"
```

```
> rownames(theDF) <- c("One", "Two", "Three", "Four", "Five", "Six",
+                      "Seven", "Eight", "Nine", "Ten")
> rownames(theDF)
```

```
[1] "One"   "Two"   "Three" "Four" "Five" "Six"   "Seven" "Eight"
[9] "Nine"  "Ten"
```

```
> # set them back to the generic index
> rownames(theDF) <- NULL
> rownames(theDF)
```

```
 [1] "1"  "2"  "3"  "4"  "5"  "6"  "7"  "8"  "9"  "10"
```

Usually a data.frame has far too many rows to print them all to the screen, so thankfully the head function prints out only the first few rows.

```
> head(theDF)
```

```
  First Second    Sport
1    10     -4   Hockey
2     9     -3 Football
3     8     -2 Baseball
4     7     -1  Curling
5     6      0    Rugby
6     5      1 Lacrosse
```

```
> head(theDF, n = 7)
```

```
  First Second      Sport
1    10     -4     Hockey
2     9     -3   Football
3     8     -2   Baseball
4     7     -1    Curling
5     6      0      Rugby
6     5      1   Lacrosse
7     4      2 Basketball
```

```
> tail(theDF)
```

```
   First Second      Sport
5      6      0      Rugby
6      5      1   Lacrosse
7      4      2 Basketball
8      3      3     Tennis
9      2      4    Cricket
10     1      5     Soccer
```

As we can with other variables, we can check the `class` of a `data.frame` using the `class` function.

```
> class(theDF)
```

```
[1] "data.frame"
```

Since each column of the `data.frame` is an individual `vector`, it can be accessed individually and each has its own `class`. Like many other aspects of R, there are multiple ways to access an individual column. There is the `$` operator and also the square brackets. Running `theDF$Sport` will give the third column in `theDF`. That allows us to specify one particular column by name.

```
> theDF$Sport
```

```
 [1] Hockey     Football   Baseball   Curling    Rugby      Lacrosse
 [7] Basketball Tennis     Cricket    Soccer
10 Levels: Baseball Basketball Cricket Curling Football ... Tennis
```

Similar to `vectors`, `data.frames` allow us to access individual elements by their position using square brackets, but instead of having one position two are specified. The first is the row number and the second is the column number. So to get the third row from the second column we use `theDF[3, 2]`.

```
> theDF[3, 2]
```

```
[1] -2
```

To specify more than one row or column use a `vector` of indices.

```
> # row 3, columns 2 through 3
> theDF[3, 2:3]
```

```
  Second    Sport
3     -2 Baseball
```

```
>
> # rows 3 and 5, column 2
> # since only one column was selected it was returned as a vector
```

```
> # hence the column names will not be printed
> theDF[c(3, 5), 2]

[1] -2  0

>
> # rows 3 and 5, columns 2 through 3
> theDF[c(3, 5), 2:3]

  Second   Sport
3     -2 Baseball
5      0   Rugby
```

To access an entire row, specify that row while not specifying any column. Likewise, to access an entire column, specify that column while not specifying any row.

```
> # all of column 3
> # since it is only one column a vector is returned
> theDF[, 3]

 [1] Hockey     Football   Baseball   Curling    Rugby      Lacrosse
 [7] Basketball Tennis     Cricket    Soccer
10 Levels: Baseball Basketball Cricket Curling Football ... Tennis

>
> # all of columns 2 through 3
> theDF[, 2:3]

   Second      Sport
1      -4     Hockey
2      -3   Football
3      -2   Baseball
4      -1    Curling
5       0      Rugby
6       1   Lacrosse
7       2 Basketball
8       3     Tennis
9       4    Cricket
10      5     Soccer

>
> # all of row 2
> theDF[2, ]

  First Second    Sport
2     9     -3 Football
```

```
>
> # all of rows 2 through 4
> theDF[2:4, ]

  First Second    Sport
2     9      -3 Football
3     8      -2 Baseball
4     7      -1  Curling
```

To access multiple columns by name, make the column argument a character vector of the names.

```
> theDF[, c("First", "Sport")]

   First       Sport
1     10      Hockey
2      9    Football
3      8    Baseball
4      7     Curling
5      6       Rugby
6      5    Lacrosse
7      4  Basketball
8      3      Tennis
9      2     Cricket
10     1      Soccer
```

Yet another way to access a specific column is to use its column name (or its number) either as second argument to the square brackets or as the only argument to either single or double square brackets.

```
> # just the "Sport" column
> # since it is one column it returns as a (factor) vector
> theDF[, "Sport"]

 [1] Hockey     Football   Baseball   Curling    Rugby      Lacrosse
 [7] Basketball Tennis     Cricket    Soccer
10 Levels: Baseball Basketball Cricket Curling Football ... Tennis

> class(theDF[, "Sport"])

[1] "factor"

>
> # just the "Sport" column
> # this returns a one column data.frame
> theDF["Sport"]
```

```
        Sport
1      Hockey
2    Football
3    Baseball
4     Curling
5       Rugby
6    Lacrosse
7  Basketball
8      Tennis
9     Cricket
10     Soccer

> class(theDF["Sport"])

[1] "data.frame"

>
> # just the "Sport" column
> # this also returns a (factor) vector
> theDF[["Sport"]]

 [1] Hockey      Football    Baseball   Curling    Rugby      Lacrosse
 [7] Basketball  Tennis      Cricket    Soccer
10 Levels: Baseball Basketball Cricket Curling Football ... Tennis

> class(theDF[["Sport"]])

[1] "factor"
```

All of these methods have differing outputs. Some return a vector, some return a single-column data.frame. To ensure a single-column data.frame while using single-square brackets, there is a third argument: drop=FALSE. This also works when specifying a single column by number.

```
> theDF[, "Sport", drop = FALSE]

        Sport
1      Hockey
2    Football
3    Baseball
4     Curling
5       Rugby
6    Lacrosse
7  Basketball
8      Tennis
9     Cricket
10     Soccer
```

```
> class(theDF[, "Sport", drop = FALSE])

[1] "data.frame"

>
> theDF[, 3, drop = FALSE]

          Sport
1         Hockey
2       Football
3       Baseball
4        Curling
5          Rugby
6       Lacrosse
7     Basketball
8         Tennis
9        Cricket
10        Soccer

> class(theDF[, 3, drop = FALSE])

[1] "data.frame"
```

In Section 4.4.2 we see that factors are stored specially. To see how they would be represented in data.frame form, use model.matrix to create a set of indicator (or dummy) variables. That is one column for each level of a factor, with a 1 if a row contains that level or a 0 otherwise.

```
> newFactor <- factor(c("Pennsylvania", "New York", "New Jersey", "New York",
+     "Tennessee", "Massachusetts", "Pennsylvania", "New York"))
> model.matrix(~newFactor - 1)

  newFactorMassachusetts newFactorNew Jersey newFactorNew York
1                      0                   0                 0
2                      0                   0                 1
3                      0                   1                 0
4                      0                   0                 1
5                      0                   0                 0
6                      1                   0                 0
7                      0                   0                 0
8                      0                   0                 1
  newFactorPennsylvania newFactorTennessee
1                     1                  0
2                     0                  0
3                     0                  0
```

```
4                    0                    0
5                    0                    1
6                    0                    0
7                    1                    0
8                    0                    0
attr(,"assign")
[1] 1 1 1 1 1
attr(,"contrasts")
attr(,"contrasts")$newFactor
[1] "contr.treatment"
```

We learn more about formulas (the argument to model.matrix) in Sections 11.2 and 12.3.2 and Chapters 15 and 16.

5.2 Lists

Often a container is needed to hold arbitrary objects of either the same type or varying types. R accomplishes this through lists. They store any number of items of any type. A list can contain all numerics or characters or a mix of the two or data.frames or, recursively, other lists.

Lists are created with the list function where each argument to the function becomes an element of the list.

```
> # creates a three element list
> list(1, 2, 3)


[[1]]
[1] 1

[[2]]
[1] 2

[[3]]
[1] 3

>
> # creates a single element list where the only element is a vector
> # that has three elements
> list(c(1, 2, 3))

[[1]]
[1] 1 2 3
```

```
>
> # creates a two element list
> # the first element is a three element vector
> # the second element is a five element vector
> (list3 <- list(c(1, 2, 3), 3:7))

[[1]]
[1] 1 2 3

[[2]]
[1] 3 4 5 6 7

>
> # two element list
> # first element is a data.frame
> # second element is a 10 element vector
> list(theDF, 1:10)

[[1]]
    First Second       Sport
1      10     -4      Hockey
2       9     -3    Football
3       8     -2    Baseball
4       7     -1     Curling
5       6      0       Rugby
6       5      1    Lacrosse
7       4      2  Basketball
8       3      3      Tennis
9       2      4     Cricket
10      1      5      Soccer

[[2]]
 [1]  1  2  3  4  5  6  7  8  9 10

>
> # three element list
> # first is a data.frame
> # second is a vector
> # third is list3, which holds two vectors
> list5 <- list(theDF, 1:10, list3)
> list5

[[1]]
    First Second       Sport
1      10     -4      Hockey
2       9     -3    Football
```

```
3        8       -2     Baseball
4        7       -1      Curling
5        6        0        Rugby
6        5        1     Lacrosse
7        4        2   Basketball
8        3        3       Tennis
9        2        4      Cricket
10       1        5       Soccer

[[2]]
 [1]  1  2  3  4  5  6  7  8  9 10

[[3]]
[[3]][[1]]
[1] 1 2 3

[[3]][[2]]
[1] 3 4 5 6 7
```

Notice in the previous block of code (where list3 was created) that enclosing an expression in parentheses displays the results after execution.

Like data.frames, lists can have names. Each element has a unique name that can be either viewed or assigned using names.

```
> names(list5)
```

NULL

```
> names(list5) <- c("data.frame", "vector", "list")
> names(list5)
```

```
[1] "data.frame" "vector"     "list"
```

```
> list5
```

```
$data.frame
  First Second      Sport
1    10     -4     Hockey
2     9     -3   Football
3     8     -2   Baseball
4     7     -1    Curling
5     6      0      Rugby
```

```
6        5        1      Lacrosse
7        4        2    Basketball
8        3        3        Tennis
9        2        4       Cricket
10       1        5        Soccer

$vector
 [1]   1   2   3   4   5   6   7   8   9  10

$list
$list[[1]]
[1]  1 2 3

$list[[2]]
[1]  3 4 5 6 7
```

Names can also be assigned to list elements during creation using name-value pairs.

```
> list6 <- list(TheDataFrame = theDF, TheVector = 1:10, TheList = list3)
> names(list6)

[1]  "TheDataFrame"  "TheVector"      "TheList"

> list6

$TheDataFrame
    First Second       Sport
1      10     -4       Hockey
2       9     -3     Football
3       8     -2     Baseball
4       7     -1      Curling
5       6      0        Rugby
6       5      1     Lacrosse
7       4      2   Basketball
8       3      3       Tennis
9       2      4      Cricket
10      1      5       Soccer

$TheVector
 [1]   1   2   3   4   5   6   7   8   9  10

$TheList
$TheList[[1]]
[1]  1 2 3
```

```
$TheList[[2]]
[1]  3  4  5  6  7
```

Creating an empty `list` of a certain size is, perhaps confusingly, done with `vector`.

```
> (emptyList <- vector(mode = "list", length = 4))

[[1]]
NULL

[[2]]
NULL

[[3]]
NULL

[[4]]
NULL
```

To access an individual element of a `list`, use double square brackets, specifying either the element number or name. Note that this allows access to only one element at a time.

```
> list5[[1]]
```

```
     First Second        Sport
1      10     -4        Hockey
2       9     -3      Football
3       8     -2      Baseball
4       7     -1       Curling
5       6      0         Rugby
6       5      1      Lacrosse
7       4      2    Basketball
8       3      3        Tennis
9       2      4       Cricket
10      1      5        Soccer
```

```
> list5[["data.frame"]]
```

```
     First Second        Sport
1      10     -4        Hockey
2       9     -3      Football
3       8     -2      Baseball
4       7     -1       Curling
5       6      0         Rugby
```

```
6       5       1    Lacrosse
7       4       2 Basketball
8       3       3      Tennis
9       2       4     Cricket
10      1       5      Soccer
```

Once an element is accessed it can be treated as if that actual element is being used, allowing nested indexing of elements.

```
> list5[[1]]$Sport
```

```
 [1] Hockey      Football    Baseball   Curling     Rugby       Lacrosse
 [7] Basketball Tennis       Cricket     Soccer
10 Levels: Baseball Basketball Cricket Curling Football ... Tennis
```

```
> list5[[1]][, "Second"]
```

```
 [1] -4 -3 -2 -1  0  1  2  3  4  5
```

```
> list5[[1]][, "Second", drop = FALSE]
```

```
    Second
1       -4
2       -3
3       -2
4       -1
5        0
6        1
7        2
8        3
9        4
10       5
```

It is possible to append elements to a list simply by using an index (either numeric or named) that does not exist.

```
> # see how long it currently is
> length(list5)
```

```
[1] 3
```

```
>
> # add a fourth element, unnamed
> list5[[4]] <- 2
> length(list5)
```

```
[1] 4
```

```
>
> # add a fifth element, named
> list5[["NewElement"]] <- 3:6
> length(list5)

[1] 5

>
> names(list5)

[1] "data.frame" "vector"      "list"         ""           "NewElement"

> list5

$data.frame
   First Second      Sport
1     10     -4     Hockey
2      9     -3   Football
3      8     -2   Baseball
4      7     -1    Curling
5      6      0      Rugby
6      5      1   Lacrosse
7      4      2 Basketball
8      3      3     Tennis
9      2      4    Cricket
10     1      5     Soccer

$vector
 [1]  1  2  3  4  5  6  7  8  9 10

$list
$list[[1]]
[1] 1 2 3

$list[[2]]
[1] 3 4 5 6 7


[[4]]
[1] 2

$NewElement
[1] 3 4 5 6
```

Occasionally appending to a list—or vector or data.frame for that matter—is fine, but doing so repeatedly is computationally expensive. So it is best to create a list as long as its final desired size and then fill it in using the appropriate indices.

5.3 `Matrices`

A very common mathematical structure that is essential to statistics is a matrix. This is similar to a data.frame in that it is rectangular with rows and columns except that every single element, regardless of column, must be the same type, most commonly all numerics. They also act similarly to vectors with element-by-element addition, multiplication, subtraction, division and equality. The nrow, ncol and dim functions work just like they do for data.frames.

```
> # create a 5x2 matrix
> A <- matrix(1:10, nrow = 5)
> # create another 5x2 matrix
> B <- matrix(21:30, nrow = 5)
> # create another 5x2 matrix
> C <- matrix(21:40, nrow = 2)
> A

     [,1] [,2]
[1,]    1    6
[2,]    2    7
[3,]    3    8
[4,]    4    9
[5,]    5   10

> B

     [,1] [,2]
[1,]   21   26
[2,]   22   27
[3,]   23   28
[4,]   24   29
[5,]   25   30

> C

     [,1] [,2] [,3] [,4] [,5] [,6] [,7] [,8] [,9] [,10]
[1,]   21   23   25   27   29   31   33   35   37    39
[2,]   22   24   26   28   30   32   34   36   38    40

> nrow(A)

[1] 5
```

```
> ncol(A)
```

```
[1] 2
```

```
> dim(A)
```

```
[1] 5 2
```

```
> # add them
> A + B
```

```
      [,1]  [,2]
[1,]    22    32
[2,]    24    34
[3,]    26    36
[4,]    28    38
[5,]    30    40
```

```
> # multiply them
> A * B
```

```
      [,1]  [,2]
[1,]    21   156
[2,]    44   189
[3,]    69   224
[4,]    96   261
[5,]   125   300
```

```
> # see if the elements are equal
> A == B
```

```
        [,1]    [,2]
[1,]   FALSE   FALSE
[2,]   FALSE   FALSE
[3,]   FALSE   FALSE
[4,]   FALSE   FALSE
[5,]   FALSE   FALSE
```

Matrix multiplication is a commonly used operation in mathematics, requiring the number of columns of the left-hand `matrix` to be the same as the number of rows of the right-hand `matrix`. Both A and B are 5X2 so we will transpose B so it can be used on the right-hand side.

```
> A %*% t(B)
```

```
      [,1]  [,2]  [,3]  [,4]  [,5]
[1,]   177   184   191   198   205
```

```
[2,]   224   233   242   251   260
[3,]   271   282   293   304   315
[4,]   318   331   344   357   370
[5,]   365   380   395   410   425
```

Another similarity with data.frames is that matrices can also have row and column names.

```
> colnames(A)

NULL

> rownames(A)

NULL

> colnames(A) <- c("Left", "Right")
> rownames(A) <- c("1st", "2nd", "3rd", "4th", "5th")
>
> colnames(B)

NULL

> rownames(B)

NULL

> colnames(B) <- c("First", "Second")
> rownames(B) <- c("One", "Two", "Three", "Four", "Five")
>
> colnames(C)

NULL

> rownames(C)

NULL

> colnames(C) <- LETTERS[1:10]
> rownames(C) <- c("Top", "Bottom")
```

There are two special vectors, letters and LETTERS, that contain the lower-case and upper-case letters, respectively.

Notice the effect when transposing a matrix and multiplying matrices. Transposing naturally flips the row and column names. Matrix multiplication keeps the row names from the left matrix and the column names from the right matrix.

```
> t(A)
```

```
        1st 2nd 3rd 4th 5th
Left      1   2   3   4   5
Right     6   7   8   9  10

> A %*% C

      A    B    C    D    E    F    G    H    I    J
1st 153  167  181  195  209  223  237  251  265  279
2nd 196  214  232  250  268  286  304  322  340  358
3rd 239  261  283  305  327  349  371  393  415  437
4th 282  308  334  360  386  412  438  464  490  516
5th 325  355  385  415  445  475  505  535  565  595
```

5.4 Arrays

An array is essentially a multidimensional vector. It must all be of the same type and individual elements are accessed in a similar fashion using square brackets. The first element is the row index, the second is the column index and the remaining elements are for outer dimensions.

```
> theArray <- array(1:12, dim = c(2, 3, 2))
> theArray

, , 1

     [,1] [,2] [,3]
[1,]    1    3    5
[2,]    2    4    6

, , 2

     [,1] [,2] [,3]
[1,]    7    9   11
[2,]    8   10   12

> theArray[1, , ]

     [,1] [,2]
[1,]    1    7
[2,]    3    9
[3,]    5   11

> theArray[1, , 1]

[1] 1 3 5
```

```
> theArray[, , 1]

     [,1] [,2] [,3]
[1,]    1    3    5
[2,]    2    4    6
```

The main difference between an array and a matrix is that matrices are restricted to two dimensions while arrays can have an arbitrary number.

5.5   Conclusion

Data come in many types and structures, which can pose a problem for some analysis environments but R handles them with aplomb. The most common data structure is the one-dimensional vector, which forms the basis of everything in R. The most powerful structure is the data.frame—something special in R that most other languages do not have—which handles mixed data types in a spreadsheet-like format. Lists are useful for storing collections of items like a hash in Perl.

Chapter 6

Reading Data into R

Now that we have seen some of R's basic functionality, it is time to load in data. As with everything in R, there are numerous ways to get data; the most common is probably reading comma separated values (CSV) files. Of course there are many other options that we will cover as well.

6.1 Reading CSVs

The best way to read data from a CSV file is to use read.table. It might be tempting to use read.csv but that is more trouble than it is worth, and all it does is call read.table with some arguments preset. The result of using read.table is a data.frame.

The first argument to read.table is the full path of the file to be loaded. The file can be sitting on disk or even on the Web. For the purposes of this book we will read from the Web.

Any CSV will work but we have posted an incredibly simple CSV at http://www.jaredlander.com/data/Tomato%20First.csv. Let's read that into R using read.table.

```
> theUrl <- "http://www.jaredlander.com/data/Tomato%20First.csv"
> tomato <- read.table (file = theUrl, header = TRUE, sep = ",")
```

This can now be seen using head.

```
> head(tomato)
```

	Round	Tomato	Price	Source	Sweet	Acid	Color	Texture
1	1	Simpson SM	3.99	Whole Foods	2.8	2.8	3.7	3.4
2	1	Tuttorosso (blue)	2.99	Pioneer	3.3	2.8	3.4	3.0
3	1	Tuttorosso (green)	0.99	Pioneer	2.8	2.6	3.3	2.8
4	1	La Fede SM DOP	3.99	Shop Rite	2.6	2.8	3.0	2.3
5	2	Cento SM DOP	5.49	D Agostino	3.3	3.1	2.9	2.8
6	2	Cento Organic	4.99	D Agostino	3.2	2.9	2.9	3.1

```
     Overall Avg.of.Totals Total.of.Avg
1      3.4          16.1         16.1
2      2.9          15.3         15.3
3      2.9          14.3         14.3
4      2.8          13.4         13.4
5      3.1          14.4         15.2
6      2.9          15.5         15.1
```

As mentioned before, the first argument is the file name in quotes (or as a character variable). Notice how we explicitly used the argument names file, header and sep. As discussed in Section 4.5, function arguments can be specified without the name of the argument (positionally indicated) but specifying the arguments is good practice. The second argument, header, indicates that the first row of data holds the column names. The third argument gives the delimiter separating data cells. Changing this to other values such as "\t" (tab delimited) or ";" (semicolon delimited) allows it to read other types of files.

One often unknown argument that is helpful to use is stringsAsFactors. Setting this to FALSE (the default is TRUE) prevents character columns from being converted to factor columns. This both saves computation time—this can be dramatic if it is a large dataset with many character columns with many unique values—and keeps the columns as character data, which are easier to work with.

Although we do not mention this argument in Section 5.1, stringsAsFactors can be used in data.frame. Re-creating that first bit of code results in an easier-to-use "Sport" column.

```
> x <- 10:1
> y <- -4:5
> q <- c("Hockey", "Football", "Baseball", "Curling", "Rugby",
+        "Lacrosse", "Basketball", "Tennis", "Cricket", "Soccer")
> theDF <- data.frame(First=x, Second=y, Sport=q, stringsAsFactors=FALSE)
> theDF$Sport

 [1] "Hockey"     "Football"   "Baseball"  "Curling"   "Rugby"
 [6] "Lacrosse"   "Basketball" "Tennis"    "Cricket"   "Soccer"
```

There are numerous other arguments to read.table, the most useful being quote and colClasses, specifying the character used for enclosing cells and the data type for each column, respectively.

Sometimes CSVs (or tab delimited files) are poorly built, where the cell separator has been used inside a cell. In this case read.csv2 (or read.delim2) should be used instead of read.table.

6.2   Excel Data

While Excel may be the world's most popular data analysis tool, it is unfortunately difficult to read Excel data into R. The simplest method would be to use Excel (or another spreadsheet program) to convert the Excel file to a CSV file. That might sound like a cop-out but it is the easiest method to use. The R community abounds with hacks to get data from Excel into R, such as using the Clipboard to copy and paste, but those are inelegant at best and can fail with large amounts of data.

A number of packages exist to tackle this problem such as gdata, XLConnect, xlsReadWrite, and others but they all have some erroneous requirement such as Java, Perl or 32-bit R, which is neither preferable nor so common anymore. The RODBC package has a function, odbcConnectExcel2007, that reads Excel files but requires a DSN[1] connection, which is not a feasible everyday strategy.

We understand that Excel 2007 files are essentially XML files. This would mean that they could theoretically be parsed using the XML package, but we have not seen this done as of yet.

6.3   Reading from Databases

Databases arguably store the vast majority of the world's data. Most of these, whether they be Microsoft SQL Server, DB2, MySQL or Microsoft Access, provide an ODBC connection. Accordingly, R makes use of ODBC through the aptly named RODBC package (which comes with base R). Like any other package, it must be loaded before use.

```
> require(RODBC)
```

The first step to reading from a database is to create a DSN. This differs by operating system but should result in a string name for that connection. This is used in odbcConnect to create a connection for R to use. Optional, but common, arguments are uid and pwd for the database username and password, respectively.

```
> db <- odbcConnect("QV Training")
```

At this point we are ready to run a query on that database using sqlQuery. This can be any valid SQL query of arbitrary complexity. sqlQuery returns a data.frame just like any other. Fortunately, sqlQuery has the stringsAsFactors argument first seen in Section 6.1. Again, setting this to TRUE is usually a good idea, as it will save processing time.

```
> # simple SELECT * query from one table
> ordersTable <- sqlQuery(db, "SELECT * FROM Orders",
        stringsAsFactors=FALSE)
> # simple SELECT * query from one table
> detailsTable <- sqlQuery(db, "SELECT * FROM [Order Details]",
        stringsAsFactors=FALSE)
> # do a join between the two tables
> longQuery <- "SELECT * FROM Orders, [Order Details]
        WHERE Orders.OrderID = [Order Details].OrderID"
> detailsJoin <- sqlQuery(db, longQuery, stringsAsFactors=FALSE)
```

---

1. A DSN is a data source connection used to describe communication to a data source, often a database.

We can easily check the results of these queries by viewing the resulting `data.frames`.

```
> head(ordersTable)
```

	OrderID	OrderDate	CustomerID	EmployeeID	ShipperID	Freight
1	10248	2008-06-29	4	2	2	43.48
2	10249	2007-06-29	79	7	2	29.20
3	10250	2008-07-03	34	2	2	79.17
4	10251	2007-12-02	1	7	2	43.41
5	10252	2008-04-04	76	5	1	23.20
6	10253	2008-07-05	34	3	2	66.54

```
> head(detailsTable)
```

	OrderID	LineNo	ProductID	Quantity	UnitPrice	Discount
1	10402	2	63	65	18.94	0.00
2	10403	1	48	70	31.83	0.15
3	10403	2	16	21	10.15	0.15
4	10404	1	42	40	13.37	0.05
5	10404	2	49	30	19.82	0.05
6	10404	3	26	30	33.93	0.05

```
> head(detailsJoin)
```

	OrderID	OrderDate	CustomerID	EmployeeID	ShipperID	Freight
1	10402	2006-04-28	20	4	1	46.63
2	10403	2006-09-28	20	4	1	26.43
3	10403	2006-09-28	20	4	1	26.43
4	10404	2006-04-19	49	6	1	72.73
5	10404	2006-04-19	49	6	1	72.73
6	10404	2006-04-19	49	6	1	72.73

	OrderID.1	LineNo	ProductID	Quantity	UnitPrice	Discount
1	10402	2	63	65	18.94	0.00
2	10403	1	48	70	31.83	0.15
3	10403	2	16	21	10.15	0.15
4	10404	1	42	40	13.37	0.05
5	10404	2	49	30	19.82	0.05
6	10404	3	26	30	33.93	0.05

While it is not necessary, it is good practice to close the ODBC connection using `odbcClose`, although it will close automatically when either R closes or we open another connection using `odbcConnect`. Only one connection may be open at a time.

6.4 Data from Other Statistical Tools

In an ideal world another tool besides R would never be needed, but in reality data are sometimes locked in a proprietary format such as those from SAS, SPSS or Octave. The foreign package provides a number of functions similar to read.table to read in data from other tools.

A partial list of functions to read data from commonly used statistical tools is in Table 6.1. The arguments for these functions are generally similar to read.table. These functions usually return the data as a data.frame but do not always succeed.

Table 6.1   Functions for Reading Data from Some Commonly Used Statistical Tools

Function	Format
read.spss	SPSS
read.dta	Stata
read.ssd	SAS
read.octave	Octave
read.mtp	Minitab
read.systat	Systat

While read.ssd can read SAS data, it requires a valid SAS license. This can be sidestepped by using Revolution R from Revolution Analytics with their special RxSasData function in their RevoScaleR package.

6.5 R Binary Files

When working with other R programmers, a good way to pass around data—or any R objects like variables and functions—is to use RData files. These are binary files that represent R objects of any kind. They can store a single object or multiple objects and can be passed among Windows, Mac and Linux without a problem.

First, let's create an RData file, remove the object that created it, and then read it back into R.

```
> # save the tomato data.frame to disk
> save(tomato, file = "data/tomato.rdata")
> # remove tomato from memory
> rm(tomato)
> # check if it still exists
> head(tomato)

Error: object 'tomato' not found

> # read it from the rdata file
```

```
> load("data/tomato.rdata")
> # check if it exists now
> head(tomato)
```

	Round	Tomato	Price	Source	Sweet	Acid	Color	Texture
1	1	Simpson SM	3.99	Whole Foods	2.8	2.8	3.7	3.4
2	1	Tuttorosso (blue)	2.99	Pioneer	3.3	2.8	3.4	3.0
3	1	Tuttorosso (green)	0.99	Pioneer	2.8	2.6	3.3	2.8
4	1	La Fede SM DOP	3.99	Shop Rite	2.6	2.8	3.0	2.3
5	2	Cento SM DOP	5.49	D Agostino	3.3	3.1	2.9	2.8
6	2	Cento Organic	4.99	D Agostino	3.2	2.9	2.9	3.1

	Overall	Avg.of.Totals	Total.of.Avg
1	3.4	16.1	16.1
2	2.9	15.3	15.3
3	2.9	14.3	14.3
4	2.8	13.4	13.4
5	3.1	14.4	15.2
6	2.9	15.5	15.1

Now let's create a few objects to store in a single RData file, remove them and then load them again.

```
> # create some objects
> n <- 20
> r <- 1:10
> w <- data.frame(n, r)
> # check them out
> n

[1] 20

> r

 [1]  1  2  3  4  5  6  7  8  9 10

> w

    n  r
1  20  1
2  20  2
3  20  3
4  20  4
5  20  5
6  20  6
7  20  7
8  20  8
9  20  9
10 20 10
```

```
> # save them
> save(n, r, w, file = "data/multiple.rdata")
> # delete them
> rm(n, r, w)
> # are they gone?
> n
```

```
Error: object 'n' not found
```

```
> r
```

```
Error: object 'r' not found
```

```
> w
```

```
Error: object 'w' not found
```

```
> # load them back
> load("data/multiple.rdata")
> # check them out again
> n
```

```
[1] 20
```

```
> r
```

```
[1]  1  2  3  4  5  6  7  8  9 10
```

```
> w
```

```
    n  r
1  20  1
2  20  2
3  20  3
4  20  4
5  20  5
6  20  6
7  20  7
8  20  8
9  20  9
10 20 10
```

6.6   Data Included with R

R and some packages come with data included, so we can easily have data to use.
Accessing these data is simple as long as we know what to look for. ggplot2, for instance,
comes with a dataset about diamonds. It can be loaded using the data function.

```
> require(ggplot2)
> data(diamonds)
> head(diamonds)
```

	carat	cut	color	clarity	depth	table	price	x	y	z
1	0.23	Ideal	E	SI2	61.5	55	326	3.95	3.98	2.43
2	0.21	Premium	E	SI1	59.8	61	326	3.89	3.84	2.31
3	0.23	Good	E	VS1	56.9	65	327	4.05	4.07	2.31
4	0.29	Premium	I	VS2	62.4	58	334	4.20	4.23	2.63
5	0.31	Good	J	SI2	63.3	58	335	4.34	4.35	2.75
6	0.24	Very Good	J	VVS2	62.8	57	336	3.94	3.96	2.48

To find a list of available data, simply type `data()` into the console.

6.7   Extract Data from Web Sites

These days a lot of data are displayed on Web pages. If we are lucky, it is stored neatly in an HTML table. If we are not so lucky, we might need to parse the text of the page.

6.7.1   Simple HTML Tables

If the data are stored neatly in an HTML table we can use `readHTMLTable` in the XML package to easily extract it. On my site there is a post about a Super Bowl pool I was asked to analyze at http://www.jaredlander.com/2012/02/another-kind-of-super-bowl-pool. In that post there is a table with three columns that we wish to extract. It is fairly simple to do with the following code.

```
> require(XML)
> theURL <- "http://www.jaredlander.com/2012/02/another-kind-of-
+       super-bowl-pool/"
> bowlPool <- readHTMLTable(theURL, which = 1, header = FALSE,
+       stringsAsFactors = FALSE)
> bowlPool
```

	V1	V2	V3
1	Participant 1	Giant A	Patriot Q
2	Participant 2	Giant B	Patriot R
3	Participant 3	Giant C	Patriot S
4	Participant 4	Giant D	Patriot T
5	Participant 5	Giant E	Patriot U
6	Participant 6	Giant F	Patriot V
7	Participant 7	Giant G	Patriot W
8	Participant 8	Giant H	Patriot X
9	Participant 9	Giant I	Patriot Y
10	Participant 10	Giant J	Patriot Z

Here the first argument was the URL but it could have also been a file on disk. The which argument allows us to choose which table to read if there are multiple tables. For this example, there was only one table but it could have easily been the second or third or fourth. We set header to FALSE to indicate that no header was in the table. Last, we used stringsAsFactors=FALSE so that the character columns would not be converted to factors.

6.7.2 Scraping Web Data

If the data are not so neatly stored, it is possible to scrape them off the page, although this is a very involved process. It requires good pattern matching and regular expressions, which are covered in Section 13.14. The idea is to figure out what common pattern surrounds different pieces of data, and this requires at least a basic knowledge of HTML.

6.8 Conclusion

Reading data is the first step to any analysis; without the data there is nothing to do. The most common way to read data into R is from a CSV using read.table. RODBC provides an excellent method for reading from any database with a DSN. Reading from data trapped in HTML tables is made easy using the XML package. R also has a special binary file format, RData, for the quick storage, loading and transfer of R objects.

Chapter 7

Statistical Graphics

One of the hardest parts of an analysis is producing quality supporting graphics. Conversely, a good graph is one of the best ways to present findings. Fortunately, R provides excellent graphing capabilities, both in the base installation and with add-on packages such as `lattice` and `ggplot2`. We will briefly present some simple graphs using base graphics and then show their counterparts in `ggplot2`. This will be supplemented throughout the book where supporting graphics—with code—will be made using `ggplot2` and occasionally base graphics.

Graphics are used in statistics primarily for two reasons: exploratory data analysis (EDA) and presenting results. Both are incredibly important but must be targeted to different audiences.

7.1 Base Graphics

When graphing for the first time with R, most people use base graphics and then move on to `ggplot2` when their needs become more complex. While base graphs can be beautiful creations, we recommend spending the most time learning about `ggplot2` in Section 7.2. This section is here for completeness and because base graphics are just needed, especially for modifying the plots generated by other functions.

Before we can go any further we need some data. Most of the datasets built into R are tiny, even by standards from ten years ago. A good dataset for example graphs is, ironically, included with `ggplot2`. In order to access it, `ggplot2` must first be installed and loaded. Then the `diamonds` data can be loaded and inspected.

```
> require(ggplot2)
> data(diamonds)
> head(diamonds)
```

	carat	cut	color	clarity	depth	table	price	x	y	z
1	0.23	Ideal	E	SI2	61.5	55	326	3.95	3.98	2.43
2	0.21	Premium	E	SI1	59.8	61	326	3.89	3.84	2.31
3	0.23	Good	E	VS1	56.9	65	327	4.05	4.07	2.31

```
4   0.29    Premium    I     VS2   62.4     58    334 4.20 4.23 2.63
5   0.31      Good     J     SI2   63.3     58    335 4.34 4.35 2.75
6   0.24 Very Good     J     VVS2  62.8     57    336 3.94 3.96 2.48
```

7.1.1 Base Histograms

The most common graph of data in a single variable is a histogram. This shows the distribution of values for that variable. Creating a histogram is very simple and illustrated in Figure 7.1 for the `carat` column in `diamonds`.

```
> hist(diamonds$carat, main = "Carat Histogram", xlab = "Carat")
```

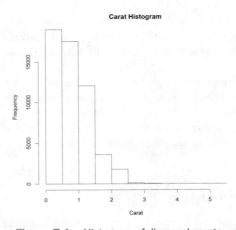

Figure 7.1   Histogram of diamond carats.

This shows the distribution of the carat size. Notice that the title was set using the `main` argument and the *x*-axis label with the `xlab` argument. More complicated histograms are easier to create with `ggplot2`. These extra capabilities are presented in Section 7.2.1.

Histograms break the data into buckets and the heights of the bars represent the number of observations that fall into each bucket. This can be sensitive to the number and size of buckets, so making a good histogram can require some experimentation.

7.1.2 Base Scatterplot

It is frequently good to see two variables in comparison with each other; this is where the scatterplot is used. Every point represents an observation in two variables where the *x*-axis represents one variable and the *y*-axis another. We will plot the price of diamonds against the carat using `formula` notation (see Figure 7.2).

```
> plot(price ~ carat, data = diamonds)
```

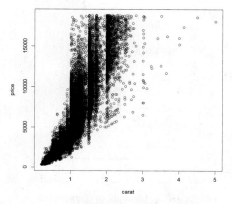

Figure 7.2   Scatterplot of diamond price versus carat.

The ~ separating `price` and `carat` indicates that we are viewing `price` against `carat` where `price` is the *y* value and `carat` is the *x* value. Formulas are explained in more detail in Chapters 15 and 16.

It is also possible to build a scatterplot by simply specifying the *x* and *y* variables without the `formula` interface. This allows plotting of variables that are not necessarily in a `data.frame`.

```
> plot(diamonds$carat, diamonds$price)
```

Scatterplots are one of the most frequently used statistical graphs and will be detailed further using `ggplot2` in Section 7.2.2.

7.1.3 Boxplots

Although boxplots are often among the first graphs taught to statistics students, they are a matter of great debate in the statistics community. Andrew Gelman from Columbia University has been very vocal in his displeasure with boxplots.[1] However, other people such as Hadley Wickham[2] and John Tukey are strong proponents of the boxplot. Given their ubiquity (deserved or not) it is important to learn them. Thankfully, R has the `boxplot` function (see Figure 7.3).

```
> boxplot(diamonds$carat)
```

The idea behind the boxplot is that the thick middle line represents the median and the box is bounded by the first and third quartiles. That is, the middle 50% of data (the Interquartile Range or IQR) is held in the box. The lines extend out to 1.5*IQR in both

---

1. `http://andrewgelman.com/2009/02/boxplot_challen/` and `http://andrewgelman.com/2009/10/better_than_a_b/`
2. `http://vita.had.co.nz/papers/boxplots.pdf`

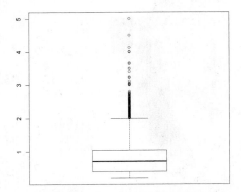

Figure 7.3   Boxplot of diamond carat.

directions. Outlier points are then plotted beyond that. It is important to note that while 50% of the data are very visible in the box, that means 50% of the data are not really displayed. That is a lot of information to not see.

As with other graphs previously discussed, more details will be provided using ggplot2 in Section 7.2.3.

Many objects, such as linear models and contingency tables, have built-in plot functions, which we will see later in the book.

7.2 ggplot2

While R's base graphics are extremely powerful and flexible and can be customized to a great extent, using them can be labor intensive. Two packages—ggplot2 and lattice—were built to make graphing easier. Over the past few years ggplot2 has far exceeded lattice in popularity and features. We re-create all the previous graphs in Section 7.1 and expand the examples with more advanced features. Neither this chapter nor this book is an exhaustive review of ggplot2. But throughout this book, where there is a plot the accompanying code (mostly with ggplot2, although some use base graphics) is included.

Initially, the ggplot2 syntax is harder to grasp, but the effort is more than worthwhile. It is much easier to delineate data by color, shape, or size and add legends with ggplot2. Graphs are quicker to build. Graphs that could take 30 lines of code with base graphics are possible with just one line in ggplot2.

The basic structure for ggplot2 starts with the ggplot function,[3] which at its most basic should take the data as its first argument. It can take more arguments, or fewer, but we will stick with that for now. After initializing the object, we add layers using

---

3. The package was previously called ggplot but early on Hadley made massive changes, so he upgraded the name to ggplot2.

the + symbol. To start, we will just discuss geometric layers such as points, lines and histograms. They are included using functions like geom_point, geom_line and geom_histogram. These functions take multiple arguments, the most important being which variable in the data gets mapped to which axis or other aesthetic using aes. Furthermore, each layer can have different aesthetic mappings and even different data.

7.2.1 ggplot2 **Histograms and Densities**

Returning to the histogram seen in Figure 7.1, we plot the distribution of diamond carats using ggplot2. This is built using ggplot and geom_histogram. Because histograms are one-dimensional displays of data, we need to specify only one aesthetic mapping, the x-axis. Figure 7.4 shows the plot.

```
> ggplot(data = diamonds) + geom_histogram(aes(x = carat))
```

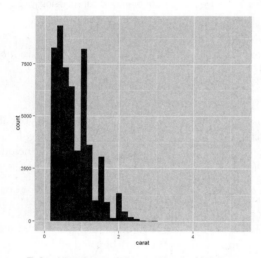

Figure 7.4   Histogram of diamond carats using ggplot2.

A similar display is the density plot, which is done by changing geom_histogram to geom_density. We also specify the color to fill in the graph using the fill argument. This differs from the color argument that we will see later. Also notice that the fill argument was entered outside the aes function. This is because we want the whole graph to be that color. We will see how it can be used inside aes later. This results in the graph shown in Figure 7.5

```
> ggplot(data = diamonds) + geom_density(aes(x = carat), fill = "grey50")
```

Whereas histograms display counts of data in buckets, density plots show the probability of observations falling within a sliding window along the variable of interest. The

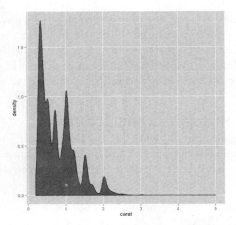

Figure 7.5   Density plot of diamond carats using `ggplot2`.

difference between the two is subtle but important. Histograms are more of a discrete measurement while density plots are more of a continuous measurement.

7.2.2 `ggplot2` **Scatterplots**

Here we not only show the `ggplot2` way of making scatterplots but also show off some of the power of `ggplot2`. We start by re-creating the simple scatterplot in Figure 7.2. Like before, we use `ggplot` to initialize the object, but this time we include `aes` inside the `ggplot` call instead of using it in the geom. The `ggplot2` version is shown in Figure 7.6.

```
> ggplot(diamonds, aes(x = carat, y = price)) + geom_point()
```

In the next few examples we will be using `ggplot(diamonds, aes(x=carat, y=price))` repeatedly, which ordinarily would require a lot of redundant typing. Fortunately we can save `ggplot` objects to variables and add layers later. We will save it to g. Notice that nothing is plotted.

```
> # save basics of ggplot object to a variable
> g <- ggplot(diamonds, aes(x = carat, y = price))
```

Going forward we can add any layer to g. Running g + `geom_point()` would re-create the graph shown in Figure 7.6.

The `diamonds` data have many interesting variables we can examine. Let's first look at color, which we will map to the color[4] aesthetic in Figure 7.7.

```
> g + geom_point(aes(color = color))
```

---

4. `ggplot` will accept both the American (color) and British (colour) spellings.

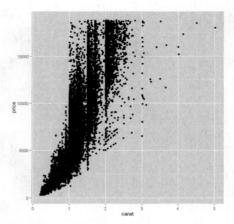

Figure 7.6   Simple `ggplot2` scatterplot.

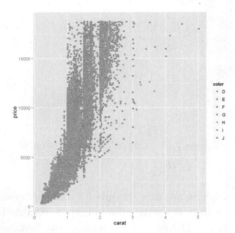

Figure 7.7   Scatterplot of diamonds data mapping diamond color to the color aesthetic.

Notice that we set `color=color` inside `aes`. This is because the designated color will be determined by the data. Also see that a legend was automatically generated. Recent versions of `ggplot2` have added flexibility with the legend, which we will discuss later.

`ggplot2` also has the ability to make faceted plots, or small multiples as Edward Tufte would say. This is done using `facet_wrap` or `facet_grid`. `facet_wrap` takes the levels of one variable, cuts up the underlying data according to them, makes a separate pane for each set, and arranges them to fit in the plot, as seen in Figure 7.8. Here the row and column placement have no real meaning. `facet_grid` acts similarly but assigns all levels of a variable to either a row or column as shown in Figure 7.9. In this case the upper left

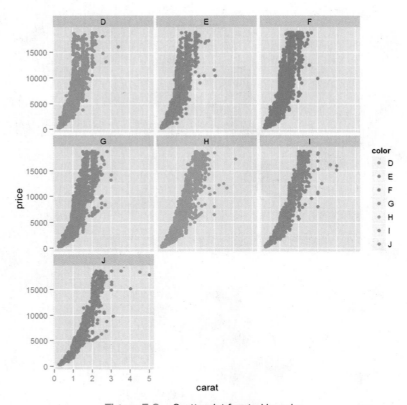

Figure 7.8   Scatterplot faceted by color.

pane displays a scatterplot where the data are only for diamonds with `Fair` cut and `I1` clarity. The pane to the right is a scatterplot where the data are only for diamonds with `Fair` cut and `SI2` clarity. The pane in the second row, first column is a scatterplot where the data are only for diamonds with `Good` cut and `I1` clarity. After understanding how to read one pane in this plot we can easily understand all the panes and make quick comparisons.

```
> g + geom_point(aes(color = color)) + facet_wrap(~color)
```

```
> g + geom_point(aes(color = color)) + facet_grid(cut ~ clarity)
```

Faceting also works with histograms or any other geom as shown in Figure 7.10.

```
> ggplot(diamonds, aes(x = carat)) + geom_histogram() + facet_wrap(~color)
```

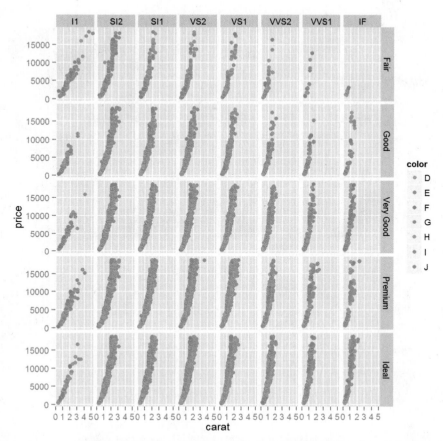

Figure 7.9 Scatterplot faceted by cut and clarity. Notice that cut is aligned vertically while clarity is aligned horizontally.

7.2.3 `ggplot2` **Boxplots and Violins Plots**

Being a complete graphics package, `ggplot2` offers a boxplot geom through `geom_boxplot`. Even though it is one-dimensional, using a y aesthetic, there needs to be some x aesthetic, so we will use 1. The result is shown in Figure 7.11.

```
> ggplot(diamonds, aes(y = carat, x = 1)) + geom_boxplot()
```

This is neatly extended to drawing multiple boxplots, one for each level of a variable, as seen in Figure 7.12.

```
> ggplot(diamonds, aes(y = carat, x = cut)) + geom_boxplot()
```

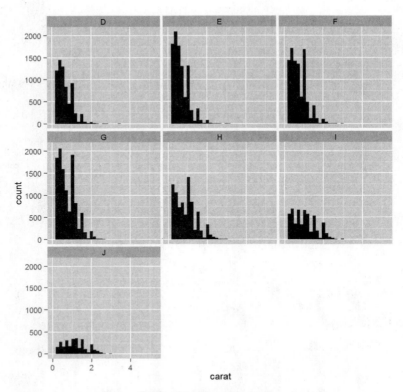

Figure 7.10   Histogram faceted by color.

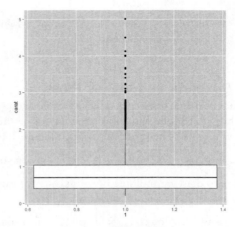

Figure 7.11   Boxplot of diamond carats using `ggplot2`.

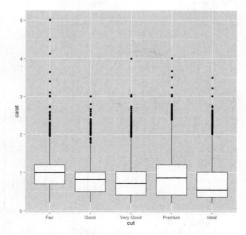

Figure 7.12   Boxplot of diamond carats by cut using `ggplot2`.

Getting fancy, we can swap out the boxplot for violin plots using `geom_violin` as shown in Figure 7.13.

```
> ggplot(diamonds, aes(y = carat, x = cut)) + geom_violin()
```

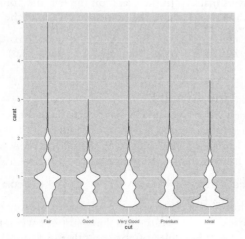

Figure 7.13   Violin plot of diamond carats by cut using `ggplot2`.

Violin plots are similar to boxplots except that the boxes are curved, giving a sense of the density of the data. This provides more information than the straight sides of ordinary boxplots.

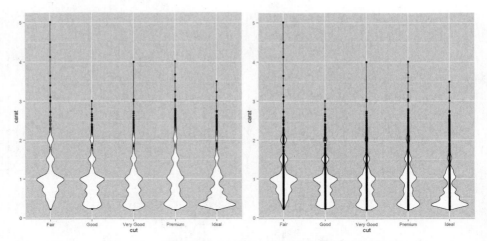

Figure 7.14   Violin plots with points. The graph on the left was built by adding the points geom and then the violin geom, while the plot on the right was built in the opposite order. The order in which the geoms are added determines the positioning of the layers.

We can use multiple layers (geoms) on the same plot, as seen in Figure 7.14. Notice that the order of the layers matters. In the graph on the left, the points are underneath the violins, while in the graph on the right, the points are on top of the violins.

```
> ggplot(diamonds, aes(y = carat, x = cut)) + geom_point() + geom_violin()
> ggplot(diamonds, aes(y = carat, x = cut)) + geom_violin() + geom_point()
```

7.2.4   ggplot2 **Line Graphs**

Line charts are often used when one variable has a certain continuity, but that is not always necessary because there is often a good reason to use a line with categorical data. Figure 7.15 shows an example of a line plot using the economics data from ggplot2. ggplot2 intelligently handles dates and plots them on a logical scale.

```
> ggplot(economics, aes(x = date, y = pop)) + geom_line()
```

While this worked just fine, it is sometimes necessary to use aes(group=1) with geom_line. Yes, it is hacky, but it gets the job done, just like when plotting a single boxplot as in Section 7.2.3. It is a quirk of ggplot2 that sometimes lines cannot be plotted without a group aesthetic.

A common task for line plots is displaying a metric over the course of a year for many years. To prepare the economics data we will use Wickham's lubridate package, which has convenient functions for manipulating dates. We need to create two new

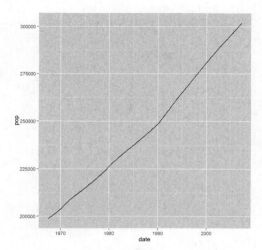

Figure 7.15   Line plot using `ggplot2`.

variables, `year` and `month`. To simplify things we will subset the data to include only years starting with 2000.

```
> # load the lubridate package
> require(lubridate)
>
> ## create year and month variables
> economics$year <- year(economics$date)
> # the label argument to month means that the result should be the
> # names of the month instead of the number
> economics$month <- month(economics$date, label=TRUE)
>
> # subset the data
> # the which function returns the indices of observations where the
> # tested condition was TRUE
> econ2000 <- economics[which(economics$year >= 2000), ]
>
> # load the scales package for better axis formatting
> require(scales)
>
> # build the foundation of the plot
> g <- ggplot(econ2000, aes(x=month, y=pop))
> # add lines color coded and grouped by year
```

```
> # the group aesthetic breaks the data into separate groups
> g <- g + geom_line(aes(color=factor(year), group=year))
> #  name the legend "Year"
> g <- g + scale_color_discrete(name="Year")
> # format the y axis
> g <- g + scale_y_continuous(labels=comma)
> # add a title and axis labels
> g <- g + labs(title="Population Growth", x="Month", y="Population")
> # plot the graph
> g
```

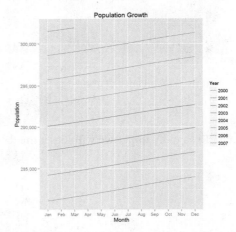

Figure 7.16   Line plot with a seperate line for each year.

Figure 7.16 contains many new concepts. The first part, `ggplot(econ2000,`
`aes(x=month, y=pop)) + geom_line(aes(color=factor(year),`
`group=year))`, is code we have seen before; it creates the line graph with a separate
line and color for each year. Notice that we converted `year` to a `factor` so
that it would get a discrete color scale. That scale was named by using
`scale_color_discrete(name="Year")`. The y-axis was formatted to have commas
using `scale_y_continuous(labels=comma)`. Last, the title, x-label and y-label were
set with `labs(title="Population Growth", x="Month", y="Population")`.
All of these pieces put together built a professional-looking, publication-quality graph.

Also note the use of `which` to subset the data. This is similar to a `where` clause in SQL.

7.2.5   Themes

A great part of `ggplot2` is the ability to use themes to easily change the way plots look.
While building a theme from scratch can be daunting, Jeffrey Arnold from the University
of Rochester has put together `ggthemes`, a package of themes to re-create commonly

used styles of graphs. Just a few styles—The Economist, Excel, Edward Tufte and The Wall Street Journal—are exhibited in Figure 7.17.

```
> require(ggthemes)
> # build a plot and store it in g2
> g2 <- ggplot(diamonds, aes(x=carat, y=price)) +
+     geom_point(aes(color=color))
>
> # apply a few themes
> g2 + theme_economist() + scale_colour_economist()
> g2 + theme_excel() + scale_colour_excel()
> g2 + theme_tufte()
> g2 + theme_wsj()
```

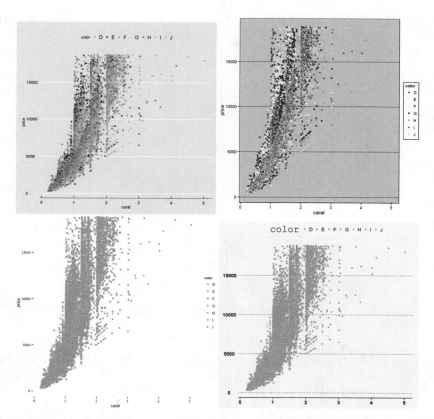

Figure 7.17   Various themes from the ggthemes package. Starting from top left and going clockwise: The Economist, Excel (for those with bosses who demand Excel output), Edward Tufte and The Wall Street Journal.

7.3 Conclusion

We have seen both basic graphs and `ggplot` graphs that are both nicer and easier to create. We have covered histograms, scatterplots, boxplots, line plots and density graphs. We have also looked at using colors and small multiples for distinguishing data. There are many other features in `ggplot2` such as jittering, stacking, dodging and alpha, which we will demonstrate in context throughout the book.

Chapter 8

Writing R functions

If we find ourselves running the same code repeatedly, it is probably a good idea to turn it into a function. In programming it is best to reduce redundancy whenever possible. There are several reasons for doing so, including maintainability and ease of reuse. R has a convenient way to make functions but it is very different from other languages, so some expectation adjustment might be necessary.

8.1 Hello, World!

This would not be a serious book about a programming language if we did not include a "Hello, World!" example, so we will start with that. Let's build a function that simply prints "Hello, World!" to the console.

```
> say.hello <- function()
+ {
+     print("Hello, World!")
+ }
```

First, note that in R the period (.) is just another character and has no special meaning,[1] unlike in other languages. This allows us to call this function say.hello.

Next, we see that functions are assigned to objects just like any other variable, using the <- operator. This is the strangest part of writing functions for people coming from other languages.

Following function are a set of parentheses that can either be empty—not have any arguments—or contain any number of arguments. We will cover those in Section 8.2.

The body of the function is enclosed in curly braces ({ and }). This is not necessary if the function contains only one line, but that is rare. Notice the indenting for the commands inside the function. While not required, it is good practice to properly indent code to ensure readability. It is here in the body that we put the lines of code we want the

---

1. One exception is that objects with names starting with a period are accessible but invisible, so they will not be found by ls.

function to perform. A semicolon (;) can be used to indicate the end of the line but is not necessary, and its use is actually frowned upon.

Calling say.hello() prints as desired.

8.2   Function Arguments

More often than not we want to pass arguments to our function. These are easily added inside the parentheses of the function declaration. We will use an argument to print "Hello Jared."

Before we do that, however, we need to briefly learn about the sprintf function. Its first argument is a string with special input characters and subsequent arguments that will be substituted into the special input characters.

```
> # one substitution
> sprintf("Hello %s", "Jared")

[1] "Hello Jared"

> # two substitutions
> sprintf("Hello %s, today is %s", "Jared", "Sunday")

[1] "Hello Jared, today is Sunday"
```

We now use sprintf to build a string to print based on a function's arguments.

```
> hello.person <- function(name)
+ {
+     print(sprintf("Hello %s", name))
+ }
> hello.person("Jared")

[1] "Hello Jared"

> hello.person("Bob")

[1] "Hello Bob"

> hello.person("Sarah")

[1] "Hello Sarah"
```

The argument name can be used as a variable inside the function (it does not exist outside the function), and can be used like any other variable and as an argument to further function calls.

We can add a second argument to be printed as well. When calling functions with more than one argument, there are two ways to specify which argument goes with which value, either positionally or by name.

```
> hello.person <- function(first, last)
+ {
+     print(sprintf("Hello %s %s", first, last))
+ }
> # by position
> hello.person("Jared", "Lander")

[1] "Hello Jared Lander"

> # by name
> hello.person(first = "Jared", last = "Lander")

[1] "Hello Jared Lander"

> # the other order
> hello.person(last = "Lander", first = "Jared")

[1] "Hello Jared Lander"

> # just specify one name
> hello.person("Jared", last = "Lander")

[1] "Hello Jared Lander"

> # specify the other
> hello.person(first = "Jared", "Lander")

[1] "Hello Jared Lander"

> # specify the second argument first then provide the first argument
> # with no name
> hello.person(last = "Lander", "Jared")

[1] "Hello Jared Lander"
```

Being able to specify the arguments by name adds a lot of flexibility to calling functions. Even partial argument names can be supplied but this should be done with care.

```
> hello.person(fir = "Jared", l = "Lander")

[1] "Hello Jared Lander"
```

8.2.1 Default Arguments

When using multiple arguments it is sometimes desirable to not have to enter a value for each. In other languages functions can be overloaded by defining the function multiple times, each with a differing number of arguments. R instead provides the ability to specify default arguments. These can be NULL, characters, numbers or any valid R object.

Let's rewrite `hello.person` to provide "Doe" as the default last name.

```
> hello.person <- function(first, last = "Doe")
+ {
+     print(sprintf("Hello %s %s", first, last))
+ }
>
> # call without specifying last
> hello.person("Jared")

[1] "Hello Jared Doe"

> # call with a different last
> hello.person("Jared", "Lander")

[1] "Hello Jared Lander"
```

8.2.2 Extra Arguments

R offers a special operator that allows functions to take an arbitrary number of arguments that do not need to be specified in the function definition. This is the dot-dot-dot argument (. . .). This should be used very carefully, although it can allow great flexibility. For now we will just see how it can absorb extra arguments; later we will find a use for it when passing arguments between functions.

```
> # call hello.person with an extra argument
> hello.person("Jared", extra = "Goodbye")

Error: unused argument (extra = "Goodbye")

> # call it with two valid arguments and a third
> hello.person("Jared", "Lander", "Goodbye")

Error: unused argument ("Goodbye")

>
> # now build hello.person with ... so that it absorbs extra arguments
> hello.person <- function(first, last = "Doe", ...)
+ {
+     print(sprintf("Hello %s %s", first, last))
+ }
> # call hello.person with an extra argument
> hello.person("Jared", extra = "Goodbye")

[1] "Hello Jared Doe"

> # call it with two valid arguments and a third
> hello.person("Jared", "Lander", "Goodbye")

[1] "Hello Jared Lander"
```

8.3 Return Values

Functions are generally used for computing some value, so they need a mechanism to supply that value back to the caller. This is called returning and is done quite easily. There are two ways to accomplish this with R. The value of the last line of code in a function is automatically returned, although this can be bad practice. The `return` command more explicitly specifies that a value should be returned and the function should be exited.

To illustrate, we will build a function that doubles its only argument and returns that value.

```
> # first build it without an explicit return
> double.num <- function(x)
+ {
+     x * 2
+ }
>
> double.num(5)

[1] 10

>
> # now build it with an explicit return
> double.num <- function(x)
+ {
+     return(x * 2)
+ }
>
> double.num(5)

[1] 10

>
> # build it again, this time with another argument after the explicit
> # return
> double.num <- function(x)
+ {
+     return(x * 2)
+
+     # below here is not executed because the function already exited
+     print("Hello!")
+     return(17)
+ }
>
> double.num(5)

[1] 10
```

8.4 `do.call`

A particularly underused trick is the `do.call` function. This allows us to specify the name of a function either as a `character` or as an object, and provide arguments as a list.

```
> do.call("hello.person", args = list(first = "Jared", last = "Lander"))

[1] "Hello Jared Lander"

> do.call(hello.person, args = list(first = "Jared", last = "Lander"))

[1] "Hello Jared Lander"
```

This is particularly useful when building a function that allows the user to specify an action. In the following example the user supplies a `vector` and a function to be run.

```
> run.this <- function(x, func = mean)
+ {
+     do.call(func, args = list(x))
+ }
>
> # finds the mean by default
> run.this(1:10)

[1] 5.5

> # specify to calculate the mean
> run.this(1:10, mean)

[1] 5.5

> # calculate the sum
> run.this(1:10, sum)

[1] 55

> # calculate the standard deviation
> run.this(1:10, sd)

[1] 3.028
```

8.5 Conclusion

Functions allow us to create reusable code that avoids repetition and allows easy modification. Important points to remember are function arguments, default values and returned values. Later in this book we will see functions that get far more complicated than the ones we have seen so far.

Chapter 9

Control Statements

Control statements allow us to control the flow of our programming and cause different things to happen depending on the values of tests. Tests result in a `logical`, TRUE, or FALSE, which is used in if-like statements. The main control statements are `if`, `else`, `ifelse` and `switch`.

9.1 `if` and `else`

The most common test is the `if` command. It essentially says: If something is TRUE, then perform some action; otherwise, do not perform that action. The thing we are testing goes inside parentheses following the `if` command. The most basic checks are equal to (==), less than (<), less than or equal to (<=), greater than (>), greater than or equal to (>=) and not equal (!=).

If these tests pass they result in TRUE, and if they fail they result in FALSE. As noted in Section 4.3.4, TRUE is numerically equivalent to 1 and FALSE is equivalent to 0.

```
> as.numeric(TRUE)

[1] 1

> as.numeric(FALSE)

[1] 0
```

These tests do not need to be used inside `if` statements. The following are some simple examples.

```
> 1 == 1   # TRUE

[1] TRUE

> 1 < 1   # FALSE

[1] FALSE
```

```
> 1 <= 1   # TRUE

[1] TRUE

> 1 > 1   # FALSE

[1] FALSE

> 1 >= 1   # TRUE

[1] TRUE

> 1 != 1   # FALSE

[1] FALSE
```

We can now show that using this test inside an `if` statement controls actions that follow.

```
> # set up a variable to hold 1
> toCheck <- 1
>
> # if toCheck is equal to 1, print hello
> if (toCheck == 1)
+ {
+       print("hello")
+ }

[1] "hello"

>
> # now if toCheck is equal to 0, print hello
> if (toCheck == 0)
+ {
+       print("hello")
+ }
> # notice nothing was printed
```

Notice that `if` statements are similar to functions in that all statements (there can be one or multiple) go inside curly braces.

Life is not always so simple that we want an action only if some relationship is TRUE. We often want a different action if that relationship is FALSE. In the following example we put an `if` statement followed by an `else` statement inside a function, so that it can be used repeatedly.

```
> # first create the function
> check.bool <- function(x)
+ {
+       if (x == 1)
```

```
+      {
+          # if the input is equal to 1, print hello
+          print("hello")
+      } else
+      {
+          # otherwise print goodbye
+          print("goodbye")
+      }
+ }
```

Notice that else is on the same line as its preceding closing curly brace (}). This is important, as the code will fail otherwise.

Now let's use that function and see if it works.

```
> check.bool(1)

[1] "hello"

> check.bool(0)

[1] "goodbye"

> check.bool("k")

[1] "goodbye"

> check.bool(TRUE)

[1] "hello"
```

Anything other than 1 caused the function to print "goodbye." That is exactly what we wanted. Passing TRUE printed "hello" because TRUE is numerically the same as 1.

Perhaps we want to successively test a few cases. That is where we can use else if. We first test a single statement, then make another test, and then perhaps fall over to catch all. We will modify check.bool to test for one condition and then another.

```
> check.bool <- function(x)
+ {
+     if (x == 1)
+     {
+         # if the input is equal to 1, print hello
+         print("hello")
+     } else if (x == 0)
+     {
+         # if the input is equal to 0, print goodbye
+         print("goodbye")
+     } else
```

```
+     {
+           # otherwise print confused
+           print("confused")
+     }
+ }
>
> check.bool(1)

[1] "hello"

> check.bool(0)

[1] "goodbye"

> check.bool(2)

[1] "confused"

> check.bool("k")

[1] "confused"
```

9.2 `switch`

If we have multiple cases to check, writing `else if` repeatedly can be cumbersome and inefficient. This is where `switch` is most useful. The first argument is the value we are testing. Subsequent arguments are a particular value and what should be the result. The last argument, if not given a value, is the default result.

To illustrate, we build a function that takes in a value and returns a corresponding result.

```
> use.switch <- function(x)
+ {
+     switch(x,
+         "a"="first",
+         "b"="second",
+         "z"="last",
+         "c"="third",
+         "other")
+ }
>
> use.switch("a")

[1] "first"

> use.switch("b")

[1] "second"
```

```
> use.switch("c")

[1] "third"

> use.switch("d")

[1] "other"

> use.switch("e")

[1] "other"

> use.switch("z")

[1] "last"
```

If the first argument is numeric, it is matched positionally to the following arguments, regardless of the names of the subsequent arguments. If the numeric argument is greater than the number of subsequent arguments, NULL is returned.

```
> use.switch(1)

[1] "first"

> use.switch(2)

[1] "second"

> use.switch(3)

[1] "last"

> use.switch(4)

[1] "third"

> use.switch(5)

[1] "other"

> use.switch(6)   # nothing is returned
> is.null(use.switch(6))

[1] TRUE
```

Here we introduced a new function, is.null, which, as the name implies, tests if an object is NULL.

9.3 ifelse

While if is like the if statement in traditional languages, ifelse is more like the if function in Excel. The first argument is the condition to be tested (much like in a traditional `if` statement), the second argument is the return value if the test is TRUE and the third argument is the return value if the test if FALSE. The beauty here—unlike with the traditional `if`—is that this works with vectorized arguments. As is often the case in R, using vectorization avoids `for` loops and speeds up our code. The nuances of `ifelse` can be tricky, so we show numerous examples.

We start with a very simple example, testing if 1 is equal to 1, and printing "Yes" if that is TRUE and "No" if it is FALSE.

```
> # see if 1 == 1
> ifelse(1 == 1, "Yes", "No")

[1] "Yes"
> # see if 1 == 0
> ifelse(1 == 0, "Yes", "No")

[1] "No"
```

This clearly gives us the results we want. `ifelse` uses all the regular equality tests seen in Section 9.1 and any other `logical` test. It is worth noting, however, that if testing just a single element (a `vector` of length 1 or a simple `is.na`) it is more efficient to use `if` than `ifelse`. This can result in a nontrivial speedup of our code.

Next we will illustrate a vectorized first argument.

```
> toTest <- c(1, 1, 0, 1, 0, 1)
> ifelse(toTest == 1, "Yes", "No")

[1] "Yes" "Yes" "No"  "Yes" "No"  "Yes"
```

This returned "Yes" for each element of `toTest` that equaled 1 and "No" for each element of `toTest` that did not equal 1.

The TRUE and FALSE arguments can even refer to the testing element.

```
> ifelse(toTest == 1, toTest * 3, toTest)

[1] 3 3 0 3 0 3

> # the FALSE argument is repeated as needed
> ifelse(toTest == 1, toTest * 3, "Zero")

[1] "3"    "3"    "Zero" "3"    "Zero" "3"
```

Now let's say that `toTest` has NA elements. In that case the corresponding result from `ifelse` is NA.

```
> toTest[2] <- NA
> ifelse(toTest == 1, "Yes", "No")

[1] "Yes" NA    "No"  "Yes" "No"  "Yes"
```

This would be the same if the TRUE and FALSE arguments are vectors.

```
> ifelse(toTest == 1, toTest * 3, toTest)

[1]   3 NA  0  3  0  3

> ifelse(toTest == 1, toTest * 3, "Zero")

[1] "3"     NA     "Zero" "3"     "Zero" "3"
```

9.4 Compound Tests

The statement being tested with if, ifelse and switch can be any argument that results in a logical TRUE or FALSE. This can be an equality check or even the result of is.numeric or is.na. Sometimes we want to test more than one relationship at a time. This is done using logical and and or operators. These are & and && for and and | and || for or. The differences are subtle but can impact our code's speed.

The double form (&& or ||) is best used in if and the single form (& or |) is necessary for ifelse. The double form compares only one element from each side, while the single form compares each element of each side.

```
> a <- c(1, 1, 0, 1)
> b <- c(2, 1, 0, 1)
>
> # this checks each element of a and each element of b
> ifelse(a == 1 & b == 1, "Yes", "No")

[1] "No"  "Yes" "No"  "Yes"

>
> # this only checks the first element of a and the first element of b,
> # returning only one result
> ifelse(a == 1 && b == 1, "Yes", "No")

[1] "No"
```

Another difference between the double and single forms is how they are processed. When using the single form, both sides of the operator are always checked. With the double form, sometimes only the left side needs to be checked. For instance, if testing 1 == 0 && 2 == 2, the left side fails, so there is no reason to check the right side. Similarly, when testing 3 == 3 || 0 == 0, the left side passes, so there is no need to check the right side. This can be particularly helpful when the right side would throw an error if the left side had failed.

There can be more than just two conditions tested. Many conditions can be strung together using multiple and or or operators. The different clauses can be grouped by parentheses just like mathematical operations. Without parentheses, the order of operations is similar to PEMDAS, seen in Section 4.1, where and is equivalent to multiplication and or is equivalent to addition, so and takes precedence over or.

9.5 Conclusion

Controlling the flow of our program, both at the command line and in functions, plays an important role when processing and analyzing our data. if statements, along with else, are the most common—and efficient—for testing single element objects, although ifelse is far more common in R programming because of its vectorized nature. switch statements are often forgotten but can come in very handy. The and (& and &&) and or (| and ||) operators allow us to combine multiple tests into one.

Chapter 10

Loops, the Un-R Way to Iterate

When starting to use R, most people use loops whenever they need to iterate over elements of a vector, list or data.frame. While it is natural to do this in other languages, with R we generally want to use vectorization. That said, sometimes loops are unavoidable, so R offers both for and while loops.

10.1 for Loops

The most commonly used loop is the for loop. It iterates over an index—provided as a vector—and performs some operations. For a first simple example, we print out the first ten numbers.

The loop is declared using for, which takes one English-seeming argument in three parts. The third part is any vector of values of any kind, most commonly numeric or character. The first part is the variable that is iteratively assigned the values in the vector from the third part. The middle part is simply the word in indicating that the variable (the first part) is in the vector (the third part).

```
> for (i in 1:10)
+ {
+     print(i)
+ }

[1] 1
[1] 2
[1] 3
[1] 4
[1] 5
[1] 6
[1] 7
[1] 8
[1] 9
[1] 10
```

Here we generated a vector holding the numbers 1 through 10, and then printed each. Notice that this could have been performed simply by using the built-in vectorization of the print function.

```
> print(1:10)

 [1]  1  2  3  4  5  6  7  8  9 10
```

Sure, it does not look exactly the same, but that is just cosmetic.

The vector in for loops does not have to be sequential; it can be any vector.

```
> # build a vector holding fruit names
> fruit <- c("apple", "banana", "pomegranate")
> # make a variable to hold their lengths, with all NA to start
> fruitLength <- rep(NA, length(fruit))
> # show it, all NAs
> fruitLength

[1] NA NA NA

> # give it names
> names(fruitLength) <- fruit
> # show it again, still NAs
> fruitLength

      apple      banana pomegranate
         NA          NA          NA

> # loop through the fruit assigning their lengths to the result vector
> for (a in fruit)
+ {
+     fruitLength[a] <- nchar(a)
+ }
> # show the lengths
> fruitLength

      apple      banana pomegranate
          5           6          11
```

Again, R's built-in vectorization could have made all of this much easier.

```
> # simply call nchar
> fruitLength2 <- nchar(fruit)
> # give it names
> names(fruitLength2) <- fruit
> # show it
> fruitLength2
```

```
       apple        banana pomegranate
           5             6          11
```

This, as expected, provides identical results, as seen next.

```
> identical(fruitLength, fruitLength2)

[1] TRUE
```

10.2 `while` Loops

Although used far less frequently in R than the `for` loop, the `while` loop is just as simple to implement. It simply runs the code inside the braces repeatedly as long as the tested condition proves true. In the following example, we print the value of x and iterate it until it reaches 5. This is a highly trivial example but shows the functionality nonetheless.

```
> x <- 1
> while (x <= 5)
+ {
+     print(x)
+     x <- x + 1
+ }

[1] 1
[1] 2
[1] 3
[1] 4
[1] 5
```

10.3 Controlling Loops

Sometimes we have to skip to the next iteration of the loop or completely break out of it. This is accomplished with `next` and `break`. We use a `for` loop to demonstrate.

```
> for (i in 1:10)
+ {
+     if (i == 3)
+     {
+         next
+     }
+     print(i)
+ }

[1] 1
[1] 2
```

```
[1]  4
[1]  5
[1]  6
[1]  7
[1]  8
[1]  9
[1]  10
```

Notice that the number 3 did not get printed.

```
> for (i in 1:10)
+ {
+     if (i == 4)
+     {
+         break
+     }
+     print(i)
+ }

[1]  1
[1]  2
[1]  3
```

Here, even though we told R to iterate over the first ten integers, it stopped after 3 because we broke the loop at 4.

10.4 Conclusion

The two primary loops are for, which iterates over a fixed sequence of elements, and while, which continues a loop as long as some condition holds true. As stated earlier, if a solution can be done without loops, via vectorization or matrix algebra, then avoid the loop. It is particularly important to avoid nested loops. Loops inside other loops are extremely slow in R.

Chapter 11

Group Manipulation

A general rule of thumb for data analysis is that manipulating the data (or "data munging," a term coined by Simple founder Josh Reich) consumes about 80% of the effort. This often requires repeated operations on different sections of the data, something Hadley Wickham coined "split-apply-combine." That is, we split the data into discrete sections based on some metric, apply a transformation of some kind to each section, and then combine all the sections together. This is somewhat like the MapReduce[1] paradigm of Hadoop.[2] There are many different ways to iterate over data in R, and we will look at some of the more convenient functions.

11.1 Apply Family

Built into R is the `apply` function and all of its relatives such as `tapply`, `lapply` and `mapply`. Each has its quirks and necessities and is best used in different situations.

11.1.1 apply

`apply` is the first member of this family that users usually learn, and it is also the most restrictive. It must be used on a `matrix`, meaning all of the elements must be of the same type whether they are `character`, `numeric` or `logical`. If used on some other object, such as a `data.frame`, it will be converted to a `matrix` first.

The first argument to `apply` is the object we are working with. The second argument is the margin to apply the function over, with 1 meaning to operate over the rows and 2 meaning to operate over the columns. The third argument is the function we want to apply. Any following arguments will be passed on to that function. `apply` will iterate over each row (or column) of the `matrix` treating them as individual inputs to the first argument of the specified function.

---

1. MapReduce is where data are split into discrete sets, computed on, and then recombined in some fashion.
2. Hadoop is a framework for distributing data and computations across a grid of computers.

To illustrate its use we start with a trivial example, summing the rows or columns of a matrix.

```
> # build the matrix
> theMatrix <- matrix(1:9, nrow = 3)
> # sum the rows
> apply(theMatrix, 1, sum)

[1] 12 15 18

> # sum the columns
> apply(theMatrix, 2, sum)

[1]  6 15 24
```

Notice that this could alternatively be accomplished using the built-in rowSums and colSums functions, yielding the same results.

```
> rowSums(theMatrix)

[1] 12 15 18

> colSums(theMatrix)

[1]  6 15 24
```

For a moment, let's set an element of theMatrix to NA to see how we handle missing data using the na.rm argument and the use of additional arguments.

```
> theMatrix[2, 1] <- NA
> apply(theMatrix, 1, sum)

[1] 12 NA 18

> apply(theMatrix, 1, sum, na.rm = TRUE)

[1] 12 13 18

> rowSums(theMatrix)

[1] 12 NA 18

> rowSums(theMatrix, na.rm = TRUE)

[1] 12 13 18
```

11.1.2 lapply and sapply

lapply works by applying a function to each element of a list and returning the results as a list.

```
> ·theList <- list(A = matrix(1:9, 3), B = 1:5, C = matrix(1:4, 2), D = 2)
> lapply(theList, sum)

$A
[1] 45

$B
[1] 15

$C
[1] 10

$D
[1] 2
```

Dealing with lists can be cumbersome, so to return the result of lapply as a vector instead, use sapply. It is exactly the same as lapply in every other way.

```
> sapply(theList, sum)

 A  B  C  D
45 15 10  2
```

Because a vector is technically a form of a list, lapply and sapply can also take a vector as their input.

```
> theNames <- c("Jared", "Deb", "Paul")
> lapply(theNames, nchar)

[[1]]
[1] 5

[[2]]
[1] 3

[[3]]
[1] 4
```

11.1.3 mapply

Perhaps the most-overlooked-when-so-useful member of the apply family is mapply, which applies a function to each element of multiple lists. Often when confronted with this scenario, people will resort to using a loop, which is certainly not necessary.

```
> ## build two lists
> firstList <- list(A = matrix(1:16, 4), B = matrix(1:16, 2), C = 1:5)
> secondList <- list(A = matrix(1:16, 4), B = matrix(1:16, 8), C = 15:1)
```

```
> # test element-by-element if they are identical
> mapply(identical, firstList, secondList)

    A     B     C
 TRUE FALSE FALSE

> ## build a simple function that adds the number of rows (or length) of
> ## each corresponding element
> simpleFunc <- function(x, y)
+ {
+     NROW(x) + NROW(y)
+ }
> # apply the function to the two lists
> mapply(simpleFunc, firstList, secondList)

 A  B  C
 8 10 20
```

11.1.4   Other `apply` Functions

There are many other members of the `apply` family that either do not get used much or have been superseded by functions in the `plyr` package. (Some would argue that `lapply` and `sapply` have been superseded, but they do have their advantages over their corresponding `plyr` functions.)

These include

- `tapply`
- `rapply`
- `eapply`
- `vapply`
- `by`

11.2   `aggregate`

People experienced with SQL generally want to run an aggregation and group by as their first R task. The way to do this is to use the aptly named `aggregate` function. There are a number of different ways to call `aggregate`, so we will look at perhaps its most convenient method, using a `formula`.

We will see `formula`s used to great extent with linear models in Chapter 16 and they play a useful role in R. `formula`s consist of a left side and a right side separated by a tilde (~). The left side represents a variable that we want to make a calculation on and the right side represents one or more variables that we want to group the calculation by.[3]

---

3. As we show in Chapter 16, the right side can be numeric, although for the `aggregate` function we will just use categorical variables.

To demonstrate `aggregate` we once again turn to the `diamonds` data in `ggplot2`.

```
> require(ggplot2)
> data(diamonds)
> head(diamonds)
```

	carat	cut	color	clarity	depth	table	price	x	y	z
1	0.23	Ideal	E	SI2	61.5	55	326	3.95	3.98	2.43
2	0.21	Premium	E	SI1	59.8	61	326	3.89	3.84	2.31
3	0.23	Good	E	VS1	56.9	65	327	4.05	4.07	2.31
4	0.29	Premium	I	VS2	62.4	58	334	4.20	4.23	2.63
5	0.31	Good	J	SI2	63.3	58	335	4.34	4.35	2.75
6	0.24	Very Good	J	VVS2	62.8	57	336	3.94	3.96	2.48

We calculate the average `price` for each type of `cut`: Fair, Good, Very Good, Premium and Ideal. The first argument to `aggregate` is the `formula` specifying that price should be broken up (or `group by` in SQL terms) by cut. The second argument is the data to use, in this case `diamonds`. The third argument is the function to apply to each subset of the data; for us this will be the mean.

```
> aggregate(price ~ cut, diamonds, mean)
```

	cut	price
1	Fair	4358.758
2	Good	3928.864
3	Very Good	3981.760
4	Premium	4584.258
5	Ideal	3457.542

For the first argument we specified that `price` should be aggregated by `cut`. Notice that we only specified the column name and did not have to identify the data because that is given in the second argument. After the third argument specifying the function, additional named arguments to that function can be passed, such as `aggregate(price ~ cut, diamonds, mean, na.rm=TRUE)`.

To group the data by more than one variable, add the additional variable to the right side of the `formula` separating it with a plus sign (+).

```
> aggregate(price ~ cut + color, diamonds, mean)
```

	cut	color	price
1	Fair	D	4291.061
2	Good	D	3405.382
3	Very Good	D	3470.467
4	Premium	D	3631.293
5	Ideal	D	2629.095
6	Fair	E	3682.312

```
7          Good    E 3423.644
8    Very Good    E 3214.652
9       Premium    E 3538.914
10         Ideal    E 2597.550
11          Fair    F 3827.003
12          Good    F 3495.750
13   Very Good    F 3778.820
14       Premium    F 4324.890
15         Ideal    F 3374.939
16          Fair    G 4239.255
17          Good    G 4123.482
18   Very Good    G 3872.754
19       Premium    G 4500.742
20         Ideal    G 3720.706
21          Fair    H 5135.683
22          Good    H 4276.255
23   Very Good    H 4535.390
24       Premium    H 5216.707
25         Ideal    H 3889.335
26          Fair    I 4685.446
27          Good    I 5078.533
28   Very Good    I 5255.880
29       Premium    I 5946.181
30         Ideal    I 4451.970
31          Fair    J 4975.655
32          Good    J 4574.173
33   Very Good    J 5103.513
34       Premium    J 6294.592
35         Ideal    J 4918.186
```

To aggregate two variables (for now we still just group by cut), they must be combined using cbind on the left side of the formula.

```
> aggregate(cbind(price, carat) ~ cut, diamonds, mean)

        cut    price     carat
1       Fair 4358.758 1.0461366
2       Good 3928.864 0.8491847
3 Very Good 3981.760 0.8063814
4    Premium 4584.258 0.8919549
5      Ideal 3457.542 0.7028370
```

This finds the mean of both price and carat for each value of cut. It is important to note that only one function can be supplied, and hence applied, to the variables. To apply more than one function it is easier to use the plyr package, which is explained in Section 11.3.

Of course, multiple variables can be supplied to both the left and right sides at the same time.

```
> aggregate(cbind(price, carat) ~ cut + color, diamonds, mean)
```

	cut	color	price	carat
1	Fair	D	4291.061	0.9201227
2	Good	D	3405.382	0.7445166
3	Very Good	D	3470.467	0.6964243
4	Premium	D	3631.293	0.7215471
5	Ideal	D	2629.095	0.5657657
6	Fair	E	3682.312	0.8566071
7	Good	E	3423.644	0.7451340
8	Very Good	E	3214.652	0.6763167
9	Premium	E	3538.914	0.7177450
10	Ideal	E	2597.550	0.5784012
11	Fair	F	3827.003	0.9047115
12	Good	F	3495.750	0.7759296
13	Very Good	F	3778.820	0.7409612
14	Premium	F	4324.890	0.8270356
15	Ideal	F	3374.939	0.6558285
16	Fair	G	4239.255	1.0238217
17	Good	G	4123.482	0.8508955
18	Very Good	G	3872.754	0.7667986
19	Premium	G	4500.742	0.8414877
20	Ideal	G	3720.706	0.7007146
21	Fair	H	5135.683	1.2191749
22	Good	H	4276.255	0.9147293
23	Very Good	H	4535.390	0.9159485
24	Premium	H	5216.707	1.0164492
25	Ideal	H	3889.335	0.7995249
26	Fair	I	4685.446	1.1980571
27	Good	I	5078.533	1.0572222
28	Very Good	I	5255.880	1.0469518
29	Premium	I	5946.181	1.1449370
30	Ideal	I	4451.970	0.9130291
31	Fair	J	4975.655	1.3411765
32	Good	J	4574.173	1.0995440
33	Very Good	J	5103.513	1.1332153
34	Premium	J	6294.592	1.2930941
35	Ideal	J	4918.186	1.0635937

11.3 `plyr`

One of the best things to ever happen to R was the development of the `plyr`[4] package by Hadley Wickham. It epitomizes the "split-apply-combine" method of data manipulation. The core of `plyr` consists of functions such as `ddply`, `llply` and `ldply`. All of the manipulation functions consist of five letters, with the last three always being `ply`. The first letter indicates the type of input and the second letter indicates the type of output. For instance, `ddply` takes in a `data.frame` and outputs a `data.frame`, `llply` takes in a `list` and outputs a `list` and `ldply` takes in a `list` and outputs a `data.frame`. A full enumeration is listed in Table 11.1.

Table 11.1   `plyr` Functions and their Corresponding Inputs and Outputs

Function	Input Type	Output Type
`ddply`	`data.frame`	`data.frame`
`llply`	`list`	`list`
`aaply`	`array/vector/matrix`	`array/vector/matrix`
`dlply`	`data.frame`	`list`
`daply`	`data.frame`	`array/vector/matrix`
`d_ply`	`data.frame`	none (used for side effects)
`ldply`	`list`	`data.frame`
`laply`	`list`	`array/vector/matrix`
`l_ply`	`list`	none (used for side effects)
`adply`	`array/vector/matrix`	`data.frame`
`alply`	`array/vector/matrix`	`list`
`a_ply`	`array/vector/matrix`	none (used for side effects)

11.3.1 `ddply`

`ddply` takes a `data.frame`, splits it according to some variable(s), performs a desired action on it and returns a `data.frame`. To learn about `ddply` we look at the `baseball` data that come with `plyr`.

```
> require(plyr)
> head(baseball)
```

```
        id year stint team lg  g  ab  r  h X2b X3b hr rbi sb cs bb
4  ansonca01 1871     1  RC1     25 120 29 39  11   3  0  16  6  2  2
44 forceda01 1871     1  WS3     32 162 45 45   9   4  0  29  8  0  4
68 mathebo01 1871     1  FW1     19  89 15 24   3   1  0  10  2  1  2
```

---

4. A play on the word *plier* because it is one of the most versatile and essential tools.

99	startjo01	1871	1	NY2	33	161	35	58	5	1	1	34	4	2	3
102	suttoez01	1871	1	CL1	29	128	35	45	3	7	3	23	3	1	1
106	whitede01	1871	1	CL1	29	146	40	47	6	5	1	21	2	2	4

	so	ibb	hbp	sh	sf	gidp
4	1	NA	NA	NA	NA	NA
44	0	NA	NA	NA	NA	NA
68	0	NA	NA	NA	NA	NA
99	0	NA	NA	NA	NA	NA
102	0	NA	NA	NA	NA	NA
106	1	NA	NA	NA	NA	NA

A common statistic in baseball is On Base Percentage (OBP), which is calculated as

$$OBP = \frac{H + BB + HBP}{AB + BB + HBP + SF} \tag{11.1}$$

where

H = Hits
BB = Bases on Balls (Walks)
HBP = Times Hit by Pitch
AB = At Bats
SF = Sacrifice Flies

Before 1954 sacrifice flies were counted as part of sacrifice hits, which includes bunts, so for players before 1954 sacrifice flies should be assumed to be 0. That will be the first change we make to the data. There are many instances of HBP (hit by pitch) that are NA, so we set those to 0 as well. We also exclude players with less than 50 at bats in a season.

```
> # subsetting with [ is faster than using ifelse
> baseball$sf[baseball$year < 1954] <- 0
> # check that it worked
> any(is.na(baseball$sf))

[1] FALSE

> # set NA hbp's to 0
> baseball$hbp[is.na(baseball$hbp)] <- 0
> # check that it worked
> any(is.na(baseball$hbp))

[1] FALSE

> # only keep players with at least 50 at bats in a season
> baseball <- baseball[baseball$ab >= 50, ]
```

Calculating the OBP for a given player in a given year is easy enough with just vector operations.

```
> # calculate OBP
> baseball$OBP <- with(baseball, (h + bb + hbp)/(ab + bb + hbp + sf))
> tail(baseball)
```

```
              id year stint team  lg   g  ab   r   h X2b X3b hr rbi sb
89499 claytro01 2007     1  TOR  AL  69 189  23  48  14   0  1  12  2
89502 cirilje01 2007     1  MIN  AL  50 153  18  40   9   2  2  21  2
89521 bondsba01 2007     1  SFN  NL 126 340  75  94  14   0 28  66  5
89523 biggicr01 2007     1  HOU  NL 141 517  68 130  31   3 10  50  4
89530 ausmubr01 2007     1  HOU  NL 117 349  38  82  16   3  3  25  6
89533  aloumo01 2007     1  NYN  NL  87 328  51 112  19   1 13  49  3
      cs  bb  so ibb hbp sh sf gidp       OBP
89499  1  14  50   0   1  3  3    8 0.3043478
89502  0  15  13   0   1  3  2    9 0.3274854
89521  0 132  54  43   3  0  2   13 0.4800839
89523  3  23 112   0   3  7  5    5 0.2846715
89530  1  37  74   3   6  4  1   11 0.3180662
89533  0  27  30   5   2  0  3   13 0.3916667
```

Here we used a new function, with. This allows us to specify the columns of a data.frame without having to specify the data.frame name each time.

To calculate the OBP for a player's entire career we cannot just average his individual season OBPs; we need to calculate and sum the numerator, and then divide by the sum of the denominator. This requires the use of ddply.

First we make a function to do that calculation, then we use ddply to run that calculation for each player.

```
> # this function assumes that the column names for the data are as
> # below
> obp <- function(data)
+ {
+     c(OBP = with(data, sum(h + bb + hbp)/sum(ab + bb + hbp + sf)))
+ }
>
> # use ddply to calculate career OBP for each player
> careerOBP <- ddply(baseball, .variables = "id", .fun = obp)
> # sort the results by OBP
> careerOBP <- careerOBP[order(careerOBP$OBP, decreasing = TRUE), ]
> # see the results
> head(careerOBP, 10)
```

```
            id       OBP
1089 willite01 0.4816861
875   ruthba01 0.4742209
658  mcgrajo01 0.4657478
```

```
356    gehrilo01  0.4477848
85     bondsba01  0.4444622
476    hornsro01  0.4339068
184     cobbty01  0.4329655
327     foxxji01  0.4290509
953    speaktr01  0.4283386
191    collied01  0.4251246
```

This nicely returns the top ten players by career on base percentage. Notice that Billy Hamilton and Bill Joyce are absent from our results because they are mysteriously missing from the baseball data.

11.3.2 llply

In Section 11.1.2 we use lapply to sum each element of a list.

```
> theList <- list(A = matrix(1:9, 3), B = 1:5, C = matrix(1:4, 2), D = 2)
> lapply(theList, sum)

$A
[1]  45

$B
[1]  15

$C
[1]  10

$D
[1]  2
```

This can be done with llpply, yielding identical results.

```
> llply(theList, sum)

$A
[1]  45

$B
[1]  15

$C
[1]  10

$D
[1]  2
```

```
> identical(lapply(theList, sum), llply(theList, sum))
```

```
[1] TRUE
```

To get the result as a vector, `laply` can be used similarly to `sapply`.

```
> sapply(theList, sum)
```

```
 A  B  C  D
45 15 10  2
```

```
> laply(theList, sum)
```

```
[1] 45 15 10  2
```

Notice, however, that while the results are the same, `laply` did not include names for the vector. These little nuances can be maddening but help dictate when to use which function.

11.3.3 `plyr` Helper Functions

`plyr` has a great deal of useful helper functions such as each, which lets us supply multiple functions to a function like `aggregate`.

```
> aggregate(price ~ cut, diamonds, each(mean, median))
```

```
        cut price.mean price.median
1      Fair   4358.758     3282.000
2      Good   3928.864     3050.500
3 Very Good   3981.760     2648.000
4   Premium   4584.258     3185.000
5     Ideal   3457.542     1810.000
```

Another great function is `idata.frame`, which creates a reference to a `data.frame` so that subsetting is much faster and more memory efficient. To illustrate this, we do a simple operation on the `baseball` data with the regular `data.frame` and an `idata.frame`.

```
> system.time(dlply(baseball, "id", nrow))
```

```
  user  system elapsed
  0.29    0.00    0.33
```

```
> iBaseball <- idata.frame(baseball)
> system.time(dlply(iBaseball, "id", nrow))
```

```
  user  system elapsed
  0.42    0.00    0.47
```

While saving less than a second in run time might seem trivial the savings can really add up with more complex operations, bigger data, more groups to split by and repeated operation.

11.3.4 Speed versus Convenience

A criticism often leveled at `plyr` is that it can run slowly. The typical response to this is that using `plyr` is a question of speed versus convenience. Most of the functionality in `plyr` can be accomplished using base functions or other packages, but few of those offer the ease of use of `plyr`. That said, in recent years Hadley Wickham has taken great steps to speed up `plyr`, including optimized R code, C++ code and parallelization.

11.4 data.table

For speed junkies there is a package called `data.table` that extends and enhances the functionality of `data.frames`. The syntax is a little different from regular `data.frames`, so it will take getting used to, which is probably the primary reason it has not seen near-universal adoption.

The secret to the speed is that `data.tables` have an index like databases. This allows faster value accessing, group by operations and joins.

Creating `data.tables` is just like creating `data.frames`, and the two are very similar.

```
> require(data.table)
> # create a regular data.frame
> theDF <- data.frame(A=1:10,
+                     B=letters[1:10],
+                     C=LETTERS[11:20],
+                     D=rep(c("One", "Two", "Three"), length.out=10))
> # create a data.table
> theDT <- data.table(A=1:10,
+                     B=letters[1:10],
+                     C=LETTERS[11:20],
+                     D=rep(c("One", "Two", "Three"), length.out=10))
> # print them and compare
> theDF

  A B C     D
1 1 a K   One
2 2 b L   Two
3 3 c M Three
4 4 d N   One
5 5 e O   Two
6 6 f P Three
7 7 g Q   One
8 8 h R   Two
```

```
9    9 i S Three
10 10 j T    One

> theDT

     A B C      D
 1:  1 a K    One
 2:  2 b L    Two
 3:  3 c M Three
 4:  4 d N    One
 5:  5 e O    Two
 6:  6 f P Three
 7:  7 g Q    One
 8:  8 h R    Two
 9:  9 i S Three
10: 10 j T    One

> # notice by default data.frame turns character data into factors
> # while data.table does not
> class(theDF$B)

[1] "factor"

> class(theDT$B)

[1] "character"
```

The data are identical—except that data.frame turned B into a factor while data.table did not—and only the way it was printed looks different.

It is also possible to create a data.table out of an existing data.frame.

```
> diamondsDT <- data.table(diamonds)
> diamondsDT

        carat       cut color clarity depth table price    x    y    z
    1:  0.23     Ideal     E     SI2  61.5    55   326 3.95 3.98 2.43
    2:  0.21   Premium     E     SI1  59.8    61   326 3.89 3.84 2.31
    3:  0.23      Good     E     VS1  56.9    65   327 4.05 4.07 2.31
    4:  0.29   Premium     I     VS2  62.4    58   334 4.20 4.23 2.63
    5:  0.31      Good     J     SI2  63.3    58   335 4.34 4.35 2.75
   ---
53936:  0.72     Ideal     D     SI1  60.8    57  2757 5.75 5.76 3.50
53937:  0.72      Good     D     SI1  63.1    55  2757 5.69 5.75 3.61
53938:  0.70 Very Good     D     SI1  62.8    60  2757 5.66 5.68 3.56
53939:  0.86   Premium     H     SI2  61.0    58  2757 6.15 6.12 3.74
53940:  0.75     Ideal     D     SI2  62.2    55  2757 5.83 5.87 3.64
```

Notice that printing the `diamonds` data would try to print out all the data but `data.table` intelligently just prints the first five and last five rows.

Accessing rows can be done similarly to accessing rows in a `data.frame`.

```
> theDT[1:2, ]

   A B C   D
1: 1 a K One
2: 2 b L Two

> theDT[theDT$A >= 7, ]

    A B C     D
1:  7 g Q   One
2:  8 h R   Two
3:  9 i S Three
4: 10 j T   One
```

While the second line in the preceding code is valid syntax, it is not necessarily efficient syntax. That line creates a vector of length `nrow(theDT)`=10 consisting of `TRUE` or `FALSE` entries, which is a vector scan. After we create a key for the `data.table` we can use different syntax to pick rows through a binary search, which will be much faster and is covered in Section 11.4.1.

Accessing individual columns must be done a little differently than accessing columns in `data.frames`. In Section 5.1 we show that multiple columns in a `data.frame` should be specified as a `character vector`. With `data.tables` the columns should be specified as a `list` of the actual names, not as `characters`.

```
> theDT[, list(A, C)]

     A C
 1:  1 K
 2:  2 L
 3:  3 M
 4:  4 N
 5:  5 O
 6:  6 P
 7:  7 Q
 8:  8 R
 9:  9 S
10: 10 T

> # just one column
> theDT[, B]

 [1] "a" "b" "c" "d" "e" "f" "g" "h" "i" "j"
```

```
> # one column while maintaining data.table structure
> theDT[, list(B)]

      B
  1:  a
  2:  b
  3:  c
  4:  d
  5:  e
  6:  f
  7:  g
  8:  h
  9:  i
 10:  j
```

If we must specify the column names as characters (perhaps because they were passed as arguments to a function), the with argument should be set to FALSE.

```
> theDT[, "B", with = FALSE]

      B
  1:  a
  2:  b
  3:  c
  4:  d
  5:  e
  6:  f
  7:  g
  8:  h
  9:  i
 10:  j

> theDT[, c("A", "C"), with = FALSE]

      A  C
  1:   1  K
  2:   2  L
  3:   3  M
  4:   4  N
  5:   5  O
  6:   6  P
  7:   7  Q
  8:   8  R
  9:   9  S
 10:  10  T
```

This time we used a vector to hold the column names instead of a list. These nuances are important to proper functions of data.tables but can lead to a great deal of frustration.

11.4.1 Keys

Now that we have a few data.tables in memory, we might be interested in seeing some information about them.

```
> # show tables
> tables()

        NAME            NROW  MB
[1,]  diamondsDT  53,940  4
[2,]  theDT             10  1
        COLS                                                                KEY
[1,]  carat,cut,color,clarity,depth,table,price,x,y,z
[2,]  A,B,C,D
Total: 5MB
```

This shows, for each data.table in memory, the name, the number of rows, the size in megabytes, the column names and the key. We have not assigned keys for any of the tables so that column is blank. The key is used to index the data.table and will provide the extra speed.

We start by adding a key to theDT. We will use the D column to index the data.table. This is done using setkey, which takes the name of the data.table as its first argument and the name of the desired column (without quotes, as is consistent with column selection) as the second argument.

```
> # set the key
> setkey(theDT, D)
> # show the data.table again
> theDT

      A B C      D
 1:   1 a K    One
 2:   4 d N    One
 3:   7 g Q    One
 4:  10 j T    One
 5:   3 c M  Three
 6:   6 f P  Three
 7:   9 i S  Three
 8:   2 b L    Two
 9:   5 e O    Two
10:   8 h R    Two
```

The data have been reordered according to column D, which is sorted alphabetically. We can confirm the key was set with `key`.

```
> key(theDT)

[1] "D"
```

Or `tables`.

```
> tables()

        NAME          NROW MB
[1,] diamondsDT 53,940 4
[2,] theDT            10 1
        COLS                                                    KEY
[1,] carat,cut,color,clarity,depth,table,price,x,y,z
[2,] A,B,C,D                                                   D
Total: 5MB
```

This adds some new functionality to selecting rows from `data.tables`. In addition to selecting rows by the row number or by some expression that evaluates to TRUE or FALSE, a value of the key column can be specified.

```
> theDT["One", ]

        D  A B C
1: One   1 a K
2: One   4 d N
3: One   7 g Q
4: One 10 j T

> theDT[c("One", "Two"), ]

        D  A B C
1: One   1 a K
2: One   4 d N
3: One   7 g Q
4: One 10 j T
5: Two   2 b L
6: Two   5 e O
7: Two   8 h R
```

More than one column can be set as the key.

```
> # set the key
> setkey(diamondsDT, cut, color)
```

To access rows according to both keys, there is a special function named J. It takes multiple arguments, each of which is a `vector` of values to select.

```
> # access some rows
> diamondsDT[J("Ideal", "E"), ]

          cut color carat clarity depth table price    x    y    z
   1: Ideal     E  0.23     SI2  61.5    55   326 3.95 3.98 2.43
   2: Ideal     E  0.26    VVS2  62.9    58   554 4.02 4.06 2.54
   3: Ideal     E  0.70     SI1  62.5    57  2757 5.70 5.72 3.57
   4: Ideal     E  0.59    VVS2  62.0    55  2761 5.38 5.43 3.35
   5: Ideal     E  0.74     SI2  62.2    56  2761 5.80 5.84 3.62
  ---
3899: Ideal     E  0.70     SI1  61.7    55  2745 5.71 5.74 3.53
3900: Ideal     E  0.51    VVS1  61.9    54  2745 5.17 5.11 3.18
3901: Ideal     E  0.56    VVS1  62.1    56  2750 5.28 5.29 3.28
3902: Ideal     E  0.77     SI2  62.1    56  2753 5.84 5.86 3.63
3903: Ideal     E  0.71     SI1  61.9    56  2756 5.71 5.73 3.54

> diamondsDT[J("Ideal", c("E", "D")), ]

          cut color carat clarity depth table price    x    y    z
   1: Ideal     E  0.23     SI2  61.5    55   326 3.95 3.98 2.43
   2: Ideal     E  0.26    VVS2  62.9    58   554 4.02 4.06 2.54
   3: Ideal     E  0.70     SI1  62.5    57  2757 5.70 5.72 3.57
   4: Ideal     E  0.59    VVS2  62.0    55  2761 5.38 5.43 3.35
   5: Ideal     E  0.74     SI2  62.2    56  2761 5.80 5.84 3.62
  ---
6733: Ideal     D  0.51    VVS2  61.7    56  2742 5.16 5.14 3.18
6734: Ideal     D  0.51    VVS2  61.3    57  2742 5.17 5.14 3.16
6735: Ideal     D  0.81     SI1  61.5    57  2748 6.00 6.03 3.70
6736: Ideal     D  0.72     SI1  60.8    57  2757 5.75 5.76 3.50
6737: Ideal     D  0.75     SI2  62.2    55  2757 5.83 5.87 3.64
```

11.4.2 data.table Aggregation

The primary benefit of indexing is faster aggregation. While aggregate and the various d*ply functions will work because data.tables are just enhanced data.frames, they will be slower than using the built-in aggregation functionality of data.table.

In Section 11.2 we calculate the mean price of diamonds for each type of cut.

```
> aggregate(price ~ cut, diamonds, mean)

        cut    price
1      Fair 4358.758
2      Good 3928.864
3 Very Good 3981.760
4   Premium 4584.258
5     Ideal 3457.542
```

To get the same result using data.table, we do this:

```
> diamondsDT[, mean(price), by = cut]

         cut      V1
1:      Fair 4358.758
2:      Good 3928.864
3: Very Good 3981.760
4:   Premium 4584.258
5:     Ideal 3457.542
```

The only difference between this and the previous result is that the columns have different names. To specify the name of the resulting column, pass the aggregation function as a named list.

```
> diamondsDT[, list(price = mean(price)), by = cut]

         cut    price
1:      Fair 4358.758
2:      Good 3928.864
3: Very Good 3981.760
4:   Premium 4584.258
5:     Ideal 3457.542
```

To aggregate on multiple columns, specify them as a list().

```
> diamondsDT[, mean(price), by = list(cut, color)]

          cut color      V1
 1:      Fair     D 4291.061
 2:      Fair     E 3682.312
 3:      Fair     F 3827.003
 4:      Fair     G 4239.255
 5:      Fair     H 5135.683
 6:      Fair     I 4685.446
 7:      Fair     J 4975.655
 8:      Good     D 3405.382
 9:      Good     E 3423.644
10:      Good     F 3495.750
11:      Good     G 4123.482
12:      Good     H 4276.255
13:      Good     I 5078.533
14:      Good     J 4574.173
15: Very Good     D 3470.467
16: Very Good     E 3214.652
```

```
17:  Very Good      F 3778.820
18:  Very Good      G 3872.754
19:  Very Good      H 4535.390
20:  Very Good      I 5255.880
21:  Very Good      J 5103.513
22:    Premium      D 3631.293
23:    Premium      E 3538.914
24:    Premium      F 4324.890
25:    Premium      G 4500.742
26:    Premium      H 5216.707
27:    Premium      I 5946.181
28:    Premium      J 6294.592
29:      Ideal      D 2629.095
30:      Ideal      E 2597.550
31:      Ideal      F 3374.939
32:      Ideal      G 3720.706
33:      Ideal      H 3889.335
34:      Ideal      I 4451.970
35:      Ideal      J 4918.186
             cut color        V1
```

To aggregate multiple arguments, pass them as a `list`. Unlike with `aggregate`, a different metric can be measured for each column.

```
> diamondsDT[, list(price = mean(price), carat = mean(carat)), by = cut]

          cut    price     carat
1:      Ideal 3457.542 0.7028370
2:    Premium 4584.258 0.8919549
3:       Good 3928.864 0.8491847
4: Very Good 3981.760 0.8063814
5:       Fair 4358.758 1.0461366

> diamondsDT[, list(price = mean(price), carat = mean(carat),
+     caratSum = sum(carat)), by = cut]

          cut    price     carat caratSum
1:      Ideal 3457.542 0.7028370 15146.84
2:    Premium 4584.258 0.8919549 12300.95
3:       Good 3928.864 0.8491847  4166.10
4: Very Good 3981.760 0.8063814  9742.70
5:       Fair 4358.758 1.0461366  1684.28
```

Finally, both multiple metrics can be calculated and multiple grouping variables can be specified at the same time.

```
> diamondsDT[, list(price = mean(price), carat = mean(carat)),
+     by = list(cut, color)]
```

	cut	color	price	carat
1:	Ideal	E	2597.550	0.5784012
2:	Premium	E	3538.914	0.7177450
3:	Good	E	3423.644	0.7451340
4:	Premium	I	5946.181	1.1449370
5:	Good	J	4574.173	1.0995440
6:	Very Good	J	5103.513	1.1332153
7:	Very Good	I	5255.880	1.0469518
8:	Very Good	H	4535.390	0.9159485
9:	Fair	E	3682.312	0.8566071
10:	Ideal	J	4918.186	1.0635937
11:	Premium	F	4324.890	0.8270356
12:	Ideal	I	4451.970	0.9130291
13:	Good	I	5078.533	1.0572222
14:	Very Good	E	3214.652	0.6763167
15:	Very Good	G	3872.754	0.7667986
16:	Very Good	D	3470.467	0.6964243
17:	Very Good	F	3778.820	0.7409612
18:	Good	F	3495.750	0.7759296
19:	Good	H	4276.255	0.9147293
20:	Good	D	3405.382	0.7445166
21:	Ideal	G	3720.706	0.7007146
22:	Premium	D	3631.293	0.7215471
23:	Premium	J	6294.592	1.2930941
24:	Ideal	D	2629.095	0.5657657
25:	Premium	G	4500.742	0.8414877
26:	Premium	H	5216.707	1.0164492
27:	Fair	F	3827.003	0.9047115
28:	Ideal	F	3374.939	0.6558285
29:	Ideal	H	3889.335	0.7995249
30:	Fair	H	5135.683	1.2191749
31:	Good	G	4123.482	0.8508955
32:	Fair	G	4239.255	1.0238217
33:	Fair	J	4975.655	1.3411765
34:	Fair	I	4685.446	1.1980571
35:	Fair	D	4291.061	0.9201227
	cut	color	price	carat

11.5 Conclusion

Aggregating data is a very important step in the analysis process. Sometimes it is the end goal, and other times it is in preparation for applying more advanced methods. No matter the reason for aggregation, there are plenty of functions to make it possible. These include `aggregate`, `apply` and `lapply` in base; `ddply`, `llply` and the rest in `plyr`; and the group by functionality in `data.table`.

Chapter 12

Data Reshaping

As noted in Chapter 11, manipulating the data takes a great deal of effort before serious analysis can begin. In this chapter we will consider when the data needs to be rearranged from column oriented to row oriented (or the opposite) and when the data are in multiple, separate sets and need to be combined into one.

There are base functions to accomplish these tasks but we will focus on those in plyr, reshape2 and data.table.

12.1 cbind and rbind

The simplest case is when we have two datasets with either identical columns (both the number of and names) or the same number of rows. In this case, either rbind or cbind work great.

As a first trivial example, we create two simple data.frames by combining a few vectors with cbind, and then stack them using rbind.

```
> # make two vectors and combine them as columns in a data.frame
> sport <- c("Hockey", "Baseball", "Football")
> league <- c("NHL", "MLB", "NFL")
> trophy <- c("Stanley Cup", "Commissioner's Trophy",
+             "Vince Lombardi Trophy")
> trophies1 <- cbind(sport, league, trophy)
> # make another data.frame using data.frame()
> trophies2 <- data.frame(sport=c("Basketball", "Golf"),
+                         league=c("NBA", "PGA"),
+                         trophy=c("Larry O'Brien Championship Trophy",
+                                  "Wanamaker Trophy"),
+                         stringsAsFactors=FALSE)
> # combine them into one data.frame with rbind
> trophies <- rbind(trophies1, trophies2)
```

Both cbind and rbind can take multiple arguments to combine an arbitrary number of objects. Note that it is possible to assign new column names to vectors in cbind.

```
> cbind(Sport = sport, Association = league, Prize = trophy)

     Sport        Association Prize
[1,] "Hockey"     "NHL"        "Stanley Cup"
[2,] "Baseball"   "MLB"        "Commissioner's Trophy"
[3,] "Football"   "NFL"        "Vince Lombardi Trophy"
```

12.2 Joins

Data do not always come so nicely aligned for combining using cbind, so they need to be joined together using a common key. This concept should be familiar to SQL users. Joins in R are not as flexible as SQL joins, but are still an essential operation in the data analysis process.

The three most commonly used functions for joins are merge in base R, join in plyr and the merging functionality in data.table. Each has pros and cons with some pros outweighing their respective cons.

To illustrate these functions I have prepared data originally made available as part of the USAID Open Government initiative.[1] The data have been chopped into eight separate files so that they can be joined together. They are all available in a zip file at http://jaredlander.com/data/US_Foreign_Aid.zip. These should be downloaded and unzipped to a folder on our computer. This can be done a number of ways (including using a mouse!) but we show how to download and unzip using R.

```
> download.file(url="http://jaredlander.com/data/US_Foreign_Aid.zip",
+               destfile="data/ForeignAid.zip")
> unzip("data/ForeignAid.zip", exdir="data")
```

To load all of these files programmatically, we use a for loop as seen in Section 10.1. We get a list of the files using dir, and then loop through that list assigning each dataset to a name specified using assign.

```
> require(stringr)
> # first get a list of the files
> theFiles <- dir("data/", pattern="\\.csv")
> ## loop through those files
> for(a in theFiles)
+ {
+     # build a good name to assign to the data
+     nameToUse <- str_sub(string=a, start=12, end=18)
```

---

1. More information about the data is available at http://gbk.eads.usaidallnet.gov/.

```
+       # read in the csv using read.table
+       # file.path is a convenient way to specify a folder and file name
+       temp <- read.table(file=file.path("data", a),
+                          header=TRUE, sep=",", stringsAsFactors=FALSE)
+       # assign them into the workspace
+       assign(x=nameToUse, value=temp)
+ }
```

12.2.1 merge

R comes with a built-in function, called merge, to merge two data.frames.

```
> Aid90s00s <- merge(x=Aid_90s, y=Aid_00s,
+                     by.x=c("Country.Name", "Program.Name"),
+                     by.y=c("Country.Name", "Program.Name"))
> head(Aid90s00s)
```

```
  Country.Name                                      Program.Name
1  Afghanistan                         Child Survival and Health
2  Afghanistan        Department of Defense Security Assistance
3  Afghanistan                             Development Assistance
4  Afghanistan Economic Support Fund/Security Support Assistance
5  Afghanistan                                  Food For Education
6  Afghanistan                    Global Health and Child Survival
  FY1990 FY1991 FY1992    FY1993   FY1994 FY1995 FY1996 FY1997 FY1998
1    NA     NA     NA       NA       NA     NA     NA     NA     NA
2    NA     NA     NA       NA       NA     NA     NA     NA     NA
3    NA     NA     NA       NA       NA     NA     NA     NA     NA
4    NA     NA     NA 14178135  2769948     NA     NA     NA     NA
5    NA     NA     NA       NA       NA     NA     NA     NA     NA
6    NA     NA     NA       NA       NA     NA     NA     NA     NA
  FY1999 FY2000  FY2001   FY2002    FY2003       FY2004     FY2005
1    NA     NA      NA  2586555  56501189     40215304   39817970
2    NA     NA      NA  2964313        NA     45635526  151334908
3    NA     NA 4110478  8762080  54538965    180539337  193598227
4    NA     NA   61144 31827014 341306822   1025522037 1157530168
5    NA     NA      NA       NA   3957312      2610006    3254408
6    NA     NA      NA       NA        NA           NA         NA
       FY2006     FY2007     FY2008     FY2009
1    40856382   72527069   28397435         NA
2   230501318  214505892  495539084  552524990
3   212648440  173134034  150529862    3675202
4  1357750249 1266653993 1400237791 1418688520
5     386891         NA         NA         NA
6         NA         NA   63064912    1764252
```

The by.x specifies the key column(s) in the left data.frame and by.y does the same for the right data.frame. The ability to specify different column names for each data.frame is the most useful feature of merge. The biggest drawback, however, is that merge can be much slower than the alternatives.

12.2.2 plyr join

Returning to Hadley Wickham's plyr package, we see it includes a join function, which works similarly to merge but is much faster. The biggest drawback, though, is that the key column(s) in each table must have the same name. We use the same data used previously to illustrate.

```
> require(plyr)
> Aid90s00sJoin <- join(x = Aid_90s, y = Aid_00s, by = c("Country.Name",
+      "Program.Name"))
> head(Aid90s00sJoin)
```

	Country.Name	Program.Name
1	Afghanistan	Child Survival and Health
2	Afghanistan	Department of Defense Security Assistance
3	Afghanistan	Development Assistance
4	Afghanistan	Economic Support Fund/Security Support Assistance
5	Afghanistan	Food For Education
6	Afghanistan	Global Health and Child Survival

	FY1990	FY1991	FY1992	FY1993	FY1994	FY1995	FY1996	FY1997	FY1998
1	NA	NA	NA	NA	NA	NA	NA	NA	NA
2	NA	NA	NA	NA	NA	NA	NA	NA	NA
3	NA	NA	NA	NA	NA	NA	NA	NA	NA
4	NA	NA	NA	14178135	2769948	NA	NA	NA	NA
5	NA	NA	NA	NA	NA	NA	NA	NA	NA
6	NA	NA	NA	NA	NA	NA	NA	NA	NA

	FY1999	FY2000	FY2001	FY2002	FY2003	FY2004	FY2005
1	NA	NA	NA	2586555	56501189	40215304	39817970
2	NA	NA	NA	2964313	NA	45635526	151334908
3	NA	NA	4110478	8762080	54538965	180539337	193598227
4	NA	NA	61144	31827014	341306822	1025522037	1157530168
5	NA	NA	NA	NA	3957312	2610006	3254408
6	NA	NA	NA	NA	NA	NA	NA

	FY2006	FY2007	FY2008	FY2009
1	40856382	72527069	28397435	NA
2	230501318	214505892	495539084	552524990
3	212648440	173134034	150529862	3675202
4	1357750249	1266653993	1400237791	1418688520
5	386891	NA	NA	NA
6	NA	NA	63064912	1764252

join has an argument for specifying a left, right, inner or full (outer) join.

We have eight `data.frames` containing foreign assistance data that we would like to combine into one `data.frame` without hand coding each join. The best way to do this is to put all the `data.frames` into a `list`, and then successively join them together using Reduce.

```
> # first figure out the names of the data.frames
> frameNames <- str_sub(string = theFiles, start = 12, end = 18)
> # build an empty list
> frameList <- vector("list", length(frameNames))
> names(frameList) <- frameNames
> # add each data.frame into the list
> for (a in frameNames)
+ {
+     frameList[[a]] <- eval(parse(text = a))
+ }
```

A lot happened in that section of code, so let's go over it carefully. First we reconstructed the names of the `data.frames` using str_sub from Hadley Wickham's stringr package, which is shown in more detail in Chapter 13. Then we built an empty `list` with as many elements as there are `data.frames`, in this case eight, using vector and assigning its mode to "list." We then set appropriate names to the `list`.

Now that the `list` is built and named, we loop through it, assigning to each element the appropriate `data.frame`. The problem is that we have the names of the `data.frames` as characters but the <- operator requires a variable, not a character. So we parse and evaluate the character, which realizes the actual variable. Inspecting, we see that the list does indeed contain the appropriate `data.frames`.

```
> head(frameList[[1]])
```

	Country.Name	Program.Name
1	Afghanistan	Child Survival and Health
2	Afghanistan	Department of Defense Security Assistance
3	Afghanistan	Development Assistance
4	Afghanistan	Economic Support Fund/Security Support Assistance
5	Afghanistan	Food For Education
6	Afghanistan	Global Health and Child Survival

	FY2000	FY2001	FY2002	FY2003	FY2004	FY2005	FY2006
1	NA	NA	2586555	56501189	40215304	39817970	40856382
2	NA	NA	2964313	NA	45635526	45635526	230501318
3	NA	4110478	8762080	54538965	180539337	193598227	212648440
4	NA	61144	31827014	341306822	1025522037	1157530168	1357750249
5	NA	NA	NA	3957312	2610006	3254408	386891
6	NA	NA	NA	NA	NA	NA	NA

```
        FY2007       FY2008       FY2009
1    72527069     28397435           NA
2   214505892    495539084    552524990
3   173134034    150529862      3675202
4  1266653993   1400237791   1418688520
5          NA           NA           NA
6          NA     63064912      1764252
```

```
> head(frameList[["Aid_00s"]])
```

```
  Country.Name                                     Program.Name
1  Afghanistan                         Child Survival and Health
2  Afghanistan      Department of Defense Security Assistance
3  Afghanistan                            Development Assistance
4  Afghanistan Economic Support Fund/Security Support Assistance
5  Afghanistan                               Food For Education
6  Afghanistan             Global Health and Child Survival
   FY2000  FY2001    FY2002      FY2003      FY2004      FY2005      FY2006
1      NA      NA   2586555    56501189    40215304    39817970    40856382
2      NA      NA   2964313          NA    45635526   151334908   230501318
3      NA 4110478   8762080    54538965   180539337   193598227   212648440
4      NA   61144  31827014   341306822  1025522037  1157530168  1357750249
5      NA      NA        NA     3957312     2610006     3254408      386891
6      NA      NA        NA          NA          NA          NA          NA
        FY2007       FY2008       FY2009
1    72527069     28397435           NA
2   214505892    495539084    552524990
3   173134034    150529862      3675202
4  1266653993   1400237791   1418688520
5          NA           NA           NA
6          NA     63064912      1764252
```

```
> head(frameList[[5]])
```

```
  Country.Name                                     Program.Name
1  Afghanistan                         Child Survival and Health
2  Afghanistan      Department of Defense Security Assistance
3  Afghanistan                            Development Assistance
4  Afghanistan Economic Support Fund/Security Support Assistance
5  Afghanistan                               Food For Education
6  Afghanistan             Global Health and Child Survival
   FY1960 FY1961    FY1962 FY1963 FY1964 FY1965 FY1966 FY1967 FY1968
1      NA     NA        NA     NA     NA     NA     NA     NA     NA
2      NA     NA        NA     NA     NA     NA     NA     NA     NA
3      NA     NA        NA     NA     NA     NA     NA     NA     NA
```

4	NA	NA	181177853	NA	NA	NA	NA	NA	NA
5	NA	NA	NA	NA	NA	NA	NA	NA	NA
6	NA	NA	NA	NA	NA	NA	NA	NA	NA

	FY1969
1	NA
2	NA
3	NA
4	NA
5	NA
6	NA

```
> head(frameList[["Aid_60s"]])
```

	Country.Name	Program.Name
1	Afghanistan	Child Survival and Health
2	Afghanistan	Department of Defense Security Assistance
3	Afghanistan	Development Assistance
4	Afghanistan	Economic Support Fund/Security Support Assistance
5	Afghanistan	Food For Education
6	Afghanistan	Global Health and Child Survival

	FY1960	FY1961	FY1962	FY1963	FY1964	FY1965	FY1966	FY1967	FY1968
1	NA	NA	NA	NA	NA	NA	NA	NA	NA
2	NA	NA	NA	NA	NA	NA	NA	NA	NA
3	NA	NA	NA	NA	NA	NA	NA	NA	NA
4	NA	NA	181177853	NA	NA	NA	NA	NA	NA
5	NA	NA	NA	NA	NA	NA	NA	NA	NA
6	NA	NA	NA	NA	NA	NA	NA	NA	NA

	FY1969
1	NA
2	NA
3	NA
4	NA
5	NA
6	NA

Having all the data.frames in a list allows us to iterate through the list, joining all the elements together (or applying any function to the elements iteratively). Rather than using a loop, we use the Reduce function to speed up the operation.

```
> allAid <- Reduce(function(...)
+ {
+     join(..., by = c("Country.Name", "Program.Name"))
+ }, frameList)
> dim(allAid)

[1] 2453    67
```

```
> require(useful)
> corner(allAid, c = 15)
```

```
  Country.Name                                       Program.Name
1 Afghanistan                          Child Survival and Health
2 Afghanistan        Department of Defense Security Assistance
3 Afghanistan                          Development Assistance
4 Afghanistan Economic Support Fund/Security Support Assistance
5 Afghanistan                                  Food For Education
  FY2000  FY2001   FY2002    FY2003     FY2004      FY2005      FY2006
1    NA      NA  2586555  56501189   40215304    39817970    40856382
2    NA      NA  2964313        NA   45635526   151334908   230501318
3    NA 4110478  8762080  54538965  180539337   193598227   212648440
4    NA   61144 31827014 341306822 1025522037  1157530168 1357750249
5    NA      NA       NA   3957312    2610006     3254408      386891
       FY2007      FY2008     FY2009     FY2010 FY1946 FY1947
1   72527069    28397435         NA         NA     NA     NA
2  214505892   495539084  552524990  316514796     NA     NA
3  173134034   150529862    3675202         NA     NA     NA
4 1266653993  1400237791 1418688520 2797488331     NA     NA
5        NA          NA         NA         NA     NA     NA
```

```
> bottomleft(allAid, c = 15)
```

```
      Country.Name       Program.Name  FY2000   FY2001    FY2002
2449      Zimbabwe Other State Assistance 1341952   322842        NA
2450      Zimbabwe Other USAID Assistance 3033599  8464897   6624408
2451      Zimbabwe          Peace Corps 2140530  1150732    407834
2452      Zimbabwe                Title I      NA       NA        NA
2453      Zimbabwe               Title II      NA       NA  31019776
        FY2003    FY2004    FY2005   FY2006     FY2007      FY2008     FY2009
2449        NA    318655     44553   883546    1164632     2455592    2193057
2450  11580999  12805688  10091759  4567577   10627613    11466426   41940500
2451        NA        NA        NA       NA         NA          NA         NA
2452        NA        NA        NA       NA         NA          NA         NA
2453        NA        NA        NA   277468  100053600   180000717  174572685
        FY2010 FY1946 FY1947
2449   1605765     NA     NA
2450  30011970     NA     NA
2451        NA     NA     NA
2452        NA     NA     NA
2453  79545100     NA     NA
```

Reduce can be a difficult function to grasp, so we illustrate it with a simple example. Let's say we have a vector of the first ten integers, 1:10, and want to sum them (forget for a moment that sum(1:10) will work perfectly). We can call Reduce(sum, 1:10), which will first add 1 and 2. It will then add 3 to that result, then 4 to that result, and so on, resulting in 55.

Likewise, we passed a `list` to a function that joins its inputs, which in this case was simply . . . , meaning that anything could be passed. Using . . . is an advanced trick of R programming that can be difficult to get right. Reduce passed the first two `data.frames` in the `list`, which were then joined. That result was then joined to the next `data.frame` and so on until they were all joined together.

12.2.3 `data.table` merge

Like many other operations in `data.table`, joining data requires a different syntax, and possibly a different way of thinking. To start, we convert two of our foreign aid datasets' `data.frames` into `data.tables`.

```
> require(data.table)
> dt90 <- data.table(Aid_90s, key = c("Country.Name", "Program.Name"))
> dt00 <- data.table(Aid_00s, key = c("Country.Name", "Program.Name"))
```

Then, doing the join is a simple operation. Note that the join requires specifying the keys for the `data.tables`, which we did during their creation.

```
> dt0090 <- dt90[dt00]
```

In this case `dt90` is the left side, `dt00` is the right side and a left join was performed.

12.3 reshape2

The next most common munging need is either melting data (going from column orientation to row orientation) or casting data (going from row orientation to column orientation). As with most other procedures in R, there are multiple functions available to accomplish these tasks but we will focus on Hadley Wickham's `reshape2` package. (We talk about Wickham a lot because his products have become so fundamental to the R developer's toolbox.)

12.3.1 `melt`

Looking at the `Aid_00s` `data.frame`, we see that each year is stored in its own column. That is, the dollar amount for a given country and program is found in a different column for each year. This is called a cross table, which, while nice for human consumption, is not ideal for graphing with `ggplot2` or for some analysis algorithms.

```
> head(Aid_00s)

  Country.Name                                    Program.Name
1  Afghanistan                      Child Survival and Health
2  Afghanistan      Department of Defense Security Assistance
```

```
3  Afghanistan                                        Development Assistance
4  Afghanistan Economic Support Fund/Security Support Assistance
5  Afghanistan                                            Food For Education
6  Afghanistan                          Global Health and Child Survival
     FY2000   FY2001    FY2002     FY2003      FY2004       FY2005       FY2006
1     NA       NA    2586555   56501189    40215304    39817970    40856382
2     NA       NA    2964313        NA     45635526   151334908   230501318
3     NA  4110478    8762080   54538965   180539337   193598227   212648440
4     NA    61144   31827014  341306822  1025522037  1157530168  1357750249
5     NA       NA         NA    3957312     2610006     3254408      386891
6     NA       NA         NA         NA          NA          NA          NA
       FY2007     FY2008     FY2009
1    72527069   28397435         NA
2   214505892  495539084  552524990
3   173134034  150529862    3675202
4  1266653993 1400237791 1418688520
5         NA         NA         NA
6         NA   63064912    1764252
```

We want it set up so that each row represents a single country-program-year entry with the dollar amount stored in one column. To achieve this we melt the data using `melt` from reshape2.

```
> require(reshape2)
> melt00 <- melt(Aid_00s, id.vars=c("Country.Name", "Program.Name"),
+                 variable.name="Year", value.name="Dollars")
> tail(melt00, 10)

        Country.Name
24521      Zimbabwe
24522      Zimbabwe
24523      Zimbabwe
24524      Zimbabwe
24525      Zimbabwe
24526      Zimbabwe
24527      Zimbabwe
24528      Zimbabwe
24529      Zimbabwe
24530      Zimbabwe
                                        Program.Name    Year
24521       Migration and Refugee Assistance FY2009
24522                      Narcotics Control FY2009
```

```
24523 Nonproliferation, Anti-Terrorism, Demining and Related FY2009
24524                            Other Active Grant Programs FY2009
24525                              Other Food Aid Programs FY2009
24526                              Other State Assistance FY2009
24527                              Other USAID Assistance FY2009
24528                                         Peace Corps FY2009
24529                                            Title I FY2009
24530                                           Title II FY2009
         Dollars
24521   3627384
24522        NA
24523        NA
24524   7951032
24525        NA
24526   2193057
24527  41940500
24528        NA
24529        NA
24530 174572685
```

The `id.vars` argument specifies which columns uniquely identify a row.

After some manipulation of the Year column and aggregating, this is now prime for plotting, as shown in Figure 12.1. The plot uses faceting allowing us to quickly see and understand the funding for each program over time.

```
> require(scales)
> # strip the "FY" out of the year column and convert it to numeric
> melt00$Year <- as.numeric(str_sub(melt00$Year, start=3, 6))
> # aggregate the data so we have yearly numbers by program
> meltAgg <- aggregate(Dollars ~ Program.Name + Year, data=melt00,
+                       sum, na.rm=TRUE)
> # just keep the first 10 characters of program name
> # then it will fit in the plot
> meltAgg$Program.Name <- str_sub(meltAgg$Program.Name, start=1,
+                                 end=10)
>
> ggplot(meltAgg, aes(x=Year, y=Dollars)) +
+     geom_line(aes(group=Program.Name)) +
+     facet_wrap(~ Program.Name) +
+     scale_x_continuous(breaks=seq(from=2000, to=2009, by=2)) +
+     theme(axis.text.x=element_text(angle=90, vjust=1, hjust=0)) +
+     scale_y_continuous(labels=multiple_format(extra=dollar,
+                                 multiple="B"))
```

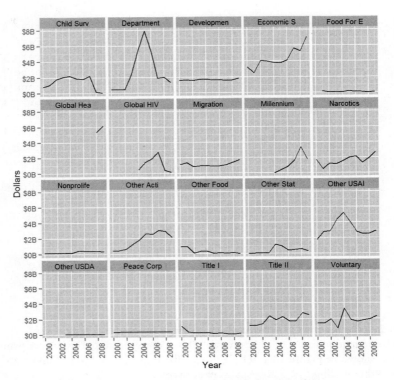

Figure 12.1   Plot of foreign assistance by year for each of the programs.

12.3.2   `dcast`

Now that we have the foreign aid data melted, we cast it back into the wide format for illustration purposes. The function for this is `dcast`, and it has trickier arguments than `melt`. The first is the data to be used, in our case `melt00`. The second argument is a `formula` where the left side specifies the columns that should remain columns and the right side specifies the columns that should become row names. The third argument is the column (as a character) that holds the values to be populated into the new columns representing the unique values of the right side of the `formula` argument.

```
> cast00 <- dcast(melt00, Country.Name + Program.Name ~ Year,
+       value.var = "Dollars")
> head(cast00)

  Country.Name                                  Program.Name 2000
1  Afghanistan                     Child Survival and Health   NA
2  Afghanistan   Department of Defense Security Assistance   NA
3  Afghanistan                        Development Assistance   NA
```

```
4  Afghanistan Economic Support Fund/Security Support Assistance   NA
5  Afghanistan                                Food For Education    NA
6  Afghanistan                      Global Health and Child Survival NA
        2001       2002        2003        2004         2005         2006
1        NA    2586555    56501189    40215304     39817970     40856382
2        NA    2964313          NA    45635526    151334908    230501318
3   4110478    8762080    54538965   180539337    193598227    212648440
4     61144   31827014   341306822  1025522037   1157530168   1357750249
5        NA         NA     3957312     2610006      3254408       386891
6        NA         NA          NA          NA           NA           NA
        2007        2008        2009
1   72527069    28397435          NA
2  214505892   495539084   552524990
3  173134034   150529862     3675202
4 1266653993  1400237791  1418688520
5        NA          NA          NA
6        NA    63064912     1764252
```

12.4 Conclusion

Getting the data just right to analyze can be a time-consuming part of our work flow, although it is often inescapable. In this chapter we examined combining multiple datasets into one and changing the orientation from column based (wide) to row based (long). We used `plyr`, `reshape2` and `data.table` along with base functions to accomplish this. This chapter combined with Chapter 11 covers most of the basics of data munging with an eye to both convenience and speed.

Chapter 13

Manipulating Strings

Strings (`character` data) often need to be constructed or deconstructed to identify observations, preprocess text, combine information or satisfy any number of other needs. R offers functions for building strings, like `paste` and `sprintf`. It also provides a number of functions for using regular expressions and examining text data, although for those purposes it is better to use Hadley Wickham's `stringr` package.

13.1 `paste`

The first function new R users reach for when putting together strings is `paste`. This function takes a series of strings, or expressions that evaluate to strings, and puts them together into one string. We start by putting together three simple strings.

```
> paste("Hello", "Jared", "and others")

[1] "Hello Jared and others"
```

Notice that spaces were put between the strings. This is because `paste` has a third argument, `sep`, that determines what to put in between entries. This can be any valid text, including empty text (`""`).

```
> paste("Hello", "Jared", "and others", sep = "/")

[1] "Hello/Jared/and others"
```

Like many functions in R, `paste` is vectorized. This means each element can be a vector of data to be put together.

```
> paste(c("Hello", "Hey", "Howdy"), c("Jared", "Bob", "David"))

[1] "Hello Jared" "Hey Bob"      "Howdy David"
```

In this case each `vector` had the same number of entries so they paired one-to-one. When the `vectors` do not have the same length they are recycled.

```
> paste("Hello", c("Jared", "Bob", "David"))
```

```
[1] "Hello Jared" "Hello Bob"     "Hello David"

> paste("Hello", c("Jared", "Bob", "David"), c("Goodbye", "Seeya"))

[1] "Hello Jared Goodbye" "Hello Bob Seeya"      "Hello David Goodbye"
```

paste also has the ability to collapse a vector of text into one vector containing all the elements with any arbitrary separator, using the collapse argument.

```
> vectorOfText <- c("Hello", "Everyone", "out there", ".")
> paste(vectorOfText, collapse = " ")

[1] "Hello Everyone out there ."

> paste(vectorOfText, collapse = "*")

[1] "Hello*Everyone*out there*."
```

13.2 sprintf

While paste is convenient for putting together short bits of text, it can become unwieldy when piecing together long pieces of text, such as when inserting a number of variables into a long piece of text. For instance, we might have a lengthy sentence that has a few spots that require the insertion of special variables. An example is "Hello Jared, your party of eight will be seated in 25 minutes" where "Jared," "eight" and "25" could be replaced with other information.

Reforming this with paste can make reading the line in code difficult.

To start, we make some variables to hold the information.

```
> person <- "Jared"
> partySize <- "eight"
> waitTime <- 25
```

Now we build the paste expression.

```
> paste("Hello ", person, ", your party of ", partySize,
+        " will be seated in ", waitTime, " minutes.", sep="")

[1] "Hello Jared, your party of eight will be seated in 25 minutes."
```

Making even a small change to this sentence would require putting the commas in just the right places.

A good alternative is the sprintf function. With this function we build one long string with special markers indicating where to insert values.

```
> sprintf("Hello %s, your party of %s will be seated in %s minutes",
+      person, partySize, waitTime)

[1] "Hello Jared, your party of eight will be seated in 25 minutes"
```

Here, each %s was replaced with its corresponding variable. While the long sentence is easier to read in code, we must maintain the order of %s's and variables.

sprintf is also vectorized. Note that the vector lengths must be multiples of each other.

```
> sprintf("Hello %s, your party of %s will be seated in %s minutes",
+        c("Jared", "Bob"), c("eight", 16, "four", 10), waitTime)

[1] "Hello Jared, your party of eight will be seated in 25 minutes"
[2] "Hello Bob, your party of 16 will be seated in 25 minutes"
[3] "Hello Jared, your party of four will be seated in 25 minutes"
[4] "Hello Bob, your party of 10 will be seated in 25 minutes"
```

13.3 Extracting Text

Often text needs to be ripped apart to be made useful, and while R has a number of functions for doing so, the stringr package is much easier to use.

First we need some data, so we use the XML package to download a table of United States presidents from Wikipedia.

```
> require(XML)
```

Then we use readHTMLTable to parse the table.

```
> load("data/presidents.rdata")
```

```
> theURL <- "http://www.loc.gov/rr/print/list/057_chron.html"
> presidents <- readHTMLTable(theURL, which=3, as.data.frame=TRUE,
+                              skip.rows=1, header=TRUE,
+                              stringsAsFactors=FALSE)
```

Now we take a look at the data.

```
> head(presidents)
```

```
        YEAR             PRESIDENT
1  1789-1797  George Washington
2  1797-1801         John Adams
3  1801-1805    Thomas Jefferson
4  1805-1809    Thomas Jefferson
5  1809-1812      James Madison
6  1812-1813      James Madison
                                      FIRST LADY    VICE PRESIDENT
1                            Martha Washington         John Adams
2                               Abigail Adams  Thomas Jefferson
3  Martha Wayles Skelton Jefferson\n   (no image)       Aaron Burr
4  Martha Wayles Skelton Jefferson\n   (no image)    George Clinton
```

```
5                              Dolley Madison    George Clinton
6                              Dolley Madison     office vacant
```

Examining it more closely, we see that the last few rows contain information we do not want, so we keep only the first 64 rows.

```
> tail(presidents$YEAR)
```

```
[1] "2001-2009"
[2] "2009-"
[3] "Presidents: Introduction (Rights/Ordering\n       Info.) | Adams\n
- Cleveland | Clinton - Harding Harrison\n       - Jefferson | Johnson
- McKinley | Monroe\n              - Roosevelt | Taft - Truman |
Tyler\n           - WilsonList of names, Alphabetically"
[4] "First Ladies: Introduction\n
(Rights/Ordering Info.) | Adams\n              - Coolidge | Eisenhower
- HooverJackson\n         - Pierce  | \n
Polk - Wilson | List\n          of names, Alphabetically"
[5] "Vice Presidents: Introduction (Rights/Ordering Info.) |
Adams - Coolidge | Curtis - Hobart Humphrey - Rockefeller | Roosevelt
- WilsonList of names, Alphabetically"
[6] "Top\n          of Page"
```

```
> presidents <- presidents[1:64, ]
```

To start, we create two new columns, one for the beginning of the term and one for the end of the term. To do this we need to split the Year column on the hyphen (-). The stringr package has the str_split function that splits a string based on some value. It returns a list with an element for each element of the input vector. Each of these elements has as many elements as necessary for the split, in this case either two (a start and stop year) or one (when the president served less than one year).

```
> require(stringr)
> # split the string
> yearList <- str_split(string = presidents$YEAR, pattern = "-")
> head(yearList)
```

```
[[1]]
[1] "1789" "1797"

[[2]]
[1] "1797" "1801"

[[3]]
[1] "1801" "1805"
```

```
[[4]]
[1] "1805" "1809"

[[5]]
[1] "1809" "1812"

[[6]]
[1] "1812" "1813"


> # combine them into one matrix
> yearMatrix <- data.frame(Reduce(rbind, yearList))
> head(yearMatrix)

    X1   X2
1 1789 1797
2 1797 1801
3 1801 1805
4 1805 1809
5 1809 1812
6 1812 1813

> # give the columns good names
> names(yearMatrix) <- c("Start", "Stop")
> # bind the new columns onto the data.frame
> presidents <- cbind(presidents, yearMatrix)
> # convert the start and stop columns into numeric
> presidents$Start <- as.numeric(as.character(presidents$Start))
> presidents$Stop <- as.numeric(as.character(presidents$Stop))
> # view the changes
> head(presidents)

       YEAR          PRESIDENT
1 1789-1797 George Washington
2 1797-1801        John Adams
3 1801-1805   Thomas Jefferson
4 1805-1809   Thomas Jefferson
5 1809-1812      James Madison
6 1812-1813      James Madison
                                    FIRST LADY     VICE PRESIDENT
1                             Martha Washington        John Adams
2                                Abigail Adams  Thomas Jefferson
3 Martha Wayles Skelton Jefferson\n  (no image)        Aaron Burr
4 Martha Wayles Skelton Jefferson\n  (no image)    George Clinton
5                               Dolley Madison    George Clinton
6                               Dolley Madison     office vacant
```

```
   Start Stop
1   1789 1797
2   1797 1801
3   1801 1805
4   1805 1809
5   1809 1812
6   1812 1813
```

```
> tail(presidents)
```

```
       YEAR       PRESIDENT        FIRST LADY    VICE PRESIDENT
59 1977-1981   Jimmy Carter    Rosalynn Carter Walter F. Mondale
60 1981-1989  Ronald Reagan      Nancy Reagan      George Bush
61 1989-1993    George Bush      Barbara Bush       Dan Quayle
62 1993-2001   Bill Clinton Hillary Rodham Clinton    Albert Gore
63 2001-2009 George W. Bush        Laura Bush   Richard Cheney
64     2009-   Barack Obama    Michelle Obama  Joseph R. Biden
   Start Stop
59   1977 1981
60   1981 1989
61   1989 1993
62   1993 2001
63   2001 2009
64   2009   NA
```

In the preceding example there was a quirk of R that can be frustrating at first pass. In order to convert the factor presidents$Start into a numeric, we first had to convert it into a character. That is because factors are simply labels on top of integers, as seen in Section 4.4.2. So when applying as.numeric to a factor, it is converted to the underlying integers.

Just like in Excel, it is possible to select specified characters from text using str_sub.

```
> # get the first 3 characters
> str_sub(string = presidents$PRESIDENT, start = 1, end = 3)
```

```
 [1] "Geo" "Joh" "Tho" "Tho" "Jam" "Jam" "Jam" "Jam" "Jam" "Joh" "And"
[12] "And" "Mar" "Wil" "Joh" "Jam" "Zac" "Mil" "Fra" "Fra" "Jam" "Abr"
[23] "Abr" "And" "Uly" "Uly" "Uly" "Rut" "Jam" "Che" "Gro" "Gro" "Ben"
[34] "Gro" "Wil" "Wil" "Wil" "The" "The" "Wil" "Wil" "Woo" "War" "Cal"
[45] "Cal" "Her" "Fra" "Fra" "Fra" "Har" "Har" "Dwi" "Joh" "Lyn" "Lyn"
[56] "Ric" "Ric" "Ger" "Jim" "Ron" "Geo" "Bil" "Geo" "Bar"
```

```
> # get the 4th through 8th characters
> str_sub(string = presidents$PRESIDENT, start = 4, end = 8)
```

```
 [1] "rge W" "n Ada" "mas J" "mas J" "es Ma" "es Ma" "es Ma" "es Ma"
 [9] "es Mo" "n Qui" "rew J" "rew J" "tin V" "liam " "n Tyl" "es K."
[17] "hary " "lard " "nklin" "nklin" "es Bu" "aham " "aham " "rew J"
[25] "sses " "sses " "sses " "herfo" "es A." "ster " "ver C" "ver C"
[33] "jamin" "ver C" "liam " "liam " "liam " "odore" "odore" "liam "
[41] "liam " "drow " "ren G" "vin C" "vin C" "bert " "nklin" "nklin"
[49] "nklin" "ry S." "ry S." "ght D" "n F. " "don B" "don B" "hard "
[57] "hard " "ald R" "my Ca" "ald R" "rge B" "l Cli" "rge W" "ack O"
```

This is good for finding a president whose term started in a year ending in 1, which means he got elected in a year ending in 0, a preponderance of which ones died in office.

```
> presidents[str_sub(string = presidents$Start, start = 4,
+     end = 4) == 1, c("YEAR", "PRESIDENT", "Start", "Stop")]
```

```
          YEAR              PRESIDENT Start Stop
3    1801-1805       Thomas Jefferson  1801 1805
14        1841 William Henry Harrison  1841 1841
15   1841-1845             John Tyler  1841 1845
22   1861-1865        Abraham Lincoln  1861 1865
29        1881      James A. Garfield  1881 1881
30   1881-1885     Chester A. Arthur   1881 1885
37        1901      William McKinley   1901 1901
38   1901-1905    Theodore Roosevelt   1901 1905
43   1921-1923     Warren G. Harding   1921 1923
48   1941-1945 Franklin D. Roosevelt   1941 1945
53   1961-1963       John F. Kennedy   1961 1963
60   1981-1989         Ronald Reagan   1981 1989
63   2001-2009        George W. Bush   2001 2009
```

13.4 Regular Expressions

Sifting through text often requires searching for patterns, and usually these patterns have to be general and flexible. This is where regular expressions are very useful. We will not make an exhaustive lesson of regular expressions but will illustrate how to use them within R.

Let's say we want to find any president with "John" in his name, either first or last. Since we do not know where in the name "John" would occur, we cannot simply use str_sub. Instead we use str_detect.

```
> # returns TRUE/FALSE if John was found in the name
> johnPos <- str_detect(string = presidents$PRESIDENT, pattern = "John")
> presidents[johnPos, c("YEAR", "PRESIDENT", "Start", "Stop")]
```

```
        YEAR   PRESIDENT Start Stop
2  1797-1801  John Adams  1797 1801
```

```
10 1825-1829 John Quincy Adams  1825 1829
15 1841-1845         John Tyler  1841 1845
24 1865-1869    Andrew Johnson  1865 1869
53 1961-1963    John F. Kennedy  1961 1963
54 1963-1965 Lyndon B. Johnson  1963 1965
55 1963-1969 Lyndon B. Johnson  1963 1969
```

This found John Adams, John Quincy Adams, John Tyler, Andrew Johnson, John F. Kennedy and Lyndon B. Johnson. Note that regular expressions are case sensitive, so to ignore case we have to put the pattern in `ignore.case`.

```
> badSearch <- str_detect(presidents$PRESIDENT, "john")
> goodSearch <- str_detect(presidents$PRESIDENT, ignore.case("John"))
> sum(badSearch)

[1] 0

> sum(goodSearch)

[1] 7
```

To show off some more interesting regular expressions we will make use of yet another table from Wikipedia, the list of United States wars. Because we only care about one column, which has some encoding issues, we put an `Rdata` file of just that one column at `http://www.jaredlander.com/data/warTimes.rdata`. We load that file using `load` and we then see a new object in our session named `warTimes`.

For some odd reason, loading `rdata` files from a URL is not as straightforward as reading in a CSV file from a URL. A connection must first be made using `url`, then that connection is loaded with `load`, and then the connection must be closed with `close`.

```
> con <- url("http://www.jaredlander.com/data/warTimes.rdata")
> load(con)
> close(con)
```

This `vector` holds the starting and stopping dates of the wars. Sometimes it has just years, sometimes it also includes months and possibly days. There are instances where it has only one year. Because of this, it is a good dataset to comb through with various text functions. The first few entries follow.

```
> head(warTimes, 10)

 [1] "September 1, 1774 ACAEA September 3, 1783"
 [2] "September 1, 1774 ACAEA March 17, 1776"
 [3] "1775ACAEA1783"
 [4] "June 1775 ACAEA October 1776"
 [5] "July 1776 ACAEA March 1777"
 [6] "June 14, 1777 ACAEA October 17, 1777"
 [7] "1777ACAEA1778"
```

```
 [8]  "1775ACAEA1782"
 [9]  "1776ACAEA1794"
[10]  "1778ACAEA1782"
```

We want to create a new column that contains information for the start of the war. To get at this information we need to split the `Time` column. Thanks to Wikipedia's encoding, the separator is generally "ACAEA," which was originally "Ã¢Â€Â'" and converted to these characters to make life easier. There are two instances where the "-" appears, once as a separator and once to make a hyphenated word. This is seen in the following code.

```
> warTimes[str_detect(string = warTimes, pattern = "-")]

[1] "6 June 1944 ACAEA mid-July 1944"
[2] "25 August-17 December 1944"
```

So when we are splitting our string, we need to search for either "ACAEA" or "-." In `str_split` the `pattern` argument can take a regular expression. In this case it will be "(ACAEA)|-," which tells the engine to search for either "(ACAEA)" or (denoted by the vertical pipe) "-" in the string. To avoid the instance, seen before, where the hyphen is used in "mid-July" we set the argument n to 2 so it returns at most only two pieces for each element of the input `vector`. The parentheses are not matched but rather act to group the characters "ACAEA" in the search.[1] This grouping capability will prove important for advanced replacement of text, which will be demonstrated later in this section.

```
> theTimes <- str_split(string = warTimes, pattern = "(ACAEA)|-", n = 2)
> head(theTimes)

[[1]]
[1] "September 1, 1774 " " September 3, 1783"

[[2]]
[1] "September 1, 1774 " " March 17, 1776"

[[3]]
[1] "1775" "1783"

[[4]]
[1] "June 1775 "    " October 1776"

[[5]]
[1] "July 1776 "  " March 1777"
```

---

1. To match parentheses, they should be prefixed with a backslash (\).

```
[[6]]
[1] "June 14, 1777 "      " October 17, 1777"
```

Seeing that this worked for the first few entries, we also check on the two instances where a hyphen was the separator.

```
> which(str_detect(string = warTimes, pattern = "-"))

[1] 147 150

> theTimes[[147]]

[1] "6 June 1944 "      " mid-July 1944"

> theTimes[[150]]

[1] "25 August"         "17 December 1944"
```

This looks correct, as the first entry shows "mid-July" still intact while the second entry shows the two dates split apart.

For our purposes we only care about the start date of the wars, so we need to build a function that extracts the first (in some cases only) element of each `vector` in the `list`.

```
> theStart <- sapply(theTimes, FUN = function(x) x[1])
> head(theStart)

[1] "September 1, 1774 " "September 1, 1774 " "1775"
[4] "June 1775 "         "July 1776 "         "June 14, 1777 "
```

The original text sometimes had spaces around the separators and sometimes did not, meaning that some of our text has trailing white spaces. The easiest way to get rid of them is with the `str_trim` function.

```
> theStart <- str_trim(theStart)
> head(theStart)

[1] "September 1, 1774" "September 1, 1774" "1775"
[4] "June 1775"         "July 1776"         "June 14, 1777"
```

To extract the word "January" wherever it might occur, use `str_extract`. In places where it is not found will be `NA`.

```
> # pull out 'January' anywhere it's found, otherwise return NA
> str_extract(string = theStart, pattern = "January")

 [1] NA        NA        NA        NA        NA        NA
 [7] NA        NA        NA        NA        NA        NA
[13] "January" NA        NA        NA        NA        NA
```

[19] NA	NA	NA	NA	NA	NA
[25] NA	NA	NA	NA	NA	NA
[31] NA	NA	NA	NA	NA	NA
[37] NA	NA	NA	NA	NA	NA
[43] NA	NA	NA	NA	NA	NA
[49] NA	NA	NA	NA	NA	NA
[55] NA	NA	NA	NA	NA	NA
[61] NA	NA	NA	NA	NA	NA
[67] NA	NA	NA	NA	NA	NA
[73] NA	NA	NA	NA	NA	NA
[79] NA	NA	NA	NA	NA	NA
[85] NA	NA	NA	NA	NA	NA
[91] NA	NA	NA	NA	NA	NA
[97] NA	NA	"January"	NA	NA	NA
[103] NA	NA	NA	NA	NA	NA
[109] NA	NA	NA	NA	NA	NA
[115] NA	NA	NA	NA	NA	NA
[121] NA	NA	NA	NA	NA	NA
[127] NA	NA	NA	NA	"January"	NA
[133] NA	NA	"January"	NA	NA	NA
[139] NA	NA	NA	NA	NA	NA
[145] "January"	"January"	NA	NA	NA	NA
[151] NA	NA	NA	NA	NA	NA
[157] NA	NA	NA	NA	NA	NA
[163] NA	NA	NA	NA	NA	NA
[169] "January"	NA	NA	NA	NA	NA
[175] NA	NA	NA	NA	NA	NA
[181] "January"	NA	NA	NA	NA	"January"
[187] NA	NA				

To find elements that contain "January" and return the entire entry—not just "January"—use str_detect and subset theStart with the results.

```
> # just return elements where 'January' was detected
> theStart[str_detect(string = theStart, pattern = "January")]
```

```
[1] "January"          "January 21"        "January 1942"
[4] "January"          "January 22, 1944"  "22 January 1944"
[7] "January 4, 1989"  "15 January 2002"   "January 14, 2010"
```

To extract the year, we search for an occurrence of four numbers together. Because we do not know specific numbers, we have to use a pattern. In a regular expression search, "[0-9]" searches for any number. We use "[0-9][0-9][0-9][0-9]" to search for four consecutive numbers.

```
> # get incidents of 4 numeric digits in a row
> head(str_extract(string = theStart, "[0-9][0-9][0-9][0-9]"), 20)

 [1] "1774" "1774" "1775" "1775" "1776" "1777" "1777" "1775" "1776"
[10] "1778" "1775" "1779" NA      "1785" "1798" "1801" NA      "1812"
[19] "1812" "1813"
```

Writing "[0-9]" repeatedly is inefficient, especially when searching for many occurences of a number. Putting "4" in curly braces after "[0-9]" causes the engine to search for any set of four numbers.

```
> # a smarter way to search for four numbers
> head(str_extract(string = theStart, "[0-9]{4}"), 20)

 [1] "1774" "1774" "1775" "1775" "1776" "1777" "1777" "1775" "1776"
[10] "1778" "1775" "1779" NA      "1785" "1798" "1801" NA      "1812"
[19] "1812" "1813"
```

Even writing "[0-9]" can be inefficient, so there is a shortcut to denote any integer. In most other languages the shortcut is "\d" but in R there needs to be two backslashes ("\\d").

```
> # "\\d" is a shortcut for "[0-9]"
> head(str_extract(string = theStart, "\\d{4}"), 20)

 [1] "1774" "1774" "1775" "1775" "1776" "1777" "1777" "1775" "1776"
[10] "1778" "1775" "1779" NA      "1785" "1798" "1801" NA      "1812"
[19] "1812" "1813"
```

The curly braces offer even more functionality: for instance, searching for a number one to three times.

```
> # this looks for any digit that occurs either once, twice or thrice
> str_extract(string = theStart, "\\d{1,3}")

  [1] "1"   "1"   "177" "177" "177" "14"  "177" "177" "177" "177"
 [11] "177" "177" NA    "178" "179" "180" NA    "18"  "181" "181"
 [21] "181" "181" "181" "181" "181" "181" "181" "181" "181" "181"
 [31] "22"  "181" "181" "5"   "182" "182" "182" NA    "6"   "183"
 [41] "23"  "183" "19"  "11"  "25"  "184" "184" "184" "184" "184"
 [51] "185" "184" "28"  "185" "13"  "4"   "185" "185" "185" "185"
 [61] "185" "185" "6"   "185" "6"   "186" "12"  "186" "186" "186"
 [71] "186" "186" "17"  "31"  "186" "20"  "186" "186" "186" "186"
 [81] "186" "17"  "1"   "6"   "12"  "27"  "187" "187" "187" "187"
 [91] "187" "187" NA    "30"  "188" "189" "22"  "189" "21"  "189"
[101] "25"  "189" "189" "189" "189" "189" "189" "2"   "189" "28"
```

```
[111] "191" "21"   "28"   "191" "191" "191" "191" "191" "191" "191"
[121] "191" "191" "191" "7"    "194" "194" NA    NA    "3"   "7"
[131] "194" "194" NA    "20"  NA    "1"   "16"  "194" "8"   "194"
[141] "17"  "9"   "194" "3"   "22"  "22"  "6"   "6"   "15"  "25"
[151] "25"  "16"  "8"   "6"   "194" "195" "195" "195" "195" "197"
[161] "28"  "25"  "15"  "24"  "19"  "198" "15"  "198" "4"   "20"
[171] "2"   "199" "199" "199" "19"  "20"  "24"  "7"   "7"   "7"
[181] "15"  "7"   "6"   "20"  "16"  "14"  "200" "19"
```

Regular expressions can search for text with anchors indicating the beginning of a line ("^") and the end of a line ("$").

```
> # extract 4 digits at the beginning of the text
> head(str_extract(string = theStart, pattern = "^\\d{4}"), 30)

 [1] NA     NA     "1775" NA     NA     NA     "1777" "1775" "1776"
[10] "1778" "1775" "1779" NA     "1785" "1798" "1801" NA     NA
[19] "1812" "1813" "1812" "1812" "1813" "1813" "1813" "1814" "1813"
[28] "1814" "1813" "1815"
```

```
> # extract 4 digits at the end of the text
> head(str_extract(string = theStart, pattern = "\\d{4}$"), 30)

 [1] "1774" "1774" "1775" "1775" "1776" "1777" "1777" "1775" "1776"
[10] "1778" "1775" "1779" NA     "1785" "1798" "1801" NA     "1812"
[19] "1812" "1813" "1812" "1812" "1813" "1813" "1813" "1814" "1813"
[28] "1814" "1813" "1815"
```

```
> # extract 4 digits at the beginning AND the end of the text
> head(str_extract(string = theStart, pattern = "^\\d{4}$"), 30)

 [1] NA     NA     "1775" NA     NA     NA     "1777" "1775" "1776"
[10] "1778" "1775" "1779" NA     "1785" "1798" "1801" NA     NA
[19] "1812" "1813" "1812" "1812" "1813" "1813" "1813" "1814" "1813"
[28] "1814" "1813" "1815"
```

Replacing text selectively is another powerful feature of regular expressions. We start by simply replacing numbers with a fixed value.

```
> # replace the first digit seen with "x"
> head(str_replace(string=theStart, pattern="\\d", replacement="x"), 30)

 [1] "September x, 1774" "September x, 1774" "x775"
 [4] "June x775"         "July x776"         "June x4, 1777"
 [7] "x777"              "x775"              "x776"
[10] "x778"              "x775"              "x779"
[13] "January"           "x785"              "x798"
```

```
[16]  "x801"                "August"              "June x8, 1812"
[19]  "x812"                "x813"                "x812"
[22]  "x812"                "x813"                "x813"
[25]  "x813"                "x814"                "x813"
[28]  "x814"                "x813"                "x815"

> # replace all digits seen with "x"
> # this means "7" -> "x" and "382" -> "xxx"
> head(str_replace_all(string=theStart, pattern="\\d", replacement="x"),
+       30)

 [1]  "September x, xxxx"  "September x, xxxx"  "xxxx"
 [4]  "June xxxx"          "July xxxx"          "June xx, xxxx"
 [7]  "xxxx"               "xxxx"               "xxxx"
[10]  "xxxx"               "xxxx"               "xxxx"
[13]  "January"            "xxxx"               "xxxx"
[16]  "xxxx"               "August"             "June xx, xxxx"
[19]  "xxxx"               "xxxx"               "xxxx"
[22]  "xxxx"               "xxxx"               "xxxx"
[25]  "xxxx"               "xxxx"               "xxxx"
[28]  "xxxx"               "xxxx"               "xxxx"

> # replace any strings of digits from 1 to 4 in length with "x"
> # this means "7" -> "x" and "382" -> "x"
> head(str_replace_all(string=theStart, pattern="\\d{1,4}",
+                       replacement="x"), 30)

 [1]  "September x, x"  "September x, x"  "x"
 [4]  "June x"          "July x"          "June x, x"
 [7]  "x"               "x"               "x"
[10]  "x"               "x"               "x"
[13]  "January"         "x"               "x"
[16]  "x"               "August"          "June x, x"
[19]  "x"               "x"               "x"
[22]  "x"               "x"               "x"
[25]  "x"               "x"               "x"
[28]  "x"               "x"               "x"
```

Not only can regular expressions substitute fixed values into a string, they can also substitute part of the search pattern. To see this, we create a vector of some HTML commands.

```
> # create a vector of HTML commands
> commands <- c("<a href=index.html>The Link is here</a>",
+               "<b>This is bold text</b>")
```

Now we would like to extract the text between the HTML tags. The pattern is a set of opening and closing angle brackets with something in between ("<.+?>"), some text (".+?") and another set of opening and closing brackets ("<.+?>"). The "." indicates a search for anything, while the "+" means to search for it one or more times with the "?" meaning it is not a greedy search. Because we do not know what the text between the tags will be, and that is what we want to substitute back into the text, we group it inside parentheses and use a back reference to reinsert it using "\\1," which indicates use of the first grouping. Subsequent groupings are referenced using subsequent numerals, up to nine. In other languages a "$" is used instead of "\\."

```
> # get the text between the HTML tags
> # the content in (.+?) is substituted using 1
> str_replace(string=commands, pattern="<.+?>(.+?)<.+>",
+             replacement="\\1")

[1] "The Link is here"  "This is bold text"
```

Since R has its own regular expression peculiarities, there is a handy help file that can be accessed with ?regex.

13.5 Conclusion

R has many facilities for dealing with text, whether creating, extracting or manipulating it. For creating text, it is best to use sprintf and if necessary paste. For all other text needs, it is best to use Hadley Wickham's stringr package. This includes pulling out text specified by character position (str_sub), regular expressions (str_detect, str_extract and str_replace) and splitting strings (str_split).

Chapter 14

Probability Distributions

Being a statistical programming language, R easily handles all the basic necessities of statistics, including drawing random numbers and calculating distribution values (the focus of this chapter), means, variances, maxmima and minima, correlation and t-tests (the focus of Chapter 15).

Probability distributions lie at the heart of statistics, so naturally R provides numerous functions for making use of them. These include functions for generating random numbers and calculating the distribution and quantile.

14.1 Normal Distribution

Perhaps the most famous, and most used, statistical distribution is the normal distribution, sometimes referred to as the Gaussian distribution, which is defined as

$$f(x; \mu, \sigma) = \frac{1}{\sqrt{2\pi}\sigma} e^{\frac{-(x-\mu)^2}{2\sigma^2}} \tag{14.1}$$

where μ is the mean and σ the standard deviation. This is the famous bell curve that describes so many phenomena in life. To draw random numbers from the normal distribution use the rnorm function, which, optionally, allows the specification of the mean and standard deviation.

```
> # 10 draws from the standard 0-1 normal distribution
> rnorm(n = 10)

 [1] -2.1654005 0.7044448 0.1545891  1.3325220 -0.1965996 1.3166821
 [7]  0.2055784 0.7698138 0.4276115 -0.6209493


> # 10 draws from the 100-20 distribution
> rnorm(n = 10, mean = 100, sd = 20)

 [1]  99.50443 86.81502 73.57329 113.36646 70.55072 95.70594
 [7]  67.10154 99.49917 111.02245 114.16694
```

The density (the probability of a particular value) for the normal distribution is calculated using dnorm.

```
> randNorm10 <- rnorm(10)
> randNorm10
```

```
[1] -1.2376217  0.2989008  1.8963171 -1.1609135 -0.9199759 0.4251059
[7] -1.1112031 -0.3353926 -0.5533266 -0.5985041
```

```
> dnorm(randNorm10)
```

```
[1] 0.18548296 0.38151338 0.06607612 0.20335569 0.26129210 0.36447547
[7] 0.21517046 0.37712348 0.34231507 0.33352345
```

```
> dnorm(c(-1, 0, 1))
```

```
[1] 0.2419707 0.3989423 0.2419707
```

dnorm returns the probability of a specific number occurring. While it is technically mathematically impossible to find the exact probability of a number from a continuous distribution, this is an estimate of the probability. Like with rnorm, a mean and standard deviation can be specified for dnorm.

To see this visually we generate a number of normal random variables, calculate their distributions and then plot them. This should result in a nicely shaped bell curve, as seen in Figure 14.1.

```
> # generate the normal variables
> randNorm <- rnorm(30000)
> # calcualte their distributions
> randDensity <- dnorm(randNorm)
> # load ggplot2
> require(ggplot2)
> # plot them
> ggplot(data.frame(x = randNorm, y = randDensity)) + aes(x = x, y = y) +
+     geom_point() + labs(x = "Random Normal Variables", y = "Density")
```

Similarly, pnorm calculates the distribution of the normal distribution; that is, the cumulative probability that a given number, or smaller number, occurs. This is defined as

$$\Phi(a) = P\{X <= a\} = \int_{-\infty}^{a} \frac{1}{\sqrt{2\pi}\sigma} e^{\frac{-(x-\mu)^2}{2\sigma^2}} \, dx \qquad (14.2)$$

```
> pnorm(randNorm10)
```

```
[1] 0.1079282 0.6174921 0.9710409 0.1228385 0.1787927 0.6646203
[7] 0.1332405 0.3686645 0.2900199 0.2747518
```

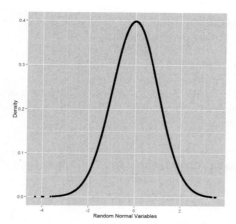

Figure 14.1   Plot of random normal variables and their densities, which results in a bell curve.

```
> pnorm(c(-3, 0, 3))

[1] 0.001349898 0.500000000 0.998650102

> pnorm(-1)

[1] 0.1586553
```

By default this is left-tailed. To find the probability that the variable falls between two points, we must calculate the two probabilities and subtract them from each other.

```
> pnorm(1) - pnorm(0)

[1] 0.3413447

> pnorm(1) - pnorm(-1)

[1] 0.6826895
```

This probability is represented by the area under the curve and illustrated in Figure 14.2, which is drawn by the following code.

```
> # a few things happen with this first line of code
> # the idea is to build a ggplot2 object that we can build upon later
> # that is why it is saved to p
> # we take randNorm and randDensity and put them into a data.frame
> # we declare the x and y axes outside of any other function
> # this just gives more flexibility
> # we add lines with geom_line()
> # x- and y-axis labels with labs(x="x", y="Density")
```

```
> p <- ggplot(data.frame(x=randNorm, y=randDensity)) + aes(x=x, y=y) +
+     geom_line() + labs(x="x", y="Density")
>
> # plotting p will print a nice distribution
> # to create a shaded area under the curve we first calculate that area
> # generate a sequence of numbers going from the far left to -1
> neg1Seq <- seq(from=min(randNorm), to=-1, by=.1)
>
> # build a data.frame of that sequence as x
> # the distribution values for that sequence as y
> lessThanNeg1 <- data.frame(x=neg1Seq, y=dnorm(neg1Seq))
>
> head(lessThanNeg1)

          x              y
1 -3.873328 0.0002203542
2 -3.773328 0.0003229731
3 -3.673328 0.0004686713
4 -3.573328 0.0006733293
5 -3.473328 0.0009577314
6 -3.373328 0.0013487051


>
> # combine this with endpoints at the far left and far right
> # the height is 0
> lessThanNeg1 <- rbind(c(min(randNorm), 0),
+                       lessThanNeg1,
+                       c(max(lessThanNeg1$x), 0))
>
> # use that shaded region as a polygon
> p + geom_polygon(data=lessThanNeg1, aes(x=x, y=y))
>
> # create a similar sequence going from -1 to 1
> neg1Pos1Seq <- seq(from=-1, to=1, by=.1)
>
> # build a data.frame of that sequence as x
> # the distribution values for that sequence as y
> neg1To1 <- data.frame(x=neg1Pos1Seq, y=dnorm(neg1Pos1Seq))
>
> head(neg1To1)

     x        y
1 -1.0 0.2419707
2 -0.9 0.2660852
3 -0.8 0.2896916
```

```
4 -0.7 0.3122539
5 -0.6 0.3332246
6 -0.5 0.3520653

>
> # combine this with endpoints at the far left and far right
> # the height is 0
> neg1To1 <- rbind(c(min(neg1To1$x), 0),
+                  neg1To1,
+                  c(max(neg1To1$x), 0))
>
> # use that shaded region as a polygon
> p + geom_polygon(data=neg1To1, aes(x=x, y=y))
```

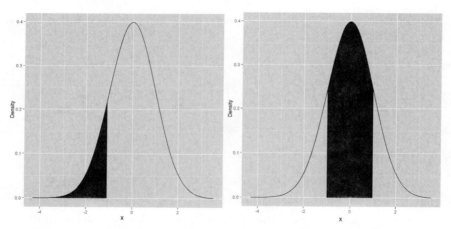

Figure 14.2   Area under a normal curve. The plot on the left shows the area to the left of -1, while the plot on the right shows the area between -1 and 1.

The distribution has a non–decreasing shape, as shown in Figure 14.3. The information displayed here is the same as in Figure 14.2 but it is shown differently. Instead of the cumulative probability being shown as a shaded region it is displayed as a single point along the *y*-axis.

```
> randProb <- pnorm(randNorm)
> ggplot(data.frame(x=randNorm, y=randProb)) + aes(x=x, y=y) +
+     geom_point() + labs(x="Random Normal Variables", y="Probability")
```

The opposite of pnorm is qnorm. Given a cumulative probability it returns the quantile.

```
> randNorm10
```

```
 [1] -1.2376217  0.2989008  1.8963171 -1.1609135 -0.9199759 0.4251059
 [7] -1.1112031 -0.3353926 -0.5533266 -0.5985041
```

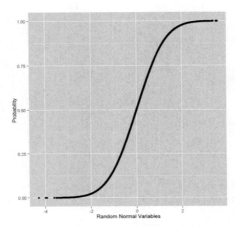

Figure 14.3   Normal distribution function.

```
> qnorm(pnorm(randNorm10))

[1] -1.2376217  0.2989008  1.8963171 -1.1609135 -0.9199759  0.4251059
[7] -1.1112031 -0.3353926 -0.5533266 -0.5985041

> all.equal(randNorm10, qnorm(pnorm(randNorm10)))

[1] TRUE
```

14.2   Binomial Distribution

Like the normal distribution, the binomial distribution is well represented in R. Its probability mass function is

$$p(x; n, p) = \binom{n}{x} p^x (1 - p)^{n-x} \tag{14.3}$$

where

$$\binom{n}{x} = \frac{n!}{x!(n - x)!} \tag{14.4}$$

and n is the number of trials and p is the probability of success of a trial. The mean is np and the variance is $np(1 - p)$. When $n = 1$ this reduces to the Bernoulli distribution.

Generating random numbers from the binomial distribution is not simply generating random numbers but rather generating the number of successes of independent trials. To simulate the number of successes out of ten trials with probability 0.4 of success, we run rbinom with n=1 (only one run of the trials), size=10 (trial size of 10), and prob=0.4 (probability of success is 0.4).

```
> rbinom(n = 1, size = 10, prob = 0.4)

[1] 6
```

That is to say that ten trials were conducted, each with 0.4 probability of success, and the number generated is the number that succeeded. As this is random, different numbers will be generated each time.

By setting n to anything greater than 1, R will generate the number of successes for each of the n sets of size trials.

```
> rbinom(n = 1, size = 10, prob = 0.4)

[1] 3

> rbinom(n = 5, size = 10, prob = 0.4)

[1] 5 3 6 5 4

> rbinom(n = 10, size = 10, prob = 0.4)

[1] 5 3 4 4 5 3 3 5 3 3
```

Setting size to 1 turns the numbers into a Bernoulli random variable, which can take on only the value 1 (success) or 0 (failure).

```
> rbinom(n = 1, size = 1, prob = 0.4)

[1] 1

> rbinom(n = 5, size = 1, prob = 0.4)

[1] 0 0 1 1 1

> rbinom(n = 10, size = 1, prob = 0.4)

[1] 0 0 0 1 0 1 0 0 1 0
```

To visualize the binomial distribution we randomly generate 10,000 experiments, each with 10 trials and 0.3 probability of success. This is seen in Figure 14.4, which shows that the most common number of successes is 3, as expected.

```
> binomData <- data.frame(Successes = rbinom(n = 10000, size = 10,
+         prob = 0.3))
> ggplot(binomData, aes(x = Successes)) + geom_histogram(binwidth = 1)
```

To see how the binomial distribution is well approximated by the normal distribution as the number of trials grows large, we run similar experiments with differing numbers of trials and graph the results, as shown in Figure 14.5, on page 181.

```
> # create a data.frame with Successes being the 10,000 random draws
> # Size equals 5 for all 10,000 rows
```

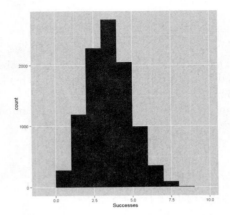

Figure 14.4   Ten thousand runs of binomial experiments with ten trials each and probability of success of 0.3.

```
> binom5 <- data.frame(Successes=rbinom(n=10000, size=5,
+           prob=.3), Size=5)
> dim(binom5)

[1] 10000      2

> head(binom5)

  Successes Size
1         1    5
2         1    5
3         2    5
4         2    5
5         3    5
6         0    5

>
> # similar to before, still 10,000 rows
> # numbers are drawn from a distribution with a different size
> # Size now equals 10 for all 10,000 rows
> binom10 <- data.frame(Successes=rbinom(n=10000, size=10,
+           prob=.3), Size=10)
> dim(binom10)

[1] 10000      2

> head(binom10)
```

```
    Successes Size
1           1   10
2           3   10
3           3   10
4           3   10
5           0   10
6           3   10

>
> binom100 <- data.frame(Successes=rbinom(n=10000, size=100,
+         prob=.3), Size=100)
>
> binom1000 <- data.frame(Successes=rbinom(n=10000, size=1000,
+         prob=.3), Size=1000)
>
> # combine them all into one data.frame
> binomAll <- rbind(binom5, binom10, binom100, binom1000)
> dim(binomAll)

[1] 40000       2

> head(binomAll, 10)

    Successes Size
1           1    5
2           1    5
3           2    5
4           2    5
5           3    5
6           0    5
7           1    5
8           1    5
9           1    5
10          1    5

> tail(binomAll, 10)

        Successes Size
39991         316 1000
39992         311 1000
39993         296 1000
39994         316 1000
39995         288 1000
39996         286 1000
39997         264 1000
```

```
39998          291 1000
39999          300 1000
40000          302 1000

>
> # build the plot
> # histograms only need an x aesthetic
> # it is faceted (broken up) based on the values of Size
> # these are 5, 10, 100, 1000
> ggplot(binomAll, aes(x=Successes)) + geom_histogram() +
+     facet_wrap(~ Size, scales="free")
```

The cumulative distribution function is

$$F(a; n, p) = P\{X <= a\} = \sum_{i=0}^{a} \binom{n}{i} p^i (1-p)^{n-i} \qquad (14.5)$$

where n and p are the number of trials and the probability of success, respectively, as before.

Similar to the normal distribution functions, dbinom and pbinom provide the density (probability of an exact value) and distribution (cumulative probability), respectively, for the binomial distribution.

```
> # probability of 3 successes out of 10
> dbinom(x = 3, size = 10, prob = 0.3)

[1] 0.2668279

> # probability of 3 or fewer successes out of 10
> pbinom(q = 3, size = 10, prob = 0.3)

[1] 0.6496107

> # both functions can be vectorized
> dbinom(x = 1:10, size = 10, prob = 0.3)

 [1] 0.1210608210 0.2334744405 0.2668279320 0.2001209490 0.1029193452
 [6] 0.0367569090 0.0090016920 0.0014467005 0.0001377810 0.0000059049

> pbinom(q = 1:10, size = 10, prob = 0.3)

 [1] 0.1493083 0.3827828 0.6496107 0.8497317 0.9526510 0.9894079
 [7] 0.9984096 0.9998563 0.9999941 1.0000000
```

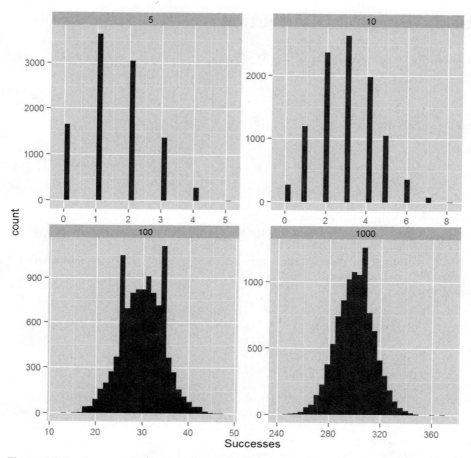

Figure 14.5   Random binomial histograms faceted by trial size. Notice that while not perfect, as the number of trials increases the distribution appears more normal. Also note the differing scales in each pane.

Given a certain probability, qbinom returns the quantile, which for this distribution is the number of successes.

```
> qbinom(p = 0.3, size = 10, prob = 0.3)

[1] 2

> qbinom(p = c(0.3, 0.35, 0.4, 0.5, 0.6), size = 10, prob = 0.3)

[1] 2 2 3 3 3
```

14.3   Poisson Distribution

Another popular distribution is the Poisson distribution, which is for count data. Its probability mass function is

$$p(x; \lambda) = \frac{\lambda^x e^{-\lambda}}{x!} \tag{14.6}$$

and the cumulative distribution is

$$F(a; \lambda) = P\{X <= a\} = \sum_{i=0}^{a} \frac{\lambda^i e^{-\lambda}}{i!} \tag{14.7}$$

where λ is both the mean and variance.

To generate random counts, the density, the distribution and quantiles use `rpois`, `dpois`, `ppois` and `qpois`, respectively.

As λ grows large the Poisson distribution begins to resemble the normal distribution. To see this we will simulate 10,000 draws from the Poisson distribution and plot their histograms to see the shape.

```
> # generate 10,000 random counts from 5 different Poisson distributions
> pois1 <- rpois(n=10000, lambda=1)
> pois2 <- rpois(n=10000, lambda=2)
> pois5 <- rpois(n=10000, lambda=5)
> pois10 <- rpois(n=10000, lambda=10)
> pois20 <- rpois(n=10000, lambda=20)
> pois <- data.frame(Lambda.1=pois1, Lambda.2=pois2,
+                    Lambda.5=pois5, Lambda.10=pois10, Lambda.20=pois20)
> # load reshape2 package to melt the data to make it easier to plot
> require(reshape2)
> # melt the data into a long format
> pois <- melt(data=pois, variable.name="Lambda", value.name="x")
> # load the stringr package to help clean up the new column name
> require(stringr)
> # clean up the Lambda to just show the value for that lambda
> pois$Lambda <- as.factor(as.numeric(str_extract(string=pois$Lambda,
+                                     pattern="\\d+")))
> head(pois)

  Lambda x
1      1 0
2      1 2
3      1 0
4      1 1
```

```
5        1 2
6        1 0

> tail(pois)

        Lambda   x
49995       20  26
49996       20  14
49997       20  26
49998       20  22
49999       20  20
50000       20  23
```

Now we will plot a separate histogram for each value of λ, as shown in Figure 14.6.

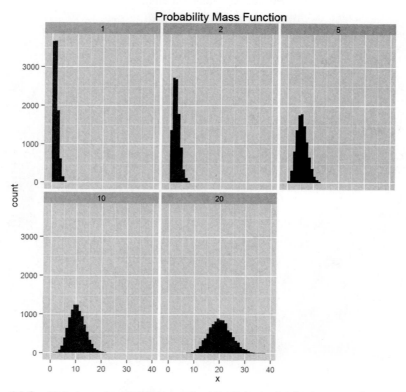

Figure 14.6   Histograms for 10,000 draws from the Poisson distribution at varying levels of λ. Notice how the histograms become more like the normal distribution.

```
> require(ggplot2)
> ggplot(pois, aes(x=x)) + geom_histogram(binwidth=1) +
+       facet_wrap(~ Lambda) + ggtitle("Probability Mass Function")
```

Another, perhaps more compelling, way to visualize this convergence to normality is within overlaid density plots, as seen in Figure 14.7.

```
> ggplot(pois, aes(x=x)) +
+       geom_density(aes(group=Lambda, color=Lambda, fill=Lambda),
+           adjust=4, alpha=1/2) +
+       scale_color_discrete() + scale_fill_discrete() +
+       ggtitle("Probability Mass Function")
```

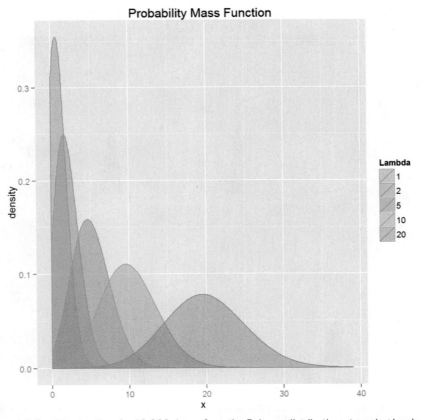

Figure 14.7   Density plots for 10,000 draws from the Poisson distribution at varying levels of λ. Notice how the density plots become more like the normal distribution.

14.4   Other Distributions

R supports many distributions, some of which are very common, while others are quite obscure. They are listed in Table 14.1; the mathematical formulas, means and variances are in Table 14.2.

Table 14.1   Statistical Distributions and their Functions

Distribution	Random Number	Density	Distribution	Quantile
Normal	rnorm	dnorm	pnorm	qnorm
Binomial	rbinom	dbinom	pbinom	qbinom
Poisson	rpois	dpois	ppois	qpois
t	rt	dt	pt	qt
F	rf	df	pf	qf
Chi-Squared	rchisq	dchisq	pchisq	qchisq
Gamma	rgamma	dgamma	pgamma	qgamma
Geometric	rgeom	dgeom	pgeom	qgeom
Negative Binomial	rnbinom	dnbinom	pnbinom	qnbinom
Exponential	rexp	dexp	pexp	qexp
Weibull	rweibull	dweibull	pweibull	qweibull
Uniform (Continuous)	runif	dunif	punif	qunif
Beta	rbeta	dbeta	pbeta	qbeta
Cauchy	rcauchy	dcauchy	pcauchy	qcauchy
Multinomial	rmultinom	dmultinom	pmultinom	qmultinom
Hypergeometric	rhyper	dhyper	phyper	qhyper
Log-normal	rlnorm	dlnorm	plnorm	qlnorm
Logistic	rlogis	dlogis	plogis	qlogis

Table 14.2   Formulas, Means and Variances for Various Statistical Distributions
(The B in the F distribution is the beta function, $B(x, y) = \int_0^1 t^{x-1}(1-t)^{y-1} dt$)

Distribution	Formula	Mean	Variance
Normal	$f(x; \mu, \sigma) = \frac{1}{\sqrt{2\pi}\sigma} e^{\frac{-(x-\mu)^2}{2\sigma^2}}$	μ	σ^2
Binomial	$p(x; n, p) = \binom{n}{x} p^x (1-p)^{n-x}$	np	$np(1-p)$
Poisson	$p(i) = \binom{n}{i} p^i (1-p)^{n-i}$	λ	λ
t	$f(x; n) = \frac{\Gamma(\frac{n+1}{2})}{\sqrt{n\pi}\Gamma(\frac{n}{2})} \left(1 + \frac{x^2}{n}\right)^{-\frac{n+1}{2}}$	0	$\frac{n}{n-2}$

Table 14.2   Formulas, Means and Variances for Various Statistical Distributions
(The B in the F distribution is the beta function, $B(x, y) = \int_0^1 t^{x-1}(1-t)^{y-1}dt$)
(*Continued*)

Distribution	Formula	Mean	Variance
F	$f(x; \lambda, s) = \dfrac{\sqrt{\frac{(n_1 x)^{n_1} n_2^{n_2}}{(n_1 x + n_2)^{n_1 + n_2}}}}{x B(\frac{n_1}{2}, \frac{n_2}{2})}$	$\dfrac{n_2}{n_2 - 2}$	$\dfrac{2 n_2^2 (n_1 + n_2 - 2)}{n_1 (n_2 - 2)^2 (n_2 - 4)}$
Chi-Squared	$f(x; n) = \dfrac{e^{-\frac{y}{2}} y^{(\frac{n}{2})-1}}{2^{\frac{n}{2}} \Gamma(\frac{n}{2})}$	n	$2n$
Gamma	$f(x; \lambda, s) = \dfrac{\lambda e^{-\lambda x}(\lambda x)^{s-1}}{\Gamma(s)}$	$\dfrac{s}{\lambda}$	$\dfrac{s}{\lambda^2}$
Geometric	$p(x; p) = p(1-p)^{x-1}$	$\dfrac{1}{\lambda}$	$\dfrac{1}{\lambda^2}$
Negative Binomial	$p(x; r, p) = \binom{x-1}{r-1} p^r (1-p)^{x-r}$	$\dfrac{r}{p}$	$\dfrac{r(1-p)}{p^2}$
Exponential	$f(x; \lambda) = \lambda e^{-\lambda x}$	$\dfrac{1}{\lambda}$	$\dfrac{1}{\lambda^2}$
Weibull	$f(x; \lambda, k) = \frac{k}{\lambda}(\frac{x}{\lambda})^{k-1} e^{-(x/\lambda)^k}$	$\lambda \Gamma(1 + \frac{1}{k})$	$\lambda^2 \Gamma(1 + \frac{2}{k}) - \mu^2$
Uniform	$f(x; a, b) = \dfrac{1}{b-a}$	$\dfrac{a+b}{2}$	$\dfrac{(b-a)^2}{12}$
Beta	$f(x; \alpha, \beta) = \frac{1}{B(\alpha, \beta)} x^{\alpha-1}(1-x)^{\beta-1}$	$\dfrac{\alpha}{\alpha+\beta}$	$\dfrac{\alpha\beta}{(\alpha+\beta)^2(\alpha+\beta+1)}$
Cauchy	$f(x; s, t) = \dfrac{s}{\pi\left(s^2 + (x-t)^2\right)}$	Undefined	Undefined
Multinomial	$p(x_1, \ldots, x_k; n, p_1, \ldots, p_k) =$ $\dfrac{n!}{x_1! \cdots x_k!} p_1^{x_1} \cdots p_k^{x_k}$	$n p_i$	$n p_i (1 - p_i)$
Hypergeometric	$p(x; N, n, m) = \dfrac{\binom{m}{x}\binom{N-m}{n-x}}{\binom{N}{n}}$	$\dfrac{nm}{N}$	$\dfrac{nm}{N}\left[\dfrac{(n-1)(m-1)}{N-1} + 1 - \dfrac{nm}{N}\right]$
Log-normal	$f(x; \mu, \sigma) = \dfrac{1}{x\sigma\sqrt{2\pi}} e^{-\frac{(\ln x - \mu)^2}{2\sigma^2}}$	$e^{\mu + \frac{\sigma^2}{2}}$	$\left(e^{\sigma^2} - 1\right) e^{2\mu + \sigma^2}$
Logistic	$f(x; \mu, s) = \dfrac{e^{-\frac{x-\mu}{s}}}{s\left(1 + e^{-\frac{x-\mu}{s}}\right)^2}$	μ	$\frac{1}{3} s^2 \pi^2$

14.5   Conclusion

R facilitates the use of many different probability distributions through the various random number, density, distribution and quantile functions outlined in Table 14.1. We focused on three distributions—normal, Bernoulli and Poisson—in detail as they are the most commonly used. The formulas for every distribution available in the base packages of R, along with their means and variances, are listed in Table 14.2.

Chapter 15

Basic Statistics

Some of the most common tools used in statistics are means, variances, correlations and t-tests. These are all well represented in R with easy-to-use functions such as mean, var, cor and t.test.

15.1 Summary Statistics

The first thing many people think of in relation to statistics is the average, or mean, as it is properly called. We start by looking at some simple numbers and later in the chapter play with bigger datasets. First we generate a random sampling of 100 numbers between 1 and 100.

```
> x <- sample(x = 1:100, size = 100, replace = TRUE)
> x
```

```
 [1] 93 98   84 62 18 12 40 13 30   4 95 18 55 46   2 24
[17] 54 91    9 57 74   6 11 38 67 13 40 87   2 85   4  6
[33] 61 28   37 61 10 87 41 10 11   4 37 84 54 69 21 33
[49] 37 44   46 78   6 50 88 74 76 31 67 68   1 23 31 51
[65] 22 64  100 12 20 56 74 61 52   4 28 62 90 66 34 11
[81] 21 78   17 94   9 80 92 83 72 43 20 44   3 43 46 72
[97] 32 61   16 12
```

sample uniformly draws size entries from x. Setting replace=TRUE means that the same number can be drawn multiple times.

Now that we have a vector of data we can calculate the mean.

```
> mean(x)
```

```
[1] 44.51
```

This is the simple arithmetic mean.

$$E[X] = \frac{\sum_{i=1}^{N} x_i}{N} \tag{15.1}$$

Simple enough. Because this is statistics, we need to consider cases where some data are missing. To create this we take x and randomly set 20% of the elements to NA.

```
> # copy x
> y <- x
> # choose a random 20 elements, using sample, to set to NA
> y[sample(x = 1:100, size = 20, replace = FALSE)] <- NA
> y

 [1] 93 98   84 62 18 12 40 NA 30   4 95 18 55 46   2 24
[17] 54 91   NA 57 NA  6 11 38 67 NA 40 87   2 NA   4  6
[33] 61 28   37 NA 10 NA 41 10 11   4 37 84 54 69 21 33
[49] 37 44   46 78  6 50 88 74 76 NA 67 68 NA 23 31 51
[65] 22 64 100 12 20 56 74 NA 52   4 NA 62 90 NA 34 11
[81] 21 78   17 NA  9 80 NA 83 NA NA 20 44 NA NA 46 NA
[97] 32 61   NA 12
```

Using mean on y will return NA. This is because, by default, if mean encounters even one element that is NA it will return NA. This is to avoid providing misleading information.

```
> mean(y)

[1] NA
```

To have the NAs removed before calculating the mean, set na.rm to TRUE.

```
> mean(y, na.rm = TRUE)

[1] 43.5875
```

To calculate the weighted mean of a set of numbers, the function weighted.mean takes a vector of numbers and a vector of weights. It also has an optional argument, na.rm, to remove NAs before calculating; otherwise, a vector with NA values will return NA.

```
> grades <- c(95, 72, 87, 66)
> weights <- c(1/2, 1/4, 1/8, 1/8)
> mean(grades)

[1] 80

> weighted.mean(x = grades, w = weights)

[1] 84.625
```

The formula for weighted.mean is in Equation 15.2, which is the same as the expected value of a random variable.

$$E[X] = \frac{\sum_{i=1}^{N} w_i x_i}{\sum_{i=1}^{N} w_i} = \sum_{i=1}^{N} p_i x_i \qquad (15.2)$$

Another vitally important metric is the variance, which is calculated with var.

```
> var(x)
```

```
[1] 865.5049
```

This calculates variance as

$$Var(x) = \frac{\sum_{i=1}^{N}(x_i - \bar{x})^2}{N - 1} \qquad (15.3)$$

which can be verified in R.

```
> var(x)
```

```
[1] 865.5049
```

```
> sum((x - mean(x))^2)/(length(x) - 1)
```

```
[1] 865.5049
```

Standard deviation is the square root of variance and is calculated with sd. Like mean and var, sd has the na.rm argument to remove NAs before computation; otherwise, any NAs will cause the answer to be NA.

```
> sqrt(var(x))
```

```
[1] 29.41947
```

```
> sd(x)
```

```
[1] 29.41947
```

```
> sd(y)
```

```
[1] NA
```

```
> sd(y, na.rm = TRUE)
```

```
[1] 28.89207
```

Other commonly used functions for summary statistics are min, max and median. Of course, all of these also have na.rm arguments.

```
> min(x)
```

```
[1] 1
```

```
> max(x)
```

```
[1] 100
```

```
> median(x)

[1] 43

> min(y)

[1] NA

> min(y, na.rm = TRUE)

[1] 2
```

The median, as calculated before, is the middle of an ordered set of numbers. For instance, the median of 5, 2, 1, 8 and 6 is 5. In the case when there is an even amount of numbers, the median is the mean of the middle two numbers. For 5, 1, 7, 4, 3, 8, 6 and 2 the median is 4.5.

A helpful function that computes the mean, minimum, maximum and median is summary. There is no need to specify na.rm because if there are NAs, they are automatically removed and their count is included in the results.

```
> summary(x)

   Min.  1st Qu.  Median   Mean  3rd Qu.    Max.
   1.00    17.75   43.00  44.51    68.25  100.00

> summary(y)

   Min.  1st Qu.  Median   Mean  3rd Qu.    Max.    NA's
   2.00    18.00   40.50  43.59    67.00  100.00      20
```

This summary also displayed the first and third quantiles. These can be computed using quantile.

```
> # calculate the 25th and 75th quantile
> quantile(x, probs = c(0.25, 0.75))

  25%   75%
17.75 68.25

> # try the same on y
> quantile(y, probs = c(0.25, 0.75))

Error: missing values and NaN's not allowed if 'na.rm' is FALSE

> # this time use na.rm=TRUE
> quantile(y, probs = c(0.25, 0.75), na.rm = TRUE)
```

```
25% 75%
18  67
```

```
> # compute other quantiles
> quantile(x, probs = c(0.1, 0.25, 0.5, 0.75, 0.99))
```

```
10%    25%    50%    75%    99%
6.00  17.75  43.00  68.25  98.02
```

Quantiles are numbers in a set where a certain percentage of the numbers are smaller than that quantile. For instance, of the numbers one through 200, the 75th quantile—the number that is larger than 75% of the numbers—is 150.25.

15.2 Correlation and Covariance

When dealing with more than one variable, we need to test their relationships with each other. Two simple, straightforward methods are correlation and covariance. To examine these concepts we look at the economics data from ggplot2.

```
> require(ggplot2)
> head(economics)
```

```
        date   pce    pop psavert uempmed unemploy year month
1 1967-06-30 507.8 198712     9.8     4.5     2944 1967   Jun
2 1967-07-31 510.9 198911     9.8     4.7     2945 1967   Jul
3 1967-08-31 516.7 199113     9.0     4.6     2958 1967   Aug
4 1967-09-30 513.3 199311     9.8     4.9     3143 1967   Sep
5 1967-10-31 518.5 199498     9.7     4.7     3066 1967   Oct
6 1967-11-30 526.2 199657     9.4     4.8     3018 1967   Nov
```

In the economics dataset, pce is personal consumption expenditures and psavert is the personal savings rate. We calculate their correlation using cor.

```
> cor(economics$pce, economics$psavert)
```

```
[1] -0.9271222
```

This very low correlation makes sense because spending and saving are opposites of each other. Correlation is defined as

$$r_{xy} = \frac{\sum_{i=1}^{n}(x_i - \bar{x})(y_i - \bar{y})}{(n-1)s_x s_y} \tag{15.4}$$

where $\bar{x}$ and $\bar{y}$ are the means of x and y, and s_x and s_y are the standard deviations of x and y. It can range between –1 and 1, with higher positive numbers meaning a closer relationship between the two variables, lower negative numbers meaning an inverse relationship and numbers near zero meaning no relationship. This can be easily checked by computing Equation 15.4.

```
> # use cor to calculate correlation
> cor(economics$pce, economics$psavert)

[1] 0.9271222

>
> ## calculate each part of correlation
> xPart <- economics$pce - mean(economics$pce)
> yPart <- economics$psavert - mean(economics$psavert)
> nMinusOne <- (nrow(economics) - 1)
> xSD <- sd(economics$pce)
> ySD <- sd(economics$psavert)
> # use correlation formula
> sum(xPart * yPart) / (nMinusOne * xSD * ySD)

[1] -0.9271222
```

To compare multiple variables at once, use cor on a matrix (only for numeric variables).

```
> cor(economics[, c(2, 4:6)])

                 pce       psavert      uempmed     unemploy
pce        1.0000000  -0.92712221   0.5145862   0.32441514
psavert   -0.9271222   1.00000000  -0.3615301  -0.07641651
uempmed    0.5145862  -0.36153012   1.0000000   0.78427918
unemploy   0.3244151  -0.07641651   0.7842792   1.00000000
```

Because this is just a table of numbers, it would be helpful to also visualize the information using a plot. For this we use the ggpairs function from the GGally package (a collection of helpful plots built on ggplot2) shown in Figure 15.1. This shows a scatterplot of every variable in the data against every other variable. Loading GGally also loads the reshape package, which causes namespace issues with the newer reshape2 package. So rather than load GGally, we call its function using the :: operator, which allows access to functions within a package without loading it.

```
> GGally::ggpairs(economics[, c(2, 4:6)], params = list(labelSize = 8))
```

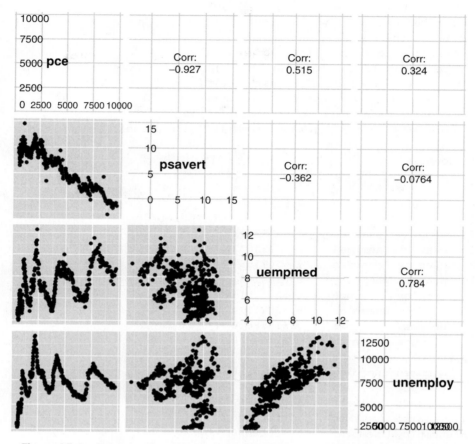

Figure 15.1   Pairs plot of economics data showing the relationship between each pair of variables as a scatterplot with the correlations printed as numbers.

This is similar to a small multiples plot except that each pane has different *x*- and *y*-axes. While this shows the original data, it does not actually show the correlation. To show that we build a heatmap of the correlation numbers, as shown in Figure 15.2. High positive correlation indicates a positive relationship between the variables, high negative correlation indicates a negative relationship between the variables and near zero correlation indicates no strong relationship.

```
> # load the reshape package for melting the data
> require(reshape2)
> # load the scales package for some extra plotting features
```

```
> require(scales)
> # build the correlation matrix
> econCor <- cor(economics[, c(2, 4:6)])
> # melt it into the long format
> econMelt <- melt(econCor, varnames=c("x", "y"),
+                     value.name="Correlation")
> # order it according to the correlation
> econMelt <- econMelt[order(econMelt$Correlation), ]
> # display the melted data
> econMelt

           x         y   Correlation
2     psavert       pce   -0.92712221
5         pce   psavert   -0.92712221
7     uempmed   psavert   -0.36153012
10    psavert   uempmed   -0.36153012
8    unemploy   psavert   -0.07641651
14    psavert  unemploy   -0.07641651
4    unemploy       pce    0.32441514
13        pce  unemploy    0.32441514
3     uempmed       pce    0.51458618
9         pce   uempmed    0.51458618
12   unemploy   uempmed    0.78427918
15    uempmed  unemploy    0.78427918
1         pce       pce    1.00000000
6     psavert   psavert    1.00000000
11    uempmed   uempmed    1.00000000
16   unemploy  unemploy    1.00000000

> ## plot it with ggplot
> # initialize the plot with x and y on the x and y axes
> ggplot(econMelt, aes(x=x, y=y)) +
+     # draw tiles filling the color based on Correlation
+     geom_tile(aes(fill=Correlation)) +
+     # make the fill (color) scale a three color gradient with muted
+     # red for the low point, white for the middle and steel blue
+     # for the high point
+     # the guide should be a colorbar with no ticks, whose height is
+     # 10 lines
+     # limits indicates the scale should be filled from -1 to 1
+     scale_fill_gradient2(low=muted("red"), mid="white",
+             high="steelblue",
+             guide=guide_colorbar(ticks=FALSE, barheight=10),
+             limits=c(-1, 1)) +
```

```
+       # use the minimal theme so there are no extras in the plot
+       theme_minimal() +
+       # make the x and y labels blank
+       labs(x=NULL, y=NULL)
```

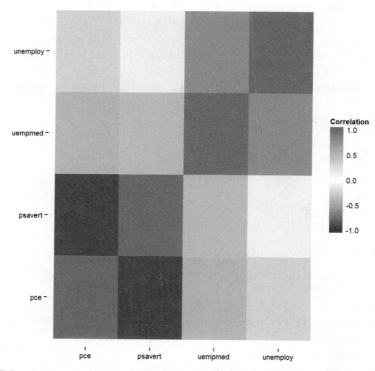

Figure 15.2   Heatmap of the correlation of the economics data. The diagonal has elements with correlation 1 because every element is perfectly correlated with itself. Red indicates highly negative correlation, blue indicates highly positive correlation and white is no correlation.

Missing data is just as much a problem with `cor` as it is with `mean` and `var`, but it is dealt with differently because multiple columns are being considered simultaneously. Instead of specifying `na.rm=TRUE` to remove NA entries, one of `"all.obs"`, `"complete.obs"`, `"pairwise.complete.obs"`, `"everything"` or `"na.or.complete"` is used. To illustrate this we first make a five-column matrix where only the fourth and fifth columns have no NA values; the other columns have one or two NAs.

```
> m <- c(9, 9, NA, 3, NA, 5, 8, 1, 10, 4)
> n <- c(2, NA, 1, 6, 6, 4, 1, 1, 6, 7)
> p <- c(8, 4, 3, 9, 10, NA, 3, NA, 9, 9)
> q <- c(10, 10, 7, 8, 4, 2, 8, 5, 5, 2)
> r <- c(1, 9, 7, 6, 5, 6, 2, 7, 9, 10)
> # combine them together
> theMat <- cbind(m, n, p, q, r)
```

The first option for use is `"everything"`, which means that the entirety of all columns must be free of NAs, otherwise the result is NA. Running this should generate a matrix of all NAs except ones on the diagonal—because a `vector` is always perfectly correlated with itself—and between q and r. With the second option—`"all.obs"`—even a single NA in any column will cause an error.

```
> cor(theMat, use = "everything")

    m  n  p      q           r
m   1 NA NA     NA          NA
n  NA  1 NA     NA          NA
p  NA NA  1     NA          NA
q  NA NA NA  1.0000000 -0.4242958
r  NA NA NA -0.4242958  1.0000000

> cor(theMat, use = "all.obs")

Error: missing observations in cov/cor
```

The third and fourth options—`"complete.obs"` and `"na.or.complete"`—work similarly to each other in that they keep only rows where every entry is not NA. That means our `matrix` will be reduced to rows 1, 4, 7, 9 and 10, and then have its correlation computed. The difference is that `"complete.obs"` will return an error if not a single complete row can be found, while `"na.or.complete"` will return NA in that case.

```
> cor(theMat, use = "complete.obs")

           m          n          p          q          r
m  1.0000000 -0.5228840 -0.2893527  0.2974398 -0.3459470
n -0.5228840  1.0000000  0.8090195 -0.7448453  0.9350718
p -0.2893527  0.8090195  1.0000000 -0.3613720  0.6221470
q  0.2974398 -0.7448453 -0.3613720  1.0000000 -0.9059384
r -0.3459470  0.9350718  0.6221470 -0.9059384  1.0000000

> cor(theMat, use = "na.or.complete")
```

```
            m           n           p           q           r
m   1.0000000  -0.5228840  -0.2893527   0.2974398  -0.3459470
n  -0.5228840   1.0000000   0.8090195  -0.7448453   0.9350718
p  -0.2893527   0.8090195   1.0000000  -0.3613720   0.6221470
q   0.2974398  -0.7448453  -0.3613720   1.0000000  -0.9059384
r  -0.3459470   0.9350718   0.6221470  -0.9059384   1.0000000
```

```
> # calculate the correlation just on complete rows
> cor(theMat[c(1, 4, 7, 9, 10), ])
```

```
            m           n           p           q           r
m   1.0000000  -0.5228840  -0.2893527   0.2974398  -0.3459470
n  -0.5228840   1.0000000   0.8090195  -0.7448453   0.9350718
p  -0.2893527   0.8090195   1.0000000  -0.3613720   0.6221470
q   0.2974398  -0.7448453  -0.3613720   1.0000000  -0.9059384
r  -0.3459470   0.9350718   0.6221470  -0.9059384   1.0000000
```

```
> # compare "complete.obs" and computing on select rows
> # should give the same result
> identical(cor(theMat, use = "complete.obs"),
+     cor(theMat[c(1, 4, 7, 9, 10), ]))
```

```
[1] TRUE
```

The final option is `"pairwise.complete"`, which is much more inclusive. It compares two columns at a time and keeps rows—for those two columns—where neither entry is NA. This is essentially the same as computing the correlation between every combination of two columns with use set to `"complete.obs"`.

```
> # the entire correlation matrix
> cor(theMat, use = "pairwise.complete.obs")
```

```
             m           n           p           q           r
m   1.00000000  -0.02511812  -0.3965859   0.4622943  -0.2001722
n  -0.02511812   1.00000000   0.8717389  -0.5070416   0.5332259
p  -0.39658588   0.87173889   1.0000000  -0.5197292   0.1312506
q   0.46229434  -0.50704163  -0.5197292   1.0000000  -0.4242958
r  -0.20017222   0.53322585   0.1312506  -0.4242958   1.0000000
```

```
> # compare the entries for m vs n to this matrix
> cor(theMat[, c("m", "n")], use = "complete.obs")
```

```
             m           n
m   1.00000000  -0.02511812
n  -0.02511812   1.00000000
```

```
> # compare the entries for m vs p to this matrix
> cor(theMat[, c("m", "p")], use = "complete.obs")


          m           p
m   1.0000000  -0.3965859
p  -0.3965859   1.0000000
```

To see `ggpairs` in all its glory, look at `tips` data from the `reshape2` package in Figure 15.3. This shows every pair of variables in relation to each other building either histograms, boxplots or scatterplots depending on the combination of continuous and

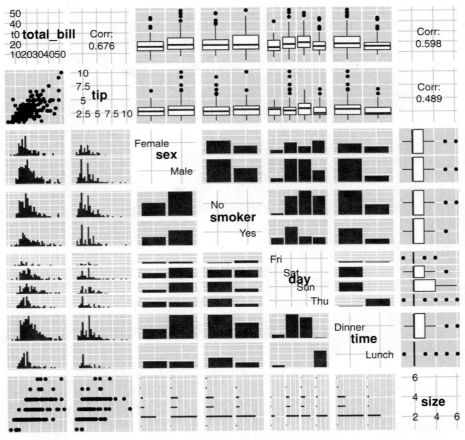

Figure 15.3   `ggpairs` plot of `tips` data using both continuous and categorial variables.

discrete variables. While a data dump like this looks really nice, it is not always the most informative form of exploratory data analysis.

```
> data(tips, package = "reshape2")
> head(tips)
```

```
  total_bill  tip     sex smoker day    time size
1      16.99 1.01  Female     No Sun Dinner    2
2      10.34 1.66    Male     No Sun Dinner    3
3      21.01 3.50    Male     No Sun Dinner    3
4      23.68 3.31    Male     No Sun Dinner    2
5      24.59 3.61  Female     No Sun Dinner    4
6      25.29 4.71    Male     No Sun Dinner    4
```

```
> GGally::ggpairs(tips)
```

No discussion of correlation would be complete without the old refrain, "Correlation does not mean causation." In other words, just because two variables are correlated does not mean they have an effect on each other. This is exemplified in xkcd[1] comic number 552. There is even an R package, RXKCD, for downloading individual comics. Running the following code should generate a pleasant surprise.

```
> require(RXKCD)
> getXKCD(which = "552")
```

Similar to correlation is covariance, which is like a variance between variables; its formula is in Equation 15.5. Notice the similarity to correlation in Equation 15.4 and variance in Equation 15.3.

$$cov(X, Y) = \frac{1}{N-1} \sum_{i=1}^{N} (x_i - \bar{x})(y_i - \bar{y}) \tag{15.5}$$

The cov function works similarly to the cor function, with the same arguments for dealing with missing data. In fact, ?cor and ?cov pull up the same help menu.

```
> cov(economics$pce, economics$psavert)
```

```
[1] -8412.231
```

```
> cov(economics[, c(2, 4:6)])
```

---

1. xkcd is a Web comic by Randall Munroe, beloved by statisticians, physicists, mathematicians and the like. It can be found at http://xkcd.com.

```
                    pce       psavert     uempmed      unemploy
pce         6810308.380 -8412.230823 2202.786256 1573882.2016
psavert       -8412.231    12.088756   -2.061893    -493.9304
uempmed        2202.786    -2.061893    2.690678    2391.6039
unemploy    1573882.202  -493.930390 2391.603889 3456013.5176
```

```
> # check that cov and cor*sd*sd are the same
> identical(cov(economics$pce, economics$psavert),
+            cor(economics$pce, economics$psavert) *
+              sd(economics$pce) * sd(economics$psavert))
```

```
[1] TRUE
```

15.3   T-Tests

In traditional statistics classes, the t-test—invented by William Gosset while working at the Guinness brewery—is taught for conducting tests on the mean of data or for comparing two sets of data. To illustrate this we continue to use the tips data from Section 15.2.

```
> head(tips)
```

```
  total_bill  tip     sex smoker day   time size
1      16.99 1.01  Female     No Sun Dinner    2
2      10.34 1.66    Male     No Sun Dinner    3
3      21.01 3.50    Male     No Sun Dinner    3
4      23.68 3.31    Male     No Sun Dinner    2
5      24.59 3.61  Female     No Sun Dinner    4
6      25.29 4.71    Male     No Sun Dinner    4
```

```
> # sex of the server
> unique(tips$sex)
```

```
[1] Female Male
Levels: Female Male
```

```
> # day of the week
> unique(tips$day)
```

```
[1] Sun  Sat  Thur Fri
Levels: Fri Sat Sun Thur
```

15.3.1   One-Sample T-Test

First we conduct a one-sample t-test on whether the average tip is equal to $2.50. This test essentially calculates the mean of data and builds a confidence interval. If the value we are testing falls within that confidence interval then we can conclude that it is the true value for the mean of the data; otherwise, we conclude that it is not the true mean.

```
> t.test(tips$tip, alternative = "two.sided", mu = 2.5)

    One Sample t-test

data:  tips$tip
t = 5.6253, df = 243, p-value = 5.08e-08
alternative hypothesis: true mean is not equal to 2.5
95 percent confidence interval:
 2.823799 3.172758
sample estimates:
mean of x
    2.998279
```

The output very nicely displays the setup and results of the hypothesis test of whether the mean is equal to \$2.50. It prints the t-statistic, the degrees of freedom and p-value. It also provides the 95% confidence interval and mean for the variable of interest. The p-value indicates that the null hypothesis[2] should be rejected, and we conclude that the mean is not equal to \$2.50.

We encountered a few new concepts here. The t-statistic is the ratio where the numerator is the difference between the estimated mean and the hypothesized mean and the denominator is the standard error of the estimated mean. It is defined in Equation 15.6.

$$\text{t-statistic} = \frac{(\bar{x} - \mu_0)}{s_{\bar{x}}/\sqrt{n}} \tag{15.6}$$

Here, $\bar{x}$ is the estimated mean, μ_0 is the hypothesized mean and $\frac{s_{\bar{x}}}{\sqrt{n}}$ is the standard error of $\bar{x}$.[3]

If the hypothesized mean is correct, then we expect the t-statistic to fall somewhere in the middle—about two standard deviations from the mean—of the t distribution. In Figure 15.4 we see that the thick black line, which represents the estimated mean, falls so far outside the distribution that we must conclude that the mean is not equal to \$2.50.

```
> ## build a t distribution
> randT <- rt(30000, df=NROW(tips)-1)
>
> # get t-statistic and other information
> tipTTest <- t.test(tips$tip, alternative="two.sided", mu=2.50)
>
> # plot it
> ggplot(data.frame(x=randT)) +
+     geom_density(aes(x=x), fill="grey", color="grey") +
+     geom_vline(xintercept=tipTTest$statistic) +
+     geom_vline(xintercept=mean(randT) + c(-2, 2)*sd(randT), linetype=2)
```

---

2. The null hypothesis is what is considered to be true, in this case that the mean is equal to \$2.50.
3. $s_{\bar{x}}$ is the standard deviation of the data and n is the number of observations.

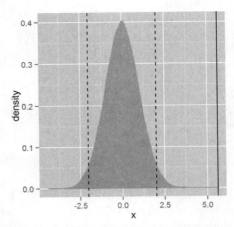

Figure 15.4   t distribution and t-statistic for tip data. The dashed lines are two standard deviations from the mean in either direction. The thick black line, the t-statistic, is so far outside the distribution that we must reject the null hypothesis and conclude that the true mean is not $2.50.

The p-value is an often misunderstood concept. Despite all the misinterpretations, a p-value is the probability, if the null hypothesis were correct, of getting as extreme, or more extreme, a result. It is a measure of how extreme the statistic—in this case, the estimated mean—is. If the statistic is too extreme, we conclude that the null hypothesis should be rejected. The main problem with p-values, however, is determining what should be considered too extreme. Ronald A. Fisher, the father of modern statistics, decided we should consider a p-value that is smaller than either 0.10, 0.05 or 0.01 to be too extreme. While those p-values have been the standard for decades, they were arbitrarily chosen, leading some modern data scientists to question their usefulness. In this example, the p-value is 5.0799885×10^{-8}; this is smaller than 0.01 so we reject the null hypothesis.

Degrees of freedom is another difficult concept to grasp but is pervasive throughout statistics. It represents the effective number of observations. Generally, the degrees of freedom for some statistic or distribution is the number of observations minus the number of parameters being estimated. In the case of the t distribution, one parameter, the standard error, is being estimated. In this example, there are `nrow(tips)-1`=243 degrees of freedom.

Next we conduct a one-sided t-test to see if the mean is greater than $2.50.

```
> t.test(tips$tip, alternative = "greater", mu = 2.5)


One Sample t-test

data:  tips$tip
t = 5.6523, df = 243, p-value = 2.54e-08
```

```
alternative hypothesis: true mean is greater than 2.5
95 percent confidence interval:
 2.852023    Inf
sample estimates:
mean of x
    2.998279
```

Once again, the p-value indicates that we should reject the null hypothesis and conclude that the mean is greater than $2.50, which coincides nicely with the confidence interval.

15.3.2 Two-Sample T-Test

More often than not the t-test is used for comparing two samples. Continuing with the `tips` data, we compare how female and male servers are tipped. Before running the t-test, however, we first need to check the variance of each sample. A traditional t-test requires both groups to have the same variance, whereas the Welch two-sample t-test can handle groups with differing variances. We explore this both numerically and visually in Figure 15.5.

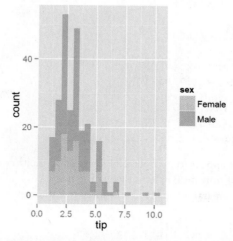

Figure 15.5   Histogram of tip amount by sex. Note that neither distribution appears to be normal.

```
> # first just compute the variance for each group;
> # using the the formula interface
> # calculate the variance of tip for each level of sex
> aggregate(tip ~ sex, data=tips, var)
```

```
        sex        tip
1 Female 1.3444282
2    Male 2.217424

> # now test for normality of tip distribution
> shapiro.test(tips$tip)


	Shapiro-Wilk normality test

data:  tips$tip
W = 0.8978, p-value = 8.2e-12

> shapiro.test(tips$tip[tips$sex == "Female"])


	Shapiro-Wilk normality test

data:  tips$tip[tips$sex == "Female"]
W = 0.9568, p-value = 0.005448

> shapiro.test(tips$tip[tips$sex == "Male"])


	Shapiro-Wilk normality test

data:  tips$tip[tips$sex == "Male"]
W = 0.8759, p-value = 3.708e-10

> # all the tests fail so inspect visually
> ggplot(tips, aes(x=tip, fill=sex)) +
+     geom_histogram(binwidth=.5, alpha=1/2)
```

Since the data do not appear to be normally distributed, neither the standard F-test (via the var.test function) nor the Bartlett test (via the bartlett.test function) will suffice. So we use the nonparametric Ansari–Bradley test to examine the equality of variances.

```
> ansari.test(tip ~ sex, tips)


	Ansari-Bradley test

data:  tip by sex
AB = 5582.5, p-value = 0.376
alternative hypothesis: true ratio of scales is not equal to 1
```

This test indicates that the variances are equal, meaning we can use the standard two–sample t–test.

```
> # setting var.equal=TRUE runs a standard two sample t-test whereas
> # var.equal=FALSE (the default) would run the Welch test
> t.test(tip ~ sex, data = tips, var.equal = TRUE)


Two Sample t-test

data:  tip by sex
t = -1.3879, df = 242, p-value = 0.1665
alternative hypothesis: true difference in means is not equal to 0
95 percent confidence interval:
 -0.6197558  0.1074167
sample estimates:
mean in group Female   mean in group Male
            2.833448             3.089618
```

According to this test, the results were not significant, and we should conclude that female and male workers are tipped roughly equally. While all this statistical rigor is nice, a simple rule of thumb would be to see if the two means are within two standard deviations of each other.

```
> require(plyr)
> tipSummary <- ddply(tips, "sex", summarize,
+                     tip.mean=mean(tip), tip.sd=sd(tip),
+                     Lower=tip.mean - 2*tip.sd/sqrt(NROW(tip)),
+                     Upper=tip.mean + 2*tip.sd/sqrt(NROW(tip)))
> tipSummary

     sex  tip.mean   tip.sd    Lower    Upper
1 Female  2.833448 1.159495 2.584827 3.082070
2   Male  3.089618 1.489102 2.851931 3.327304
```

A lot happened in that code. First, ddply was used to split the data according to the levels of sex. It then applied the summarize function to each subset of the data. This function applied the indicated functions to the data, creating a new data.frame.

As usual, we prefer visualizing the results rather than comparing numerical values. This requires reshaping the data a bit. The results, in Figure 15.6, clearly show the confidence intervals overlapping, suggesting that the means for the two sexes are roughly equivalent.

```
> ggplot(tipSummary, aes(x=tip.mean, y=sex)) + geom_point() +
+     geom_errorbarh(aes(xmin=Lower, xmax=Upper), height=.2)
```

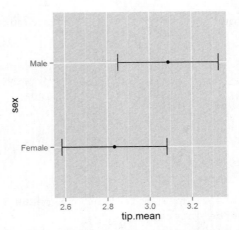

Figure 15.6   Plot showing the mean and two standard errors of tips broken down by the sex of the server.

15.3.3   Paired Two-Sample T-Test

For testing paired data (for example, measurements on twins, before and after treatment effects, father and son comparisons) a paired t-test should be used. This is simple enough to do by setting the paired argument in t.test to TRUE. To illustrate, we use data collected by Karl Pearson on the heights of fathers and sons that is located in the UsingR package. Heights are generally normally distributed, so we will forgo the tests of normality and equal variance.

```
> require(UsingR)
> head(father.son)

   fheight   sheight
1 65.04851 59.77827
2 63.25094 63.21404
3 64.95532 63.34242
4 65.75250 62.79238
5 61.13723 64.28113
6 63.02254 64.24221

> t.test(father.son$fheight, father.son$sheight, paired = TRUE)


Paired t-test

data:  father.son$fheight and father.son$sheight
t = -11.7885, df = 1077, p-value < 2.2e-16
alternative hypothesis: true difference in means is not equal to 0
```

```
95 percent confidence interval:
 -1.1629160 -0.8310296
sample estimates:
mean of the differences
          -0.9969728
```

This test shows that we should reject the null hypothesis and conclude that fathers and sons (at least for this dataset) have different heights. We visualize this data using a density plot of the differences, as shown in Figure 15.7. In it we see a distribution with a mean not at zero and a confidence interval that barely excludes zero which agrees with the test.

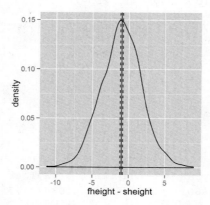

Figure 15.7   Density plot showing the difference of heights of fathers and sons.

```
> heightDiff <- father.son$fheight - father.son$sheight
> ggplot(father.son, aes(x=fheight - sheight)) +
+       geom_density() +
+       geom_vline(xintercept=mean(heightDiff)) +
+       geom_vline(xintercept=mean(heightDiff) +
+               2*c(-1, 1)*sd(heightDiff)/sqrt(nrow(father.son)),
+               linetype=2)
```

15.4 ANOVA

After comparing two groups, the natural next step is comparing multiple groups. Every year, far too many students in introductory statistics classes are forced to learn the ANOVA (analysis of variance) test and memorize its formula, which is

$$F = \frac{\sum_i n_i (\bar{Y}_i - \bar{Y})^2 / (K - 1)}{\sum_{ij} (Y_{ij} - \bar{Y}_i)^2 / (N - K)} \tag{15.7}$$

where n_i is the number of observations in group i, $\bar{Y}_i$ is the mean of group i, $\bar{Y}$ is the overall mean, Y_{ij} is observation j in group i, N is the total number of observations and K is the number of groups.

Not only is this a laborious formula that often turns off a lot of students to statistics, it is also a bit of an old-fashioned way of comparing groups. Even so, there is an R function—albeit rarely used—to conduct the ANOVA test. This also uses the `formula` interface where the left side is the variable of interest and the right side contains the variables that control grouping. To see this we compare tips by day of the week, which has `levels` Fri, Sat, Sun, Thur.

```
> tipAnova <- aov(tip ~ day - 1, tips)
```

In the `formula` the right side was `day - 1`. This might seem odd at first but will make more sense when comparing it to a call without `-1`.

```
> tipIntercept <- aov(tip ~ day, tips)
> tipAnova$coefficients

   dayFri   daySat   daySun  dayThur
 2.734737 2.993103 3.255132 2.771452

> tipIntercept$coefficients

(Intercept)      daySat      daySun     dayThur
 2.73473684  0.25836661  0.52039474  0.03671477
```

Here we see that just using `tip ~ day` includes only Saturday, Sunday and Thursday, along with an intercept, while `tip ~ day - 1` compares Friday, Saturday, Sunday and Thursday with no intercept. The importance of the intercept is made clear in Chapter 16, but for now it suffices that having no intercept makes the analysis more straightforward.

The ANOVA tests whether any group is different from any other group but it does not specify which group is different. So printing a summary of the test just returns a single p-value.

```
> summary(tipAnova)

             Df  Sum Sq  Mean Sq  F value Pr(>F)
day           4  2203.0    550.8    290.1 <2e-16 ***
Residuals   240   455.7      1.9
---
Signif. codes:  0 '***' 0.001 '**' 0.01 '*' 0.05 '.' 0.1 ' ' 1
```

Since the test had a significant p-value, we would like to see which group differed from the others. The simplest way is to make a plot of the group means and confidence intervals and see which overlap. Figure 15.8 shows that tips on Sunday differ (just barely, at the 90% confidence level) from both Thursday and Friday.

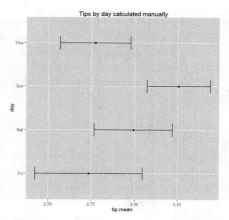

Figure 15.8   Means and confidence intervals of tips by day. This shows that Sunday tips differ from Thursday and Friday tips.

```
> tipsByDay <- ddply(tips, "day", summarize,
+                    tip.mean=mean(tip), tip.sd=sd(tip),
+                    Length=NROW(tip),
+                    tfrac=qt(p=.90, df=Length-1),
+                    Lower=tip.mean - tfrac*tip.sd/sqrt(Length),
+                    Upper=tip.mean + tfrac*tip.sd/sqrt(Length)
+                    )
>
> ggplot(tipsByDay, aes(x=tip.mean, y=day)) + geom_point() +
+     geom_errorbarh(aes(xmin=Lower, xmax=Upper), height=.3)
```

The use of NROW instead of nrow is to guarantee computation. Where nrow works only on data.frames and matrices, NROW returns the length of objects that have only one dimension.

```
> nrow(tips)

[1] 244

> NROW(tips)

[1] 244

> nrow(tips$tip)

NULL

> NROW(tips$tip)

[1] 244
```

To confirm the results from the ANOVA, individual t-tests could be run on each pair of groups just like in Section 15.3.2. Traditional texts encourage adjusting the p-value to accommodate the multiple comparisons. However, some professors, including Andrew Gelman, suggest not worrying about adjustments for multiple comparisons.

An alternative to the ANOVA is to fit a linear regression with one categorical variable and no intercept. This is discussed in Section 16.1.1.

15.5   Conclusion

Whether computing simple numerical summaries or conducting hypothesis tests, R has functions for all of them. Means, variances and standard deviations are computed with mean, var and sd, respectively. Correlation and covariance are computed with cor and cov. For t-tests t.test is used, while aov is for ANOVA.

Chapter 16

Linear Models

The workhorse of statistical analysis is the linear model, particularly regression. Originally invented by Francis Galton to study the relationships between parents and children, which he described as regressing to the mean, it has become one of the most widely used modeling techniques and has spawned other models such as generalized linear models, regression trees, penalized regression and many others. In this chapter we focus on simple and multiple regression and some basic generalized linear models.

16.1 Simple Linear Regression

In its simplest form regression is used to determine the relationship between two variables. That is, given one variable, it tells us what we can expect from the other variable. This powerful tool, which is frequently taught and can accomplish a great deal of analysis with minimal effort, is called simple linear regression.

Before we go any further, we clarify some terminology. The outcome variable (what we are trying to predict) is called the response, and the input variable (what we are using to predict) is the predictor. Fields outside of statistics use other terms, such as measured variable, outcome variable and experimental variable for response, and covariate, feature and explanatory variable for predictor. Worst of all are the terms dependent (response) and independent (predictor) variables. These very names are misnomers. According to probability theory, if variable y is dependent on variable x then variable x *cannot* be independent of variable y. So we stick with the terms response and predictor exclusively.

The general idea behind simple linear regression is using the predictor to come up with some average value of the response. The relationship is defined as

$$y = a + bx + \epsilon \qquad (16.1)$$

where

$$b = \frac{\sum_{i=1}^{n}(x_i - \bar{x})(y_i - \bar{y})}{\sum_{i=1}^{n}(x_i - \bar{x})^2} \qquad (16.2)$$

$$a = \bar{y} - b \qquad (16.3)$$

and

$$\epsilon \sim \mathcal{N}(0, 1) \tag{16.4}$$

which is to say that there are normally distributed errors.

Equation 16.1 is essentially describing a straight line that goes through the data where *a* is the *y*-intercept and *b* is the slope. This is illustrated using fathers' and sons' height data, which are plotted in Figure 16.1. In this case we are using the fathers' heights as the predictor and the sons' heights as the response. The blue line running through the points is the regression line and the grey band around it represents the uncertainty in the fit.

```
> require(UsingR)
> require(ggplot2)
> head(father.son)

    fheight     sheight
1   65.04851    59.77827
2   63.25094    63.21404
3   64.95532    63.34242
4   65.75250    62.79238
5   61.13723    64.28113
6   63.02254    64.24221

> ggplot(father.son, aes(x=fheight, y=sheight)) + geom_point() +
+       geom_smooth(method="lm") + labs(x="Fathers", y="Sons")
```

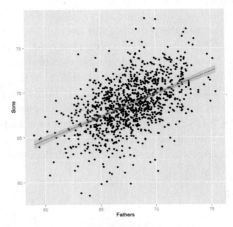

Figure 16.1   Using fathers' heights to predict sons' heights using simple linear regression. The fathers' heights are the predictors and the sons' heights are the responses. The blue line running through the points is the regression line and the grey band around it represents the uncertainty in the fit.

While that code generated a nice graph showing the results of the regression (generated with geom_smooth(method="lm")), it did not actually make those results available to us. To actually calculate a regression use the lm function.

```
> heightsLM <- lm(sheight ~ fheight, data = father.son)
> heightsLM


Call:
lm(formula = sheight ~ fheight, data = father.son)

Coefficients:
(Intercept)        fheight
    33.8866         0.5141
```

Here we once again see the formula notation that specifies to regress sheight (the response) on fheight (the predictor), using the father.son data, and adds the intercept term automatically. The results show coefficients for (Intercept) and fheight which is the slope for the fheight, predictor. The interpretation of this is that, for every extra inch of height in a father, we expect an extra half inch in height for his son. The intercept in this case does not make much sense because it represents the height of a son whose father had zero height, which obviously cannot exist in reality.

While the point estimates for the coefficients are nice, they are not very helpful without the standard errors, which give the sense of uncertainty about the estimate and are similar to standard deviations. To quickly see a full report on the model use summary.

```
> summary(heightsLM)


Call:
lm(formula = sheight ~ fheight, data = father.son)

Residuals:
    Min       1Q  Median      3Q     Max
-8.8772  -1.5144  -0.0079  1.6285  8.9685

Coefficients:
              Estimate Std. Error t value Pr(>|t|)
(Intercept)   33.88660    1.83235   18.49   <2e-16 ***
fheight        0.51409    0.02705   19.01   <2e-16 ***
---
Signif. codes:  0 '***' 0.001 '**' 0.01 '*' 0.05 '.' 0.1 ' ' 1

Residual standard error: 2.437 on 1076 degrees of freedom
Multiple R-squared:  0.2513,  Adjusted R-squared:  0.2506
F-statistic:  361.2 on 1 and 1076 DF,  p-value: <2.2e-16
```

This prints out a lot more information about the model, including the standard errors, t-test values and p-values for the coefficients, the degrees of freedom, residual summary statistics (seen in more detail in Section 18.1) and the results of an F-test. This is all diagnostic information to check the fit of the model, and is covered in more detail in Section 16.2 about multiple regression.

16.1.1   ANOVA Alternative

An alternative to running an ANOVA test (discussed in Section 15.4) is to fit a regression with just one categorical variable and no intercept term. To see this we use the `tips` data in the `reshape2` package on which we will fit a regression.

```
> data(tips, package = "reshape2")
> head(tips)

  total_bill  tip    sex smoker day   time size
1      16.99 1.01 Female     No Sun Dinner    2
2      10.34 1.66   Male     No Sun Dinner    3
3      21.01 3.50   Male     No Sun Dinner    3
4      23.68 3.31   Male     No Sun Dinner    2
5      24.59 3.61 Female     No Sun Dinner    4
6      25.29 4.71   Male     No Sun Dinner    4

> tipsAnova <- aov(tip ~ day - 1, data = tips)
> # putting -1 in the formula indicates that the intercept should not
> # be included in the model; the categorical variable day is
> # automatically setup to have a coefficient for each level
> tipsLM <- lm(tip ~ day - 1, data = tips)
> summary(tipsAnova)

           Df Sum Sq Mean Sq F value Pr(>F)
day         4 2203.0   550.8   290.1 <2e-16 ***
Residuals 240  455.7     1.9
---
Signif. codes:  0 '***' 0.001 '**' 0.01 '*' 0.05 '.' 0.1 ' ' 1

> summary(tipsLM)


Call:
lm(formula = tip ~ day - 1, data = tips)

Residuals:
    Min      1Q  Median      3Q     Max
-2.2451 -0.9931 -0.2347  0.5382  7.0069
```

```
Coefficients:
         Estimate Std. Error t value Pr(>|t|)
dayFri     2.7347     0.3161   8.651 7.46e-16 ***
daySat     2.9931     0.1477  20.261  < 2e-16 ***
daySun     3.2551     0.1581  20.594  < 2e-16 ***
dayThur    2.7715     0.1750  15.837  < 2e-16 ***
---
Signif. codes:  0 '***' 0.001 '**' 0.01 '*' 0.05 '.' 0.1 ' ' 1

Residual standard error: 1.378 on 240 degrees of freedom
Multiple R-squared:  0.8286, Adjusted R-squared:  0.8257
F-statistic:  290.1 on 4 and 240 DF,  p-value: <2.2e-16
```

Notice that the F–value or F–statistic is the same for both, as are the degrees of freedom. This shows that the ANOVA and regression were derived along the same lines and can accomplish the same analysis. Visualizing the coefficients and standard errors should show the same results as computing them using the ANOVA formula. This is seen in Figure 16.2. The point estimates for the mean are identical and the confidence intervals are similar, the difference due to slightly different calculations.

```
> # first calculate the means and CI manually
> require(plyr)
> tipsByDay <- ddply(tips, "day", summarize,
+                        tip.mean=mean(tip), tip.sd=sd(tip),
+                        Length=NROW(tip),
+                        tfrac=qt(p=.90, df=Length-1),
+                        Lower=tip.mean - tfrac*tip.sd/sqrt(Length),
+                        Upper=tip.mean + tfrac*tip.sd/sqrt(Length)
+                        )
>
> # now extract them from the summary for tipsLM
> tipsInfo <- summary(tipsLM)
> tipsCoef <- as.data.frame(tipsInfo$coefficients[, 1:2])
> tipsCoef <- within(tipsCoef, {
+     Lower <- Estimate - qt(p=0.90, df=tipsInfo$df[2]) * `Std. Error`
+     Upper <- Estimate + qt(p=0.90, df=tipsInfo$df[2]) * `Std. Error`
+     day <- rownames(tipsCoef)
+ })
> # plot them both
> ggplot(tipsByDay, aes(x=tip.mean, y=day)) + geom_point() +
+     geom_errorbarh(aes(xmin=Lower, xmax=Upper), height=.3) +
+     ggtitle("Tips by day calculated manually")
>
> ggplot(tipsCoef, aes(x=Estimate, y=day)) + geom_point() +
```

```
+        geom_errorbarh(aes(xmin=Lower, xmax=Upper), height=.3) +
+        ggtitle("Tips by day calculated from regression model")
```

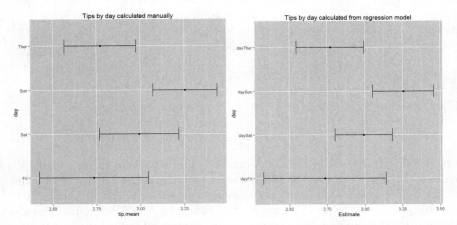

Figure 16.2   Regression coefficients and confidence intervals as taken from a regression model and calculated manually. The point estimates for the mean are identical and the confidence intervals are very similar, the difference due to slightly different calculations. The *y*-axis labels are also different because when dealing with factors `lm` tacks on the name of the variable to the level value.

A new function and a new feature were used here. First, we introduced `within`, which is similar to `with` in that it lets us refer to columns in a `data.frame` by name but different in that we can create new columns within that `data.frame`, hence the name. Second, one of the columns was named `Std. Error` with a space. In order to refer to a variable with spaces in its name, even as a column in a `data.frame`, we must enclose the name in back ticks.

16.2 Multiple Regression

The logical extension of simple linear regression is multiple regression, which allows for multiple predictors. The idea is still the same; we are still making predictions or inferences[1] on the response, but we now have more information in the form of multiple predictors. The math requires some matrix algebra but fortunately the `lm` function is used with very little extra effort.

In this case the relationship between the response and the *p* predictors (*p* − 1 predictors and the intercept) is modeled as

$$Y = X\beta + \epsilon \tag{16.5}$$

---

1. Prediction is the use of known predictors to predict an unknown response while inference is figuring out how predictors affect a response.

where $\boldsymbol{Y}$ is the nx1 response vector

$$\boldsymbol{Y} = \begin{bmatrix} Y_1 \\ Y_2 \\ Y_3 \\ \vdots \\ Y_n \end{bmatrix} \tag{16.6}$$

$\boldsymbol{X}$ is the nxp matrix (n rows and $p - 1$ predictors plus the intercept)

$$\boldsymbol{X} = \begin{bmatrix} 1 & X_{11} & X_{12} & \cdots & X_{1,p-1} \\ 1 & X_{21} & X_{22} & \cdots & X_{2,p-1} \\ \vdots & \vdots & \vdots & \ddots & \vdots \\ 1 & X_{n1} & X_{n2} & \cdots & X_{n,p-1} \end{bmatrix} \tag{16.7}$$

$\boldsymbol{\beta}$ is the px1 vector of coefficients (one for each predictor and intercept)

$$\boldsymbol{\beta} = \begin{bmatrix} \beta_0 \\ \beta_1 \\ \beta_2 \\ \vdots \\ \beta_{p-1} \end{bmatrix} \tag{16.8}$$

and $\boldsymbol{\epsilon}$ is the nx1 vector of normally distributed errors

$$\boldsymbol{\epsilon} = \begin{bmatrix} \epsilon_1 \\ \epsilon_2 \\ \epsilon_3 \\ \vdots \\ \epsilon_n \end{bmatrix} \tag{16.9}$$

with

$$\epsilon_i \sim \mathcal{N}(0, 1) \tag{16.10}$$

which seems more complicated than simple regression but the algebra actually gets easier. The solution for the coefficients is simply written as in Equation 16.11.

$$\hat{\boldsymbol{\beta}} = (\boldsymbol{X}^T \boldsymbol{X})^{-1} \boldsymbol{X}^T \boldsymbol{Y} \tag{16.11}$$

To see this in action we use New York City condo evaluations for fiscal year 2011–2012, obtained through NYC Open Data. NYC Open Data is an initiative by New York City to make government more transparent and work better. It provides data on all manner of city services to the public for analysis, scrutiny and app building (through `http://nycbigapps.com/`). It has been surprisingly popular, spawning hundreds of mobile apps and being copied in other cities such as Chicago and Washington, DC. Its Web site is at `https://data.cityofnewyork.us/`.

The original data were separated by borough with one file each for Manhattan,[2] Brooklyn,[3] Queens,[4] the Bronx[5] and Staten Island,[6] and contained extra information we will not be using. So we combined the five files into one, cleaned up the column names and posted it at `http://www.jaredlander.com/data/housing.csv`. To access the data, either download it from that URL and use `read.table` on the now local file, or read it directly from the URL.

```
> housing <- read.table("http://www.jaredlander.com/data/housing.csv",
+                        sep = ",", header = TRUE,
+                        stringsAsFactors = FALSE)
```

A few reminders about what that code does: `sep` specifies that commas were used to separate columns; `header` means the first row contains the column names; and `stringsAsFactors` leaves `character` columns as they are and does not convert them to `factors`, which speeds up loading time and also makes them easier to work with. Looking at the data, we see that we have a lot of columns and some bad names, so we should rename those.

```
> names(housing) <- c("Neighborhood", "Class", "Units", "YearBuilt",
+                      "SqFt", "Income", "IncomePerSqFt", "Expense",
+                      "ExpensePerSqFt", "NetIncome", "Value",
+                      "ValuePerSqFt", "Boro")
> head(housing)
```

	Neighborhood	Class	Units	YearBuilt	SqFt	Income
1	FINANCIAL	R9-CONDOMINIUM	42	1920	36500	1332615
2	FINANCIAL	R4-CONDOMINIUM	78	1985	126420	6633257
3	FINANCIAL	RR-CONDOMINIUM	500	NA	554174	17310000
4	FINANCIAL	R4-CONDOMINIUM	282	1930	249076	11776313
5	TRIBECA	R4-CONDOMINIUM	239	1985	219495	10004582
6	TRIBECA	R4-CONDOMINIUM	133	1986	139719	5127687

---

2. https://data.cityofnewyork.us/Finances/DOF-Condominium-Comparable-Rental-Income-Manhattan/dvzp-h4k9

3. https://data.cityofnewyork.us/Finances/DOF-Condominium-Comparable-Rental-Income-Brooklyn-/bss9-579f

4. https://data.cityofnewyork.us/Finances/DOF-Condominium-Comparable-Rental-Income-Queens-FY/jcih-dj9q

5. https://data.cityofnewyork.us/Property/DOF-Condominium-Comparable-Rental-Income-Bronx-FY-/3qfc-4tta

6. https://data.cityofnewyork.us/Finances/DOF-Condominium-Comparable-Rental-Income-Staten-Is/tkdy-59zg

	IncomePerSqFt	Expense	ExpensePerSqFt	NetIncome	Value
1	36.51	342005	9.37	990610	7300000
2	52.47	1762295	13.94	4870962	30690000
3	31.24	3543000	6.39	13767000	90970000
4	47.28	2784670	11.18	8991643	67556006
5	45.58	2783197	12.68	7221385	54320996
6	36.70	1497788	10.72	3629899	26737996

	ValuePerSqFt	Boro
1	200.00	Manhattan
2	242.76	Manhattan
3	164.15	Manhattan
4	271.23	Manhattan
5	247.48	Manhattan
6	191.37	Manhattan

For this data the response is the value per square foot and the predictors are everything else. However, we ignore the income and expense variables, as they are actually just estimates based on an arcane requirement that condos be compared to rentals for valuation purposes. The first step is to visualize the data in some exploratory data analysis. The natural place to start is with a histogram of ValuePerSqFt, which is shown in Figure 16.3.

```
> ggplot(housing, aes(x=ValuePerSqFt)) +
+     geom_histogram(binwidth=10) + labs(x="Value per Square Foot")
```

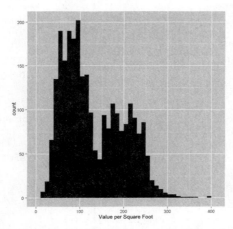

Figure 16.3   Histogram of value per square foot for NYC condos. It appears to be bimodal.

The bimodal nature of the histogram means there is something left to be explored. Mapping color to Boro in Figure 16.4a and faceting on Boro in Figure 16.4b reveal that

Brooklyn and Queens make up one mode and Manhattan makes up the other, while there is not much data on the Bronx and Staten Island.

```
> ggplot(housing, aes(x=ValuePerSqFt, fill=Boro)) +
+     geom_histogram(binwidth=10) + labs(x="Value per Square Foot")
> ggplot(housing, aes(x=ValuePerSqFt, fill=Boro)) +
+     geom_histogram(binwidth=10) + labs(x="Value per Square Foot") +
+     facet_wrap(~Boro)
```

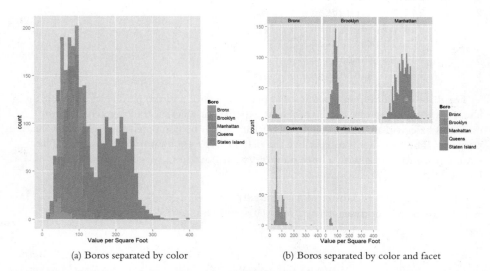

(a) Boros separated by color   (b) Boros separated by color and facet

Figure 16.4   Histograms of value per square foot. These illustrate structure in the data revealing that Brooklyn and Queens make up one mode and Manhattan makes up the other, while there is not much data on the Bronx and Staten Island.

Next we should look at histograms for square footage and the number of units.

```
> ggplot(housing, aes(x=SqFt)) + geom_histogram()
> ggplot(housing, aes(x=Units)) + geom_histogram()
> ggplot(housing[housing$Units < 1000, ],
+       aes(x=SqFt)) + geom_histogram()
> ggplot(housing[housing$Units < 1000, ],
+       aes(x=Units)) + geom_histogram()
```

Figure 16.5 shows that there are quite a few buildings with an incredible number of units. Plotting scatterplots in Figure 16.6 of the value per square foot versus both number of units and square footage, with and without those outlying buildings, gives us an idea whether we can remove them from the analysis.

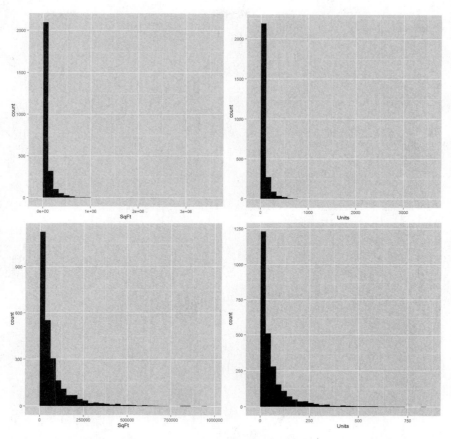

Figure 16.5   Histograms for total square feet and number of units. The distributions are
highly right skewed in the top two graphs, so they were repeated after removing buildings with
more than 1,000 units.

```
> ggplot(housing, aes(x = SqFt, y = ValuePerSqFt)) + geom_point()
> ggplot(housing, aes(x = Units, y = ValuePerSqFt)) + geom_point()
> ggplot(housing[housing$Units < 1000, ], aes(x = SqFt,
+      y = ValuePerSqFt)) + geom_point()
> ggplot(housing[housing$Units < 1000, ], aes(x = Units,
+      y = ValuePerSqFt)) + geom_point()

> # how many need to be removed?
> sum(housing$Units >= 1000)
[1] 6
```

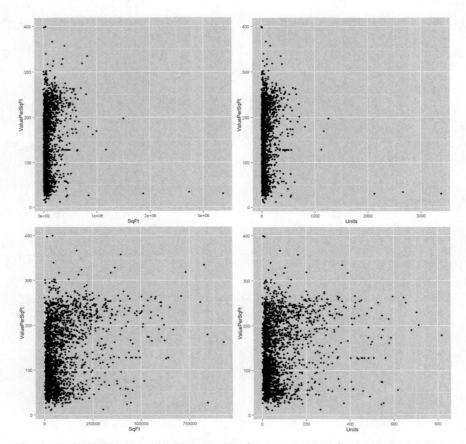

Figure 16.6   Scatterplots of value per square foot versus square footage and value versus number of units, both with and without the buildings that have over 1,000 units.

```
> # remove them
> housing <- housing[housing$Units < 1000, ]
```

Even after we remove the outliers, it still seems like a log transformation of some data could be helpful. Figures 16.7 and 16.8 show that taking the log of square footage and number of units might prove helpful. It also shows what happens when taking the log of value.

```
> # plot ValuePerSqFt against SqFt
> ggplot(housing, aes(x=SqFt, y=ValuePerSqFt)) + geom_point()
> ggplot(housing, aes(x=log(SqFt), y=ValuePerSqFt)) + geom_point()
```

```
> ggplot(housing, aes(x=SqFt, y=log(ValuePerSqFt))) + geom_point()
> ggplot(housing, aes(x=log(SqFt), y=log(ValuePerSqFt))) +
+     geom_point()
```

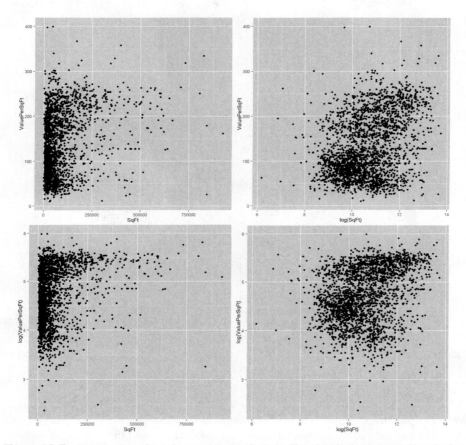

Figure 16.7   Scatterplots of value versus square footage. The plots indicate that taking the log of SqFt might be useful in modeling.

```
> # plot ValuePerSqFt against Units
> ggplot(housing, aes(x=Units, y=ValuePerSqFt)) + geom_point()
> ggplot(housing, aes(x=log(Units), y=ValuePerSqFt)) + geom_point()
> ggplot(housing, aes(x=Units, y=log(ValuePerSqFt))) + geom_point()
> ggplot(housing, aes(x=log(Units), y=log(ValuePerSqFt))) +
+     geom_point()
```

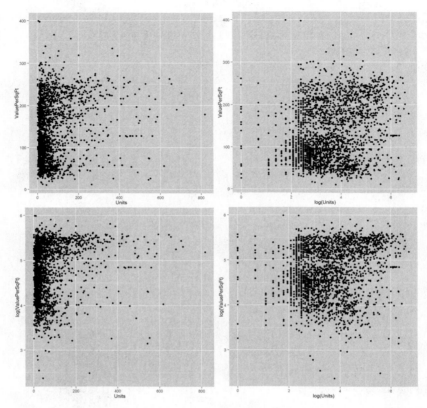

Figure 16.8   Scatterplots of value versus number of units. It is not yet certain whether taking logs will be useful in modeling.

Now that we have viewed our data a few different ways, it is time to start modeling. We already saw from Figure 16.4 that accounting for the different boroughs will be important and the various scatterplots indicated that Units and SqFt will be important as well.

Fitting the model uses the formula interface in lm. Now that there are multiple predictors, we separate them on the right side of the formula using plus signs (+).

```
> house1 <- lm(ValuePerSqFt ~ Units + SqFt + Boro, data = housing)
> summary(house1)


Call:
lm(formula = ValuePerSqFt ~ Units + SqFt + Boro, data = housing)
```

```
Residuals:
      Min        1Q    Median        3Q       Max
 -168.458   -22.680     1.493    26.290   261.761

Coefficients:
                     Estimate  Std. Error  t value  Pr(>|t|)
(Intercept)         4.430e+01   5.342e+00    8.293   < 2e-16 ***
Units              -1.532e-01   2.421e-02   -6.330  2.88e-10 ***
SqFt                2.070e-04   2.129e-05    9.723   < 2e-16 ***
BoroBrooklyn        3.258e+01   5.561e+00    5.858  5.28e-09 ***
BoroManhattan       1.274e+02   5.459e+00   23.343   < 2e-16 ***
BoroQueens          3.011e+01   5.711e+00    5.272  1.46e-07 ***
BoroStaten Island  -7.114e+00   1.001e+01   -0.711     0.477
---
Signif. codes:  0 '***' 0.001 '**' 0.01 '*' 0.05 '.' 0.1 ' ' 1

Residual standard error: 43.2 on 2613 degrees of freedom
Multiple R-squared:  0.6034, Adjusted R-squared:  0.6025
F-statistic:  662.6 on 6 and 2613 DF,  p-value: < 2.2e-16
```

The first thing to notice is that in some versions of R there is a message warning us that Boro was converted to a factor. This is because Boro was stored as a character, and for modeling purposes character data must be represented using indicator variables, which is how factors are treated inside modeling functions, as seen on page 60 in Section 5.1.

The summary function prints out information about the model, including how the function was called, quantiles for the residuals, coefficient estimates, standard errors and p-values for each variable, and the degrees of freedom, p-value and F-statistic for the model. There is no coefficient for the Bronx because that is the baseline level of Boro, and all the other Boro coefficients are relative to that baseline.

The coefficients represent the effect of the predictors on the response and the standard errors are the uncertainty in the estimation of the coefficients. The t value (t-statistic) and p-value for the coefficients are numerical measures of statistical significance, though these should be viewed with caution as most modern data scientists do not like to look at the statistical significance of individual coefficients but rather judge the model as a whole as covered in Chapter 18.

The model p-value and F-statistic are measures of its goodness of fit. The degrees of freedom for a regression are calculated as the number of observations minus the number of coefficients. In this example, there are nrow(housing) - length(coef(house1))=2613 degrees of freedom.

A quick way to grab the coefficients from a model is to either use the coef function or get them from the model using the $ operator on the model object.

```
> house1$coefficients

     (Intercept)                 Units                  SqFt
    4.430325e+01         -1.532405e-01          2.069727e-04
    BoroBrooklyn          BoroManhattan           BoroQueens
    3.257554e+01          1.274259e+02          3.011000e+01
BoroStaten Island
   -7.113688e+00

> coef(house1)

     (Intercept)                 Units                  SqFt
    4.430325e+01         -1.532405e-01          2.069727e-04
    BoroBrooklyn          BoroManhattan           BoroQueens
    3.257554e+01          1.274259e+02          3.011000e+01
BoroStaten Island
   -7.113688e+00

> # works the same as coef
> coefficients(house1)

     (Intercept)                 Units                  SqFt
    4.430325e+01         -1.532405e-01          2.069727e-04
    BoroBrooklyn          BoroManhattan           BoroQueens
    3.257554e+01          1.274259e+02          3.011000e+01
BoroStaten Island
   -7.113688e+00
```

As a repeated theme, we prefer visualizations over tables of information, and a great way of visualizing regression results is a coefficient plot like the one shown in Figure 16.2. Rather than build it from scratch, we use the convenient coefplot package that we wrote. Figure 16.9 shows the result, where each coefficient is plotted as a point with a thick line representing the one standard error confidence interval and a thin line representing the two standard error confidence interval. There is a vertical line indicating 0. In general, a good rule of thumb is that if the two standard error confidence interval does not contain 0, it is statistically significant.

```
> require(coefplot)
> coefplot(house1)
```

Figure 16.9 shows that, as expected, being located in Manhattan has the largest effect on value per square foot. Surprisingly, the number of units or square feet in a building has little effect on value. This is a model with purely additive terms. Interactions between variables can be equally powerful. To enter them in a formula, separate the desired variables with a * instead of +. Doing so results in the individual variables plus the interaction term being included in the model. To include just the interaction term, and

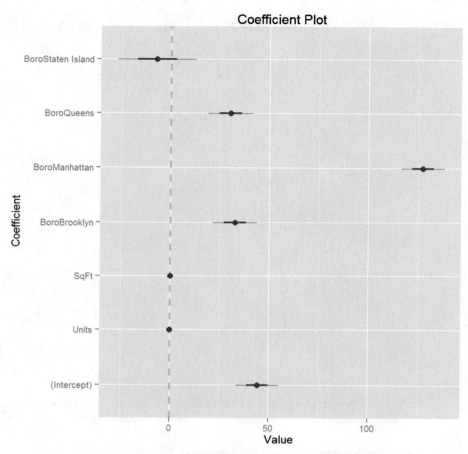

Figure 16.9   Coefficient plot for condo value regression.

not the individual variables, use `:` instead. The results of interacting `Units` and `SqFt` are shown in Figure 16.10.

```
> house2 <- lm(ValuePerSqFt ~ Units * SqFt + Boro, data = housing)
> house3 <- lm(ValuePerSqFt ~ Units:SqFt + Boro, data = housing)
> house2$coefficients

        (Intercept)               Units                 SqFt
       4.093685e+01        -1.024579e-01         2.362293e-04
        BoroBrooklyn        BoroManhattan           BoroQueens
       3.394544e+01         1.272102e+02         3.040115e+01
    BoroStaten Island          Units:SqFt
       -8.419682e+00        -1.809587e-07
```

```
> house3$coefficients
```

```
        (Intercept)       BoroBrooklyn      BoroManhattan
       4.804972e+01       3.141208e+01       1.302084e+02
         BoroQueens  BoroStaten Island          Units:SqFt
       2.841669e+01      -7.199902e+00       1.088059e-07
```

```
> coefplot(house2)
> coefplot(house3)
```

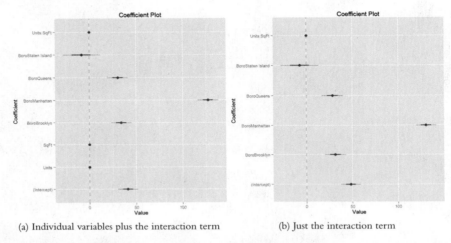

(a) Individual variables plus the interaction term   (b) Just the interaction term

Figure 16.10   Coefficient plots for models with interaction terms. (a) includes individual variables and the interaction term, while (b) only includes the interaction term.

If three variables all interact together, the resulting coefficients will be the three individual terms, three two-way interactions and one three-way interaction.

```
> house4 <- lm(ValuePerSqFt ~ SqFt * Units * Income, housing)
> house4$coefficients
```

```
        (Intercept)                SqFt               Units
       1.116433e+02      -1.694688e-03        7.142611e-03
             Income           SqFt:Units         SqFt:Income
       7.250830e-05        3.158094e-06       -5.129522e-11
       Units:Income  SqFt:Units:Income
      -1.279236e-07        9.107312e-14
```

Interacting (from now on, unless otherwise specified, interacting will refer to the * operator) a continuous variable like SqFt with a factor like Boro results in individual terms for the continuous variable and each non-baseline level of the factor plus an interaction term between the continuous variable and each non-baseline `level` of the factor. Interacting two (or more) `factor`s yields terms for all the individual non-baseline `level`s in both `factor`s and an interaction term for every combination of non-baseline `level`s of the `factor`s.

```
> house5 <- lm(ValuePerSqFt ~ Class * Boro, housing)
> house5$coefficients
```

```
                             (Intercept)
                               47.041481
                    ClassR4-CONDOMINIUM
                                4.023852
                    ClassR9-CONDOMINIUM
                               -2.838624
                    ClassRR-CONDOMINIUM
                                3.688519
                            BoroBrooklyn
                               27.627141
                           BoroManhattan
                               89.598397
                              BoroQueens
                               19.144780
                        BoroStaten Island
                               -9.203410
      ClassR4-CONDOMINIUM:BoroBrooklyn
                                4.117977
      ClassR9-CONDOMINIUM:BoroBrooklyn
                                2.660419
      ClassRR-CONDOMINIUM:BoroBrooklyn
                              -25.607141
     ClassR4-CONDOMINIUM:BoroManhattan
                               47.198900
     ClassR9-CONDOMINIUM:BoroManhattan
                               33.479718
     ClassRR-CONDOMINIUM:BoroManhattan
                               10.619231
        ClassR4-CONDOMINIUM:BoroQueens
                               13.588293
        ClassR9-CONDOMINIUM:BoroQueens
                               -9.830637
        ClassRR-CONDOMINIUM:BoroQueens
                               34.675220
ClassR4-CONDOMINIUM:BoroStaten Island
                                      NA
```

```
ClassR9-CONDOMINIUM:BoroStaten Island
                                   NA
ClassRR-CONDOMINIUM:BoroStaten Island
                                   NA
```

Because neither `SqFt` nor `Units` appears to be significant in any model, it would be good to test their ratio. To simply divide one variable by another in a `formula`, the division must be wrapped in the `I` function.

```
> house6 <- lm(ValuePerSqFt ~ I(SqFt/Units) + Boro, housing)
> house6$coefficients

     (Intercept)      I(SqFt/Units)         BoroBrooklyn
     43.754838763        0.004017039         30.774343209
   BoroManhattan         BoroQueens  BoroStaten Island
    130.769502685        29.767922792         -6.134446417
```

The `I` function is used to preserve a mathematical relationship in a `formula` and prevent it from being interpreted according to `formula` rules. For instance, using `(Units + SqFt)^2` in a formula is the same as using `Units * SqFt`, whereas `I(Units + SqFt)^2` will include the square of the sum of the two variables as a term in the `formula`.

```
> house7 <- lm(ValuePerSqFt ~ (Units + SqFt)^2, housing)
> house7$coefficients

  (Intercept)            Units            SqFt      Units:SqFt
 1.070301e+02   -1.125194e-01    4.964623e-04   -5.159669e-07

> house8 <- lm(ValuePerSqFt ~ Units * SqFt, housing)
> identical(house7$coefficients, house8$coefficients)

[1] TRUE

> house9 <- lm(ValuePerSqFt ~ I(Units + SqFt)^2, housing)
> house9$coefficients

   (Intercept) I(Units + SqFt)
  1.147034e+02    2.107231e-04
```

We have fit numerous models from which we need to pick the "best" one. Model selection is discussed in Section 18.2. In the meantime, visualizing the coefficients from multiple models is a handy tool. Figure 16.11 shows a coefficient plot for models `house1`, `house2` and `house3`.

```
> # also from the coefplot package
> multiplot(house1, house2, house3)
```

Regression is often used for prediction, which in R is enabled by the `predict` function. For this example, new data are available at `http://www.jaredlander.com/data/housingNew.csv`.

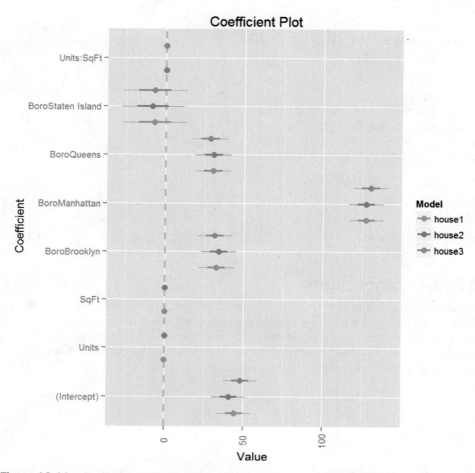

Figure 16.11 Coefficient plot for multiple condo models. The coefficients are plotted in the same spot on the *y*-axis for each model. If a model does not contain a particular coefficient, it is simply not plotted.

```
> housingNew <- read.table("http://www.jaredlander.com/data/
+ housingNew.csv", sep = ",", header = TRUE, stringsAsFactors = FALSE)
```

Making the prediction can be as simple as calling `predict`, although caution must be used when dealing with `factor` predictors to ensure that they have the same `levels` as those used in building the model.

```
> # make prediction with new data and 95% confidence bounds
> housePredict <- predict(house1, newdata = housingNew, se.fit = TRUE,
+                         interval = "prediction", level = .95)
> # view predictions with upper and lower bounds based on
```

```
> # standard errors
> head(housePredict$fit)

        fit         lwr         upr
1   74.00645  -10.813887  158.8268
2   82.04988   -2.728506  166.8283
3  166.65975   81.808078  251.5114
4  169.00970   84.222648  253.7968
5   80.00129   -4.777303  164.7799
6   47.87795  -37.480170  133.2361

> # view the standard errors for the prediction
> head(housePredict$se.fit)

       1        2        3        4        5        6
2.118509 1.624063 2.423006 1.737799 1.626923 5.318813
```

16.3   Conclusion

Perhaps one of the most versatile tools in statistical analysis, regression is well handled using R's lm function. It takes the formula interface, where a response is modeled on a set of predictors. Other useful arguments to the function are weights, which specifies the weights attributed to observations (both probability and count weights), and subset, which will fit the model only on a subset of the data.

Chapter 17

Generalized Linear Models

Not all data can be appropriately modeled with linear regression, because they are binomial (TRUE/FALSE) data, count data or some other form. To model these types of data, generalized linear models were developed. They are still modeled using a linear predictor, $\mathbf{X}\boldsymbol{\beta}$, but they are transformed using some link function. To the R user, fitting a generalized linear model requires barely any more effort than running a linear regression.

17.1 Logistic Regression

A very powerful and common model—especially in fields such as marketing and medicine—is logistic regression. The examples in this section will use a subset of data from the 2010 American Community Survey (ACS) for New York State.[1] ACS data contain a lot of information, so we have made a subset of it with 22,745 rows and 18 columns available at http://jaredlander.com/data/acs_ny.csv.

```
> acs <- read.table("http://jaredlander.com/data/acs_ny.csv", sep = ",",
+       header = TRUE, stringsAsFactors = FALSE)
```

Logistic regression models are formulated as

$$p(y_i = 1) = \text{logit}^{-1}(\mathbf{X}_i\boldsymbol{\beta}) \tag{17.1}$$

where y_i is the ith response and $\mathbf{X}_i\boldsymbol{\beta}$ is the linear predictor. The inverse logit function

$$\text{logit}^{-1}(x) = \frac{e^x}{1 + e^x} = \frac{1}{1 + e^{-x}} \tag{17.2}$$

transforms the continuous output from the linear predictor to fall between 0 and 1. This is the inverse of the link function.

---

1. The ACS is a large-scale survey very similar to the decennial census, except that is conducted on a more frequent basis.

We now formulate a question that asks whether a household has an income greater than $150,000 (See Figure 17.1). To do this we need to create a new binary variable with TRUE for income above that mark and FALSE for income below.

```
> acs$Income <- with(acs, FamilyIncome >= 150000)
> require(ggplot2)
> require(useful)
> ggplot(acs, aes(x=FamilyIncome)) +
+     geom_density(fill="grey", color="grey") +
+     geom_vline(xintercept=150000) +
+     scale_x_continuous(label=multiple.dollar, limits=c(0, 1000000))
```

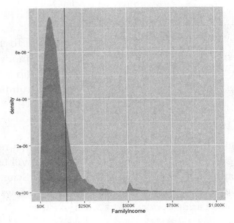

Figure 17.1   Density plot of family income with a vertical line indicating the $150,000 mark.

```
> head(acs)
```

	Acres	FamilyIncome	FamilyType	NumBedrooms	NumChildren	NumPeople
1	1-10	150	Married	4	1	3
2	1-10	180	Female Head	3	2	4
3	1-10	280	Female Head	4	0	2
4	1-10	330	Female Head	2	1	2
5	1-10	330	Male Head	3	1	2
6	1-10	480	Male Head	0	3	4

	NumRooms	NumUnits	NumVehicles	NumWorkers	OwnRent
1	9	Single detached	1	0	Mortgage
2	6	Single detached	2	0	Rented
3	8	Single detached	3	1	Mortgage
4	4	Single detached	1	0	Rented
5	5	Single attached	1	0	Mortgage
6	1	Single detached	0	0	Rented

```
    YearBuilt HouseCosts ElectricBill FoodStamp HeatingFuel Insurance
1   1950-1959       1800           90        No         Gas      2500
2  Before 1939       850           90        No         Oil         0
3   2000-2004       2600          260        No         Oil      6600
4   1950-1959       1800          140        No         Oil         0
5  Before 1939       860          150        No         Gas       660
6  Before 1939       700          140        No         Gas         0
        Language Income
1        English  FALSE
2        English  FALSE
3 Other European  FALSE
4        English  FALSE
5        Spanish  FALSE
6        English  FALSE
```

Running a logistic regression is done very similarly to running a linear regression. It still uses the formula interface but the function is glm rather than lm (glm can actually fit linear regressions as well), and a few more options need to be set.

```
> income1 <- glm(Income ~ HouseCosts + NumWorkers + OwnRent +
+                    NumBedrooms + FamilyType,
+                data=acs, family=binomial(link="logit"))
> summary(income1)


Call:
glm(formula = Income ~ HouseCosts + NumWorkers + OwnRent + NumBedrooms +
    FamilyType, family = binomial(link = "logit"), data = acs)

Deviance Residuals:
    Min      1Q  Median      3Q     Max
-2.8452 -0.6246 -0.4231 -0.1743  2.9503

Coefficients:
                      Estimate Std. Error z value Pr(>|z|)
(Intercept)         -5.738e+00  1.185e-01 -48.421   <2e-16 ***
HouseCosts           7.398e-04  1.724e-05  42.908   <2e-16 ***
NumWorkers           5.611e-01  2.588e-02  21.684   <2e-16 ***
OwnRentOutright      1.772e+00  2.075e-01   8.541   <2e-16 ***
OwnRentRented       -8.886e-01  1.002e-01  -8.872   <2e-16 ***
NumBedrooms          2.339e-01  1.683e-02  13.895   <2e-16 ***
FamilyTypeMale Head  3.336e-01  1.472e-01   2.266   0.0235 *
FamilyTypeMarried    1.405e+00  8.704e-02  16.143   <2e-16 ***
---
Signif. codes:  0 '***' 0.001 '**' 0.01 '*' 0.05 '.' 0.1 ' ' 1

(Dispersion parameter for binomial family taken to be 1)
```

```
    Null deviance: 22808  on 22744  degrees of freedom
Residual deviance: 18073  on 22737  degrees of freedom
AIC: 18089

Number of Fisher Scoring iterations: 6

> require(coefplot)
> coefplot(income1)
```

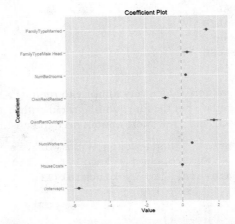

Figure 17.2   Coefficient plot for logistic regression on family income greater than $150,000, based on the American Community Survey.

The output from summary and coefplot for glm is similar to that of lm. There are coefficient estimates, standard errors, p-values—both overall and for the coefficients—and a measure of correctness, which in this case is the deviance and AIC. A general rule of thumb is that adding a variable (or a level of a factor) to a model should result in a drop in deviance of two; otherwise, the variable is not useful in the model. Interactions and all the other formula concepts work the same.

Interpreting the coefficients from a logistic regression necessitates taking the inverse logit.

```
> invlogit <- function(x)
+ {
+     1/(1 + exp(-x))
+ }
> invlogit(income1$coefficients)

    (Intercept)          HouseCosts         NumWorkers
     0.003211572         0.500184950        0.636702036
```

```
       OwnRentOutright          OwnRentRented          NumBedrooms
            0.854753527            0.291408659          0.558200010
     FamilyTypeMale Head      FamilyTypeMarried
            0.582624773            0.802983719
```

17.2   Poisson Regression

Another popular member of the generalized linear models is Poisson regression, which, much like the Poisson distribution, is used for count data. It, like all other generalized linear models, is called using glm. To illustrate we continue using the ACS data with the number of children (NumChildren) as the response.

The formulation for Poisson regression is

$$y_i \sim pois(\theta_i) \tag{17.3}$$

where y_i is the ith response and

$$\theta_i = e^{X_i\beta} \tag{17.4}$$

is the mean of the distribution for the ith observation.

Before fitting a model, we look at the histogram of the number of children in each household.

```
> ggplot(acs, aes(x = NumChildren)) + geom_histogram(binwidth = 1)
```

While Figure 17.3 does not show data that have a perfect Poisson distribution it is close enough to fit a good model. The coefficient plot is shown in Figure 17.4.

```
> children1 <- glm(NumChildren ~ FamilyIncome + FamilyType + OwnRent,
+                 data=acs, family=poisson(link="log"))
> summary(children1)


Call:
glm(formula = NumChildren ~ FamilyIncome + FamilyType + OwnRent,
    family = poisson(link = "log"), data = acs)

Deviance Residuals:
    Min      1Q  Median      3Q     Max
-1.9950 -1.3235 -1.2045  0.9464  6.3781

Coefficients:
                      Estimate Std. Error z value Pr(>|z|)
(Intercept)         -3.257e-01  2.103e-02 -15.491  < 2e-16 ***
FamilyIncome         5.420e-07  6.572e-08   8.247  < 2e-16 ***
FamilyTypeMale Head -6.298e-02  3.847e-02  -1.637    0.102
```

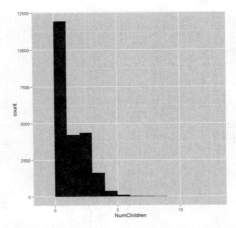

Figure 17.3   Histogram of the number of children per household from the American Community Survey. The distribution is not perfectly Poisson but it is sufficiently so for modeling with Poisson regression.

```
FamilyTypeMarried     1.440e-01   2.147e-02    6.707 1.98e-11 ***
OwnRentOutright      -1.974e+00   2.292e-01   -8.611  < 2e-16 ***
OwnRentRented         4.086e-01   2.067e-02   19.773  < 2e-16 ***
---
Signif. codes:  0 '***' 0.001 '**' 0.01 '*' 0.05 '.' 0.1 ' ' 1


(Dispersion parameter for poisson family taken to be 1)

    Null deviance: 35240  on 22744  degrees of freedom
Residual deviance: 34643  on 22739  degrees of freedom
AIC: 61370

Number of Fisher Scoring iterations: 5

> coefplot(children1)
```

The output here is similar to that for logistic regression, and the same rule of thumb for deviance applies.

A particular concern with Poisson regression is overdispersion, which means that the variability seen in the data is greater than is theorized by the Poisson distribution where the mean and variance are the same.

Overdispersion is defined as

$$OD = \frac{1}{n-p} \sum_{i=1}^{n} z_i^2 \qquad (17.5)$$

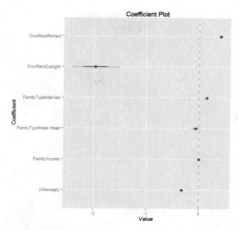

Figure 17.4   Coefficient plot for a logistic regression on ACS data.

where

$$z_i = \frac{y_i - \hat{y}_i}{sd(\hat{y}_i)} = \frac{y_i - u_i\hat{\theta}_i}{\sqrt{u_i\hat{\theta}_i}} \tag{17.6}$$

are the studentized residuals.

Calculating overdispersion in R is as follows.

```
> # the standardized residuals
> z <- (acs$NumChildren - children1$fitted.values) /
+      sqrt(children1$fitted.values)
> # Overdispersion Factor
> sum(z^2) / children1$df.residual

[1] 1.469747

> # Overdispersion p-value
> pchisq(sum(z^2), children1$df.residual)

[1] 1
```

Generally an overdispersion ratio of 2 or greater indicates overdispersion. While this overdispersion ratio is less than 2, the p-value is 1, meaning that there is a statistically significant overdispersion. So we refit the model to account for the overdispersion using the quasipoisson family, which actually uses the negative binomial distribution.

```
> children2 <- glm(NumChildren ~ FamilyIncome + FamilyType + OwnRent,
+                  data=acs, family=quasipoisson(link="log"))
> multiplot(children1, children2)
```

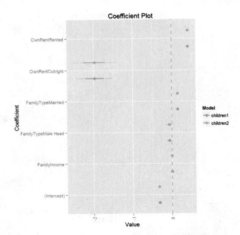

Figure 17.5   Coefficient plot for Poisson models. The first model, `children1`, does not account for overdispersion, while `children2` does. Because the overdispersion was not too big, the coefficient estimates in the second model have just a bit more uncertainty.

Figure 17.5 shows a coefficient plot for a model that accounts for overdispersion and one that does not. Since the overdispersion was not very large, the second model adds just a little uncertainty to the coefficient estimates.

17.3 Other Generalized Linear Models

Other common generalized linear models supported by the `glm` function are gamma, inverse gaussian and quasibinomial. Different link functions can be supplied, such as the following: logit, probit, cauchit, log and cloglog for binomial; inverse, identity and log for gamma; log, identity and sqrt for Poisson; and 1/mu^2, inverse, identity and log for inverse gaussian.

Multinomial regression, for classifying multiple categories, requires either running multiple logistic regressions (a tactic well supported in statistical literature) or using the `polr` function or the `multinom` function from the `nnet` package.

17.4 Survival Analysis

While not technically part of the family of generalized linear models, survival analysis is another important extension to regression. It has many applications, such as clinical medical trials, server failure times, number of accidents and time to death after a treatment or disease.

Data used for survival analysis are different from most other data in that they are censored, meaning there is unknown information, typically about what happens to a subject after a given amount of time. For an example, we look at the `bladder` data from the `survival` package.

```
> require(survival)
> head(bladder)

  id rx number size stop event enum
1  1  1      1    3    1     0    1
2  1  1      1    3    1     0    2
3  1  1      1    3    1     0    3
4  1  1      1    3    1     0    4
5  2  1      2    1    4     0    1
6  2  1      2    1    4     0    2
```

The columns of note are stop (when an event occurs or the patient leaves the study) and event (whether an event occurred at the time). Even if event is 0, we do not know if an event could have occurred later; this is why it is called censored. Making use of that structure requires the Surv function.

```
> # first look at a piece of the data
> bladder[100:105, ]

    id rx number size stop event enum
100 25  1      2    1   12     1    4
101 26  1      1    3   12     1    1
102 26  1      1    3   15     1    2
103 26  1      1    3   24     1    3
104 26  1      1    3   31     0    4
105 27  1      1    2   32     0    1
```

```
> # now look at the response variable built by build.y
> survObject <- with(bladder[100:105, ], Surv(stop, event))
> # nicely printed form
> survObject

[1] 12   12   15   24   31+  32+
```

```
> # see its matrix form
> survObject[, 1:2]

     time status
[1,]   12      1
[2,]   12      1
[3,]   15      1
[4,]   24      1
[5,]   31      0
[6,]   32      0
```

This shows that for the first three rows where an event occurred, the time is known to be 12, whereas the bottom two rows had no event, so the time is censored because an event could have occurred afterward.

Perhaps the most common modeling technique in survival analysis is using a Cox proportional hazards model, which in R is done with coxph. The model is fitted using the familiar formula interface supplied to coxph. The survfit function builds the survival curve that can then be plotted as shown in Figure 17.6. The survival curve shows the percentage of participants surviving at a given time. The summary is similar to other summaries but tailored to survival analysis.

```
> cox1 <- coxph(Surv(stop, event) ~ rx + number + size + enum,
+                   data=bladder)
> summary(cox1)


Call:
coxph(formula = Surv(stop, event) ~ rx + number + size + enum,
    data = bladder)

  n= 340, number of events= 112

            coef exp(coef) se(coef)      z Pr(>|z|)
rx      -0.59739   0.55024  0.20088 -2.974  0.00294 **
number   0.21754   1.24301  0.04653  4.675 2.93e-06 ***
size    -0.05677   0.94481  0.07091 -0.801  0.42333
enum    -0.60385   0.54670  0.09401 -6.423 1.34e-10 ***
---
Signif. codes:  0 '***' 0.001 '**' 0.01 '*' 0.05 '.' 0.1 ' ' 1

        exp(coef) exp(-coef) lower .95 upper .95
rx         0.5502     1.8174    0.3712    0.8157
number     1.2430     0.8045    1.1347    1.3617
size       0.9448     1.0584    0.8222    1.0857
enum       0.5467     1.8291    0.4547    0.6573


Concordance= 0.753  (se = 0.029 )
Rsquare= 0.179   (max possible= 0.971 )
Likelihood ratio test= 67.21  on 4 df,   p=8.804e-14
Wald test            = 64.73  on 4 df,   p=2.932e-13
Score (logrank) test = 69.42  on 4 df,   p=2.998e-14


> plot(survfit(cox1), xlab="Days", ylab="Survival Rate",
+         conf.int=TRUE)
```

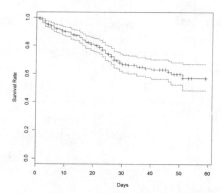

Figure 17.6 Survival curve for Cox proportional hazards model fitted on bladder data.

In this data, the `rx` variable indicates placebo versus treatment, which is a natural stratification of the patients. Passing `rx` to `strata` in the `formula` splits the data into two for analysis and will result in two survival curves like those in Figure 17.7.

```
> cox2 <- coxph(Surv(stop, event) ~ strata(rx) + number + size + enum,
+               data=bladder)
> summary(cox2)

Call:
coxph(formula = Surv(stop, event) ~ strata(rx) + number + size +
    enum, data = bladder)

  n= 340, number of events= 112

          coef exp(coef) se(coef)      z Pr(>|z|)
number  0.21371   1.23826  0.04648  4.598 4.27e-06 ***
size   -0.05485   0.94662  0.07097 -0.773     0.44
enum   -0.60695   0.54501  0.09408 -6.451 1.11e-10 ***
---
Signif. codes:  0 '***' 0.001 '**' 0.01 '*' 0.05 '.' 0.1 ' ' 1

        exp(coef) exp(-coef) lower .95 upper .95
number     1.2383     0.8076    1.1304    1.3564
size       0.9466     1.0564    0.8237    1.0879
enum       0.5450     1.8348    0.4532    0.6554

Concordance= 0.74  (se = 0.04 )
Rsquare= 0.166   (max possible= 0.954 )
Likelihood ratio test= 61.84  on 3 df,   p=2.379e-13
Wald test            = 60.04  on 3 df,   p=5.751e-13
Score (logrank) test = 65.05  on 3 df,   p=4.896e-14
```

```
> plot(survfit(cox2), xlab="Days", ylab="Survival Rate",
+       conf.int=TRUE, col=1:2)
> legend("bottomleft", legend=c(1, 2), lty=1, col=1:2,
+         text.col=1:2, title="rx")
```

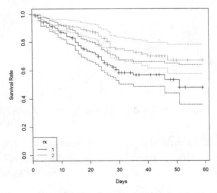

Figure 17.7   Survival curve for Cox proportional hazards model fitted on bladder data stratified on rx.

As an aside, this was a relatively simple legend to produce but it took a lot more effort than it would with `ggplot2`.

Testing the assumption of proportional hazards is done with `cox.zph`.

```
> cox.zph(cox1)
```

	rho	chisq	p
rx	0.0299	0.0957	7.57e-01
number	0.0900	0.6945	4.05e-01
size	-0.1383	2.3825	1.23e-01
enum	0.4934	27.2087	1.83e-07
GLOBAL	NA	32.2101	1.73e-06

```
> cox.zph(cox2)
```

	rho	chisq	p
number	0.0966	0.785	3.76e-01
size	-0.1331	2.197	1.38e-01
enum	0.4972	27.237	1.80e-07
GLOBAL	NA	32.101	4.98e-07

An Andersen-Gill analysis is similar to survival analysis, except it takes intervalized data and can handle multiple events such as counting the number of emergency room visits as opposed to whether or not there is an emergency room visit. It is also performed using coxph, except an additional variable is passed to Surv, and the data must be clustered on an identification column (id) to keep track of multiple events. The corresponding survival curves are seen in Figure 17.8.

```
> head(bladder2)

  id rx number size start stop event enum
1  1  1      1    3     0    1     0    1
2  2  1      2    1     0    4     0    1
3  3  1      1    1     0    7     0    1
4  4  1      5    1     0   10     0    1
5  5  1      4    1     0    6     1    1
6  5  1      4    1     6   10     0    2
> ag1 <- coxph(Surv(start, stop, event) ~ rx + number + size + enum +
+                 cluster(id), data=bladder2)
> ag2 <- coxph(Surv(start, stop, event) ~ strata(rx) + number + size +
+                 enum + cluster(id), data=bladder2)
> plot(survfit(ag1), conf.int=TRUE)
> plot(survfit(ag2), conf.int=TRUE, col=1:2)
> legend("topright", legend=c(1, 2), lty=1, col=1:2,
+          text.col=1:2, title="rx")
```

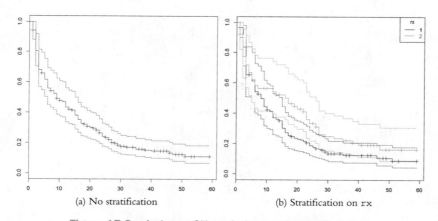

(a) No stratification   (b) Stratification on rx

Figure 17.8   Andersen-Gill survival curves for bladder2 data.

17.5 Conclusion

Generalized linear models extend regression beyond linear relationships between the predictors and response. The most prominent types are logistic for binary data, Poisson for count data and survival analysis. Their uses go far beyond that, but those are by far the most common.

Chapter 18

Model Diagnostics

Building a model can be a never-ending process in which we constantly improve the model by adding interactions, taking away variables, doing transformations and so on. However, at some point we need to confirm that we have the best model at the time, or even a good model. That leads to the question: How do we judge the quality of a model? In almost all cases the answer has to be: in relation to other models. This could be an analysis of residuals, the results of an ANOVA test or a Wald test, drop-in deviance, the AIC or BIC score, cross-validation error or bootstrapping.

18.1 Residuals

One of the first-taught ways of assessing model quality is an analysis of the residuals, which is the difference between the actual response and the fitted values, values predicted by the model. This is a direct result of the formulation in Equation 16.1 where the errors, akin to residuals, are normally distributed. The basic idea is that if the model is appropriately fitted to the data, the residuals should be normally distributed as well. To see this, we start with the housing data to which we fit a regression and visualize with a coefficient plot, as shown in Figure 18.1.

```
> # read in the data
> housing <- read.table("data/housing.csv", sep=",", header=TRUE,
+                       stringsAsFactors=FALSE)
> # give the data good names
> names(housing) <- c("Neighborhood", "Class", "Units", "YearBuilt",
+                     "SqFt", "Income", "IncomePerSqFt", "Expense",
+                     "ExpensePerSqFt", "NetIncome", "Value",
+                     "ValuePerSqFt", "Boro")
> # eliminate some outliers
> housing <- housing[housing$Units < 1000, ]
> head(housing)
```

```
   Neighborhood           Class Units YearBuilt    SqFt    Income
1    FINANCIAL R9-CONDOMINIUM    42      1920   36500   1332615
2    FINANCIAL R4-CONDOMINIUM    78      1985  126420   6633257
3    FINANCIAL RR-CONDOMINIUM   500        NA  554174  17310000
4    FINANCIAL R4-CONDOMINIUM   282      1930  249076  11776313
5      TRIBECA R4-CONDOMINIUM   239      1985  219495  10004582
6      TRIBECA R4-CONDOMINIUM   133      1986  139719   5127687
  IncomePerSqFt Expense ExpensePerSqFt NetIncome     Value
1         36.51  342005           9.37    990610   7300000
2         52.47 1762295          13.94   4870962  30690000
3         31.24 3543000           6.39  13767000  90970000
4         47.28 2784670          11.18   8991643  67556006
5         45.58 2783197          12.68   7221385  54320996
6         36.70 1497788          10.72   3629899  26737996
  ValuePerSqFt      Boro
1       200.00 Manhattan
2       242.76 Manhattan
3       164.15 Manhattan
4       271.23 Manhattan
5       247.48 Manhattan
6       191.37 Manhattan

>
> # fit a model
> house1 <- lm(ValuePerSqFt ~ Units + SqFt + Boro, data=housing)
> summary(house1)


Call:
lm(formula = ValuePerSqFt ~ Units + SqFt + Boro, data = housing)

Residuals:
     Min      1Q   Median      3Q      Max
-168.458  -22.680    1.493   26.290  261.761

Coefficients:
                     Estimate  Std. Error  t value  Pr(>|t|)
(Intercept)         4.430e+01   5.342e+00    8.293   < 2e-16 ***
Units              -1.532e-01   2.421e-02   -6.330  2.88e-10 ***
SqFt                2.070e-04   2.129e-05    9.723   < 2e-16 ***
BoroBrooklyn        3.258e+01   5.561e+00    5.858  5.28e-09 ***
BoroManhattan       1.274e+02   5.459e+00   23.343   < 2e-16 ***
BoroQueens          3.011e+01   5.711e+00    5.272  1.46e-07 ***
BoroStaten Island  -7.114e+00   1.001e+01   -0.711     0.477
---
```

```
Signif. codes:  0 '***' 0.001 '**' 0.01 '*' 0.05 '.' 0.1 ' ' 1

Residual standard error: 43.2 on 2613 degrees of freedom
Multiple R-squared:  0.6034, Adjusted R-squared:  0.6025
F-statistic:  662.6 on 6 and 2613 DF,  p-value: <2.2e-16

>
> # visualize the model
> require(coefplot)
> coefplot(house1)
```

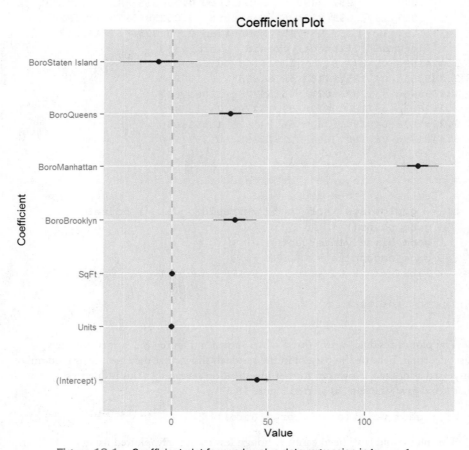

Figure 18.1   Coefficient plot for condo value data regression in house1.

For linear regression, three important residual plots are fitted values against residuals, Q-Q plots and the histogram of the residuals. The first is easy enough with ggplot2. Fortunately, ggplot2 has a handy trick for dealing with lm models. We can use the model as the data source and `ggplot2` "fortifies" it, creating new columns, for easy plotting.

```
> require(ggplot2)
> # see what a fortified lm model looks like
> head(fortify(house1))

  ValuePerSqFt Units    SqFt      Boro          .hat   .sigma
1       200.00    42   36500  Manhattan 0.0009594821 43.20952
2       242.76    78  126420  Manhattan 0.0009232393 43.19848
3       164.15   500  554174  Manhattan 0.0089836758 43.20347
4       271.23   282  249076  Manhattan 0.0035168641 43.17583
5       247.48   239  219495  Manhattan 0.0023865978 43.19289
6       191.37   133  139719  Manhattan 0.0008934957 43.21225
        .cooksd  .fitted    .resid   .stdresid
1 5.424169e-05 172.8475  27.15248   0.6287655
2 2.285253e-04 185.9418  56.81815   1.3157048
3 1.459368e-03 209.8077 -45.65775  -1.0615607
4 2.252653e-03 180.0672  91.16278   2.1137487
5 8.225193e-04 180.5341  66.94589   1.5513636
6 8.446170e-06 180.2661  11.10385   0.2571216

> # save a plot to an object
> # notice we are using the created columns for the x- and y-axes
> # they are .fitted and .resid
> h1 <- ggplot(aes(x=.fitted, y=.resid), data = house1) +
+       geom_point() +
+       geom_hline(yintercept = 0) +
+       geom_smooth(se = FALSE) +
+       labs(x="Fitted Values", y="Residuals")
>
> # print the plot
> h1
```

The plot of residuals versus fitted values shown in Figure 18.2 is at first glance disconcerting, because the pattern in the residuals shows that they are not as randomly dispersed as desired. However, further investigation reveals that this is due to the structure that Boro gives the data, as seen in Figure 18.3.

```
> h1 + geom_point(aes(color = Boro))
```

This plot could have been easily, although less attractively, plotted using the built-in plotting function, as shown in Figure 18.4.

```
> # basic plot
> plot(house1, which=1)
```

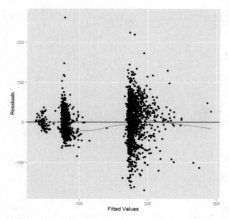

Figure 18.2   Plot of residuals versus fitted values for `house1`. This clearly shows a pattern in the data that does not appear to be random.

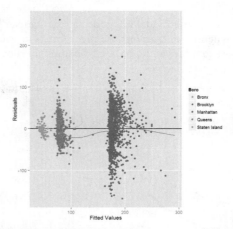

Figure 18.3   Plot of residuals versus fitted values for `house1` colored by `Boro`. The pattern in the residuals is revealed to be the result of the effect of `Boro` on the model. Notice that the points sit above the *x*-axis and the smoothing curve because `geom_point` was added after the other geoms, meaning it gets layered on top.

```
> # same plot but colored by Boro
> plot(house1, which=1, col=as.numeric(factor(house1$model$Boro)))
> # corresponding legend
> legend("topright", legend=levels(factor(house1$model$Boro)), pch=1,
+        col=as.numeric(factor(levels(factor(house1$model$Boro)))),
+        text.col=as.numeric(factor(levels(factor(house1$model$Boro)))),
+        title="Boro")
```

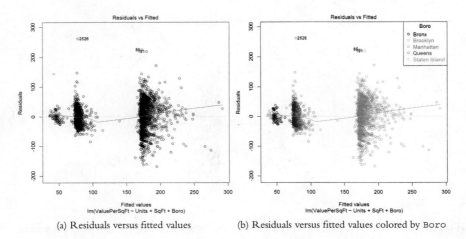

Figure 18.4   Base graphics plots for residuals versus fitted values.

Next up is the Q-Q plot. If the model is a good fit, the standardized residuals should all fall along a straight line when plotted against the theoretical quantiles of the normal distribution. Both the base graphics and `ggplot2` versions are shown in Figure 18.5.

```
> plot(house1, which = 2)
> ggplot(house1, aes(sample = .stdresid)) + stat_qq() + geom_abline()
```

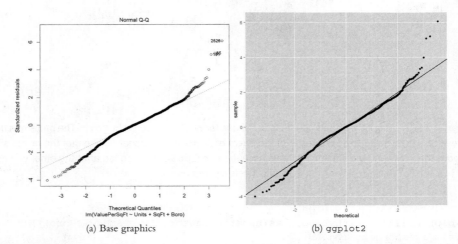

Figure 18.5   Q-Q plot for `house1`. The tails drift away from the ideal theoretical line, indicating that we do not have the best fit.

Another diagnostic is a histogram of the residuals. This time we will not be showing the base graphics alternative because a histogram is a standard plot that we have shown repeatedly. The histogram in Figure 18.6 is not normally distributed, meaning that our model is not an entirely correct specification.

```
> ggplot(house1, aes(x = .resid)) + geom_histogram()
```

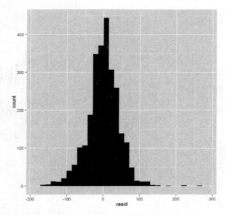

Figure 18.6   Histogram of residuals from `house1`. This does not look normally distributed, meaning our model is incomplete.

18.2   Comparing Models

All of this measuring of model fit only really makes sense when comparing multiple models, because all of these measures are relative. So we will fit a number of models in order to compare them to each other.

```
> house2 <- lm(ValuePerSqFt ~ Units * SqFt + Boro, data=housing)
> house3 <- lm(ValuePerSqFt ~ Units + SqFt * Boro + Class,
+              data=housing)
> house4 <- lm(ValuePerSqFt ~ Units + SqFt * Boro + SqFt*Class,
+              data=housing)
> house5 <- lm(ValuePerSqFt ~ Boro + Class, data=housing)
```

As usual, our first step is to visualize the models together using `multiplot` from the `coefplot` package. The result is in Figure 18.7 and shows that `Boro` is the only variable with a significant effect on `ValuePerSqFt` as do certain condominium types.

```
> multiplot(house1, house2, house3, house4, house5, pointSize = 2)
```

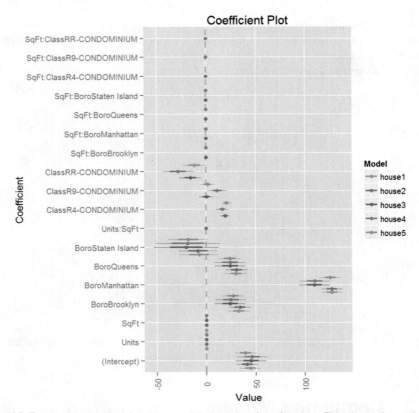

Figure 18.7 Coefficient plot of various models based on housing data. This shows that only `Boro` and some condominium types matter.

While we do not promote using ANOVA for a multisample test, we do believe it serves a useful purpose in testing the relative merits of different models. Simply passing multiple model objects to anova will return a table of results including the residual sum of squares (RSS), which is a measure of error, the lower the better.

```
> anova(house1, house2, house3, house4, house5)

Analysis of Variance Table

Model 1: ValuePerSqFt ~ Units + SqFt + Boro
Model 2: ValuePerSqFt ~ Units * SqFt + Boro
Model 3: ValuePerSqFt ~ Units + SqFt * Boro + Class
Model 4: ValuePerSqFt ~ Units + SqFt * Boro + SqFt * Class
Model 5: ValuePerSqFt ~ Boro + Class
```

```
   Res.Df        RSS Df Sum of Sq        F    Pr(>F)
1    2613 4877506
2    2612 4847886  1      29620 17.0360 3.783e-05 ***
3    2606 4576769  6     271117 25.9888 < 2.2e-16 ***
4    2603 4525783  3      50986  9.7749 2.066e-06 ***
5    2612 4895630 -9    -369847 23.6353 < 2.2e-16 ***
---
Signif. codes:  0 '***' 0.001 '**' 0.01 '*' 0.05 '.' 0.1 ' ' 1
```

This shows that the fourth model, house4, has the lowest RSS, meaning it is the best model of the bunch. The problem with RSS is that it always improves when an additional variable is added to the model. This can lead to excessive model complexity and overfitting. Another metric, which penalizes model complexity, is the Akaike Information Criterion (AIC). As with RSS, the model with the lowest AIC—even negative values—is considered optimal. The BIC (Bayesian Information Criterion) is a similar measure where, once again, lower is better.

The formula for AIC is

$$AIC = -2\ln(\mathcal{L}) + 2p \tag{18.1}$$

where $\ln(\mathcal{L})$ is the maximized log-likelihood and p is the number of coefficients in the model. As the model improves the log-likelihood gets bigger, and because that term is negated the AIC gets lower. However, adding coefficients increases the AIC; this penalizes model complexity. The formula for BIC is similar except that instead of multiplying the number of coefficients by 2 it multiplies it by the natural log of the number of rows. This is seen in Equation 18.2.

$$BIC = -2\ln(\mathcal{L}) + \ln(n) \cdot p \tag{18.2}$$

The AIC and BIC for our models are calculated using the AIC and BIC functions, respectively.

```
> AIC(house1, house2, house3, house4, house5)

       df      AIC
house1  8 27177.78
house2  9 27163.82
house3 15 27025.04
house4 18 27001.69
house5  9 27189.50

> BIC(house1, house2, house3, house4, house5)

       df      BIC
house1  8 27224.75
house2  9 27216.66
house3 15 27113.11
```

```
house4 18 27107.37
house5  9 27242.34
```

When called on `glm` models, anova returns the deviance of the model, which is another measure of error. The general rule of thumb—according to Andrew Gelman—is that for every added variable in the model, the deviance should drop by two. For categorical (`factor`) variables, the deviance should drop by two for each `level`.

To illustrate we make a binary variable out of `ValuePerSqFt` and fit a few logistic regression models.

```
> # create the binary variable based on whether ValuePerSqFt is above 150
> housing$HighValue <- housing$ValuePerSqFt >= 150
>
> # fit a few models
> high1 <- glm(HighValue ~ Units + SqFt + Boro,
+              data=housing, family=binomial(link="logit"))
> high2 <- glm(HighValue ~ Units * SqFt + Boro,
+              data=housing, family=binomial(link="logit"))
> high3 <- glm(HighValue ~ Units + SqFt * Boro + Class,
+              data=housing, family=binomial(link="logit"))
> high4 <- glm(HighValue ~ Units + SqFt * Boro + SqFt*Class,
+              data=housing, family=binomial(link="logit"))
> high5 <- glm(HighValue ~ Boro + Class,
+              data=housing, family=binomial(link="logit"))
>
> # test the models using ANOVA (deviance), AIC and BIC
> anova(high1, high2, high3, high4, high5)

Analysis of Deviance Table

Model 1: HighValue ~ Units + SqFt + Boro
Model 2: HighValue ~ Units * SqFt + Boro
Model 3: HighValue ~ Units + SqFt * Boro + Class
Model 4: HighValue ~ Units + SqFt * Boro + SqFt * Class
Model 5: HighValue ~ Boro + Class
  Resid. Df Resid. Dev Df  Deviance
1      2613     1687.5
2      2612     1678.8  1     8.648
3      2606     1627.5  6    51.331
4      2603     1606.1  3    21.420
5      2612     1662.3 -9   -56.205

> AIC(high1, high2, high3, high4, high5)

      df      AIC
high1  7 1701.484
high2  8 1694.835
```

```
high3 14 1655.504
high4 17 1640.084
high5  8 1678.290
```

```
> BIC(high1, high2, high3, high4, high5)
```

```
      df     BIC
high1  7 1742.580
high2  8 1741.803
high3 14 1737.697
high4 17 1739.890
high5  8 1725.257
```

Here, once again, the fourth model is the best. Notice that the fourth model added three variables (the three indicator variables for Class interacted with SqFt) and its deviance dropped by 21, which is greater than two for each additional variable.

18.3   Cross-Validation

Residual diagnostics and model tests such as ANOVA and AIC are a bit old fashioned and came along before modern computing horsepower. The preferred method to assess model quality—at least by most data scientists—is cross-validation, sometimes called k-fold cross-validation. The data are broken into k (usually five or ten) non-overlapping sections. Then a model is fitted on $k - 1$ sections of the data, which is then used to make predictions based on the kth section. This is repeated k times until every section has been held out for testing once and included in model fitting $k - 1$ times. Cross-validation provides a measure of the predictive accuracy of a model, which is largely considered a good means of assessing model quality.

There are a number of packages and functions that assist in performing cross-validation. Each has its own limitations or quirks, so rather than going through a number of incomplete functions, we show one that works well for generalized linear models (including linear regression), and then build a generic framework that can be used generally for an arbitrary model type.

The boot package by Brian Ripley has cv.glm for performing cross-validation on. As the name implies, it works only for generalized linear models, which will suffice for a number of situations.

```
> require(boot)
> # refit house1 using glm instead of lm
> houseG1 <- glm(ValuePerSqFt ~ Units + SqFt + Boro,
+               data=housing, family=gaussian(link="identity"))
>
> # ensure it gives the same results as lm
> identical(coef(house1), coef(houseG1))

[1] TRUE
```

```
>
> # run the cross-validation with 5 folds
> houseCV1 <- cv.glm(housing, houseG1, K=5)
> # check the error
> houseCV1$delta

[1] 1878.596 1876.691
```

The results from `cv.glm` include `delta`, which has two numbers, the raw cross-validation error based on the cost function (in this case the mean squared error, which is a measure of correctness for an estimator and is defined in Equation 18.3) for all the folds and the adjusted cross-validation error. This second number compensates for not using leave-one-out cross-validation, which is like k-fold cross-validation except that each fold is the all but one data point with one point held out. This is very accurate but highly computationally intensive.

$$\text{MSE} = \frac{1}{n} \sum_{i=1}^{n} (\hat{y}_i - y_i)^2 \tag{18.3}$$

While we got a nice number for the error, it helps us only if we can compare it to other models, so we run the same process for the other models we built, rebuilding them with `glm` first.

```
> # refit the models using glm
> houseG2 <- glm(ValuePerSqFt ~ Units * SqFt + Boro, data=housing)
> houseG3 <- glm(ValuePerSqFt ~ Units + SqFt * Boro + Class,
+                data=housing)
> houseG4 <- glm(ValuePerSqFt ~ Units + SqFt * Boro + SqFt*Class,
+                data=housing)
> houseG5 <- glm(ValuePerSqFt ~ Boro + Class, data=housing)
>
> # run cross-validation
> houseCV2 <- cv.glm(housing, houseG2, K=5)
> houseCV3 <- cv.glm(housing, houseG3, K=5)
> houseCV4 <- cv.glm(housing, houseG4, K=5)
> houseCV5 <- cv.glm(housing, houseG5, K=5)
>
> ## check the error results
> # build a data.frame of the results
> cvResults <- as.data.frame(rbind(houseCV1$delta, houseCV2$delta,
+                                  houseCV3$delta, houseCV4$delta,
+                                  houseCV5$delta))
> ## do some cleaning up to make the results more presentable
> # give better column names
> names(cvResults) <- c("Error", "Adjusted.Error")
> # add model name
> cvResults$Model <- sprintf("houseG%s", 1:5)
```

```
>
> # check the results
> cvResults

     Error Adjusted.Error    Model
1 1878.596       1876.691 houseG1
2 1862.247       1860.900 houseG2
3 1767.268       1764.953 houseG3
4 1764.370       1760.102 houseG4
5 1882.631       1881.067 houseG5
```

Once again, the fourth model, houseG4, is the superior model. Figure 18.8 shows how much ANOVA, AIC and cross-validation agree on the relative merits of the different models. The scales are all different but the shapes of the plots are identical.

```
> # visualize the results
> # test with ANOVA
> cvANOVA <-anova(houseG1, houseG2, houseG3, houseG4, houseG5)
> cvResults$ANOVA <- cvANOVA$`Resid. Dev`
> # measure with AIC
> cvResults$AIC <- AIC(houseG1, houseG2, houseG3, houseG4, houseG5)$AIC
>
> # make the data.frame suitable for plotting
> require(reshape2)
> cvMelt <- melt(cvResults, id.vars="Model", variable.name="Measure",
+                value.name="Value")
> cvMelt

     Model       Measure        Value
1  houseG1         Error     1878.596
2  houseG2         Error     1862.247
3  houseG3         Error     1767.268
4  houseG4         Error     1764.370
5  houseG5         Error     1882.631
6  houseG1 Adjusted.Error     1876.691
7  houseG2 Adjusted.Error     1860.900
8  houseG3 Adjusted.Error     1764.953
9  houseG4 Adjusted.Error     1760.102
10 houseG5 Adjusted.Error     1881.067
11 houseG1         ANOVA  4877506.411
12 houseG2         ANOVA  4847886.327
13 houseG3         ANOVA  4576768.981
14 houseG4         ANOVA  4525782.873
15 houseG5         ANOVA  4895630.307
16 houseG1           AIC    27177.781
17 houseG2           AIC    27163.822
```

```
18  houseG3            AIC    27025.042
19  houseG4            AIC    27001.691
20  houseG5            AIC    27189.499

>
> ggplot(cvMelt, aes(x=Model, y=Value)) +
+     geom_line(aes(group=Measure, color=Measure)) +
+     facet_wrap(~Measure, scales="free_y") +
+     theme(axis.text.x=element_text(angle=90, vjust=.5)) +
+     guides(color=FALSE)
```

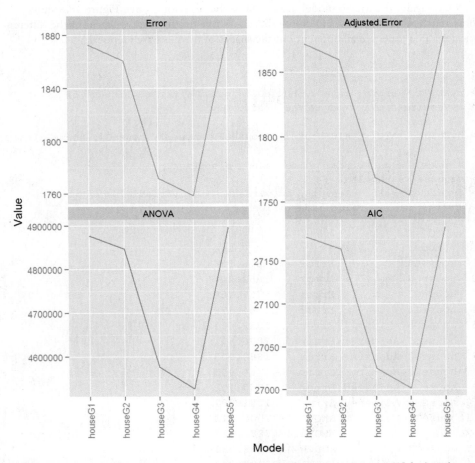

Figure 18.8   Plots for cross-validation error (raw and adjusted), ANOVA and AIC for housing models. The scales are different, as they should be, but the shapes are identical, indicating that `houseG4` truly is the best model.

We now present a general framework (loosely borrowed from cv.glm) for running our own cross-validation on models other than glm. This is not universal and will not work for all models, but gives a general idea for how it should be done. In practice it should be abstracted into smaller parts and made more robust.

```
> cv.work <- function(fun, k = 5, data,
+                          cost = function(y, yhat) mean((y - yhat)^2),
+                          response="y", ...)
+ {
+     # generate folds
+     folds <- data.frame(Fold=sample(rep(x=1:k, length.out=nrow(data))),
+                         Row=1:nrow(data))
+
+     # start the error at 0
+     error <- 0
+
+     ## loop through each of the folds
+     ## for each fold:
+     ## fit the model on the training data
+     ## predict on the test data
+     ## compute the error and accumulate it
+     for(f in 1:max(folds$Fold))
+     {
+         # rows that are in test set
+         theRows <- folds$Row[folds$Fold == f]
+
+         ## call fun on data[-theRows, ]
+         ## predict on data[theRows, ]
+         mod <- fun(data=data[-theRows, ], ...)
+         pred <- predict(mod, data[theRows, ])
+
+         # add new error weighted by the number of rows in this fold
+         error <- error +
+             cost(data[theRows, response], pred) *
+             (length(theRows)/nrow(data))
+     }
+
+     return(error)
+ }
```

Applying that function to the various housing models we get their cross-validation errors.

```
> cv1 <- cv.work(fun=lm, k=5, data=housing, response="ValuePerSqFt",
+                formula=ValuePerSqFt ~ Units + SqFt + Boro)
> cv2 <- cv.work(fun=lm, k=5, data=housing, response="ValuePerSqFt",
+                formula=ValuePerSqFt ~ Units * SqFt + Boro)
```

```
> cv3 <- cv.work(fun=lm, k=5, data=housing, response="ValuePerSqFt",
+                formula=ValuePerSqFt ~ Units + SqFt * Boro + Class)
> cv4 <- cv.work(fun=lm, k=5, data=housing, response="ValuePerSqFt",
+                formula=ValuePerSqFt ~ Units + SqFt * Boro + SqFt*Class)
> cv5 <- cv.work(fun=lm, k=5, data=housing, response="ValuePerSqFt",
+                formula=ValuePerSqFt ~ Boro + Class)
> cvResults <- data.frame(Model=sprintf("house%s", 1:5),
+                         Error=c(cv1, cv2, cv3, cv4, cv5))
> cvResults

    Model      Error
1  house1   1875.582
2  house2   1859.388
3  house3   1766.066
4  house4   1764.343
5  house5   1880.926
```

This gives very similar results to cv.glm and again shows that the fourth parameterization is still the best. These measures do not always agree so nicely but it is great when they do.

18.4 Bootstrap

Sometimes, for one reason or another, there is not a good analytic solution to a problem and another tactic is needed. This is especially true for measuring uncertainty for confidence intervals. To overcome this, Bradley Efron introduced the bootstrap in 1979. Since then the bootstrap has grown to revolutionize modern statistics and is indispensable.

The idea is that we start with n rows of data. Some statistic (whether a mean, regression or some arbitrary function) is applied to the data. Then the data are sampled, creating a new dataset. This new set still has n rows except that there are repeats and other rows are entirely missing. The statistic is applied to this new dataset. The process is repeated R times (typically around 1,200), which generates an entire distribution for the statistic. This distribution can then be used to find the mean and confidence interval (typically 95%) for the statistic.

The boot package is a very robust set of tools for making the bootstrap easy to compute. Some care is needed when setting up the function call, but that can be handled easily enough.

Starting with a simple example, we analyze the batting average of Major League Baseball as a whole since 1990. The baseball data have information such as at bats (ab) and hits (h).

```
> require(plyr)
> baseball <- baseball[baseball$year >= 1990, ]
> head(baseball)
```

	id	year	stint	team	lg	g	ab	r	h	X2b	X3b	hr	rbi	sb
67412	alomasa02	1990	1	CLE	AL	132	445	60	129	26	2	9	66	4
67414	anderbr01	1990	1	BAL	AL	89	234	24	54	5	2	3	24	15
67422	baergca01	1990	1	CLE	AL	108	312	46	81	17	2	7	47	0
67424	baineha01	1990	1	TEX	AL	103	321	41	93	10	1	13	44	0
67425	baineha01	1990	2	OAK	AL	32	94	11	25	5	0	3	21	0
67442	bergmda01	1990	1	DET	AL	100	205	21	57	10	1	2	26	3

	cs	bb	so	ibb	hbp	sh	sf	gidp	OBP
67412	1	25	46	2	2	5	6	10	0.3263598
67414	2	31	46	2	5	4	5	4	0.3272727
67422	2	16	57	2	4	1	5	4	0.2997033
67424	1	47	63	9	0	0	3	13	0.3773585
67425	2	20	17	1	0	0	4	4	0.3813559
67442	2	33	17	3	0	1	2	7	0.3750000

The proper way to compute the batting average is to divide total hits by total at bats. This means we cannot simply run mean(h/ab) and sd(h/ab) to get the mean and standard deviation. Rather, the batting average is calculated as sum(h)/sum(ab) and its standard deviation is not easily calculated. This problem is a great candidate for using the bootstrap.

We calculate the overall batting average with the original data. Then we sample *n* rows with replacement and calculate the batting average again. We do this repeatedly until a distribution is formed. Rather that doing this manually, though, we use boot.

The first argument to boot is the data. The second argument is the function that is to be computed on the data. This function must take at least two arguments (unless sim="parametric" in which case only the first argument is necessary). The first is the original data and the second is a vector of indices, frequencies or weights. Additional named arguments can be passed into the function from boot.

```
> ## build a function for calculating batting average
> # data is the data
> # boot will pass varying sets of indices
> # some rows will be represented multiple times in a single pass
> # other rows will not be represented at all
> # on average about 63% of the rows will be present
> # this funciton is called repeatedly by boot
> bat.avg <- function(data, indices=1:NROW(data), hits="h",
+                     at.bats="ab")
+ {
+     sum(data[indices, hits], na.rm=TRUE) /
+         sum(data[indices, at.bats], na.rm=TRUE)
+ }
>
```

```
> # test it on the original data
> bat.avg(baseball)

[1] 0.2745988

>
> # bootstrap it
> # using the baseball data, call bat.avg 1,200 times
> # pass indices to the function
> avgBoot <- boot(data=baseball, statistic=bat.avg, R=1200, stype="i")
>
> # print original measure and estimates of bias and standard error
> avgBoot


ORDINARY NONPARAMETRIC BOOTSTRAP


Call:
boot(data = baseball, statistic = bat.avg, R = 1200, stype = "i")


Bootstrap Statistics :
       original        bias       std. error
t1*    0.2745988 1.071011e-05 0.0006843765

> # print the confidence interval
> boot.ci(avgBoot, conf=.95, type="norm")

BOOTSTRAP CONFIDENCE INTERVAL CALCULATIONS
Based on 1200 bootstrap replicates

CALL :
boot.ci(boot.out = avgBoot, conf = 0.95, type = "norm")

Intervals :
Level      Normal
95%    ( 0.2732,  0.2759 )
Calculations and Intervals on Original Scale
```

Visualizing the distribution is as simple as plotting a histogram of the replicate results. Figure 18.9 shows the histogram for the batting average with vertical lines two standard errors on either side of the original estimate. These mark the (roughly) 95% confidence interval.

```
> ggplot() +
+     geom_histogram(aes(x=avgBoot$t), fill="grey", color="grey") +
```

```
+       geom_vline(xintercept=avgBoot$t0 + c(-1, 1)*2*sqrt(var(avgBoot$t)),
+                  linetype=2)
```

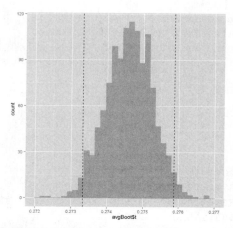

Figure 18.9   Histogram of the batting average bootstrap. The vertical lines are two standard errors from the original estimate in each direction. They make up the bootstrapped 95% confidence interval.

The bootstrap is an incredibly powerful tool that holds a great deal of promise. The `boot` package offers far more than what we have shown here, including the ability to bootstrap time series and censored data. The beautiful thing about the bootstrap is its near universal applicability. It can be used in just about any situation where an analytical solution is impractical or impossible. There are some instances where the bootstrap is inappropriate, such as for measuring uncertainty of biased estimators like those from the lasso, although such limitations are rare.

18.5 Stepwise Variable Selection

A common, though becoming increasingly discouraged, way to select variables for a model is stepwise selection. This is the process of iteratively adding and removing variables from a model and testing the model at each step, usually using AIC.

The `step` function iterates through possible models. The `scope` argument specifies a lower and upper bound on possible models. The `direction` argument specifies whether variables are just added into the model, just subtracted from the model or added and subtracted as necessary. When run, `step` prints out all the iterations it has taken to arrive at what it considers the optimal model.

```
> # the lowest model is the null model, basically the straight average
> nullModel <- lm(ValuePerSqFt ~ 1, data=housing)
> # the largest model we will accept
```

```
> fullModel <- lm(ValuePerSqFt ~ Units + SqFt*Boro + Boro*Class,
+                 data=housing)
> # try different models
> # start with nullModel
> # do not go above fullModel
> # work in both directions
> houseStep <- step(nullModel,
+                   scope=list(lower=nullModel, upper=fullModel),
+                   direction="both")


Start:  AIC=22151.56
ValuePerSqFt ~ 1


        Df Sum of Sq       RSS    AIC
+ Boro   4   7160206   5137931  19873
+ SqFt   1   1310379  10987758  21858
+ Class  3   1264662  11033475  21873
+ Units  1    778093  11520044  21982
<none>              12298137  22152


Step:  AIC=19872.83
ValuePerSqFt ~ Boro


        Df Sum of Sq       RSS    AIC
+ Class  3    242301   4895630  19752
+ SqFt   1    185635   4952296  19778
+ Units  1     83948   5053983  19832
<none>              5137931  19873
- Boro   4   7160206  12298137  22152


Step:  AIC=19752.26
ValuePerSqFt ~ Boro + Class


            Df Sum of Sq       RSS    AIC
+ SqFt       1    182170   4713460  19655
+ Units      1    100323   4795308  19700
+ Boro:Class 9    111838   4783792  19710
<none>                  4895630  19752
- Class      3    242301   5137931  19873
- Boro       4   6137845  11033475  21873


Step:  AIC=19654.91
ValuePerSqFt ~ Boro + Class + SqFt
```

```
              Df Sum of Sq      RSS   AIC
+ SqFt:Boro    4    113219  4600241 19599
+ Boro:Class   9     94590  4618870 19620
+ Units        1     37078  4676382 19636
<none>                      4713460 19655
- SqFt         1    182170  4895630 19752
- Class        3    238836  4952296 19778
- Boro         4   5480928 10194388 21668


Step:  AIC=19599.21
ValuePerSqFt ~ Boro + Class + SqFt + Boro:SqFt


              Df Sum of Sq     RSS   AIC
+ Boro:Class   9     68660 4531581 19578
+ Units        1     23472 4576769 19588
<none>                     4600241 19599
- Boro:SqFt    4    113219 4713460 19655
- Class        3    258642 4858883 19737


Step:  AIC=19577.81
ValuePerSqFt ~ Boro + Class + SqFt + Boro:SqFt + Boro:Class


              Df Sum of Sq     RSS   AIC
+ Units        1     20131 4511450 19568
<none>                     4531581 19578
- Boro:Class   9     68660 4600241 19599
- Boro:SqFt    4     87289 4618870 19620


Step:  AIC=19568.14
ValuePerSqFt ~ Boro + Class + SqFt + Units + Boro:SqFt + Boro:Class


              Df Sum of Sq     RSS   AIC
<none>                     4511450 19568
- Units        1     20131 4531581 19578
- Boro:Class   9     65319 4576769 19588
- Boro:SqFt    4     75955 4587405 19604

> # reveal the chosen model
> houseStep


Call:
lm(formula = ValuePerSqFt ~ Boro + Class + SqFt + Units + Boro:SqFt +
    Boro:Class, data = housing)
```

```
Coefficients:
                                       (Intercept)
                                         4.848e+01
                                       BoroBrooklyn
                                         2.655e+01
                                       BoroManhattan
                                         8.672e+01
                                       BoroQueens
                                         1.999e+01
                                   BoroStaten Island
                                        -1.132e+01
                                 ClassR4-CONDOMINIUM
                                         6.586e+00
                                 ClassR9-CONDOMINIUM
                                         4.553e+00
                                 ClassRR-CONDOMINIUM
                                         8.130e+00
                                              SqFt
                                         1.373e-05
                                              Units
                                        -8.296e-02
                                  BoroBrooklyn:SqFt
                                         3.798e-05
                                 BoroManhattan:SqFt
                                         1.594e-04
                                   BoroQueens:SqFt
                                         2.753e-06
                              BoroStaten Island:SqFt
                                         4.362e-05
                 BoroBrooklyn:ClassR4-CONDOMINIUM
                                         1.933e+00
                BoroManhattan:ClassR4-CONDOMINIUM
                                         3.436e+01
                  BoroQueens:ClassR4-CONDOMINIUM
                                         1.274e+01
             BoroStaten Island:ClassR4-CONDOMINIUM
                                                NA
                 BoroBrooklyn:ClassR9-CONDOMINIUM
                                        -3.440e+00
                BoroManhattan:ClassR9-CONDOMINIUM
                                         1.497e+01
                  BoroQueens:ClassR9-CONDOMINIUM
                                        -9.967e+00
             BoroStaten Island:ClassR9-CONDOMINIUM
                                                NA
```

```
      BoroBrooklyn:ClassRR-CONDOMINIUM
                      -2.901e+01
      BoroManhattan:ClassRR-CONDOMINIUM
                      -6.850e+00
       BoroQueens:ClassRR-CONDOMINIUM
                       2.989e+01
  BoroStaten Island:ClassRR-CONDOMINIUM
                              NA
```

Ultimately, `step` decided that `fullModel` was optimal with the lowest AIC. While this works, it is a bit of a brute force method and has its own theoretical problems. Lasso regression arguably does a better job of variable selection and is discussed in Section 19.1.

18.6 Conclusion

Determining the quality of a model is an important step in the model-building process. This can take the form of traditional tests of fit such as ANOVA or more modern techniques like cross-validation. The bootstrap is another means of determining model uncertainty, especially for models where confidence intervals are impractical to calculate. These can all be shaped by helping select which variables are included in a model and which are excluded.

Chapter 19

Regularization and Shrinkage

In today's era of high dimensional (many variables) data, methods are needed to prevent overfitting. Traditionally, this has been done with variable selection, as described in Chapter 18, although with a large number of variables that can become computationally prohibitive. These methods can take a number of forms; we focus on regularization and shrinkage. For these we will use `glmnet` from the `glmnet` package and `bayesglm` from the `arm` package.

19.1 Elastic Net

One of the most exciting algorithms to be developed in the past five years is the Elastic Net, which is a dynamic blending of lasso and ridge regression. The lasso uses an L1 penalty to perform variable selection and dimension reduction, while the ridge uses an L2 penalty to shrink the coefficients for more stable predictions. The formula for the Elastic Net is

$$\min_{\beta_0, \beta \in \mathbb{R}^{p+1}} \left[\frac{1}{2N} \sum_{i=1}^{N} \left(y_i - \beta_0 - x_i^T \beta \right)^2 + \lambda P_\alpha \left(\beta \right) \right] \tag{19.1}$$

where

$$P_\alpha \left(\beta \right) = (1 - \alpha) \frac{1}{2} ||\beta||_{l_2}^2 + \alpha ||\beta||_{l_1} \tag{19.2}$$

where λ is a complexity parameter controlling the amount of shrinkage (0 is no penalty and ∞ is complete penalty) and α regulates how much of the solution is ridge versus lasso with $\alpha = 0$ being complete ridge and $\alpha = 1$ being complete lasso. Γ, not seen here, is a vector of penalty factors—one value per variable—that multiplies λ for fine tuning of the penalty applied to each variable; again 0 is no penalty and ∞ is complete penalty.

A fairly new package (this is a relatively new algorithm) is `glmnet`, which fits generalized linear models with the Elastic Net. It is written by Trevor Hastie, Robert Tibshirani and Jerome Friedman from Stanford University who also published the landmark papers on the Elastic Net.

Because it is designed for speed and larger, sparser data, `glmnet` requires a little more effort to use than most other modeling functions in R. Where functions like `lm` and `glm` take a `formula` to specify the model, `glmnet` requires a `matrix` of predictors (excluding an intercept, as it is added automatically) and a response `matrix`.

Even though it is not incredibly high dimensional, we will look at the American Community Survey (ACS) data for New York State. We will throw every possible predictor into the model and see which are selected.

```
> acs <- read.table("http://jaredlander.com/data/acs_ny.csv", sep = ",",
+       header = TRUE, stringsAsFactors = FALSE)
```

Because `glmnet` requires a predictor `matrix`, it will be good to have a convenient way of building that `matrix`. This can be done simply enough using `model.matrix`, which at its most basic takes in a `formula` and a `data.frame` and returns a design `matrix`. As an example we create some fake data and run `model.matrix` on it.

```
> # build a data.frame where the first three columns are numeric
> testFrame <-
+       data.frame(First=sample(1:10, 20, replace=TRUE),
+                  Second=sample(1:20, 20, replace=TRUE),
+                  Third=sample(1:10, 20, replace=TRUE),
+                  Fourth=factor(rep(c("Alice", "Bob", "Charlie", "David"),
+                                    5)),
+                  Fifth=ordered(rep(c("Edward", "Frank", "Georgia",
+                                      "Hank", "Isaac"), 4)),
+                  Sixth=rep(c("a", "b"), 10), stringsAsFactors=F)
> head(testFrame)
```

```
  First Second Third  Fourth   Fifth Sixth
1     3      8     6   Alice  Edward     a
2     3     16     4     Bob   Frank     b
3     9     14     6 Charlie Georgia     a
4     9      2     2   David    Hank     b
5     5     17     6   Alice   Isaac     a
6     6      3     4     Bob  Edward     b
```

```
>
> head(model.matrix(First ~ Second + Fourth + Fifth, testFrame))
```

```
  (Intercept) Second FourthBob FourthCharlie FourthDavid     Fifth.L
1           1      8         0             0           0  -0.6324555
2           1     16         1             0           0  -0.3162278
3           1     14         0             1           0   0.0000000
4           1      2         0             0           1   0.3162278
5           1     17         0             0           0   0.6324555
6           1      3         1             0           0  -0.6324555
```

```
      Fifth.Q          Fifth.C      Fifth^4
1   0.5345225  -3.162278e-01   0.1195229
2  -0.2672612   6.324555e-01  -0.4780914
3  -0.5345225  -4.095972e-16   0.7171372
4  -0.2672612  -6.324555e-01  -0.4780914
5   0.5345225   3.162278e-01   0.1195229
6   0.5345225  -3.162278e-01   0.1195229
```

This works very well and is simple, but first there are a few things to notice. As expected, Fourth gets converted into indicator variables with one less column than levels in Fourth. Initially, the parameterization of Fifth might seem odd, as there is one less column than there are levels, but their values are not just 1s and 0s. This is because Fifth is an ordered factor where one level is greater or less than another level.

Not creating an indicator variable for the base level of a factor is essential for most linear models to avoid multicollinearity.[1] However, it is generally considered undesirable for the predictor matrix to be designed this way for the Elastic Net. It is possible to have model.matrix return indicator variables for all levels of a factor, although doing so can take some creative coding.[2] To make the process easier we incorporated a solution in the build.x function in the useful package.

```
> require(useful)
> # always use all levels
> head(build.x(First ~ Second + Fourth + Fifth, testFrame,
+               contrasts=FALSE))

   (Intercept) Second FourthAlice FourthBob FourthCharlie FourthDavid
1            1      8           1         0             0           0
2            1     16           0         1             0           0
3            1     14           0         0             1           0
4            1      2           0         0             0           1
5            1     17           1         0             0           0
6            1      3           0         1             0           0
   FifthEdward FifthFrank FifthGeorgia FifthHank FifthIsaac
1            1          0            0         0          0
2            0          1            0         0          0
3            0          0            1         0          0
4            0          0            0         1          0
5            0          0            0         0          1
6            1          0            0         0          0
```

---

1. This is a characteristic of a matrix in linear algebra where the columns are not linearly independent. While this is an important concept, we do not need to concern ourselves with it much in the context of this book.

2. The difficulty is evidenced in this Stack Overflow question asked by us: http://stackoverflow.com/questions/4560459/all-levels-of-a-factor-in-a-model-matrix-in-r/15400119

```
> # just use all levels for Fourth
> head(build.x(First ~ Second + Fourth + Fifth, testFrame,
+               contrasts=c(Fourth=FALSE, Fifth=TRUE)))
```

```
  (Intercept) Second FourthAlice FourthBob FourthCharlie FourthDavid
1           1      8           1         0             0           0
2           1     16           0         1             0           0
3           1     14           0         0             1           0
4           1      2           0         0             0           1
5           1     17           1         0             0           0
6           1      3           0         1             0           0
      Fifth.L    Fifth.Q       Fifth.C       Fifth^4
1 -0.6324555  0.5345225 -3.162278e-01    0.1195229
2 -0.3162278 -0.2672612  6.324555e-01   -0.4780914
3  0.0000000 -0.5345225 -4.095972e-16    0.7171372
4  0.3162278 -0.2672612 -6.324555e-01   -0.4780914
5  0.6324555  0.5345225  3.162278e-01    0.1195229
6 -0.6324555  0.5345225 -3.162278e-01    0.1195229
```

Using build.x appropriately on acs builds a nice predictor matrix for use in glmnet. We control the desired matrix by using a formula for our model specification just like we would in lm, interactions and all.

```
> # make a binary Income variable for building a logistic regression
> acs$Income <- with(acs, FamilyIncome >= 150000)
>
> head(acs)
```

```
  Acres FamilyIncome  FamilyType NumBedrooms NumChildren NumPeople
1  1-10          150     Married           4           1         3
2  1-10          180 Female Head           3           2         4
3  1-10          280 Female Head           4           0         2
4  1-10          330 Female Head           2           1         2
5  1-10          330   Male Head           3           1         2
6  1-10          480   Male Head           0           3         4
  NumRooms          NumUnits NumVehicles NumWorkers  OwnRent
1        9 Single detached            1          0 Mortgage
2        6 Single detached            2          0   Rented
3        8 Single detached            3          1 Mortgage
4        4 Single detached            1          0   Rented
5        5 Single attached            1          0 Mortgage
6        1 Single detached            0          0   Rented
  YearBuilt HouseCosts ElectricBill FoodStamp HeatingFuel Insurance
1 1950-1959       1800           90        No         Gas      2500
2 Before 1939        850           90        No         Oil         0
3 2000-2004       2600          260        No         Oil      6600
```

```
4  1950-1959        1800          140        No      Oil         0
5 Before 1939        860          150        No      Gas       660
6 Before 1939        700          140        No      Gas         0
         Language Income
1         English  FALSE
2         English  FALSE
3 Other European  FALSE
4         English  FALSE
5         Spanish  FALSE
6         English  FALSE

>
> # build predictor matrix
> # do not include the intercept as glmnet will add that automatically
> acsX <- build.x(Income ~ NumBedrooms + NumChildren + NumPeople +
+                 NumRooms + NumUnits + NumVehicles + NumWorkers +
+                 OwnRent + YearBuilt + ElectricBill + FoodStamp +
+                 HeatingFuel + Insurance + Language - 1,
+             data=acs, contrasts=FALSE)
>
> # check class and dimensions
> class(acsX)

[1] "matrix"

> dim(acsX)


[1] 22745     44


>
> # view the top left and top right of the data
> topleft(acsX, c=6)

  NumBedrooms NumChildren NumPeople NumRooms NumUnitsMobile home
1           4           1         3        9                   0
2           3           2         4        6                   0
3           4           0         2        8                   0
4           2           1         2        4                   0
5           3           1         2        5                   0
  NumUnitsSingle attached
1                       0
2                       0
3                       0
4                       0
5                       1
```

```
> topright(acsX, c=6)


  Insurance LanguageAsian Pacific LanguageEnglish LanguageOther
1     2500                     0               1               0
2        0                     0               1               0
3     6600                     0               0               0
4        0                     0               1               0
5      660                     0               0               0
  LanguageOther European LanguageSpanish
1                      0               0
2                      0               0
3                      1               0
4                      0               0
5                      0               1

>
> # build response predictor
> acsY <- build.y(Income ~ NumBedrooms + NumChildren + NumPeople +
+                      NumRooms + NumUnits + NumVehicles + NumWorkers +
+                      OwnRent + YearBuilt + ElectricBill + FoodStamp +
+                      HeatingFuel + Insurance + Language - 1, data=acs)
>
> head(acsY)

[1] FALSE FALSE FALSE FALSE FALSE FALSE

> tail(acsY)

[1] TRUE TRUE TRUE TRUE TRUE TRUE
```

Now that the data are properly stored we can run `glmnet`. As seen in Equation 19.1, λ controls the amount of shrinkage. By default `glmnet` fits the regularization path on 100 different values of λ. The decision of which is best then falls upon the user with cross-validation being a good measure. Fortunately, the `glmnet` package has a function, `cv.glmnet`, that computes the cross-validation automatically. By default $\alpha = 1$, meaning only the lasso is calculated. Selecting the best α requires an additional layer of cross-validation.

```
> require(glmnet)
> set.seed(1863561)
> # run the cross-validated glmnet
> acsCV1 <- cv.glmnet(x = acsX, y = acsY, family = "binomial", nfold = 5)
```

The most important information returned from `cv.glmnet` are the cross-validation error and which value of λ minimizes the cross-validation error. Additionally, it also returns the largest value of λ with a cross-validation error that is within one standard error of the minimum. Theory suggests that the simpler model, even though it is slightly less accurate, should be preferred due to its parsimony. The cross-validation errors for differing values of λ are seen in Figure 19.1. The top row of numbers indicates how many variables (factor levels are counted as individual variables) are in the model for a given value of log(λ).

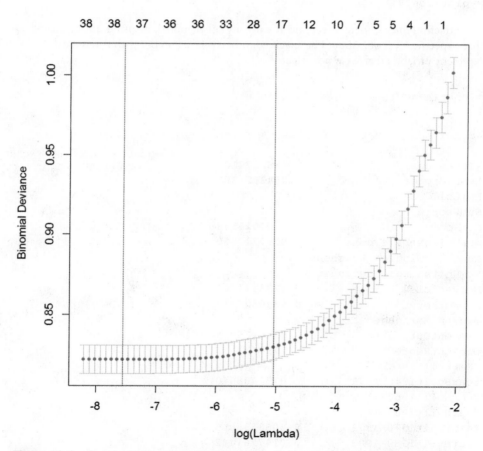

Figure 19.1 Cross-validation curve for the `glmnet` fitted on the American Community Survey data. The top row of numbers indicates how many variables (factor levels are counted as individual variables) are in the model for a given value of log(λ). The dots represent the cross-validation error at that point and the vertical lines are the confidence interval for the error. The leftmost vertical line indicates the value of λ where the error is minimized and the rightmost vertical line is the next largest value of λ error that is within one standard error of the minimum.

```
> acsCV1$lambda.min

[1] 0.0005258299

> acsCV1$lambda.1se

[1] 0.006482677


> plot(acsCV1)
```

Extracting the coefficients is done as with any other model, by using coef, except that a specific level of λ should be specified; otherwise, the entire path is returned. Dots represent variables that were not selected.

```
> coef(acsCV1, s = "lambda.1se")


45 x 1 sparse Matrix of class "dgCMatrix"
                                    1
(Intercept)              -5.0552170103
NumBedrooms               0.0542621380
NumChildren               .
NumPeople                 .
NumRooms                  0.1102021934
NumUnitsMobile home      -0.8960712560
NumUnitsSingle attached   .
NumUnitsSingle detached   .
NumVehicles               0.1283171343
NumWorkers                0.4806697219
OwnRentMortgage           .
OwnRentOutright           0.2574766773
OwnRentRented            -0.1790627645
YearBuilt15               .
YearBuilt1940-1949       -0.0253908040
YearBuilt1950-1959        .
YearBuilt1960-1969        .
YearBuilt1970-1979       -0.0063336086
YearBuilt1980-1989        0.0147761442
YearBuilt1990-1999        .
YearBuilt2000-2004        .
YearBuilt2005             .
YearBuilt2006             .
YearBuilt2007             .
YearBuilt2008             .
```

```
YearBuilt2009                    .
YearBuilt2010                    .
YearBuiltBefore 1939        -0.1829643904
ElectricBill                 0.0018200312
FoodStampNo                  0.7071289660
FoodStampYes                     .
HeatingFuelCoal             -0.2635263281
HeatingFuelElectricity           .
HeatingFuelGas                   .
HeatingFuelNone                  .
HeatingFuelOil                   .
HeatingFuelOther                 .
HeatingFuelSolar                 .
HeatingFuelWood             -0.7454315355
Insurance                    0.0004973315
LanguageAsian Pacific        0.3606176925
LanguageEnglish                  .
LanguageOther                    .
LanguageOther European       0.0389641675
LanguageSpanish                  .
```

It might seem weird that some `levels` of a `factor` were selected and others were not, but it ultimately makes sense because the lasso eliminates variables that are highly correlated with each other.

Another thing to notice is that there are no standard errors and hence no confidence intervals for the coefficients. The same is true of any predictions made from a `glmnet` model. This is due to the theoretical properties of the lasso and ridge, and is an open problem. Recent advancements have led to the ability to perform significance tests on lasso regressions, although the existing R package requires that the model be fitted using the `lars` package, not `glmnet`, at least until the research extends the testing ability to cover the Elastic Net as well.

Visualizing where variables enter the model along the λ path can be illuminating and is seen in Figure 19.2.

```
> # plot the path
> plot(acsCV1$glmnet.fit, xvar = "lambda")
> # add in vertical lines for the optimal values of lambda
> abline(v = log(c(acsCV1$lambda.min, acsCV1$lambda.1se)), lty = 2)
```

Setting α to 0 causes the results to be from the ridge. In this case, every variable is kept in the model but is just shrunk closer to 0. Figure 19.3, on page 283, shows the cross-validation curve. Notice in Figure 19.4, on page 284, that for every value of λ there are still all the variables, just at different sizes.

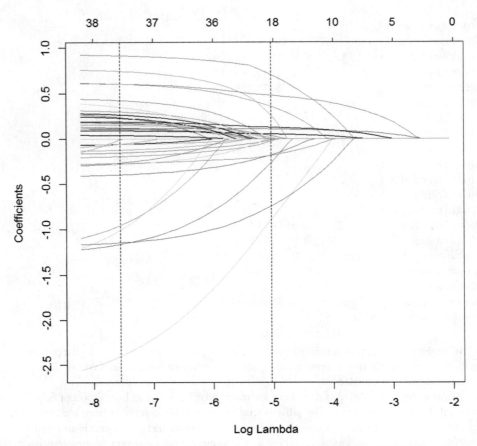

Figure 19.2   Coefficient profile plot of the `glmnet` model fitted on the ACS data. Each line represents a coefficient's value at different values of λ. The leftmost vertical line indicates the value of λ where the error is minimized and the rightmost vertical line is the next largest value of λ error that is within one standard error of the minimum.

```
> # fit the ridge model
> set.seed(71623)
> acsCV2 <- cv.glmnet(x = acsX, y = acsY, family = "binomial", nfold = 5,
+     alpha = 0)

> # look at the lambda values
> acsCV2$lambda.min
```

```
[1] 0.01272576

> acsCV2$lambda.1se

[1] 0.04681018

>
> # look at the coefficients
> coef(acsCV2, s = "lambda.1se")

45 x 1 sparse Matrix of class "dgCMatrix"
                                    1
(Intercept)             -4.8197810188
NumBedrooms              0.1027963294
NumChildren              0.0308893447
NumPeople               -0.0203037177
NumRooms                 0.0918136969
NumUnitsMobile home     -0.8470874369
NumUnitsSingle attached  0.1714879712
NumUnitsSingle detached  0.0841095530
NumVehicles              0.1583881396
NumWorkers               0.3811651456
OwnRentMortgage          0.1985621193
OwnRentOutright          0.6480126218
OwnRentRented           -0.2548147427
YearBuilt15             -0.6828640400
YearBuilt1940-1949      -0.1082928305
YearBuilt1950-1959       0.0602009151
YearBuilt1960-1969       0.0081133932
YearBuilt1970-1979      -0.0816541923
YearBuilt1980-1989       0.1593567244
YearBuilt1990-1999       0.1218212609
YearBuilt2000-2004       0.1768690849
YearBuilt2005            0.2923210334
YearBuilt2006            0.2309044444
YearBuilt2007            0.3765019705
YearBuilt2008           -0.0648999685
YearBuilt2009            0.2382560699
YearBuilt2010            0.3804282473
YearBuiltBefore 1939    -0.1648659906
ElectricBill             0.0018576432
FoodStampNo              0.3886474609
FoodStampYes            -0.3886013004
HeatingFuelCoal         -0.7005075763
```

```
HeatingFuelElectricity    -0.1370927269
HeatingFuelGas             0.0873505398
HeatingFuelNone           -0.5983944720
HeatingFuelOil             0.1241958119
HeatingFuelOther          -0.1872564710
HeatingFuelSolar          -0.0870480957
HeatingFuelWood           -0.6699727752
Insurance                  0.0003881588
LanguageAsian Pacific      0.3982023046
LanguageEnglish           -0.0851389569
LanguageOther              0.1804675114
LanguageOther European     0.0964194255
LanguageSpanish           -0.1274688978

>
> # plot the cross-validation error path
> plot(acsCV2)


> # plot the coefficient path
> plot(acsCV2$glmnet.fit, xvar = "lambda")
> abline(v = log(c(acsCV2$lambda.min, acsCV2$lambda.1se)), lty = 2)
```

Finding the optimal value of α requires an additional layer of cross-validation, and unfortunately glmnet does not do that automatically. This will require us to run cv.glmnet at various levels of α, which will take a fairly large chunk of time if performed sequentially, making this a good time to use parallelization. The most straightforward way to run code in parallel is to the use the parallel, doParallel and foreach packages.

```
> require(parallel)
Loading required package: parallel
> require(doParallel)
Loading required package: doParallel
Loading required package: foreach
Loading required package: iterators
```

First, we build some helper objects to speed along the process. When a two-layered cross-validation is run, an observation should fall in the same fold each time, so we build a vector specifying fold membership. We also specify the sequence of α values that foreach will loop over. It is generally considered better to lean toward the lasso rather than the ridge, so we consider only α values greater than 0.5.

```
> # set the seed for repeatability of random results
> set.seed(2834673)
>
> # create folds, we want observations to be in the same fold each time
> # it is run
```

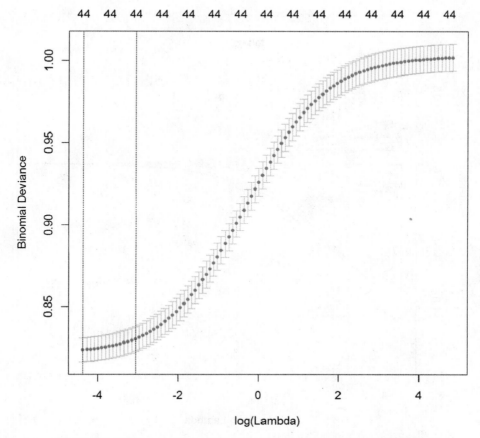

Figure 19.3   Cross-validation curve for ridge regression fitted on ACS data.

```
> theFolds <- sample(rep(x = 1:5, length.out = nrow(acsX)))
>
> # make sequence of alpha values
> alphas <- seq(from = 0.5, to = 1, by = 0.05)
```

Before running a parallel job, a cluster (even on a single machine) must be started and registered with makeCluster and registerDoParallel. After the job is done the cluster should be stopped with stopCluster. Setting .errorhandling to ''remove'' means that if an error occurs, that iteration will be skipped. Setting .inorder to FALSE means that the order of combining the results does not matter and they can be combined whenever returned, which yields significant speed improvements. Because we are using the default combination function, list, which takes multiple arguments at once, we can speed up the process by setting .multicombine to TRUE. We specify in .packages that glmnet should be loaded on each of the workers, again

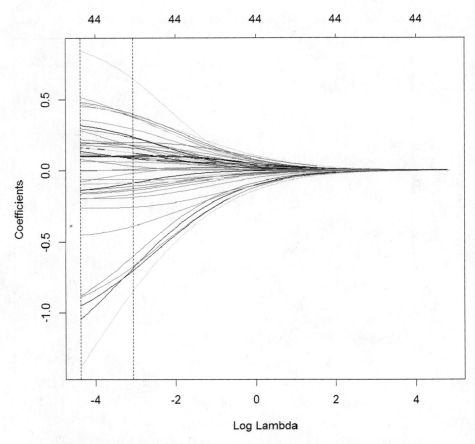

Figure 19.4   Coefficient profile plot for ridge regression fitted on ACS data.

leading to performance improvements. The operator `%dopar%` tells `foreach` to work in parallel. Parallel computing can be dependent on the `environment`, so we explicitly load some variables into the `foreach environment` using `.export`, namely, `acsX`, `acsY`, `alphas` and `theFolds`.

```
> # set the seed for repeatability of random results
> set.seed(5127151)
>
> # start a cluster with two workers
> cl <- makeCluster(2)
> # register the workers
> registerDoParallel(cl)
>
> # keep track of timing
```

```
> before <- Sys.time()
>
> # build foreach loop to run in parallel
> ## several arguments
> acsDouble <- foreach(i=1:length(alphas), .errorhandling="remove",
+                       .inorder=FALSE, .multicombine=TRUE,
+                       .export=c("acsX", "acsY", "alphas", "theFolds"),
+                       .packages="glmnet") %dopar%
+ {
+     print(alphas[i])
+     cv.glmnet(x=acsX, y=acsY, family="binomial", nfolds=5,
+               foldid=theFolds, alpha=alphas[i])
+ }
>
> # stop timing
> after <- Sys.time()
>
> # make sure to stop the cluster when done
> stopCluster(cl)
>
> # time difference
> # this will depend on speed, memory & number of cores of the machine
> after - before

Time difference of 1.443783 mins
```

The results in acsDouble should be a list with 11 instances of cv.glmnet objects. We can use sapply to check the class of each element of the list.

```
> sapply(acsDouble, class)

 [1] "cv.glmnet" "cv.glmnet" "cv.glmnet" "cv.glmnet" "cv.glmnet"
 [6] "cv.glmnet" "cv.glmnet" "cv.glmnet" "cv.glmnet" "cv.glmnet"
[11] "cv.glmnet"
```

The goal is to find the best combination of λ and α, so we need to build some code to extract the cross–validation error (including the confidence interval) and λ from each element of the list.

```
> # function for extracting info from cv.glmnet object
> extractGlmnetInfo <- function(object)
+ {
+     # find lambdas
+     lambdaMin <- object$lambda.min
+     lambda1se <- object$lambda.1se
+
+     # figure out where those lambdas fall in the path
+     whichMin <- which(object$lambda == lambdaMin)
```

```
+       which1se <- which(object$lambda == lambda1se)
+
+       # build a one line data.frame with each of the selected lambdas and
+       # its corresponding error figures
+       data.frame(lambda.min=lambdaMin, error.min=object$cvm[whichMin],
+                  lambda.1se=lambda1se, error.1se=object$cvm[which1se])
+ }
>
> # apply that function to each element of the list
> # combine it all into a data.frame
> alphaInfo <- Reduce(rbind, lapply(acsDouble, extractGlmnetInfo))
>
> # could also be done with ldply from plyr
> alphaInfo2 <- plyr::ldply(acsDouble, extractGlmnetInfo)
> identical(alphaInfo, alphaInfo2)

[1] TRUE

>
> # make a column listing the alphas
> alphaInfo$Alpha <- alphas
> alphaInfo

      lambda.min error.min  lambda.1se error.1se Alpha
1   0.0009582333 0.8220267 0.008142621 0.8275331  0.50
2   0.0009560545 0.8220226 0.007402382 0.8273936  0.55
3   0.0008763832 0.8220197 0.006785517 0.8272771  0.60
4   0.0008089692 0.8220184 0.006263554 0.8271786  0.65
5   0.0008244253 0.8220168 0.005816158 0.8270917  0.70
6   0.0007694636 0.8220151 0.005428414 0.8270161  0.75
7   0.0007213721 0.8220139 0.005585323 0.8276118  0.80
8   0.0006789385 0.8220130 0.005256774 0.8275519  0.85
9   0.0006412197 0.8220123 0.004964731 0.8274993  0.90
10  0.0006074713 0.8220128 0.004703430 0.8274524  0.95
11  0.0005770977 0.8220125 0.004468258 0.8274120  1.00
```

Now that we have this nice, unintelligible set of numbers, we should plot it to easily pick out the best combination of α and λ, which is where the plot shows minimum error. Figure 19.5 indicates that by using the one standard error methodology, the optimal α and λ are 0.75 and 0.0054284, respectively.

```
> ## prepare the data.frame for plotting multiple pieces of information
> require(reshape2)
> require(stringr)
>
> # melt the data into long format
> alphaMelt <- melt(alphaInfo, id.vars="Alpha", value.name="Value",
```

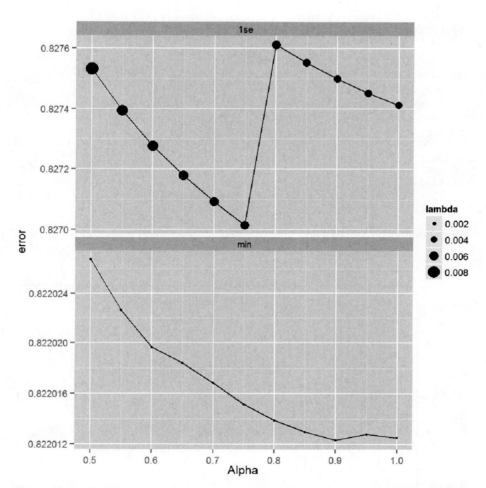

Figure 19.5   Plot of α versus error for `glmnet` cross-validation on the ACS data. The lower the error the better. The size of the dot represents the value of lambda. The top pane shows the error using the one standard error methodology (0.0054) and the bottom pane shows the error by selecting the λ (6e-04) that minimizes the error. In the top pane the error is minimized for an α of 0.75 and in the bottom pane the optimal α is 0.9.

```
+                         variable.name="Measure")
> alphaMelt$Type <- str_extract(string=alphaMelt$Measure,
+                               pattern="(min)|(1se)")
>
> # some housekeeping
> alphaMelt$Measure <- str_replace(string=alphaMelt$Measure,
+                                  pattern="\\.(min|1se)",
+                                  replacement="")
```

```
> alphaCast <- dcast(alphaMelt, Alpha + Type ~ Measure,
+                     value.var="Value")
>
> ggplot(alphaCast, aes(x=Alpha, y=error)) +
+     geom_line(aes(group=Type)) +
+     facet_wrap(~Type, scales="free_y", ncol=1) +
+     geom_point(aes(size=lambda))
```

Now that we have found the optimal value of α (0.75), we refit the model and check the results.

```
> set.seed(5127151)
> acsCV3 <- cv.glmnet(x = acsX, y = acsY, family = "binomial", nfold = 5,
+     alpha = alphaInfo$Alpha[which.min(alphaInfo$error.1se)])
```

After fitting the model we check the diagnostic plots shown in Figures 19.6 and 19.7.

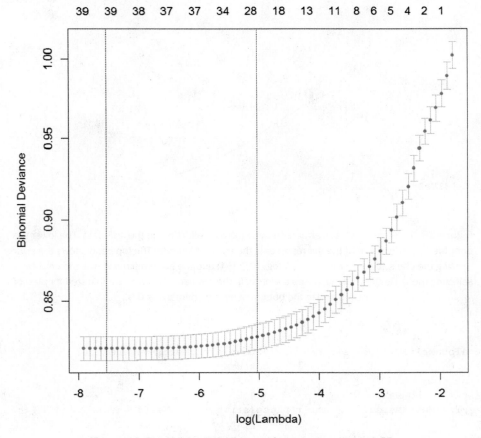

Figure 19.6   Cross-validation curve for `glmnet` with $\alpha = 0.75$.

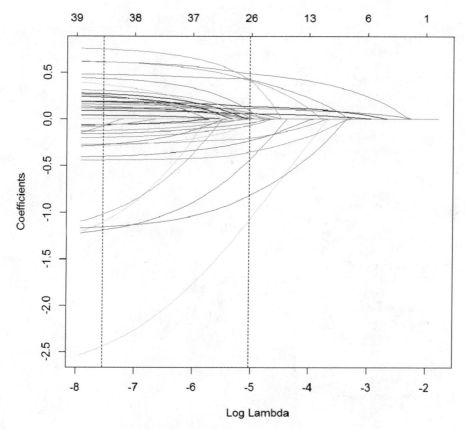

Figure 19.7   Coefficient path for `glmnet` with $\alpha = 0.75$.

```
> plot(acsCV3)
```

```
> plot(acsCV3$glmnet.fit, xvar = "lambda")
> abline(v = log(c(acsCV3$lambda.min, acsCV3$lambda.1se)), lty = 2)
```

Viewing the coefficient plot for a `glmnet` object is not yet implemented in `coefplot`, so we build it manually. Figure 19.8 shows that the number of workers in the family and not being on foodstamps are the strongest indicators of having high income, and using coal heat and living in a mobile home are the strongest indicators of having low income. There are no standard errors because `glmnet` does not calculate them.

```
> theCoef <- as.matrix(coef(acsCV3, s = "lambda.1se"))
> coefDF <- data.frame(Value = theCoef,
+       Coefficient = rownames(theCoef))
> coefDF <- coefDF[nonzeroCoef(coef(acsCV3, s = "lambda.1se")), ]
> ggplot(coefDF, aes(x = X1, y = reorder(Coefficient, X1))) +
```

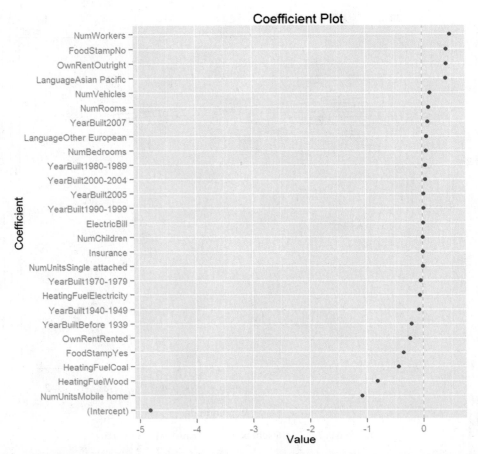

Figure 19.8 Coefficient plot for `glmnet` on ACS data. This shows that the number of workers in the family and not being on foodstamps are the strongest indicators of having high income, and using coal heat and living in a mobile home are the strongest indicators of having low income. There are no standard errors because `glmnet` does not calculate them.

```
+       geom_vline(xintercept = 0, color = "grey", linetype = 2) +
+       geom_point(color = "blue") + labs(x = "Value",
+       y = "Coefficient", title = "Coefficient Plot")
```

19.2 Bayesian Shrinkage

For Bayesians, shrinkage can come in the form of weakly informative priors.[3] This can be particularly useful when a model is built on data that does not have a large enough number

---

3. From a Bayesian point of view, the penalty terms in the Elastic Net could be considered log-priors as well.

of rows for some combinations of the variables. For this example, we blatantly steal an example from Andrew Gelman's and Jennifer Hill's book, *Data Analysis Using Regression and Multilevel/Hierarchical Models*, examining voter preference. The data have been cleaned up and posted at http://jaredlander.com/data/ideo.rdata.

```
> load("data/ideo.rdata")
> head(ideo)
```

```
    Year        Vote Age Gender  Race
1   1948    democrat  NA    male white
2   1948  republican  NA  female white
3   1948    democrat  NA  female white
4   1948  republican  NA  female white
5   1948    democrat  NA    male white
6   1948  republican  NA  female white
                              Education             Income
1     grade school of less (0-8 grades)  34 to 67 percentile
2 high school (12 grades or fewer, incl  96 to 100 percentile
3 high school (12 grades or fewer, incl  68 to 95 percentile
4 some college(13 grades or more,but no  96 to 100 percentile
5 some college(13 grades or more,but no  68 to 95 percentile
6 high school (12 grades or fewer, incl  96 to 100 percentile
                      Religion
1              protestant
2              protestant
3 catholic (roman catholic)
4              protestant
5 catholic (roman catholic)
6              protestant
```

To show the need for shrinkage, we fit a separate model for each election year and then display the resulting coefficients for the black level of Race.

```
> ## fit a bunch of models
> # figure out the years we will be fitting the models on
> theYears <- unique(ideo$Year)
>
> # create an empty list
> # as many elements as years
> # it holds the results
> # preallocating the object makes the code run faster
> results <- vector(mode="list", length=length(theYears))
> # give good names to the list
> names(results) <- theYears
>
> ## loop through the years
```

```
> # fit a model on the subset of data for that year
> for(i in theYears)
+ {
+     results[[as.character(i)]] <- glm(Vote ~ Race + Income + Gender +
+                                     Education,
+                              data=ideo, subset=Year==i,
+                              family=binomial(link="logit"))
+ }
```

Now that we have all of these models, we can plot the coefficients with `multiplot`. Figure 19.9 shows the coefficient for the `black level` of Race for each model. The result for the model from 1964 is clearly far different from the other models. Figure 19.9 shows standard errors, which threw off the scale so much that we had to restrict the plot window to still see variation in the other points. Fitting a series of models like this and

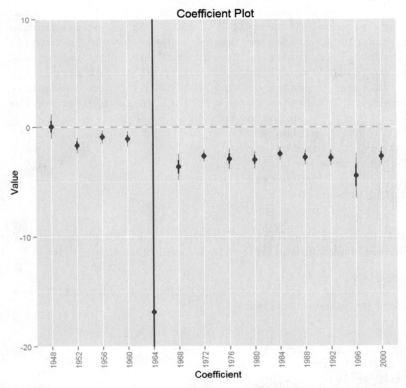

Figure 19.9   Plot showing the coefficient for the `black level` of Race for each of the models. The coefficient for 1964 has a standard error that is orders of magnitude bigger than for the other years. It is so out of proportion that the plot had to be truncated to still see variation in the other data points.

then plotting the coefficients over time has been termed the "secret weapon" by Gelman due to its usefulness and simplicity.

```
> require(coefplot)
> # get the coefficient information
> voteInfo <- multiplot(results, coefficients="Raceblack", plot=FALSE)
> head(voteInfo)

        Value Coefficient   HighInner     LowInner    HighOuter
1    0.07119541   Raceblack    0.6297813   -0.4873905    1.1883673
2   -1.68490828   Raceblack   -1.3175506   -2.0522659   -0.9501930
3   -0.89178359   Raceblack   -0.5857195   -1.1978476   -0.2796555
4   -1.07674848   Raceblack   -0.7099648   -1.4435322   -0.3431811
5  -16.85751152   Raceblack  382.1171424 -415.8321655  781.0917963
6   -3.65505395   Raceblack   -3.0580572   -4.2520507   -2.4610605
      LowOuter Model
1    -1.045976  1948
2    -2.419624  1952
3    -1.503912  1956
4    -1.810316  1960
5  -814.806819  1964
6    -4.849047  1968

>
> # plot it restricting the window to (-20, 10)
> multiplot(results, coefficients="Raceblack", secret.weapon=TRUE) +
+     coord_flip(xlim=c(-20, 10))
```

By comparing the model for 1964 to the other models, we can see that something is clearly wrong with the estimate. To fix this we put a prior on the coefficients in the model. The simplest way to do this is to use Gelman's bayesglm function in the arm package. By default it sets a Cauchy prior with scale 2.5. Because the arm package namespace interferes with the coefplot namespace, we do not load the package but rather just call the function using the :: operator.

```
> resultsB <- vector(mode="list", length=length(theYears))
> # give good names to the list
> names(resultsB) <- theYears
>
> ## loop through the years
> ## fit a model on the subset of data for that year
> for(i in theYears)
+ {
+     # fit model with Cauchy priors with a scale of 2.5
+     resultsB[[as.character(i)]] <-
+         arm::bayesglm(Vote ~ Race + Income + Gender + Education,
```

```
+                                data=ideo[ideo$Year == i, ],
+                                family=binomial(link="logit"),
+                                prior.scale=2.5, prior.df=1)
+ }
>
> # build the coefficient plot
> multiplot(resultsB, coefficients="Raceblack", secret.weapon=TRUE)
```

Simply adding Cauchy priors dramatically shrinks both the estimate and the standard error of the coefficient, as seen in Figure 19.10. Remember, the models were fitted independently, meaning that it was simply the prior that did the fix and not information from the other years. It turns out that the survey conducted in 1964 underrepresented black respondents, which led to a highly inaccurate measure.

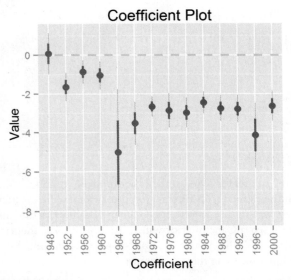

Figure 19.10   Coefficient plot (the secret weapon) for the `black level` of Race for each of the models with a Cauchy prior. A simple change like adding a prior dramatically changed the point estimate and standard error.

The default prior is a Cauchy with scale 2.5, which is the same as a t distribution with 1 degree of freedom. These arguments, `prior.scale` and `prior.df`, can be changed to represent a t distribution with any degrees of freedom. Setting both to infinity (`Inf`) makes them normal priors, which is identical to running an ordinary `glm`.

19.3 Conclusion

Regularization and shrinkage play important roles in modern statistics. They help fit models to poorly designed data, and prevent overfitting of complex models. The former is done using Bayesian methods, in this case the simple `bayesglm`; the latter is done with the lasso, ridge or Elastic Net using `glmnet`. Both are useful tools to have.

Chapter 20

Nonlinear Models

A key tenet of linear models is a linear relationship, which is actually reflected in the coefficients, not the predictors. While this is a nice simplifying assumption, in reality nonlinearity often holds. Fortunately, modern computing makes fitting nonlinear models not much more difficult than fitting linear models. Typical implementations are nonlinear least squares, splines, decision trees and random forests and generalized additive models (GAMs).

20.1 Nonlinear Least Squares

The nonlinear least squares model uses squared error loss to find the optimal parameters of a generic (nonlinear) function of the predictors.

$$y_i = f(x_i, \beta) \tag{20.1}$$

A common application for a nonlinear model is using the location of WiFi-connected devices to determine the location of the WiFi hotspot. In a problem like this, the locations of the devices in a two-dimensional grid are known, and they report their distance to the hotspot but with some random noise due to the fluctuation of the signal strength. A sample dataset is available at http://jaredlander.com/data/wifi.rdata.

```
> load("data/wifi.rdata")
> head(wifi)

  Distance        x         y
1 21.87559 28.60461 68.429628
2 67.68198 90.29680 29.155945
3 79.25427 83.48934  0.371902
4 44.73767 61.39133 80.258138
5 39.71233 19.55080 83.805855
6 56.65595 71.93928 65.551340
```

This dataset is easy to plot with ggplot2. The x- and y-axes are the device's positions in the grid and the color represents how far the device is from the hotspot, blue being closer and red being farther (see Figure 20.1).

```
> require(ggplot2)
> ggplot(wifi, aes(x=x, y=y, color=Distance)) + geom_point() +
+     scale_color_gradient2(low="blue", mid="white", high="red",
+                               midpoint=mean(wifi$Distance))
```

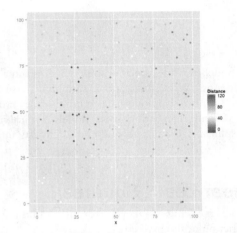

Figure 20.1   Plot of WiFi device position colored by distance from the hotspot. Blue points are closer and red points are farther.

The distance between a device i and the hotspot is

$$d_i = \sqrt{(\beta_x - x_i)^2 + (\beta_y - y_i)^2} \qquad (20.2)$$

where β_x and β_y are the unknown x- and y-coordinates of the hotspot.

A standard function in R for computing nonlinear least squares is nls. Since these problems are usually intractable, numerical methods are used, which can be sensitive to starting values, so best guesses need to be specified. The function takes a formula—just like lm—except the equation and coefficients are explicitly specified. The starting values for the coefficients are given in a named list.

```
> # specify the square root model
> # starting values are at the center of the grid
> wifiMod1 <- nls(Distance ~ sqrt((betaX - x)^2 + (betaY - y)^2),
+     data = wifi, start = list(betaX = 50, betaY = 50))
> summary(wifiMod1)
```

```
Formula: Distance ~ sqrt((betaX - x)^2 + (betaY - y)^2)

Parameters:
       Estimate Std. Error t value Pr(>|t|)
betaX    17.851     1.289   13.85   <2e-16 ***
betaY    52.906     1.476   35.85   <2e-16 ***
---
Signif. codes:  0 '***' 0.001 '**' 0.01 '*' 0.05 '.' 0.1 ' ' 1

Residual standard error: 13.73 on 198 degrees of freedom

Number of iterations to convergence: 6
Achieved convergence tolerance: 3.846e-06
```

This estimates that the hotspot is located at 17.8506668, 52.9056438. Plotting this in Figure 20.2, we see that the hotspot is located amidst the "close" blue points, indicating a good fit.

```
> ggplot(wifi, aes(x = x, y = y, color = Distance)) + geom_point() +
+       scale_color_gradient2(low = "blue", mid = "white", high = "red",
+               midpoint = mean(wifi$Distance)) +
+       geom_point(data = as.data.frame(t(coef(wifiMod1))),
+                       aes(x = betaX, y = betaY), size = 5, color = "green")
```

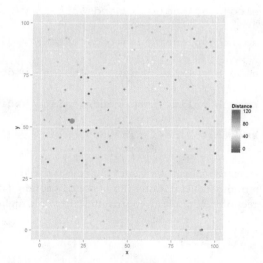

Figure 20.2   Plot of WiFi devices. The hotspot is the large green dot. Its position in the middle of the blue dots indicates a good fit.

20.2 Splines

A smoothing spline can be used to fit a smooth to data that exhibit nonlinear behavior and even make predictions on new data. A spline is a function f that is a linear combination of N functions (one for each unique data point) that are transformations of the variable x.

$$f(x) = \sum_{j=1}^{N} N_J(x)\theta_j \tag{20.3}$$

The goal is to find the function f that minimizes

$$RSS(f, \lambda) = \sum_{i=1}^{N}\{y_i - f(x_i)\}^2 + \lambda \int \{f''(t)\}^2 \, dt \tag{20.4}$$

where λ is the smoothing parameter. Small λs make for a rough smooth and large λs make for a smooth smooth.

This is accomplished in R using `smooth.spline`. It returns a list of items where `x` holds the unique values of the data, `y` are the corresponding fitted values and `df` is the degrees of freedom used. We demonstrate with the `diamonds` data.

```
> data(diamonds)
> # fit with a few different degrees of freedom
> # the degrees of freedom must be greater than 1
> # but less than the number of unique x values in the data
> diaSpline1 <- smooth.spline(x=diamonds$carat, y=diamonds$price)
> diaSpline2 <- smooth.spline(x=diamonds$carat, y=diamonds$price,
+                             df=2)
> diaSpline3 <- smooth.spline(x=diamonds$carat, y=diamonds$price,
+                             df=10)
> diaSpline4 <- smooth.spline(x=diamonds$carat, y=diamonds$price,
+                             df=20)
> diaSpline5 <- smooth.spline(x=diamonds$carat, y=diamonds$price,
+                             df=50)
> diaSpline6 <- smooth.spline(x=diamonds$carat, y=diamonds$price,
+                             df=100)
```

To plot these we extract the information from the objects, build a `data.frame`, then add a new layer on top of the standard scatterplot of the `diamonds` data. Figure 20.3 shows this. Fewer degrees of freedom leads to straighter fits while higher degrees of freedom leads to more interpolating lines.

```
> get.spline.info <- function(object)
+ {
+     data.frame(x=object$x, y=object$y, df=object$df)
+ }
```

```
>
> require(plyr)
> # combine results into one data.frame
> splineDF <- ldply(list(diaSpline1, diaSpline2, diaSpline3,
+                        diaSpline4, diaSpline5, diaSpline6),
                    get.spline.info)
> head(splineDF)

     x        y       df
1 0.20 361.9112 101.9053
2 0.21 397.1761 101.9053
```

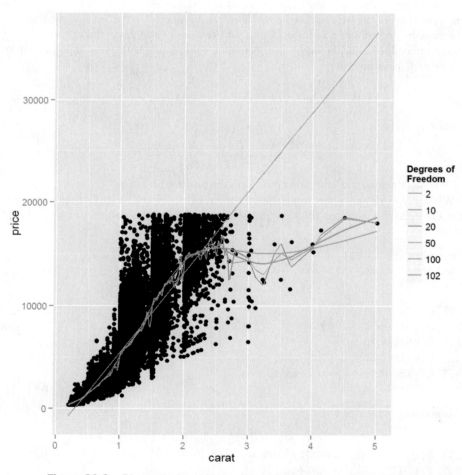

Figure 20.3   Diamonds data with a number of different smoothing splines.

```
3 0.22 437.9095 101.9053
4 0.23 479.9756 101.9053
5 0.24 517.0467 101.9053
6 0.25 542.2470 101.9053

>
> g <- ggplot(diamonds, aes(x=carat, y=price)) + geom_point()
> g + geom_line(data=splineDF,
+                    aes(x=x, y=y, color=factor(round(df, 0)),
+        group=df)) + scale_color_discrete("Degrees of \nFreedom")
```

Making predictions on new data is done, as usual, with predict.

Another type of spline is the basis spline, which creates new predictors based on transformations of the original predictors. The best basis spline is the natural cubic spline because it creates smooth transitions at interior breakpoints and forces linear behavior beyond the endpoints of the input data. A natural cubic spline with K breakpoints (knots) is made of K basis functions

$$N_1(X) = 1, N_2(X) = X, N_{k+2} = d_k(X) - d_{K-1}(X) \tag{20.5}$$

where

$$d_k(X) = \frac{(X - \xi_k)_+^3 - (X - \xi_K)_+^3}{\xi_K - \xi_k} \tag{20.6}$$

and ξ is the location of a knot and t_+ denotes the positive part of t.

While the math may seem complicated, natural cubic splines are easily fitted using ns from the splines package. It takes a predictor variable and the number of new variables to return.

```
> require(splines)
> head(ns(diamonds$carat, df = 1))

              1
[1,] 0.00500073
[2,] 0.00166691
[3,] 0.00500073
[4,] 0.01500219
[5,] 0.01833601
[6,] 0.00666764

> head(ns(diamonds$carat, df = 2))

              1            2
[1,] 0.013777685 -0.007265289
[2,] 0.004593275 -0.002422504
[3,] 0.013777685 -0.007265289
```

```
[4,]  0.041275287 -0.021735857
[5,]  0.050408348 -0.026525299
[6,]  0.018367750 -0.009684459

> head(ns(diamonds$carat, df = 3))

                  1          2           3
[1,] -0.03025012 0.06432178 -0.03404826
[2,] -0.01010308 0.02146773 -0.01136379
[3,] -0.03025012 0.06432178 -0.03404826
[4,] -0.08915435 0.19076693 -0.10098109
[5,] -0.10788271 0.23166685 -0.12263116
[6,] -0.04026453 0.08566738 -0.04534740

> head(ns(diamonds$carat, df = 4))

                 1           2          3           4
[1,] 3.214286e-04 -0.04811737 0.10035562 -0.05223825
[2,] 1.190476e-05 -0.01611797 0.03361632 -0.01749835
[3,] 3.214286e-04 -0.04811737 0.10035562 -0.05223825
[4,] 8.678571e-03 -0.13796549 0.28774667 -0.14978118
[5,] 1.584524e-02 -0.16428790 0.34264579 -0.17835789
[6,] 7.619048e-04 -0.06388053 0.13323194 -0.06935141
```

These new predictors can then be used in any model just like any other predictor. More knots means a more interpolating fit. Plotting the result of a natural cubic spline overlaid on data is easy with `ggplot2`. Figure 20.4a shows this for the `diamonds` data and

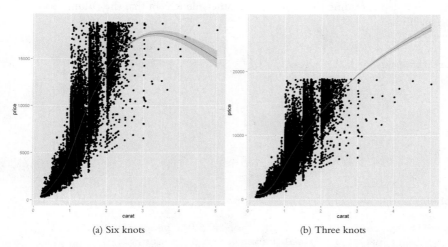

(a) Six knots   (b) Three knots

Figure 20.4   Scatterplot of price versus carat with a regression fitted on a natural cubic spline.

six knots, and Figure 20.4b shows it with three knots. Notice that having six knots fits the data more smoothly.

```
> g <- ggplot(diamonds, aes(x = carat, y = price)) + geom_point()
> g + stat_smooth(method = "lm", formula = y ~ ns(x, 6), color = "blue")
> g + stat_smooth(method = "lm", formula = y ~ ns(x, 3), color = "red")
```

20.3   Generalized Additive Models

Another method for fitting nonlinear models is generalized additive models (GAMs), which fit a separate smoothing function on each predictor independently. As the name implies, these are general and work in a number of regression contexts, meaning the response can be continuous, binary, count and other types. Like many of the best modern techniques in machine learning, this is the brainchild of Trevor Hastie and Robert Tibshirani based on work from John Chambers, the creator of S, the precursor of R.

They are specified as

$$E(Y|X_1, X_2, \ldots, X_p) = \alpha + f_1(X_1) + f_2(X_2) + \cdots + f_p(X_p) \qquad (20.7)$$

where $X_1, X_2, \ldots, X_p$ are ordinary predictors and the f_j's are any smoothing functions.

The mgcv package fits GAMs with a syntax very similar to glm. To illustrate we use data on credit scores from the University of California–Irvine Machine Learning Repository at http://archive.ics.uci.edu/ml/datasets/Statlog+(German+Credit+Data). The data are stored in a space-separated text file with no headers where categorical data have been labeled with nonobvious codes. This arcane file format goes back to a time when data storage was more limited but has, for some reason, persisted.

The first step is reading the data like any other file except that the column names need to be specified.

```
> # make vector of column names
> creditNames <- c("Checking", "Duration", "CreditHistory",
+     "Purpose", "CreditAmount", "Savings", "Employment",
+     "InstallmentRate", "GenderMarital", "OtherDebtors",
+     "YearsAtResidence", "RealEstate", "Age",
+     "OtherInstallment", "Housing", "ExistingCredits", "Job",
+     "NumLiable", "Phone", "Foreign", "Credit")
>
> # use read.table to read the file
> # specify that headers are not included
> # the col.names are from creditNames
> theURL <- "http://archive.ics.uci.edu/ml/
+             machine-learning-databases/statlog/german/german.data
> credit <- read.table(the URL sep = " ", header = FALSE,
+                     col.names = creditNames,
```

```
+                       stringsAsFactors = FALSE)
>
> head(credit)

  Checking Duration CreditHistory Purpose CreditAmount Savings
1    A11        6        A34        A43          1169     A65
2    A12       48        A32        A43          5951     A61
3    A14       12        A34        A46          2096     A61
4    A11       42        A32        A42          7882     A61
5    A11       24        A33        A40          4870     A61
6    A14       36        A32        A46          9055     A65
  Employment InstallmentRate GenderMarital OtherDebtors
1     A75           4             A93          A101
2     A73           2             A92          A101
3     A74           2             A93          A101
4     A74           2             A93          A103
5     A73           3             A93          A101
6     A73           2             A93          A101
  YearsAtResidence RealEstate Age OtherInstallment Housing
1        4          A121      67        A143          A152
2        2          A121      22        A143          A152
3        3          A121      49        A143          A152
4        4          A122      45        A143          A153
5        4          A124      53        A143          A153
6        4          A124      35        A143          A153
  ExistingCredits  Job NumLiable Phone Foreign Credit
1       2 A173         1    A192   A201     1
2       1 A173         1    A191   A201     2
3       1 A172         2    A191   A201     1
4       1 A173         2    A191   A201     1
5       2 A173         2    A191   A201     2
6       1 A172         2    A192   A201     1
```

Now comes the unpleasant task of translating the codes to meaningful data. To save time and effort we decode only the variables we care about for a simple model. The simplest way of decoding is to create named vectors where the name is the code and the value is the new data.

```
> # before
> head(credit[, c("CreditHistory", "Purpose", "Employment", "Credit")])

  CreditHistory Purpose Employment Credit
1      A34        A43      A75        1
2      A32        A43      A73        2
```

```
3              A34     A46        A74        1
4              A32     A42        A74        1
5              A33     A40        A73        2
6              A32     A46        A73        1


>
> creditHistory <- c(A30 = "All Paid", A31 = "All Paid This Bank",
+     A32 = "Up To Date", A33 = "Late Payment",
+     A34 = "Critical Account")
>
> purpose <- c(A40 = "car (new)", A41 = "car (used)",
+     A42 = "furniture/equipment", A43 = "radio/television",
+     A44 = "domestic appliances", A45 = "repairs",
+     A46 = "education",  A47 = "(vacation - does not exist?)",
+     A48 = "retraining", A49 = "business", A410 = "others")
>
> employment <- c(A71 = "unemployed", A72 = "< 1 year",
+     A73 = "1 - 4 years", A74 = "4 - 7 years", A75 = ">= 7 years")
>
> credit$CreditHistory <- creditHistory[credit$CreditHistory]
> credit$Purpose <- purpose[credit$Purpose]
> credit$Employment <- employment[credit$Employment]
>
> # code credit as good/bad
> credit$Credit <- ifelse(credit$Credit == 1, "Good", "Bad")
> # make good the base levels
> credit$Credit <- factor(credit$Credit, levels = c("Good", "Bad"))
>
> # after
> head(credit[, c("CreditHistory", "Purpose", "Employment",
    "Credit")])

    CreditHistory                 Purpose  Employment Credit
1 Critical Account     radio/television  >= 7 years   Good
2       Up To Date     radio/television  1 - 4 years   Bad
3 Critical Account             education  4 - 7 years  Good
4       Up To Date furniture/equipment  4 - 7 years  Good
5     Late Payment            car (new)  1 - 4 years   Bad
6       Up To Date             education  1 - 4 years  Good
```

Viewing the data will help give a sense of the relationship between the variables. Figures 20.5 and 20.6 show that there is not a clear linear relationship, so a GAM may be appropriate.

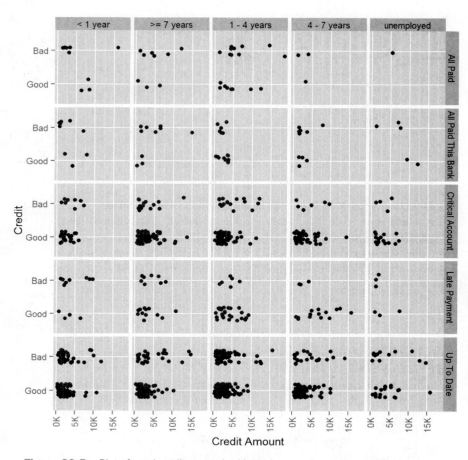

Figure 20.5 Plot of good credit versus bad based on credit amount, credit history and employment status.

```
> require(useful)
> ggplot(credit, aes(x=CreditAmount, y=Credit)) +
+     geom_jitter(position = position_jitter(height = .2)) +
+     facet_grid(CreditHistory ~ Employment) +
+     xlab("Credit Amount") +
+     theme(axis.text.x=element_text(angle=90, hjust=1, vjust=.5)) +
+     scale_x_continuous(labels=multiple)
>
> ggplot(credit, aes(x=CreditAmount, y=Age)) +
+     geom_point(aes(color=Credit)) +
+     facet_grid(CreditHistory ~ Employment) +
```

```
+     xlab("Credit Amount") +
+     theme(axis.text.x=element_text(angle=90, hjust=1, vjust=.5)) +
+     scale_x_continuous(labels=multiple)
```

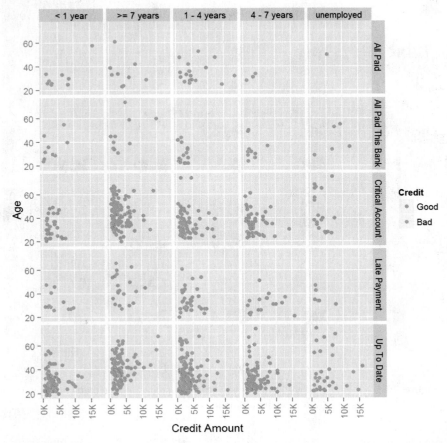

Figure 20.6   Plot of age versus credit amount faceted by credit history and employment status, color coded by credit.

Using gam is very similar to using other modeling functions like lm and glm that take a formula argument. The difference is that continuous variables, such as CreditAmount and Age, can be transformed using a nonparametric smoothing function such as a spline or tensor product.[1]

_____

1. Tensor products are a way of representing transformation functions of predictors, possibly measured on different units.

```
> require(mgcv)
> # fit a logistic GAM
> # apply a tensor product on CreditAmount and a spline on Age
> creditGam <- gam(Credit ~ te(CreditAmount) + s(Age) + CreditHistory +
+                  Employment,
+                  data=credit, family=binomial(link="logit"))
> summary(creditGam)
```

```
Family: binomial
Link function: logit

Formula:
Credit ~ te(CreditAmount) + s(Age) + CreditHistory + Employment

Parametric coefficients:
```

	Estimate	Std. Error	z value	Pr(>|z|)
(Intercept)	0.662840	0.372377	1.780	0.07507
CreditHistoryAll Paid This Bank	0.008412	0.453267	0.019	0.98519
CreditHistoryCritical Account	-1.809046	0.376326	-4.807	1.53e-06
CreditHistoryLate Payment	-1.136008	0.412776	-2.752	0.00592
CreditHistoryUp To Date	-1.104274	0.355208	-3.109	0.00188
Employment>= 7 years	-0.388518	0.240343	-1.617	0.10598
Employment1 - 4 years	-0.380981	0.204292	-1.865	0.06220
Employment4 - 7 years	-0.820943	0.252069	-3.257	0.00113
Employmentunemployed	-0.092727	0.334975	-0.277	0.78192

(Intercept)	.
CreditHistoryAll Paid This Bank	
CreditHistoryCritical Account	***
CreditHistoryLate Payment	**
CreditHistoryUp To Date	**
Employment>= 7 years	
Employment1 - 4 years	.
Employment4 - 7 years	**
Employmentunemployed	

```
---
Signif. codes:  0 '***' 0.001 '**' 0.01 '*' 0.05 '.' 0.1 ' ' 1

Approximate significance of smooth terms:
```

	edf	Ref.df	Chi.sq	p-value	
te(CreditAmount)	2.415	2.783	20.79	0.000112	***
s(Age)	1.932	2.435	6.13	0.068957	.

```
---
Signif. codes:  0 '***' 0.001 '**' 0.01 '*' 0.05 '.' 0.1 ' ' 1
```

```
R-sq.(adj) =  0.0922    Deviance explained = 8.57%
UBRE score = 0.1437   Scale est. = 1          n = 1000
```

The smoother is fitted automatically in the fitting process and can be viewed after the fact. Figure 20.7 shows `CreditAmount` and `Age` with their applied smoothers, a tensor product and a spline, respectively. The gray, shaded area represents the confidence interval for the smooths.

```
> plot(creditGam, select = 1, se = TRUE, shade = TRUE)
> plot(creditGam, select = 2, se = TRUE, shade = TRUE)
```

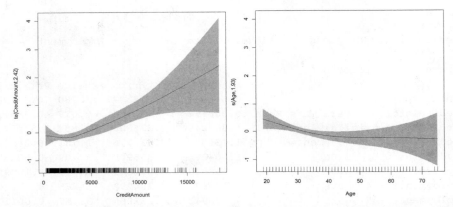

Figure 20.7   The smoother result for fitting a GAM on credit data. The shaded region represents two pointwise standard deviations.

20.4   Decision Trees

A relatively modern technique for fitting nonlinear models is the decision tree. Decision trees work for both regression and classification by performing binary splits on the recursive predictors.

For regression trees, the predictors are partitioned into M regions $R_1, R_2, \ldots, R_M$ and the response y is modeled as the average for a region with

$$\hat{f}(x) = \sum_{m=1}^{M} \hat{c}_m I(x \in R_m) \tag{20.8}$$

where

$$\hat{c}_m = \text{avg}(y_i | x_i \in R_m) \tag{20.9}$$

is the average y value for the region.

The method for classification trees is similar. The predictors are partitioned into M regions and the proportion of each class in each of the regions, $\hat{p}_{mk}$, is calculated as

$$\hat{p}_{mk} = \frac{1}{N_m} \sum_{x_i \in R_m} I(y_i = k) \tag{20.10}$$

where N_m is the number of items in region m and the summation counts the number of observations of class k in region m.

Trees can be calculated with the rpart function in rpart. Like other modeling functions, it uses the formula interface but does not take interactions.

```
> require(rpart)
> creditTree <- rpart(Credit ~ CreditAmount + Age +
+     CreditHistory + Employment, data = credit)
```

Printing the object displays the tree in text form.

```
> creditTree

n= 1000

node), split, n, loss, yval, (yprob)
      * denotes terminal node

1) root 1000 300 Good (0.7000000 0.3000000)
   2) CreditHistory=Critical Account,Late Payment,Up To
      Date 911 247 Good (0.7288694 0.2711306)
     4) CreditAmount< 7760.5 846 211 Good (0.7505910 0.2494090) *
     5) CreditAmount>=7760.5 65   29 Bad (0.4461538 0.5538462)
      10) Age>=29.5 40   17 Good (0.5750000 0.4250000)
        20) Age< 38.5 19    4 Good (0.7894737 0.2105263) *
        21) Age>=38.5 21    8 Bad (0.3809524 0.6190476) *
      11) Age< 29.5 25    6 Bad (0.2400000 0.7600000) *
   3) CreditHistory=All Paid,All Paid This Bank 89   36
      Bad (0.4044944 0.5955056) *
```

The printed tree has one line per node. The first node is the root for all the data and shows that there are 1,000 observations of which 300 are considered "Bad." The next level of indentation is the first split, which is on CreditHistory. One direction—where CreditHistory equals either "Critical Account," "Late Payment" or "Up To Date"—contains 911 observations of which 247 are considered "Bad." This has a 73% probability of having good credit. The other direction—where CreditHistory equals either "All Paid" or "All Paid This Bank"—has a 60% probability of having bad credit. The next level of indentation represents the next split.

Continuing to read the results this way could be laborious; plotting will be easier. Figure 20.8 shows the splits. Nodes split to the left meet the criteria while nodes to the right do not. Each terminal node is labelled by the predicted class, either "Good" or "Bad." The percentage is read from left to right, with the probability of being "Good" on the left.

```
> require(rpart.plot)
> rpart.plot(creditTree, extra = 4)
```

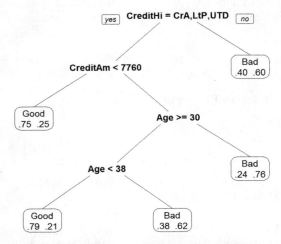

Figure 20.8   Display of decision tree based on credit data. Nodes split to the left meet the criteria while nodes to the right do not. Each terminal node is labeled by the predicted class, either "Good" or "Bad." The percentage is read from left to right, with the probability of being "Good" on the left.

While trees are easy to interpret and fit data nicely, they tend to be unstable with high variance due to overfitting. A slight change in the training data can cause a significant difference in the model.

20.5   Random Forests

Random forests are a type of ensemble method. An ensemble method is a process in which numerous models are fitted and the results are combined for stronger predictions. While this provides great predictions, inference and explainability are often limited. Random forests are composed of a number of decision trees where the included predictors are chosen at random. The name comes from randomly building trees to make a forest.

In the case of the credit data we will use `CreditHistory`, `Purpose`, `Employment`, `Duration`, `Age` and `CreditAmount`. Some trees will have just `CreditHistory` and `Employment`, another will have `Purpose`, `Employment` and `Age`, while another will have `CreditHistory`, `Purpose`, `Employment` and `Age`. All of these different trees cover all the bases and make for a random forest that should have strong predictive power.

Fitting the random forest is done with `randomForest` from the `randomForest` package. Normally, `randomForest` can be used with a `formula`, but sometimes that fails and individual predictor and response `matrices` should be supplied.

```
> require(useful)
> require(randomForest)
> # build the predictor and response matrices
> creditFormula <- Credit ~ CreditHistory + Purpose + Employment +
+       Duration + Age + CreditAmount
> creditX <- build.x(creditFormula, data=credit)
> creditY <- build.y(creditFormula, data=credit)
>
> # fit the random forest
> creditForest <- randomForest(x=creditX, y=creditY)
>
> creditForest

Call:
 randomForest(x = creditX, y = creditY)
               Type of random forest: classification
                     Number of trees: 500
No. of variables tried at each split: 4

        OOB estimate of  error rate: 28.2%
Confusion matrix:
     Good Bad class.error
Good  649  51  0.07285714
Bad   231  69  0.77000000
```

The displayed information shows that 500 trees were built and four variables were assessed at each split; the confusion matrix shows that this is not exactly the best fit and that there is room for improvement.

20.6 Conclusion

With modern computing power, the previously necessary simplifying assumptions of linearity and normality are starting to give way to nonparametric techniques. Popular implementations are nonlinear least squares, splines, generalized additive models, decision trees and random forests. As with every other method, these all have their benefits and costs.

Chapter 21

Time Series and Autocorrelation

A big part of statistics, particularly for financial and econometric data, is analyzing time series, data that are autocorrelated over time. That is, one observation depends on previous observations and the order matters. Special care needs to be taken to account for this dependency. R has a number of built-in functions and packages to make working with time series easier.

21.1 Autoregressive Moving Average

One of the most common ways of fitting time series models is to use autoregressive (AR), moving average (MA) or both (ARMA). These models are well represented in R and are fairly easy to work with. The formula for an ARMA(p, q) is

$$X_t - \Phi_1 X_{t-1} - \cdots - \Phi_p X_{t-p} = Z_t + \theta_1 Z_{t-1} + \cdots + \theta_q Z_{t-q} \qquad (21.1)$$

where

$$Z_t \sim \text{WN}(0, \sigma^2) \qquad (21.2)$$

is white noise, which is essentially random data.

AR models can be thought of as linear regressions of the current value of the time series against previous values. MA models are, similarly, linear regressions of the current value of the time series against current and previous residuals.

For an illustration, we will make use of the World Bank API to download gross domestic product (GDP) for a number of countries from 1960 through 2011.

```
> # load the World Bank API package
> require(WDI)
> # pull the data
> gdp <- WDI(country=c("US", "CA", "GB", "DE", "CN", "JP", "SG", "IL"),
```

```
+                 indicator=c("NY.GDP.PCAP.CD", "NY.GDP.MKTP.CD"),
+                 start=1960, end=2011)
> # give it good names
> names(gdp) <- c("iso2c", "Country", "Year", "PerCapGDP", "GDP")
```

After downloading, we can inspect the data, which are stored in long country-year
format with a plot of per capita GDP shown in Figure 21.1a. Figure 21.1b shows absolute
GDP, illustrating that while China's GDP has jumped significantly in the past ten years, its
per capita GDP has only marginally increased.

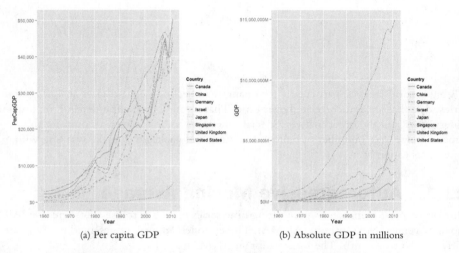

(a) Per capita GDP   (b) Absolute GDP in millions

Figure 21.1   GDP for a number of nations from 1960 to 2011.

```
> head(gdp)

  iso2c Country Year PerCapGDP          GDP
1    CA  Canada 1960  2294.569 41093453545
2    CA  Canada 1961  2231.294 40767969454
3    CA  Canada 1962  2255.230 41978852041
4    CA  Canada 1963  2354.839 44657169109
5    CA  Canada 1964  2529.518 48882938810
6    CA  Canada 1965  2739.586 53909570342

> require(ggplot2)
> require(scales)
> # per capita GDP
> ggplot(gdp, aes(Year, PerCapGDP, color=Country, linetype=Country)) +
+     geom_line() + scale_y_continuous(label=dollar)
>
> require(useful)
```

```
> # absolute GDP
> ggplot(gdp, aes(Year, GDP, color=Country, linetype=Country)) +
+     geom_line() +
+     scale_y_continuous(label=multiple_format(extra=dollar,
+                                               multiple="M"))
```

First we will only look at only one time series, so we extract the data for the United States. See Figure 21.2.

```
> # get US data
> us <- gdp$PerCapGDP[gdp$Country == "United States"]
> # convert it to a time series
> us <- ts(us, start = min(gdp$Year), end = max(gdp$Year))
> us

Time Series:
Start = 1960
End = 2011
Frequency = 1
 [1]    2881.100   2934.553   3107.937   3232.208   3423.396   3664.802
 [7]    3972.123   4152.020   4491.424   4802.642   4997.757   5360.178
[13]    5836.224   6461.736   6948.198   7516.680   8297.292   9142.795
[19]   10225.307  11301.682  12179.558  13526.187  13932.678  15000.086
[25]   16539.383  17588.810  18427.288  19393.782  20703.152  22039.227
[31]   23037.941  23443.263  24411.143  25326.736  26577.761  27559.167
[37]   28772.356  30281.636  31687.052  33332.139  35081.923  35912.333
[43]   36819.445  38224.739  40292.304  42516.393  44622.642  46349.115
[49]   46759.560  45305.052  46611.975  48111.967

> plot(us, ylab = "Per Capita GDP", xlab = "Year")
```

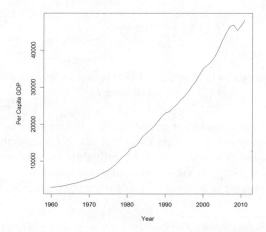

Figure 21.2   Time series plot of U.S. Per Capita GDP.

Another way to assess a time series is to view its autocovariance function (ACF) and partial autocovariance function (PACF). In R this is done with the appropriately named acf and pacf functions.

The ACF shows the correlation of a time series with lags of itself. That is, how much the time series is correlated with itself at one lag, at two lags, at three lags and so on.

The PACF is a little more complicated. The autocorrelation at lag one can have lingering effects on the autocorrelation at lag two and onward. The partial autocorrelation is the amount of correlation between a time series and lags of itself that is not explained by a previous lag. So, the partial autocorrelation at lag two is the correlation between the time series and its second lag that is not explained by the first lag.

The ACF and PACF for the U.S. Per Capita GDP data are shown in Figure 21.3. Vertical lines that extend beyond the horizontal line indicate autocorrelations and partial autocorrelations that are significant at those lags.

```
> acf(us)
> pacf(us)
```

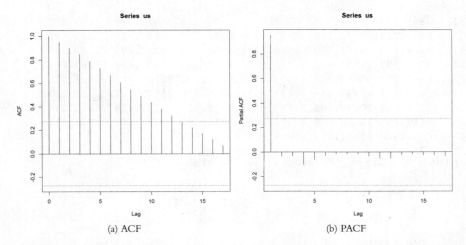

(a) ACF   (b) PACF

Figure 21.3   ACF and PACF of U.S. Per Capita GDP. These plots are indicative of a time series that is not stationary.

This time series needs a number of transformations before it can be properly modeled. Its upward trend shows that it is not stationary[1] (the data are in current U.S. dollars, so inflation is not the cause). That can be fixed by diffing the series or applying some other transformation. Diffing is the process of subtracting one observation from another and can be done on any number of observations. For instance, we start with a series

---

1. Being stationary requires that the mean and variance of a time series are constant for the whole series.

$x = [\, 1\; 4\; 8\; 2\; 6\; 6\; 5\; 3 \,]$. Diffing it yields $x^{(1)} = [\, 3\; 4\; -6\; 4\; 0\; -1\; -2 \,]$, which is the difference between successive elements. Diffing twice iteratively diffs the diffs, so $x^{(2)} = [\, 1\; -10\; 10\; -4\; -1\; -1 \,]$. Observe that for each level of diffing, there is one fewer element in the series. Doing this in R involves the diff function. The differences argument controls how many diffs are iteratively calculated. The lag determines which elements get subtracted from each other. A lag of 1 subtracts successive elements, while a lag of 2 subtracts elements that are two indices away from each other.

```
> x <- c(1, 4, 8, 2, 6, 6, 5, 3)
> # one diff
> diff(x, differences = 1)

[1]   3   4  -6   4   0  -1  -2

> # two iterative diffs
> diff(x, differences = 2)

[1]    1  -10   10   -4   -1   -1

> # equivalent to one diff
> diff(x, lag = 1)

[1]   3   4  -6   4   0  -1  -2

> # diff elements that are two indices apart
> diff(x, lag = 2)

[1]   7  -2  -2   4  -1  -3
```

Figuring out the correct number of diffs can be a tiresome process. Fortunately, the forecast package has a number of functions to make working with time series data easier, including determining the optimal number of diffs. The result is shown in Figure 21.4.

```
> require(forecast)
> ndiffs(x = us)

[1] 2

> plot(diff(us, 2))
```

While R offers individual ar and ma functions, a better option is the arima function, which can fit both AR and MA models and the combined ARMA model. It is even more robust in that it can diff the series and fit seasonal effects. Traditionally, the right order of each component of the model is determined by analyzing the ACF and PACF. This can be highly subjective, so fortunately forecast contains auto.arima, which will figure out the best specification.

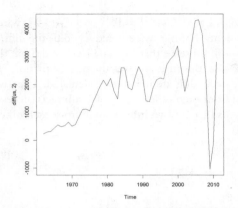

Figure 21.4   Plot of the U.S. Per Capita GDP diffed twice.

```
> usBest <- auto.arima(x = us)
> usBest

Series: us
ARIMA(2,2,1)

Coefficients:
          ar1       ar2       ma1
       0.4181   -0.2567   -0.8102
s.e.   0.1632    0.1486    0.1111

sigma^2 estimated as 269726:  log likelihood=-384.05
AIC=776.1   AICc=776.99   BIC=783.75
```

The function determined that an ARMA(2,1) (an AR(2) component and an MA(1) component) with two diffs is the optimal model based on minimum AICC (that is, AIC that is "corrected" to give a greater penalty to model complexity). The two diffs actually make this an ARIMA model rather than an ARMA model where the I stands for integrated. If this model is a good fit, then the residuals should resemble white noise. Figure 21.5 shows the ACF and PACF of the residuals for the ideal model. They resemble the pattern for white noise, confirming our model selection.

```
> acf(usBest$residuals)
> pacf(usBest$residuals)
```

The coefficients for an ARIMA model are the AR and MA components.

```
> coef(usBest)

       ar1         ar2         ma1
 0.4181109  -0.2567494  -0.8102419
```

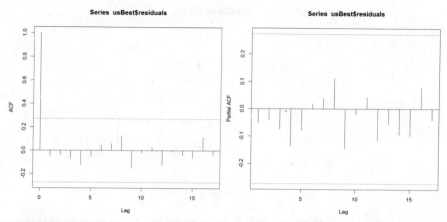

Figure 21.5   ACF and PACF plots for the residuals of ideal model chosen by `auto.arima`.

Making predictions based on an ARIMA model is much the same as with any other model type, using the `predict` function.

```
> # predict 5 years into the future and include the standard error
> predict(usBest, n.ahead = 5, se.fit = TRUE)

$pred
Time Series:
Start = 2012
End = 2016
Frequency = 1
[1] 49292.41 50289.69 51292.41 52344.45 53415.70

$se
Time Series:
Start = 2012
End = 2016
Frequency = 1
[1]   519.3512 983.3778 1355.0380 1678.3930 2000.3464
```

Visualizing this is easy enough but using the `forecast` function makes it even easier, as seen in Figure 21.6.

```
> # make a prediction for 5 years out
> theForecast <- forecast(object = usBest, h = 5)
> # plot it
> plot(theForecast)
```

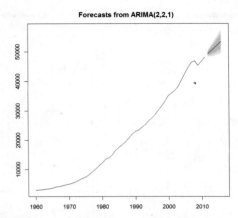

Figure 21.6   Five year prediction of U.S. GDP. The think line is the point estimate and the shaded regions represent the confidence intervals.

21.2 VAR

When dealing with multiple time series where each depends on its own past, others' pasts and others' presents, things get more complicated. The first thing we will do is convert all of the GDP data into a multivariate time series. To do this we first cast the data.frame to wide format then call ts to convert it. The result is shown in Figure 21.7.

```
> # load reshape2
> require(reshape2)
> # cast the data.frame to wide format
> gdpCast <- dcast(Year ~ Country,
+                  data=gdp[, c("Country", "Year", "PerCapGDP")],
+                  value.var="PerCapGDP")
> head(gdpCast)
```

	Year	Canada	China	Germany	Israel	Japan	Singapore
1	1960	2294.569	92.01123	NA	1365.683	478.9953	394.6489
2	1961	2231.294	75.87257	NA	1595.860	563.5868	437.9432
3	1962	2255.230	69.78987	NA	1132.383	633.6403	429.5377
4	1963	2354.839	73.68877	NA	1257.743	717.8669	472.1830
5	1964	2529.518	83.93044	NA	1375.943	835.6573	464.3773
6	1965	2739.586	97.47010	NA	1429.319	919.7767	516.2622

	United Kingdom	United States
1	1380.306	2881.100
2	1452.545	2934.553
3	1513.651	3107.937

```
4         1592.614      3232.208
5         1729.400      3423.396
6         1850.955      3664.802

> # remove first 10 rows since Germany did not have
>
> # convert to time series
> gdpTS <- ts(data=gdpCast[, -1], start=min(gdpCast$Year),
+             end=max(gdpCast$Year))
>
> # build a plot and legend using base graphics
> plot(gdpTS, plot.type="single", col=1:8)
> legend("topleft", legend=colnames(gdpTS), ncol=2, lty=1,
+        col=1:8, cex=.9)
```

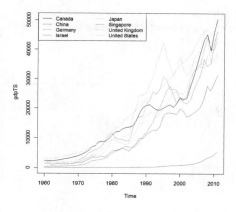

Figure 21.7   Time series plot of GDP data for all countries in the data. This is the same information as in Figure 21.1a, but this was built using base graphics.

Before proceeding we have to deal with the NAs for Germany. For some reason the World Bank does not have data on Germany's GDP before 1970. There are other resources, such as the St. Louis Federal Reserve Economic Data (FRED), but their data do not agree well with the World Bank data, so we remove Germany from our data.

```
> gdpTS <- gdpTS[, which(colnames(gdpTS) != "Germany")]
```

The most common way of fitting a model to multiple time series is to use a vector autoregressive (VAR) model. The equation for a VAR is

$$\mathbf{X}_t = \Phi_1 \mathbf{X}_{t-1} + \cdots + \Phi_p \mathbf{X}_{t-p} + \mathbf{Z}_t \tag{21.3}$$

where

$$\{Z_t\} \sim \text{WN}(0, \Sigma) \tag{21.4}$$

is white noise.

While `ar` can compute a VAR, it often has problems with singular `matrices` when the AR order is high, so it is better to use `VAR` from the `vars` package. To check whether the data should be diffed, we use the `ndiffs` function on `gdpTS` and then apply that number of diffs. The diffed data are shown in Figure 21.8, which exhibits greater stationarity than Figure 21.7.

```
> numDiffs <- ndiffs(gdpTS)
> numDiffs

[1] 1

> gdpDiffed <- diff(gdpTS, differences=numDiffs)
> plot(gdpDiffed, plot.type="single", col=1:7)
> legend("bottomleft", legend=colnames(gdpDiffed), ncol=2, lty=1,
+         col=1:7, cex=.9)
```

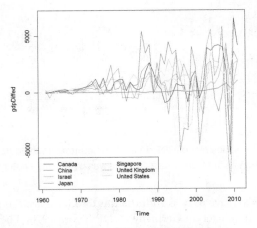

Figure 21.8   Differenced GDP data.

Now that the data are prepared, we can fit a VAR using `VAR`. This essentially fits a separate regression using `lm` of each time series on the lags of itself and the other series. This is evidenced in the coefficient plot for the Canada and Japan models, shown in Figure 21.9.

```
> require(vars)
> # fit the model
```

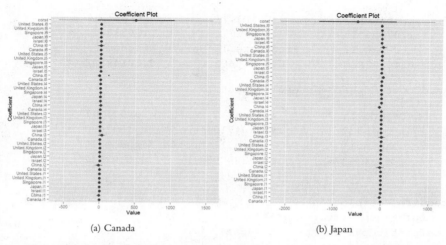

(a) Canada

(b) Japan

Figure 21.9 Coefficient plots for VAR model of GDP data for Canada and Japan.

```
> gdpVar <- VAR(gdpDiffed, lag.max = 12)
> # chosen order
> gdpVar$p

AIC(n)
     6

>
> # names of each of the models
> names(gdpVar$varresult)

[1] "Canada"          "China"           "Israel"
[4] "Japan"           "Singapore"       "United.Kingdom"
[7] "United.States"

>
> # each model is actually an lm object
> class(gdpVar$varresult$Canada)

[1] "lm"

> class(gdpVar$varresult$Japan)

[1] "lm"

>
> # each model has its own coefficients
> head(coef(gdpVar$varresult$Canada))
```

```
         Canada.11            China.11            Israel.11
      -1.07854513          -7.28241774           1.06538174
          Japan.11         Singapore.11 United.Kingdom.11
      -0.45533608          -0.03827402           0.60149182

> head(coef(gdpVar$varresult$Japan))

         Canada.11            China.11            Israel.11
        1.8045012          -19.7904918           -0.1507690
          Japan.11         Singapore.11 United.Kingdom.11
        1.3344763            1.5738029            0.5707742

>
> require(coefplot)
> coefplot(gdpVar$varresult$Canada)
> coefplot(gdpVar$varresult$Japan)
```

Predictions for this model are done just like with any other model, using the predict function.

```
> predict(gdpVar, n.ahead = 5)

$Canada
          fcst       lower       upper         CI
[1,]  -12459.46  -13284.63  -11634.30   825.1656
[2,]   15067.05   14106.02   16028.08   961.0344
[3,]   20632.99   19176.30   22089.69  1456.6943
[4,] -103830.42 -105902.11 -101758.73  2071.6904
[5,]  124483.19  119267.39  129699.00  5215.8046


$China
          fcst       lower       upper         CI
[1,]   -470.5917   -523.6101   -417.5733   53.01843
[2,]    899.5380    826.2362    972.8399   73.30188
[3,]   1730.8087   1596.4256   1865.1918  134.38308
[4,]  -3361.7713  -3530.6042  -3192.9384  168.83288
[5,]   2742.1265   2518.9867   2965.2662  223.13974


$Israel
          fcst       lower       upper         CI
[1,]   -6686.711   -7817.289   -5556.133  1130.578
[2,]  -39569.216  -40879.912  -38258.520  1310.696
[3,]   62192.139   60146.978   64237.300  2045.161
[4,]  -96325.105 -101259.427  -91390.783  4934.322
[5,]  -12922.005  -24003.839   -1840.171 11081.834
```

```
$Japan
             fcst         lower         upper       CI
[1,]    -14590.8574   -15826.761   -13354.954  1235.903
[2,]    -52051.5807   -53900.387   -50202.775  1848.806
[3,]      -248.4379    -3247.875     2750.999  2999.437
[4,]    -51465.6686   -55434.880   -47496.457  3969.212
[5,]   -111005.8032  -118885.682  -103125.924  7879.879
```

```
$Singapore
           fcst        lower        upper        CI
[1,]    -35923.80   -36071.93   -35775.67   148.1312
[2,]     54502.69    53055.85    55949.53  1446.8376
[3,]    -43551.08   -47987.48   -39114.68  4436.3991
[4,]    -99075.95  -107789.86   -90362.04  8713.9078
[5,]    145133.22   135155.64   155110.81  9977.5872
```

```
$United.Kingdom
           fcst        lower        upper        CI
[1,]    -19224.96   -20259.35   -18190.56  1034.396
[2,]     31194.77    30136.87    32252.67  1057.903
[3,]     27813.08    24593.47    31032.68  3219.604
[4,]    -66506.90   -70690.12   -62323.67  4183.226
[5,]     93857.98    88550.03    99165.94  5307.958
```

```
$United.States
           fcst        lower        upper        CI
[1,]     -657.2679   -1033.322    -281.2137   376.0542
[2,]    11088.0517   10614.924   11561.1792   473.1275
[3,]     2340.6277    1426.120    3255.1350   914.5074
[4,]    -5790.0143   -7013.843   -4566.1855  1223.8288
[5,]    24306.5309   23013.525   25599.5373  1293.0064
```

21.3 GARCH

A problem with ARMA models is that they do not handle extreme events or high volatility well. To overcome this a good tool to use is generalized autoregressive conditional heteroskedasticity or the GARCH family of models, which in addition to modeling the mean of the process also model the variance.

The model for the variance in a GARCH(m, s) is

$$\epsilon_t = \sigma_t e_t \tag{21.5}$$

where

$$\sigma_t^2 = \alpha_0 + \alpha_1 \epsilon_{t-1}^2 + \cdots + \alpha_m \epsilon_{t-m}^2 + \beta_1 \sigma_{t-1}^2 + \cdots + \beta_s \sigma_{t-s}^2 \qquad (21.6)$$

and

$$e \sim \text{GWN}(0, 1) \qquad (21.7)$$

is generalized white noise.

For this example we download AT&T ticker data using the `quantmod` package.

```
> require(quantmod)
> att <- getSymbols("T", auto.assign = FALSE)
```

This loads the data into an `xts` object from the `xts` package, which is a more robust time series object that, among many other improvements, can handle irregularly spaced events. These objects even have improved plotting over `ts`, as seen in Figure 21.10.

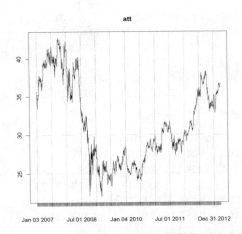

Figure 21.10   Time series plot of AT&T ticker data.

```
> require(xts)
> # show data
> head(att)

           T.Open T.High T.Low T.Close T.Volume T.Adjusted
2007-01-03  35.67  35.78 34.78   34.95 33694300      25.06
2007-01-04  34.95  35.24 34.07   34.50 44285400      24.74
2007-01-05  34.40  34.54 33.95   33.96 36561800      24.35
2007-01-08  33.40  34.01 33.21   33.81 40237400      24.50
```

```
2007-01-09  33.85  34.41 33.66   33.94 40082600      24.59
2007-01-10  34.20  35.00 31.94   34.03 29964300      24.66
```

```
> plot(att)
```

For those used to financial terminal charts, the chartSeries function should be comforting. It created the chart shown in Figure 21.11.

```
> chartSeries(att)
> addBBands()
> addMACD(32, 50, 12)
```

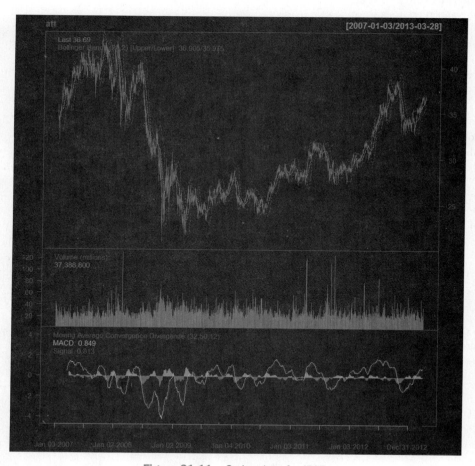

Figure 21.11   Series chart for AT&T.

We are only interested in the closing price, so we create a variable holding just that.

```
> attClose <- att$T.Close
> class(attClose)

[1] "xts" "zoo"

> head(attClose)

           T.Close
2007-01-03    34.95
2007-01-04    34.50
2007-01-05    33.96
2007-01-08    33.81
2007-01-09    33.94
2007-01-10    34.03
```

The package most widely considered to be the best for fitting GARCH models is rugarch. There are other packages for fitting GARCH models, such as tseries, fGarch and bayesGARCH, but we will focus on rugarch.

Generally, a GARCH(1,1) will be sufficient so we will fit that model to the data. The first step is setting up the model specification using ugarchspec. We specify the volatility to be modeled as a GARCH(1, 1) and the mean to be modeled as an ARMA(1, 1). We also specify that the innovation distribution should be the t distribution.

```
> require(rugarch)
> attSpec <- ugarchspec(variance.model=list(model="sGARCH",
+                                            garchOrder=c(1, 1)),
+                       mean.model=list(armaOrder=c(1, 1)),
+                       distribution.model="std")
```

The next step is to fit the model using ugarchfit.

```
> attGarch <- ugarchfit(spec = attSpec, data = attClose)
```

Printing the model spits out a lot of information, including the coefficients, standard errors, AIC and BIC. Most of this, such as the statistics on residuals, tests, AIC and BIC are diagnostic measures on the quality of the fit. The optimal parameters, seen near the top, are the crux of the model.

```
> attGarch

*---------------------------------------*
*          GARCH Model Fit              *
*---------------------------------------*
```

```
Conditional Variance Dynamics
-----------------------------------
GARCH Model : sGARCH(1,1)
Mean Model  : ARFIMA(1,0,1)
Distribution    : std

Optimal Parameters
------------------------------------
         Estimate   Std. Error   t value  Pr(>|t|)
mu       35.159848   1.328210   26.47160  0.000000
ar1       0.997009   0.001302  765.82269  0.000000
ma1      -0.009937   0.026801   -0.37078  0.710800
omega     0.001335   0.000692    1.92969  0.053645
alpha1    0.069952   0.014968    4.67328  0.000003
beta1     0.925012   0.015400   60.06615  0.000000
shape     7.581676   1.404834    5.39685  0.000000

Robust Standard Errors:
         Estimate   Std. Error   t value  Pr(>|t|)
mu       35.159848   0.541745   64.9011   0.000000
ar1       0.997009   0.001155  862.8530   0.000000
ma1      -0.009937   0.028813   -0.3449   0.730171
omega     0.001335   0.000795    1.6781   0.093319
alpha1    0.069952   0.018096    3.8657   0.000111
beta1     0.925012   0.018992   48.7047   0.000000
shape     7.581676   1.332371    5.6904   0.000000

LogLikelihood : -776.0355

Information Criteria
------------------------------------

Akaike        0.99750
Bayes         1.02139
Shibata       0.99746
Hannan-Quinn  1.00638

Q-Statistics on Standardized Residuals
------------------------------------
             statistic p-value
Lag[1]          0.5528  0.4572
Lag[p+q+1][3]   3.2738  0.0704
```

```
Lag[p+q+5][7]      6.8829   0.2295
d.o.f=2
H0 : No serial correlation
```

Q-Statistics on Standardized Squared Residuals

```
                statistic p-value
Lag[1]           0.005088 0.94314
Lag[p+q+1][3]    3.989786 0.04578
Lag[p+q+5][7]    5.817106 0.32442
d.o.f=2
```

ARCH LM Tests

```
               Statistic DoF P-Value
ARCH Lag[2]       2.229    2  0.3281
ARCH Lag[5]       4.597    5  0.4670
ARCH Lag[10]      9.457   10  0.4893
```

Nyblom stability test

```
Joint Statistic:  1.5032
Individual Statistics:
mu      0.18923
ar1     0.09786
ma1     0.24465
omega   0.13823
alpha1  0.62782
beta1   0.52974
shape   0.47109
```

```
Asymptotic Critical Values (10% 5% 1%)
Joint Statistic:          1.69 1.9 2.35
Individual Statistic:     0.35 0.47 0.75
```

Sign Bias Test

```
                    t-value    prob sig
Sign Bias           0.8259 0.4090
Negative Sign Bias  0.8228 0.4108
Positive Sign Bias  0.3965 0.6918
Joint Effect        3.0136 0.3895
```

```
Adjusted Pearson Goodness-of-Fit Test:
- - - - - - - - - - - - - - - - - - - - - - - - - - - - - - - - - - -
  group statistic p-value(g-1)
1    20    28339         0
2    30    44012         0
3    40    59699         0
4    50    75391         0
```

```
Elapsed time : 0.8640492
```

Figure 21.12 shows a time series plot and the ACF of the residuals from the model.

```
> # attGarch is an S4 object so its slots are accessed by @
> # the slot fit is a list, so its elements are accessed as usual with $
> plot(attGarch@fit$residuals, type="l")
> plot(attGarch, which=10)
```

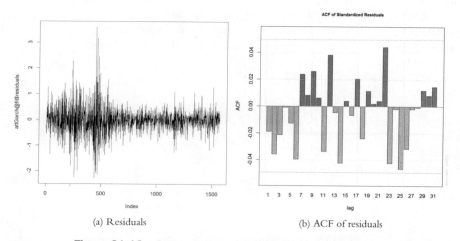

(a) Residuals   (b) ACF of residuals

Figure 21.12   Residual plots from GARCH model on AT&T data.

To judge the quality of this model, we build a few models with different mean specifications—all GARCH(1, 1)—and compare their AICs.

```
> # ARMA(1,1)
> attSpec1 <- ugarchspec(variance.model=list(model="sGARCH",
+                                            garchOrder=c(1, 1)),
+                   mean.model=list(armaOrder=c(1, 1)),
+                   distribution.model="std")
```

```
> # ARMA(0,0)
> attSpec2 <- ugarchspec(variance.model=list(model="sGARCH",
+                                              garchOrder=c(1, 1)),
+                       mean.model=list(armaOrder=c(0, 0)),
+                       distribution.model="std")
> # ARMA(0,2)
> attSpec3 <- ugarchspec(variance.model=list(model="sGARCH",
+                                              garchOrder=c(1, 1)),
+                       mean.model=list(armaOrder=c(0, 2)),
+                       distribution.model="std")
> # ARMA(1,2)
> attSpec4 <- ugarchspec(variance.model=list(model="sGARCH",
+                                              garchOrder=c(1, 1)),
+                       mean.model=list(armaOrder=c(1, 2)),
+                       distribution.model="std")
>
> attGarch1 <- ugarchfit(spec=attSpec1, data=attClose)
> attGarch2 <- ugarchfit(spec=attSpec2, data=attClose)
> attGarch3 <- ugarchfit(spec=attSpec3, data=attClose)
> attGarch4 <- ugarchfit(spec=attSpec4, data=attClose)
>
> infocriteria(attGarch1)


Akaike        0.9974974
Bayes         1.0213903
Shibata       0.9974579
Hannan-Quinn  1.0063781

> infocriteria(attGarch2)


Akaike        5.108533
Bayes         5.125600
Shibata       5.108513
Hannan-Quinn  5.114877

> infocriteria(attGarch3)


Akaike        3.406478
Bayes         3.430371
Shibata       3.406438
Hannan-Quinn  3.415359
```

```
> infocriteria(attGarch4)


Akaike         0.9963163
Bayes          1.0236224
Shibata        0.9962647
Hannan-Quinn 1.0064656
```

This shows that the first and fourth models were the best, according to AIC and BIC and the other criteria.

Predicting with objects from rugarch is done through the ugarchboot function, which can then be plotted as seen in Figure 21.13.

```
> attPred <- ugarchboot(attGarch, n.ahead=50,
+                        method = c("Partial", "Full")[1])
> plot(attPred, which=2)
```

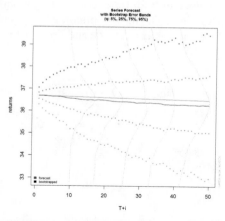

Figure 21.13   Predictions for GARCH model on AT&T data.

Because this is stock data, it is worth computing the model on the log returns instead of the actual closing prices.

```
> # diff the logs, drop the first one which is now NA
> attLog <- diff(log(attClose))[-1]
> # build the specification
> attLogSpec <- ugarchspec(variance.model=list(model="sGARCH",
+                                               garchOrder=c(1, 1)),
+                           mean.model=list(armaOrder=c(1, 1)),
+                           distribution.model="std")
```

```
> # fit the model
> attLogGarch <- ugarchfit(spec=attLogSpec, data=attLog)
> infocriteria(attLogGarch)


Akaike        -5.870043
Bayes         -5.846138
Shibata       -5.870083
Hannan-Quinn  -5.861158
```

This led to a significant drop in AIC.

It is important to remember that the purpose of GARCH models is not to fit the signal better but to capture the volatility better.

21.4 Conclusion

Time series play a crucial role in many fields, particularly finance and some physical sciences. The basic building block in R for time series is the ts object, which has been greatly extended by the xts object. The most common types of models are ARMA, VAR and GARCH, which are fitted by the arima, VAR and ugarchfit functions, respectively.

Chapter 22

Clustering

Clustering, which plays a big role in modern machine learning, is the partitioning of data into groups. This can be done in a number of ways, the two most popular being K-means and hierarchical clustering. In terms of a `data.frame`, a clustering algorithm finds out which rows are similar to each other. Rows that are grouped together are supposed to have high similarity to each other and low similarity with rows outside the grouping.

22.1 K-means

One of the more popular algorithms for clustering is K-means. It divides the observations into discrete groups based on some distance metric. For this example, we use the wine dataset from the University of California–Irvine Machine Learning Repository, available at `http://archive.ics.uci.edu/ml/datasets/Wine`.

```
> wine <- read.table("data/wine.csv", header = TRUE, sep = ",")
> head(wine)
```

	Cultivar	Alcohol	Malic.acid	Ash	Alcalinity.of.ash	Magnesium
1	1	14.23	1.71	2.43	15.6	127
2	1	13.20	1.78	2.14	11.2	100
3	1	13.16	2.36	2.67	18.6	101
4	1	14.37	1.95	2.50	16.8	113
5	1	13.24	2.59	2.87	21.0	118
6	1	14.20	1.76	2.45	15.2	112

	Total.phenols	Flavanoids	Nonflavanoid.phenols	Proanthocyanins
1	2.80	3.06	0.28	2.29
2	2.65	2.76	0.26	1.28
3	2.80	3.24	0.30	2.81
4	3.85	3.49	0.24	2.18
5	2.80	2.69	0.39	1.82
6	3.27	3.39	0.34	1.97

```
   Color.intensity  Hue OD280.OD315.of.diluted.wines Proline
1             5.64 1.04                          3.92    1065
2             4.38 1.05                          3.40    1050
3             5.68 1.03                          3.17    1185
4             7.80 0.86                          3.45    1480
5             4.32 1.04                          2.93     735
6             6.75 1.05                          2.85    1450
```

Because the first column is the cultivar, and that might be too correlated with group membership, we exclude that from the analysis.

```
> wineTrain <- wine[, which(names(wine) != "Cultivar")]
```

For K-means we need to specify the number of clusters, and then the algorithm assigns observations into that many clusters. There are heuristic rules for determining the number of clusters, which we will get to later. In R, K-means is done with the aptly named kmeans function. Its first two arguments are the data to be clustered, which must be all numeric (K-means does not work with categorical data), and the number of centers (clusters). Because there is a random component to the clustering, we set the seed to generate reproducible results.

```
> set.seed(278613)
> wineK3 <- kmeans(x = wineTrain, centers = 3)
```

Printing the K-means objects displays the size of the clusters, the cluster mean for each column, the cluster membership for each row and similarity measures.

```
> wineK3

K-means clustering with 3 clusters of sizes 62, 47, 69

Cluster means:
    Alcohol  Malic.acid      Ash Alcalinity.of.ash Magnesium
1  12.92984    2.504032 2.408065          19.89032 103.59677
2  13.80447    1.883404 2.426170          17.02340 105.51064
3  12.51667    2.494203 2.288551          20.82319  92.34783
  Total.phenols Flavanoids Nonflavanoid.phenols Proanthocyanins
1      2.111129   1.584032            0.3883871        1.503387
2      2.867234   3.014255            0.2853191        1.910426
3      2.070725   1.758406            0.3901449        1.451884
  Color.intensity       Hue OD280.OD315.of.diluted.wines   Proline
1        5.650323 0.8839677                      2.365484  728.3387
2        5.702553 1.0782979                      3.114043 1195.1489
3        4.086957 0.9411594                      2.490725  458.2319
```

```
Clustering vector:
  [1] 2 2 2 2 1 2 2 2 2 2 2 2 2 2 2 2 2 2 2 1 1 1 2 2 1 1 2 2 1 2 2 2
 [33] 2 2 2 1 1 2 2 1 1 2 2 1 1 2 2 2 2 2 2 2 2 2 2 2 2 2 2 3 1 3 1 3
 [65] 3 1 3 3 1 1 1 3 3 2 1 3 3 3 1 3 3 1 1 3 3 3 3 3 1 1 3 3 3 3 3 1
 [97] 1 3 1 3 1 3 3 3 1 3 3 3 3 1 3 3 1 3 3 3 3 3 3 3 1 3 3 3 3 3 3 3
[129] 3 3 1 3 3 1 1 1 1 3 3 3 1 1 3 3 1 1 3 1 1 3 3 3 3 1 1 1 3 1 1 1
[161] 3 1 3 1 1 3 1 1 1 1 3 3 1 1 1 1 1 3
```

```
Within cluster sum of squares by cluster:
[1]   566572.5 1360950.5 443166.7
 (between_SS / total_SS =   86.5 %)
```

```
Available components:

[1] "cluster"      "centers"      "totss"         "withinss"
[5] "tot.withinss" "betweenss"    "size"
```

Plotting the result of K-means clustering can be difficult because of the high dimensional nature of the data. To overcome this, the plot.kmeans function in useful performs multidimensional scaling to project the data into two dimensions, and then color codes the points according to cluster membership. This is seen in Figure 22.1.

```
> require(useful)
> plot(wineK3, data = wineTrain)
```

If we pass the original wine data and specify that Cultivar is the true membership column, the shape of the points will be coded by Cultivar, so we can see how that compares to the colors in Figure 22.2. A strong correlation between the color and shape would indicate a good clustering.

```
> plot(wineK3, data = wine, class = "Cultivar")
```

K-means can be subject to random starting conditions, so it is considered good practice to run it with a number of random starts. This is accomplished with the nstart argument.

```
> set.seed(278613)
> wineK3N25 <- kmeans(wineTrain, centers = 3, nstart = 25)
> # see the cluster sizes with 1 start
> wineK3$size

[1] 62 47 69

> # see the cluster sizes with 25 starts
> wineK3N25$size

[1] 62 47 69
```

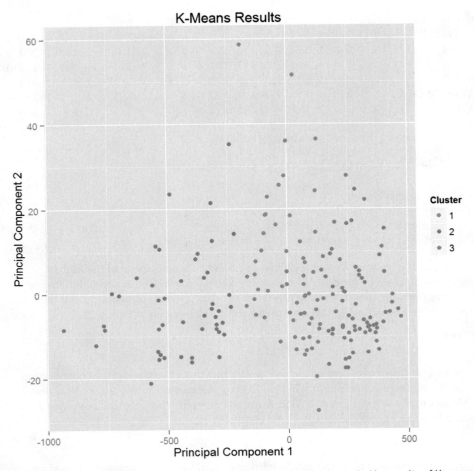

Figure 22.1   Plot of wine data scaled into two dimensions and color coded by results of K-means clustering.

For our data the results did not change. For other datasets the number of starts can have a significant impact.

Choosing the right number of clusters is important in getting a good partitioning of the data. According to David Madigan, the chair of the Department of Statistics, Columbia University, a good metric for determining the optimal number of clusters is Hartigan's Rule (J. A. Hartigan is one of the authors of the most popular K-means algorithm). It essentially compares the ratio of the within-cluster sum of squares for a clustering with k clusters and one with $k + 1$ clusters, accounting for the number of rows and clusters.

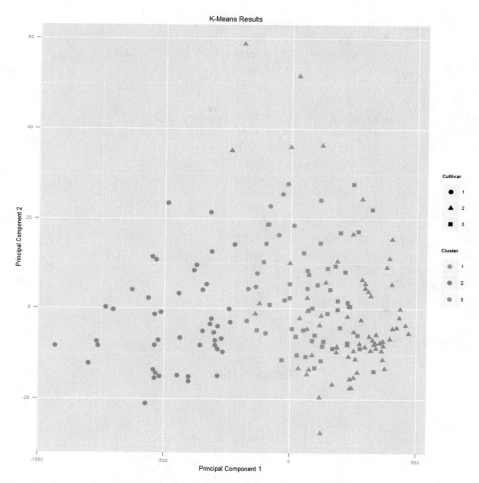

Figure 22.2 Plot of wine data scaled into two dimensions and color coded by results of K-means clustering. The shapes indicate the cultivar. A strong correlation between the color and shape would indicate a good clustering.

If that number is greater than 10, then it is worth using $k + 1$ clusters. Fitting this repeatedly can be a chore and computationally inefficient if not done right. The useful package has the FitKMeans function for doing just that. The results are plotted in Figure 22.3.

```
> wineBest <- FitKMeans(wineTrain, max.clusters=20, nstart=25,
+                 seed=278613)
> wineBest
```

	Clusters	Hartigan	AddCluster
1	2	505.429310	TRUE
2	3	160.411331	TRUE
3	4	135.707228	TRUE
4	5	78.445289	TRUE
5	6	71.489710	TRUE
6	7	97.582072	TRUE
7	8	46.772501	TRUE
8	9	33.198650	TRUE
9	10	33.277952	TRUE
10	11	33.465424	TRUE
11	12	17.940296	TRUE
12	13	33.268151	TRUE
13	14	6.434996	FALSE
14	15	7.833562	FALSE
15	16	46.783444	TRUE
16	17	12.229408	TRUE
17	18	10.261821	TRUE
18	19	-13.576343	FALSE
19	20	56.373939	TRUE

```
> PlotHartigan(wineBest)
```

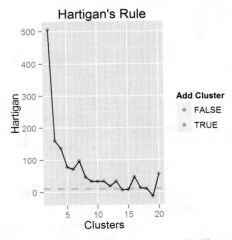

Figure 22.3   Plot of Hartigan's Rule for a series of different cluster sizes.

According to this metric we should use 13 clusters. Again, this is just a rule of thumb and should not be strictly adhered to. Because we know there are three cultivars it would seem natural to choose three clusters. Then again, the results of the clustering with three clusters did only a fairly good job of aligning the clusters with the cultivars, so it might not be that good of a fit. Figure 22.4 shows the cluster assignment going down the left side and the cultivar across the top. Cultivar 1 is mostly alone in its own cluster, and cultivar 2 is just a little worse, while cultivar 3 is not clustered well at all. If this were truly a good fit, the diagonals would be the largest segments.

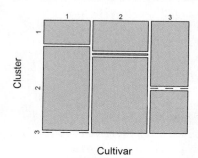

Figure 22.4   Confusion matrix for clustering of wine data by cultivars.

```
> table(wine$Cultivar, wineK3N25$cluster)


     1  2  3
1 13 46  0
2 20  1 50
3 29  0 19
```

```
> plot(table(wine$Cultivar, wineK3N25$cluster),
+     main="Confusion Matrix for Wine Clustering",
+     xlab="Cultivar", ylab="Cluster")
```

An alternative to Hartigan's Rule is the Gap statistic, which compares the within-cluster dissimilarity for a clustering of the data with that of a bootstrapped sample of data. It is measuring the gap between reality and expectation. This can be calculated (for numeric data only) using clusGap in cluster. It takes a bit of time to run because it is doing a lot of simulations.

```
> require(cluster)
> theGap <- clusGap(wineTrain, FUNcluster = pam, K.max = 20)
> gapDF <- as.data.frame(theGap$Tab)
> gapDF
```

```
      logW     E.logW        gap       SE.sim
1   9.655294  9.947093  0.2917988  0.03367473
2   8.987942  9.258169  0.2702262  0.03498740
3   8.617563  8.862178  0.2446152  0.03117947
4   8.370194  8.594228  0.2240346  0.03193258
5   8.193144  8.388382  0.1952376  0.03243527
6   7.979259  8.232036  0.2527773  0.03456908
7   7.819287  8.098214  0.2789276  0.03089973
8   7.685612  7.987350  0.3017378  0.02825189
9   7.591487  7.894791  0.3033035  0.02505585
10  7.496676  7.818529  0.3218525  0.02707628
11  7.398811  7.750513  0.3517019  0.02492806
12  7.340516  7.691724  0.3512081  0.02529801
13  7.269456  7.638362  0.3689066  0.02329920
14  7.224292  7.591250  0.3669578  0.02248816
15  7.157981  7.545987  0.3880061  0.02352986
16  7.104300  7.506623  0.4023225  0.02451914
17  7.054116  7.469984  0.4158683  0.02541277
18  7.006179  7.433963  0.4277835  0.02542758
19  6.971455  7.401962  0.4305071  0.02616872
20  6.932463  7.369970  0.4375070  0.02761156
```

Figure 22.5 shows the Gap statistic for a number of different clusters. The optimal number of clusters is the smallest number producing a gap within one standard deviation of the number of clusters that minimizes the gap.

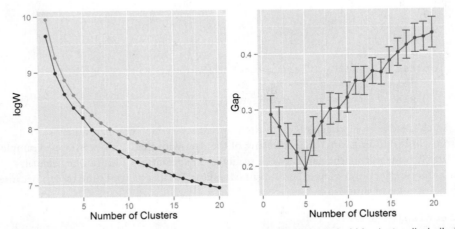

Figure 22.5   Gap curves for wine data. The blue curve is the observed within-cluster dissimilarity, and the green curve is the expected within-cluster dissimilarity. The red curve represents the Gap statistic (expected-observed) and the error bars are the standard deviation of the gap.

```
> # logW curves
> ggplot(gapDF, aes(x=1:nrow(gapDF))) +
+     geom_line(aes(y=logW), color="blue") +
+     geom_point(aes(y=logW), color="blue") +
+     geom_line(aes(y=E.logW), color="green") +
+     geom_point(aes(y=E.logW), color="green") +
+     labs(x="Number of Clusters")
>
> # gap curve
> ggplot(gapDF, aes(x=1:nrow(gapDF))) +
+     geom_line(aes(y=gap), color="red") +
+     geom_point(aes(y=gap), color="red") +
+     geom_errorbar(aes(ymin=gap-SE.sim, ymax=gap+SE.sim), color="red") +
+     labs(x="Number of Clusters", y="Gap")
```

22.2 PAM

Two problems with K-means clustering are that it does not work with categorical data and it is susceptible to outliers. An alternative is K-medoids. Instead of the center of a cluster being the mean of the cluster, the center is one of the actual observations in the cluster. This is akin to the median, which is likewise robust against outliers.

The most common K-medoids algorithm is Partitioning Around Medoids (PAM). The `cluster` package contains the pam function. For this example, we look at some data from the World Bank, including both numerical measures such as GDP and categorical information such as region and income level.

Now we use the country codes to download a number of indicators from the World Bank using WDI.

```
> indicators <- c("BX.KLT.DINV.WD.GD.ZS", "NY.GDP.DEFL.KD.ZG",
+                  "NY.GDP.MKTP.CD", "NY.GDP.MKTP.KD.ZG",
+                  "NY.GDP.PCAP.CD", "NY.GDP.PCAP.KD.ZG",
+                  "TG.VAL.TOTL.GD.ZS")
> require(WDI)
>
> # pull info on these indicators for all countries in our list
> # not all countries have information for every indicator
> # some countries do not have any data
> wbInfo <- WDI(country="all", indicator=indicators, start=2011,
+               end=2011, extra=TRUE)
> # get rid of aggregated info
> wbInfo <- wbInfo[wbInfo$region != "Aggregates", ]
> # get rid of countries where all the indicators are NA
> wbInfo <- wbInfo[which(rowSums(!is.na(wbInfo[, indicators])) > 0), ]
> # get rid of any rows where the iso is missing
> wbInfo <- wbInfo[!is.na(wbInfo$iso2c), ]
```

The data have a few missing values, but fortunately pam handles missing values well. Before we run the clustering algorithm we clean up the data some more, using the country names as the row names of the data.frame and ensuring the categorical variables are factors with the proper levels.

```
> # set rownames so we can know the country without using that for
> # clustering
> rownames(wbInfo) <- wbInfo$iso2c
> # refactorize region, income and lending to account for any changes
> # in the levels
> wbInfo$region <- factor(wbInfo$region)
> wbInfo$income <- factor(wbInfo$income)
> wbInfo$lending <- factor(wbInfo$lending)
```

Now we fit the clustering using pam from the cluster package. Figure 22.6 shows a silhouette plot of the results. Each line represents an observation, and each grouping of lines is a cluster. Observations that fit the cluster well have large positive lines and observations that do not fit well have small or negative lines. A bigger average width for a cluster means a better clustering.

```
> # find which columns to keep
> # not those in this vector
> keep.cols <- which(!names(wbInfo) %in% c("iso2c", "country", "year",
+                                           "capital", "iso3c"))
> # fit the clustering
> wbPam <- pam(x=wbInfo[, keep.cols], k=12, keep.diss=TRUE,
+              keep.data=TRUE)
>
> # show the medoid observations
> wbPam$medoids
```

	BX.KLT.DINV.WD.GD.ZS	NY.GDP.DEFL.KD.ZG	NY.GDP.MKTP.CD
PT	5.507851973	0.6601427	2.373736e+11
HT	2.463873387	6.7745103	7.346157e+09
BY	7.259657119	58.3675854	5.513208e+10
BE	19.857364384	2.0299163	5.136611e+11
MX	1.765034004	5.5580395	1.153343e+12
GB	1.157530889	2.6028860	2.445408e+12
IN	1.741905033	7.9938177	1.847977e+12
CN	3.008038634	7.7539567	7.318499e+12
DE	1.084936891	0.8084950	3.600833e+12
NL	1.660830419	1.2428287	8.360736e+11
JP	0.001347863	-2.1202280	5.867154e+12
US	1.717849686	2.2283033	1.499130e+13

	NY.GDP.MKTP.KD.ZG	NY.GDP.PCAP.CD	NY.GDP.PCAP.KD.ZG
PT	-1.6688187	22315.8420	-1.66562016
HT	5.5903433	725.6333	4.22882080
BY	5.3000000	5819.9177	5.48896865
BE	1.7839242	46662.5283	0.74634396
MX	3.9106137	10047.1252	2.67022734
GB	0.7583280	39038.4583	0.09938161
IN	6.8559233	1488.5129	5.40325582
CN	9.3000000	5444.7853	8.78729922
DE	3.0288866	44059.8259	3.09309213
NL	0.9925175	50076.2824	0.50493944
JP	-0.7000000	45902.6716	-0.98497734
US	1.7000000	48111.9669	0.96816270

	TG.VAL.TOTL.GD.ZS	region	longitude	latitude	income	lending
PT	58.63188	2	-9.135520	38.7072	2	4
HT	49.82197	3	-72.328800	18.5392	3	3
BY	156.27254	2	27.576600	53.9678	6	2
BE	182.42266	2	4.367610	50.8371	2	4
MX	61.62462	3	-99.127600	19.4270	6	2
GB	45.37562	2	-0.126236	51.5002	2	4
IN	40.45037	6	77.225000	28.6353	4	1
CN	49.76509	1	116.286000	40.0495	6	2
DE	75.75581	2	13.411500	52.5235	2	4
NL	150.41895	2	4.890950	52.3738	2	4
JP	28.58185	1	139.770000	35.6700	2	4
US	24.98827	5	-77.032000	38.8895	2	4

```
>
> # make a silhouette plot
> plot(wbPam, which.plots=2, main="")
```

Because we are dealing with country level information, it would be informative to view the clustering on a world map. As we are working with World Bank data, we will use the World Bank shapefile of the world available at http://maps.worldbank.org/overlays/2712. It can be downloaded in a browser as any other file or using R. While this is slower than using a browser, it can be nice if we have to programmatically download many files.

```
> download.file(url="http://jaredlander.com/data/worldmap.zip",
+               destfile="data/worldmap.zip", method="curl")
```

The file needs to be unzipped, which can be done through the operating system or in R.

```
> unzip(zipfile = "data/worldmap.zip", exdir = "data")
```

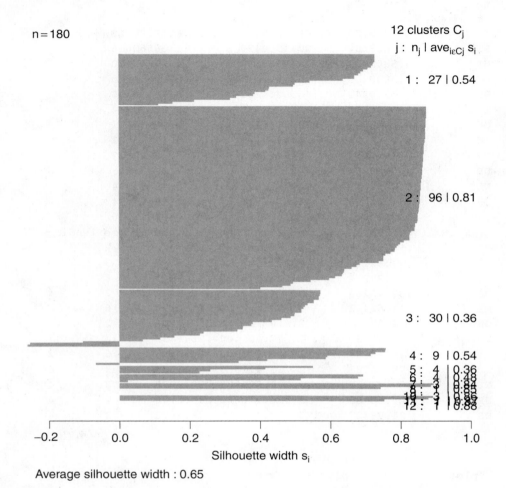

n=180

12 clusters C_j

$j : n_j \mid ave_{i \varepsilon C_j} s_i$

1 : 27 | 0.54

2 : 96 | 0.81

3 : 30 | 0.36

4 : 9 | 0.54
5 : 4 | 0.36
6 : 4 | 0.48
7 : 3 | 0.84
8 : 3 | 0.85
10 : 3 | 0.86
12 : 1 | 0.88

Silhouette width s_i

Average silhouette width : 0.65

Figure 22.6   Silhouette plot for country clustering. Each line represents an observation, and each grouping of lines is a cluster. Observations that fit the cluster well have large positive lines and observations that do not fit well have small or negative lines. A bigger average width for a cluster means a better clustering.

Of the four files, we only need to worry about the one ending in `.shp` because R will handle the rest. We read it in using `readShapeSpatial` from `maptools`.

```
         name             CntryName FipsCntry
0 Fips Cntry:                 Aruba        AA
1 Fips Cntry:     Antigua & Barbuda        AC
2 Fips Cntry: United Arab Emirates        AE
```

```
3 Fips Cntry:           Afghanistan         AF
4 Fips Cntry:               Algeria         AG
5 Fips Cntry:            Azerbaijan         AJ
```

```
> require(maptools)
> world <- readShapeSpatial(
+     "data/world_country_admin_boundary_shapefile_with_fips_codes.shp"
+     )
> head(world@data)
```

There are some blatant discrepancies between the two-digit code in the World Bank shapefile and the two-digit code in the World Bank data pulled using WDI. Notably, Austria should be "AT," Australia "AU," Myanmar (Burma) "MM," Vietnam "VN" and so on.

```
> require(plyr)
> world@data$FipsCntry <- as.character(
+     revalue(world@data$FipsCntry,
+             replace=c(AU="AT", AS="AU", VM="VN", BM="MM", SP="ES",
+                       PO="PT", IC="IL", SF="ZA", TU="TR", IZ="IQ",
+                       UK="GB", EI="IE", SU="SD", MA="MG", MO="MA",
+                       JA="JP", SW="SE", SN="SG"))
+     )
```

In order to use ggplot2 we need to convert this shapefile object into a data.frame, which requires a few steps.

```
> # make an id column using the rownames
> world@data$id <- rownames(world@data)
> # fortify it, this is a special ggplot2 function that converts
> # shapefiles to data.frames
> require(ggplot2)
> require(rgeos)
> world.df <- fortify(world, region = "id")
> head(world.df)
```

```
      long      lat order  hole piece group id
1 -69.88223 12.41111     1 FALSE     1   0.1  0
2 -69.94695 12.43667     2 FALSE     1   0.1  0
3 -70.05904 12.54021     3 FALSE     1   0.1  0
4 -70.05966 12.62778     4 FALSE     1   0.1  0
5 -70.03320 12.61833     5 FALSE     1   0.1  0
6 -69.93224 12.52806     6 FALSE     1   0.1  0
```

Before we can join this to the clustering, we need to join `FipsCntry` back into `world.df`.

```
> world.df <- join(world.df,
+                   world@data[, c("id", "CntryName", "FipsCntry")],
+                   by="id")
> head(world.df)

        long      lat order  hole piece group id CntryName FipsCntry
1 -69.88223 12.41111     1 FALSE     1   0.1  0     Aruba        AA
2 -69.94695 12.43667     2 FALSE     1   0.1  0     Aruba        AA
3 -70.05904 12.54021     3 FALSE     1   0.1  0     Aruba        AA
4 -70.05966 12.62778     4 FALSE     1   0.1  0     Aruba        AA
5 -70.03320 12.61833     5 FALSE     1   0.1  0     Aruba        AA
6 -69.93224 12.52806     6 FALSE     1   0.1  0     Aruba        AA
```

Now we can take the steps of joining in data from the clustering and the original World Bank data.

```
> clusterMembership <- data.frame(FipsCntry=names(wbPam$clustering),
+                                 Cluster=wbPam$clustering,
+                                 stringsAsFactors=FALSE)
> head(clusterMembership)

   FipsCntry Cluster
AE        AE       1
AF        AF       2
AG        AG       2
AL        AL       2
AM        AM       2
AO        AO       3
```

```
> world.df <- join(world.df, clusterMembership, by="FipsCntry")
> world.df$Cluster <- as.character(world.df$Cluster)
> world.df$Cluster <- factor(world.df$Cluster, levels=1:12)
> 1

[1] 1
```

Building the plot itself requires a number of `ggplot2` commands to format it correctly. Figure 22.7 shows the map, color coded by cluster membership; the gray countries either do not have World Bank information or were not properly matched up between the two datasets.

```
> ggplot() +
+     geom_polygon(data=world.df, aes(x=long, y=lat, group=group,
+                                     fill=Cluster, color=Cluster)) +
+       labs(x=NULL, y=NULL) + coord_equal() +
+     theme(panel.grid.major=element_blank(),
+           panel.grid.minor=element_blank(),
+           axis.text.x=element_blank(), axis.text.y=element_blank(),
+           axis.ticks=element_blank(), panel.background=element_blank())
```

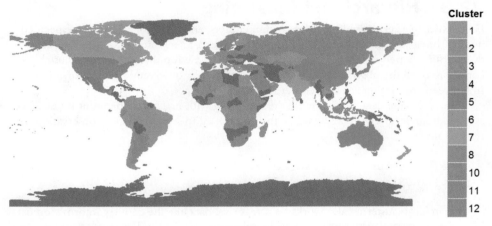

Figure 22.7   Map of PAM clustering of World Bank data. Gray countries either do not have World Bank information or were not properly matched up between the two datasets.

Much like with K-means, the number of clusters in a K-medoids clustering must be specified. Something similar to Hartigan's Rule can be built using the dissimilarity information returned by pam.

```
> wbPam$clusinfo
```

	size	max_diss	av_diss	diameter	separation
[1,]	27	122871463849	46185193372	200539326122	1.967640e+10
[2,]	96	22901202940	7270137217	31951289020	3.373324e+09
[3,]	30	84897264072	21252371506	106408660458	3.373324e+09
[4,]	9	145646809734	59174398936	251071168505	4.799168e+10
[5,]	4	323538875043	146668424920	360634547126	2.591686e+11

```
 [6,]   4 327624060484 152576296819 579061061914 3.362014e+11
 [7,]   3 111926243631  40573057031 121719171093 2.591686e+11
 [8,]   1            0            0            0 1.451345e+12
 [9,]   1            0            0            0 8.278012e+11
[10,]   3  61090193130  23949621648  71848864944 1.156755e+11
[11,]   1            0            0            0 1.451345e+12
[12,]   1            0            0            0 7.672801e+12
```

22.3   Hierarchical Clustering

Hierarchical clustering builds clusters within clusters, and does not require a prespecified number of clusters like K-means and K-medoids do. A hierarchical clustering can be thought of as a tree and displayed as a dendrogram; at the top there is just one cluster consisting of all the observations, and at the bottom each observation is an entire cluster. In between are varying levels of clustering.

Using the wine data, we can build the clustering with hclust. The result is visualized as a dendrogram in Figure 22.8. While the text is hard to see, it labels the observations at the end nodes.

```
> wineH <- hclust(d = dist(wineTrain))
> plot(wineH)
```

Hierarchical clustering also works on categorical data like the country information data. However, its dissimilarity matrix must be calculated differently. The dendrogram is shown in Figure 22.9.

```
> # calculate distance
> keep.cols <- which(!names(wbInfo) %in% c("iso2c", "country", "year",
+                                          "capital", "iso3c"))
> wbDaisy <- daisy(x=wbInfo[, keep.cols])
>
> wbH <- hclust(wbDaisy)
> plot(wbH)
```

There are a number of different ways to compute the distance between clusters and they can have a significant impact on the results of a hierarchical clustering. Figure 22.10 shows the resulting tree from four different linkage methods: single, complete, average and centroid. Average linkage is generally considered the most appropriate.

```
> wineH1 <- hclust(dist(wineTrain), method = "single")
> wineH2 <- hclust(dist(wineTrain), method = "complete")
```

Cluster Dendrogram

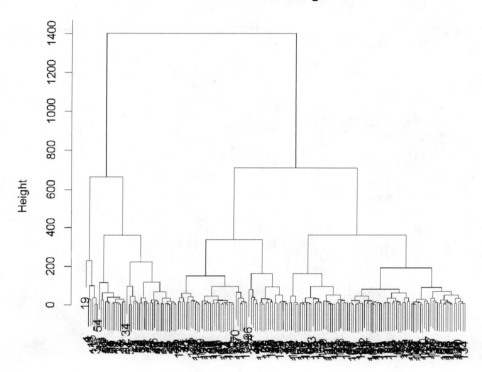

dist(wineTrain)
hclust (*, "complete")

Figure 22.8   Hierarchical clustering of wine data.

```
> wineH3 <- hclust(dist(wineTrain), method = "average")
> wineH4 <- hclust(dist(wineTrain), method = "centroid")
>
> plot(wineH1, labels = FALSE, main = "Single")
> plot(wineH2, labels = FALSE, main = "Complete")
> plot(wineH3, labels = FALSE, main = "Average")
> plot(wineH4, labels = FALSE, main = "Centroid")
```

Cluster Dendrogram

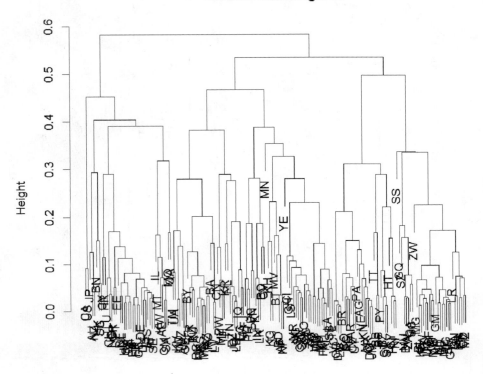

wbDaisy
hclust (*, "complete")

Figure 22.9   Hierarchical clustering of country information data.

Cutting the resulting tree produced by hierarchical clustering splits the observations into defined groups. There are two ways to cut it, either specifying the number of clusters, which determines where the cuts take place, or specifying where to make the cut, which determines the number of clusters. Figure 22.11 demonstrates cutting the tree by specifying the number of clusters.

```
> # plot the tree
> plot(wineH)
> # split into 3 clusters
```

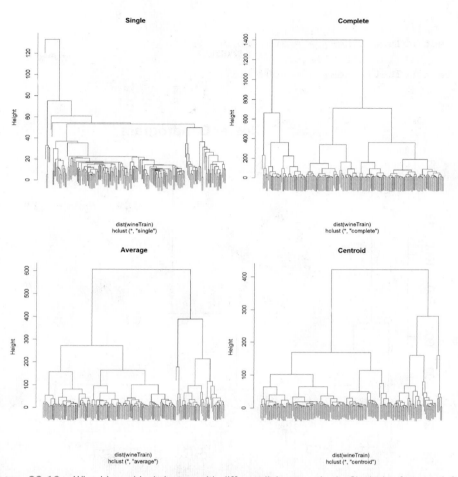

Figure 22.10   Wine hierarchical clusters with different linkage methods. Clockwise from top left: single, complete, centroid, average.

```
> rect.hclust(wineH, k = 3, border = "red")
> # split into 13 clusters
> rect.hclust(wineH, k = 13, border = "blue")
```

Figure 22.12 demonstrates cutting the tree by specifying the height of the cuts.

```
> # plot the tree
> plot(wineH)
```

```
> # split into 3 clusters
> rect.hclust(wineH, h = 200, border = "red")
> # split into 13 clusters
> rect.hclust(wineH, h = 800, border = "blue")
```

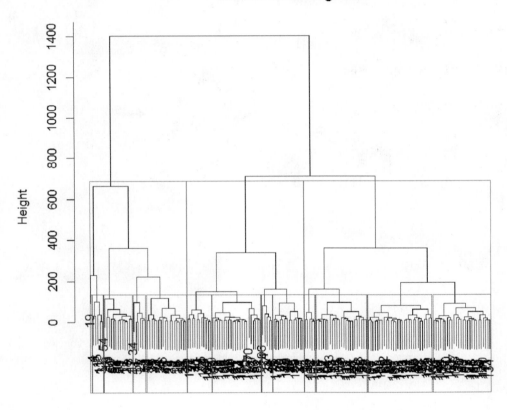

Cluster Dendrogram

dist(wineTrain)
hclust (*, "complete")

Figure 22.11   Hierarchical clustering of wine data split into three groups (red) and 13 groups (blue).

Cluster Dendrogram

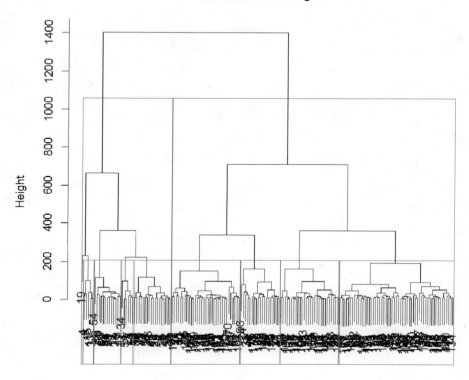

dist(wineTrain)
hclust (*, "complete")

Figure 22.12 Hierarchical clustering of wine data split by the height of cuts.

22.4 Conclusion

Clustering is a popular technique for segmenting data. The primary options for clustering in R are kmeans for K-means, pam in cluster for K-medoids and hclust for hierarchical clustering. Speed can sometimes be a problem with clustering, especially hierarchical clustering, so it is worth considering replacement packages like fastcluster, which has a drop-in replacement function, hclust, which operates just like the standard hclust, only faster.

Chapter 23

Reproducibility, Reports and Slide Shows with `knitr`

Successfully delivering the results of an analysis can be just as important as the analysis itself, so it is vital to communicate them in an effective way. This can be a written report, a Web site of results, a slide show or a dashboard. In this chapter we focus on the first three, which are made remarkably easy using `knitr`, a package written by Yihui Xie.

`knitr` was initially created as a replacement for `Sweave` for the creation of PDF documents using LaTeX interweaved with R code and the generated results. It has since added the capability to work with Markdown for generating HTML documents. While interweaving R code in LaTeX and Markdown requires using a somewhat different syntax for each, the programs are similar enough to make them both easy to work with. First we discuss working with LaTeX documents, and then Markdown.

The combination of `knitr` and RStudio is so powerful that it was possible to write this entire book inside the RStudio IDE using `knitr` to insert and run R code and graphics.

23.1 Installing a LaTeX Program

LaTeX (pronounced "lay-tech") is a markup language based on the TeX typesetting system created by Donald Knuth. It is regularly used for writing scientific papers and books, including this one. Like any other program, LaTeX must be installed before it can be used.

Each of the operating systems uses a different LaTeX distribution. Table 23.1 lists OS-specific distributions and download locations.

Table 23.1   LaTeX Distributions and their Locations

OS	Distribution	URL
Windows	MiKTeX	http://miktex.org/
Mac	MacTeX	http://www.tug.org/mactex/
Linux	TeX Live	http://www.tug.org/texlive/

23.2 LaTeX Primer

This is not intended to be anywhere near a comprehensive lesson in LaTeX, but it should be enough to get started with making documents. LaTeX documents should be saved with a `.tex` extension to identify them as such. While RStudio is intended for working with R, it is a suitable text editor for LaTeX and is the environment we will be using.

The very first line in a LaTeX file declares the type of document, the most common being "article" and "book." This is done with `\documentclass{...}`, replacing `...` with the desired document class.

Immediately following the declaration of the `documentclass` is the preamble. This is where commands that affect the document go, such as what packages to load (LaTeX packages) using `\usepackage{...}` and making an index with `\makeindex`.

In order to include images, it is advisable to use the `graphicx` package. This allows us to specify the type of image file that will be used by entering `\DeclareGraphics Extensions{.png,.jpg}`, which means LaTeX will first search for files ending in `.png` and then search for files ending in `.jpg`. This will be explained more when dealing with images later.

This is also where the title, author and date are declared with `\title`, `\author` and `\date`, respectively. New shortcuts can be created here such as `\newcommand {\dataframe}{\texttt{data.frame}}`, so that every time `\dataframe{}` is typed it will be printed as `data.frame`, which appears in a typewriter font because of the `\texttt{...}`.

The actual document starts with `\begin{document}` and ends with `\end{document}`. That is where all the content goes. So far our LaTeX document looks like the following example.

```
\documentclass{article}
% this is a comment
% all content following a % on a line will be commented out as if it
never existed to latex

\usepackage{graphicx} % use graphics
\DeclareGraphicsExtensions{.png,.jpg} % search for png then jpg

% define shortcut for dataframe
\newcommand{\dataframe}{\texttt{data.frame}}

\title{A Simple Article}
\author{Jared P. Lander\\ Lander Analytics}
% the \\ puts what follows on the next line
\date{April 14th, 2013}

\begin{document}
```

(Continues)

(Continued)

```
\maketitle

Some Content

\end{document}
```

Content can be split into sections using \section{Section Name}. All text following this command will be part of that section until another \section{...} is reached. Sections (and subsections and chapters) are automatically numbered by LaTeX. If given a label using \label{...} they can be referred to using \ref{...}. The table of contents is automatically numbered and is created using \tableofcontents. We can now further build out our document with some sections and a table of contents. Normally, LaTeX must be run twice for cross references and the table of contents but RStudio, and most other LaTeX editors, will do that automatically.

```
\documentclass{article}
% this is a comment
% all content following a % on a line will be commented out as if it
never existed to latex

\usepackage{graphicx} % use graphics
\DeclareGraphicsExtensions{.png,.jpg} % search for png then jpg

% define shortcut for dataframe
\newcommand{\dataframe}{\texttt{data.frame}}

\title{A Simple Article}
\author{Jared P. Lander\\ Lander Analytics}
% the \\ puts what follows on the next line
\date{April 14th, 2013}

\begin{document}
\maketitle % create the title page
\tableofcontents % build table of contents

\section{Getting Started}
\label{sec:GettingStarted}
This is the first section of our article. The only thing it will talk
about is building \dataframe{}s and not much else.

A new paragraph is started simply by leaving a blank line. That is all
that is required. Indenting will happen automatically.
```

(Continues)

(Continued)

```
\section{More Information}
\label{sec:MoreInfo}
Here is another section. In section~\ref{sec:GettingStarted} we learned
some basics and now we will see just a little more. Suppose this section is
getting too long so it should be broken up into subsections.

\subsection{First Subsection}
\label{FirstSub}
Content for a subsection.

\subsection{Second Subsection}
\label{SecondSub}
More content that is nested in section~\ref{sec:MoreInfo}

\section{Last Section}
\label{sec:LastBit}
This section was just created to show how to stop a preceding sub-
section, section or chapter. Note that chapters are only available in
books, not articles.

\makeindex % create the index

\end{document}
```

While there is certainly a lot more to be learned about LaTeX, this should provide
enough of a start for using it with `knitr`. A great reference is the "Not So Short
Introduction to LaTeX," which can be found at `http://tobi.oetiker.ch/lshort/`
`lshort.pdf`.

23.3   Using `knitr` with LaTeX

Writing a LaTeX document with R code is fairly straightforward. Regular text is written
using normal LaTeX conventions and the R code is delineated by special commands. All R
code is preceded by `<<label-name,option1='value1',option2='value2'>>=`
and is followed by `@`. While editing, RStudio nicely colors the background of the editor
according to what is being written, LaTeX or R code. This is seen in Figure 23.1, and is
called a "chunk."

These documents are saved as `.Rnw` files. During the knitting process an `.Rnw` file is
converted to a `.tex` file, which is then compiled to a PDF. If using the console, this is
accomplished by calling the `knit` function, passing the `.Rnw` file as the first argument. In
RStudio this is done by clicking the 📄 **Compile PDF** button in the toolbar or pressing
`Ctrl+Shift+I` on the keyboard.

Chunks are the workforce of `knitr` and are essential to understand. A typical use is to
show both the code and results. It is possible to do one or the other, or neither as well, but

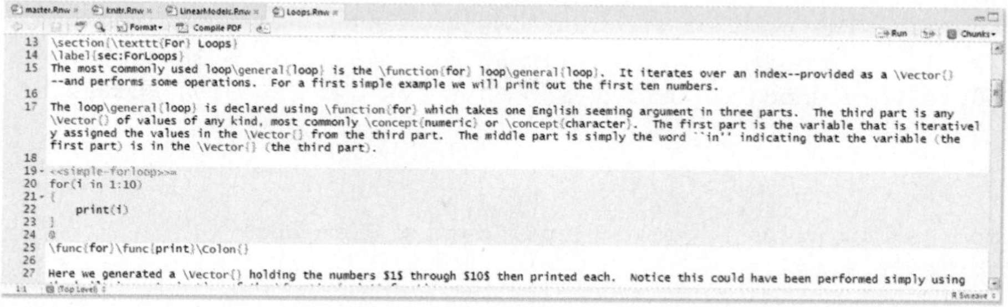

Figure 23.1   Screenshot of LaTeX and R code in RStudio text editor. Notice that the code section is gray.

for now we will focus on getting code printed and evaluated. Suppose we want to illustrate loading `ggplot2`, viewing the head of the `diamonds` data, and then fitting a regression. The first step is to build a chunk.

```
<<diamonds-model>>=
# load ggplot
require(ggplot2)

# load and view the diamonds data
data(diamonds)
head(diamonds)

# fit the model
mod1 <- lm(price ~ carat + cut, data=diamonds)
# view a summary
summary(mod1)
@
```

This will then print both the code and the result in the final document as shown next.

```
> # load ggplot
> require(ggplot2)
>
> # load and view the diamonds data
> data(diamonds)
> head(diamonds)
```

	carat	cut	color	clarity	depth	table	price	x	y	z
1	0.23	Ideal	E	SI2	61.5	55	326	3.95	3.98	2.43
2	0.21	Premium	E	SI1	59.8	61	326	3.89	3.84	2.31
3	0.23	Good	E	VS1	56.9	65	327	4.05	4.07	2.31

```
4  0.29    Premium     I     VS2   62.4     58     334 4.20 4.23 2.63
5  0.31       Good     J     SI2   63.3     58     335 4.34 4.35 2.75
6  0.24 Very Good      J    VVS2   62.8     57     336 3.94 3.96 2.48


>
> # fit the model
> mod1 <- lm(price ~ carat + cut, data = diamonds)
> # view a summary
> summary(mod1)


Call:
lm(formula = price ~ carat + cut, data = diamonds)

Residuals:
     Min        1Q   Median        3Q      Max
-17540.7    -791.6    -37.6     522.1  12721.4

Coefficients:
              Estimate Std. Error  t value Pr(>|t|)
(Intercept)   -2701.38      15.43 -175.061  < 2e-16 ***
carat          7871.08      13.98  563.040  < 2e-16 ***
cut.L          1239.80      26.10   47.502  < 2e-16 ***
cut.Q          -528.60      23.13  -22.851  < 2e-16 ***
cut.C           367.91      20.21   18.201  < 2e-16 ***
cut^4            74.59      16.24    4.593 4.37e-06 ***
---
Signif. codes:  0 '***' 0.001 '**' 0.01 '*' 0.05 '.' 0.1 ' ' 1

Residual standard error: 1511 on 53934 degrees of freedom
Multiple R-squared:  0.8565,    Adjusted R-squared:  0.8565
F-statistic: 6.437e+04 on 5 and 53934 DF,  p-value: < 2.2e-16
```

So far, the only thing supplied to the chunk was the label, in this case "diamonds-model." It is best to avoid periods and spaces in chunk labels. Options can be passed to the chunk to control display and evaluation and are entered after the label, separated by commas. Some common `knitr` chunk options are listed in Table 23.2. These options can be strings, numbers, TRUE/FALSE or any R object that evaluates to one of these.

Displaying images is made incredibly easy with `knitr`. Simply running a command that generates a plot inserts the image immediately following that line of code, with further code and results printed after that.

The following chunk will print 1 + 1 followed by the result, `plot(1:10)` followed by an image, and 2 + 2 followed by the result.

Table 23.2   Common knitr Chunk Options

Option	Effect
eval	Results printed when TRUE
echo	Code printed when TRUE
include	When FALSE, code is evaluated but neither the code nor results are printed.
cache	If the code has not changed, the results will be available but not evaluated again in order to save compilation time.
fig.cap	Caption text for images. Images will automatically be put into a special figure environment and be given a label based on the chunk label.
fig.scap	The short version of the image caption to be used in the list of captions
out.width	Width of displayed image
fig.show	Controls when images are shown. 'as.is' prints them when they appear in code and 'hold' prints them all at the end.
dev	Type of image to be printed, such as .png, .jpg, etc.
engine	knitr can handle code in other languages like Python, BASH, Perl, C++ and SAS.
prompt	Specifies the prompt character put before lines of code. If FALSE, there will be no prompt.
comment	For easier reproducibility, result lines can be commented out.

```
<<inline-plot>>=
1 + 1
plot(1:10)
2 + 2
@
```

```
> 1 + 1

[1]  2

> plot(1:10)
```

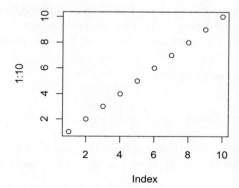

```
> 2 + 2
```

```
[1] 4
```

Adding the `fig.cap` option will put the image in a figure environment, which gets placed in a convenient spot with a caption. Running the same chunk with `fig.cap` set to `"Simple plot of the numbers 1 through 10."` will display 1 + 1 followed by the result, `plot(1:10)`, and then 2 + 2 followed by the result. The image, along with the caption, will be place where there is room, which very well could be in between lines of code. Setting `out.width` to `'.75\\linewidth'` (including the quote marks) will make the image's width 75% of the width of the line. While `\linewidth` is a LATEX command, because it is in an R string the backslash (\\) needs to be escaped with another backslash. The resulting plot is shown in Figure 23.2.

```
<<figure-plot,fig.cap="Simple plot of the numbers 1 through 10.",
fig.scap="Simple plot of the numbers 1 through 10",
out.width='.75\\linewidth'>>=
1 + 1
plot(1:10)
2 + 2
@
```

```
> 1 + 1
```

```
[1] 2
```

```
> plot(1:10)
```

```
> 2 + 2
```

```
[1] 4
```

This just scratches the surface of what is possible with LATEX and `knitr`. More information can be found on Yihui's site at `http://yihui.name/knitr/`. When using `knitr` it is considered good form to use a formal citation of the form `Yihui Xie (2013). knitr: A general-purpose package for dynamic report generation in R. R package version 1.2`. Proper citations can be found, for some packages, using the `citation` function.

```
> citation(package = "knitr")
```

```
To cite the 'knitr' package in publications use:

  Yihui Xie (2013). knitr: A general-purpose package for
  dynamic report generation in R. R package version 1.4.1.
```

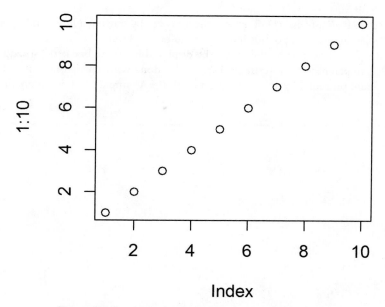

Figure 23.2 Simple plot of the numbers 1 through 10.

Yihui Xie (2013) Dynamic Documents with R and knitr. Chapman and Hall/CRC. ISBN 978-1482203530

Yihui Xie (2013) knitr: A Comprehensive Tool for Reproducible Research in R. In Victoria Stodden, Friedrich Leisch and Roger D. Peng, editors, Implementing Reproducible Computational Research. Chapman and Hall/CRC. ISBN 978-1466561595

23.4 Markdown Tips

While LaTeX is a great tool for composing a book or an article, an easier tool is Markdown, which is ideal for Web sites and presentations.[1] It is a simplified version of HTML that does away with the tedium typically involved in writing a Web page. There is also much less structure in Markdown than in LaTeX, meaning less control but easier writing.

Line breaks are created by leaving a blank line between blocks of text. Italics can be generated by putting an underscore (_) on both sides of a word, and bold is generated by putting two underscores on each side. Lists are created by putting each element on its own

---

1. LaTeX can produce presentations using Beamer but Markdown slide shows, as seen in Section 23.6, are quicker to build and allow for more interactivity.

line starting with an asterisk (*). Text is made a header by starting a line with a pound symbol (#), the number of pounds indicating the header level.

Links are created by putting the text to be displayed in square brackets ([ ]) and the linked URL in parentheses. Inserting images is also done with square brackets and parentheses and preceded by an exclamation mark (!). A sample Markdown document is shown next.

```
# Title - Also a Header 1

_this will be italicized_

_ _this will be bolded_ _

## Header 2

Build a list

* Item 1
* Item 2
* Item 3

This is a link

[My Website](http://www.jaredlander.com)

## Another Header 2

This inserts an image

![Alt text goes in here](location-of-image.png)

#### Header 4
```

RStudio provides a handy quick reference guide to Markdown, accessed by clicking the
MD button in the toolbar.

23.5 Using `knitr` and Markdown

The work flow for writing Markdown documents is similar to that for LaTeX documents: Normal text (flavored with Markdown) is written and R code is put in chunks. The style of the chunks is different but the idea is the same. A file that contains both Markdown and R code is saved as an `.Rmd` file, and then knitted to a Markdown file (`.md`), which is compiled to an HTML file. In the console this is done with the `knit` function, and in RStudio with the ⟨Knit HTML⟩ button or `Ctrl+Shift+H`.

Chunks for Markdown documents start with ```` ```{r label-name, ```` `option1='value1',option2='value2'}` and end with ```` ``` ````. Otherwise, everything else is the same with exceptions for HTML conventions such as `out.width='75%'` as opposed to `out.width='.75\linewidth'`. Following is the same chunk from earlier, but modified to meet the conventions needed for a Markdown document.

```
```{r figure-plot,fig.cap="Simple plot of the numbers 1 through 10.",
fig.scap="Simple plot of the numbers 1 through 10",
out.width='.75\\linewidth'}
1 + 1
plot(1:10)
2 + 2
```
```

23.6 pandoc

Creating reproducible presentations without leaving the friendly confines of the R environment has long been possible using LaTeX's Beamer mode, which creates a PDF where each page is a slide. However, writing all that LaTeX code can be unnecessarily time consuming. A simpler option is to write a Markdown document and compile it into an HTML5 slide show using pandoc, a great conversion utility written by John MacFarlane that is used from the command line.

Before it can be used, pandoc must be downloaded and installed from `http://johnmacfarlane.net/pandoc/installing.html`.

Pandoc can be used to convert files from one type to another. In our example we convert from Markdown to HTML5, in particular the slidy slide show format. (Other slide formats, such as s5, dzslides and slideous, are available.)

Slides are indicated by the header command (#), which also provides the slide title. While there are varying levels of headers, the highest level header in the deck that is immediately followed by content is used for slide titles. This can be overwritten by setting the `--slide-level` option when calling pandoc, which will be seen later. An example scenario would be using header 1 (#) to create sections, header 2 (##) to create subsections and header 3 (###) to create slides.

The first three lines of the Markdown file should each start with a percent symbol (%). The first is the title of the talk, the second is the author's name and the third is the date. These are used to create the title slide.

Aside from these caveats, and a few others, regular Markdown should be used. An example slide show code follows.

```
% Example Slideshow
% Jared P. Lander
% April 14th, 2013


# First Section


### First Slide in First Section
A list of things to cover
* First Item
* Second Item
* Third Item


### Some R Code
The code below will generate some results and a plot.

```{r figure-plot,fig.cap="Simple plot of the numbers 1 through 10.",
fig.scap="Simple plot of the numbers 1 through 10",out.width='50%',
fig.show='hold'}
1 + 1
plot(1:10)
2 + 2
```


Second Section

First Subsection

Another Slide
Some more information goes here

Second Subsection

Some Links
[My Website](http://www.jaredlander.com)

[R Bloggers](http://www.r-bloggers.com)
```

Running `knit` on this file, or pressing the ⚗ **Knit HTML** button or `Ctrl+Shift+H` creates both an `.md` file and an `.html` file. Pandoc should be used on the `.md` file, which we will call `example.md`, with the following line of code from the command line.

```
pandoc -s -S --toc -t slidy --self-contained
    --slide-level 3 example.md -o output.html
```

This calls pandoc on `example.md` and creates `output.html` with a number of options. `-s` builds a stand-alone file, `-S` runs it in smart mode, `--toc` creates a table of contents, `-t slidy` makes the final product a slidy slide show, `--self-contained` puts all of the content into a single HTML file with no other files needed (even images are encoded directly into the file), `--slide-level 3` means header 3 creates new slides, `example.md` specifies the input file and `-o output.html` provides the name for the output file.

This two-step process of generating the knitted Markdown file using `knit` (or the button or keyboard shortcut) and then going to the command line to run the preceding pandoc command can be tedious and error prone. Fortunately, at least for RStudio users, an option can be set to make this a one-step process. The following change to the R options makes the Knit button use pandoc for the conversion from Markdown to HTML.

```
> options(rstudio.markdownToHTML = function(inputFile, outputFile)
+ {
+ system(paste(
+ "pandoc -s -S --webtex --toc -t slidy --self-contained --slide-level 3",
+ shQuote(inputFile), "-o", shQuote(outputFile))
+ )
+ }
+ )
```

Now using the Knit button goes straight to the slide show format, which will even show up in the RStudio preview window.

Another alternative to using pandoc is the `slidify` package, written by Ramnath Vaidyanathan from McGill University. It uses a somewhat different syntax than pandoc but has a lot more power, and it even automatically changes the functionality of the Knit button in RStudio. Chunks of R code are still written as usual.

23.7 Conclusion

Writing reproducible, and maintainable, documents and slide shows from within R has never been easier, thanks to Yihui's `knitr` package. It allows seamless integration of R code, with results including images and either LaTeX or Markdown text.

On top of that, the RStudio IDE is a fantastic text editor. This entire book was written using `knitr` from within RStudio, without ever having to use Microsoft Word or a LaTeX editor.

Chapter 24

Building R Packages

As of late-July 2013, there were 4,714 packages on CRAN and another 671 on Bioconductor, with more being added daily. In the past, building a package had the potential to be mystifying and complicated but that is no longer the case, especially when using Hadley Wickham's devtools package.

All packages submitted to CRAN (or Bioconductor) must follow specific guidelines, including the folder structure of the package, inclusion of DESCRIPTION and NAMESPACE files and proper help files.

24.1 Folder Structure

An R package is essentially a folder of folders, each containing specific files. At the very minimum there must be two folders, one called R where the included functions go, and the other called man where the documentation files are placed. It used to be that the documentation had to be be written manually, but thanks to roxygen2 that is no longer necessary, as is seen in Section 24.3. Starting with R 3.0.0, CRAN is very strict in requiring that all files must end with a blank line and that code examples must be shorter than 105 characters.

In addition to the R and man folders, other common folders are src for compiled code such as C++ and FORTRAN, data for data that is included in the package and inst for files that should be available to the end user. No files from the other folders are available in a human-readable form (except the INDEX, LICENSE and NEWS files in the root folder) when a package is installed. Table 24.1 lists the most common folders used in an R package.

24.2 Package Files

The root folder of the package must contain at least a DESCRIPTION file and a NAMESPACE file, which are described in Sections 24.2.1 and 24.2.2. Other files like NEWS, LICENSE and README are recommended but not necessary. Table 24.2 lists commonly used files.

Table 24.1   **Folders Used in R Packages**
(While there are other possible folders, these are the most common)

Folder	Explanation
R	Files containing R code. Filenames must end in .R, .S, .q, .r, or .s as an extension, with .r being the most common.
man	Documentation files ending in .Rd, one for each function in the R folder. These can be generated automatically using roxygen2.
src	Compiled code such as C/C++/FORTRAN
data	Data included in the package
inst	Files to be included in the installed package for the end user
test	Code that tests the functions in the R folder

Table 24.2   **Files Used in R Packages**
(While there are other possible files, these are the most common)

File	Explanation
DESCRIPTION	Package information including dependencies
NAMESPACE	List of functions exposed to end user and functions imported from other packages
NEWS	What has been updated in each version
LICENSE	Copyright information
README	Basic description of package

24.2.1 DESCRIPTION **File**

The DESCRIPTION file contains information about the package, such as its name, version, author and other packages it depends on. The information is entered, each on one line, as Item1: Value1. Table 24.3 lists a number of fields that are used in DESCRIPTION files.

The Package field specifies the name of the package. This is the name that appears on CRAN and how users access the package.

Type is a bit archaic; it can be either Package or one other type, Frontend, which is used for building a graphical front end to R and will not be helpful for building an R package of functions.

Title is a short description of the package. It should be relatively brief and cannot end in a period. Description is a complete description of the package, which can be several sentences long but no longer than a paragraph.

Table 24.3   Fields in the DESCRIPTION File

Field	Required	Explanation
Package	Yes	Name of package
Type	No	Just use `Package`
Title	Yes	Short description of package
Version	Yes	Current version: `v.s.ss`
Date	No	Latest build date
Author	Yes	Name of author
Maintainer	Yes	Author name and email address
Description	Yes	Complete description of package
License	Yes	License type
Depends	No	Comma separated list of packages to be loaded
Imports	No	Comma separated list of packages to use but not load
Suggests	No	Comma separated list of packages that are nice to have
Collate	No	List (no commas) of R files in the R directory in processing order
ByteCompile	No	If the package should be byte-compiled on installation

Version is the package version and usually consists of three period-separated integers; for example, 1.15.2. Date is the release date of the current version.

The Author and Maintainer fields are similar but both are necessary. Author can be multiple people, separated by commas, and Maintainer is the person in charge, or rather the person who gets complained to, and should be a name followed by an email address inside angle brackets (<>). An example is Maintainer: Jared P. Lander <packages@jaredlander.com>. CRAN is actually very strict about the Maintainer field and can reject a package for not having the proper format.

License information goes in the appropriately named License field. It should be either an abbreviation of one of the standard specifications such as GPL-2 or BSD or the string 'file LICENSE' referring to the LICENSE file in the package's root folder.

Things get tricky with the Depends, Imports and Suggests fields. Often a package requires functions from other packages. In that case the other package, for example, ggplot2, should be listed in either the Depends or Imports field as a comma-separated list. If ggplot2 is listed in Depends, then when the package is loaded so will ggplot2, and its functions will be available to functions in the package and to the end user. If ggplot2 is listed in Imports, then when the package is loaded ggplot2 will not be loaded, and its functions will be available to functions in the package but not the end user. Packages should be listed in one or the other, not both. Packages listed in either of these fields will be automatically installed from CRAN when the package is installed. If the package depends on a specific version of another package, then that package name should be followed by the version number in parentheses; for example, Depends: ggplot2 (>= 0.9.1). Packages that are needed for the examples in the documentation, vignettes or testing but are not necessary for the package's functionality should be listed in Suggests.

The Collate field specifies the R code files contained in the R folder. This will be populated automatically if the package is documented using roxygen2 and devtools.

A relatively new feature is byte-compilation, which can significantly speed up R code. Setting ByteCompile to TRUE will ensure the package is byte-compiled when installed by the end user.

The DESCRIPTION file from coefplot is shown next.

```
Package: coefplot

Type: Package

Title: Plots Coefficients from Fitted Models

Version: 1.1.9

Date: 2013-01-23

Author: Jared P. Lander

Maintainer: Jared P. Lander <packages@jaredlander.com>

Description: Plots the coefficients from a model object

License: BSD

LazyLoad: yes

Depends:

    ggplot2

Imports:

    plyr,

    stringr,

    reshape2,

    useful,

    scales,

    proto

Collate:

    'coefplot.r'

    'coefplot-package.r'

    'multiplot.r'

    'extractCoef.r'

    'buildPlottingFrame.r'
```

(Continues)

(*Continued*)

```
        'buildPlot.r'
        'dodging.r'
   ByteCompile: TRUE
```

24.2.2   NAMESPACE **File**

The NAMESPACE file specifies which functions are exposed to the end user (not all functions in a package should be) and which other packages are imported into the NAMESPACE. Functions that are exported are listed as export(multiplot) and imported packages are listed as import(plyr). Building this file by hand can be quite tedious, so fortunately roxygen2 and devtools can, and should, build this file automatically.

R has three object-oriented systems: S3, S4 and Reference Classes. S3 is the oldest and simplest of the systems and is what we will focus on in this book. It consists of a number of generic functions such as print, summary, coef and coefplot. The generic functions exist only to dispatch object-specific functions. Typing print into the console shows this.

```
> print
function (x, ...)
UseMethod("print")
<bytecode: 0x00000000081e2bb0>
<environment: namespace:base>
```

It is a single-line function containing the command UseMethod("print"), which tells R to call another function depending on the class of the object passed. These can be seen with methods(print). To save space we show only 20 of the results. Functions not exposed to the end user are marked with an asterisk (*). All of the names are print and the object class separated by a period.

```
> methods(print)

   [1]  print.aareg*              print.abbrev*
   [3]  print.acf*                print.AES*
   [5]  print.agnes*              print.anova
   [7]  print.Anova*              print.anova.gam
   [9]  print.anova.lme*          print.anova.loglm*
  [11]  print.aov*                print.aovlist*
  [13]  print.ar*                 print.Arima*
```

```
[15] print.arima0*                    print.arma*
[17] print.AsIs                       print.aspell*
[19] print.aspell_inspect_context*    print.balance*
 [ reached getOption("max.print") -- omitted 385 entries ]
```

```
Non-visible functions are asterisked
```

When print is called on an object, it then calls one of these functions depending on the type of object. For instance, a data.frame is sent to print.data.frame and an lm object is sent to print.lm.

These different object-specific functions that get called by generic S3 functions must be declared in the NAMESPACE in addition to the functions that are exported. This is indicated as S3Method(coefplot, lm) to say that coefplot.lm is registered with the coefplot generic function.

The NAMESPACE file from coefplot is shown next.

```
S3method(coefplot,default)

S3method(coefplot,glm)

S3method(coefplot,lm)

S3method(coefplot,rxGlm)

S3method(coefplot,rxLinMod)

S3method(coefplot,rxLogit)

S3method(extract.coef,default)

S3method(extract.coef,glm)

S3method(extract.coef,lm)

S3method(extract.coef,rxGlm)

S3method(extract.coef,rxLinMod)

S3method(extract.coef,rxLogit)

export(buildModelCI)

export(coefplot)

export(coefplot.default)

export(coefplot.glm)

export(coefplot.lm)

export(coefplot.rxGlm)

export(coefplot.rxLinMod)

export(coefplot.rxLogit)

export(collidev)
```

(Continues)

(Continued)

```
export(extract.coef)
export(multiplot)
export(plotcoef)
export(pos_dodgev)
import(ggplot2)
import(plyr)
import(proto)
import(reshape2)
import(scales)
import(stringr)
import(useful)
```

Even with a small package like `coefplot`, building the NAMESPACE file by hand can be tedious and error prone, so it is best to let `devtools` and `roxygen2` build it.

24.2.3 Other Package Files

The NEWS file is for detailing what is new or changed in each version. The three most recent entries in the `coefplot` NEWS file are shown next. Notice how it is good practice to thank people who helped with or inspired the update. This file will be available to the end user's installation.

Version 1.1.9

Refactoring of code to make new models easier to add.
For now this means certain functionality will be lost, such as the shortening of coefficient names, plot a factor variable numerically.

Version 1.1.8

Minor changes to plotting to reflect change in gpplot2_0.9.2.

Version 1.1.7

Thanks to Felipe Carrillo I have fixed a bug in multiplot. Previously, if multiple models with the same formula but different data.frames were inputed then they would all have the same name (even if specified with the "names" argument) and only one model would be plotted. This now works as expected, plotting all the models regardless of identical formulas.

The LICENSE file is for specifying more detailed information about the package's license and will be available to the end user's installation. The LICENSE file from coefplot is shown here.

> Copyright (c) 2013, under the Simplified BSD License.
> For more information on FreeBSD see: http://www.opensource.org/licenses/
> bsd-license.php
> All rights reserved.

The README file is purely informational and is not included in the end user's installation. Its biggest benefit may be for packages hosted on GitHub, where the README will be the information displayed on the project's home page.

24.3 Package Documentation

A very strict requirement for R packages to be accepted by CRAN is proper documentation. Each exported function in a package needs its own .Rd file that is written in a LaTeX-like syntax. This can be difficult to write for even simple functions like the following one.

```
> simple.ex <- function(x, y)
+ {
+     return(x * y)
+ }
```

Even though it has only two arguments and simply returns the product of the two, it has a lot of necessary documentation, shown here.

```
\name{simple.ex}

\alias{simple.ex}

\title{within.distance}

\usage{simple.ex(x, y)}

\arguments{

    \item{x}{A numeric}

    \item{y}{A second numeric}

}

\value{x times y}

\description{Compute distance threshold}

\details{This is a simple example of a function}
```

(Continues)

(Continued)

```
\author{Jared P. Lander}
\examples{
    simple.ex(3, 5)
}
```

Rather than taking this two-step approach, it is better to write function documentation along with the function. That is, the documentation is written in a specially commented out block right above the function, as shown here.

```
> #' @title simple.ex
> #' @description Simple Example
> #' @details This is a simple example of a function
> #' @aliases simple.ex
> #' @author Jared P. Lander
> #' @export simple.ex
> #' @param x A numeric
> #' @param y A second numeric
> #' @return x times y
> #' @examples
> #' simple.ex(5, 3)
> simple.ex <- function(x, y)
+ {
+     return(x * y)
+ }
```

Running `document` from `devtools` will automatically generate the appropriate `.Rd` file based on the block of code above the function. The code is indicated by `#'` at the beginning of the line. Table 24.4 lists a number of commonly used `roxygen2` tags.

Every argument must be documented with a `@param` tag, including the dots (...), which are written as `\dots`. There must be an exact correspondence between `@param` tags and arguments; one more or less will cause an error.

It is considered good form to show examples of a function's usage. This is done on the lines following the `@examples` tag. In order to be accepted by CRAN all of the examples must work without error. In order to show, but not run, the examples wrap them in `\dontrun{...}`.

Knowing the type of object is important when using a function, so `@return` should be used to describe the returned object. If the object is a list, the `@return` tag should be an itemized list of the form `\item{name a}{description a}\item{name b}{description b}`.

Help pages are typically arrived at by typing `?FunctionName` into the console. The `@aliases` tag uses a space-separated list to specify the names that will lead to a particular help file. For instance, using `@aliases coefplot plotcoef` will result in both `?coefplot` and `?plotcoef` leading to the same help file.

Table 24.4 **Tags Used in `roxygen2` Documentation of Functions**

Tag	Explanation
@param	The name of an argument and a short description
@inheritParams	Copies the @param tags from another function so that they do not need be to rewritten
@examples	Examples of the function being used
@return	Description of the object that is returned by the function
@author	Name of the author of the function
@aliases	Names by which a user can search for the function
@export	Lists the function as an export in the NAMESPACE file
@import	Lists a package as an import in the NAMESPACE file
@seealso	A list of other functions to see
@title	Title of help file
@description	Short description of the function
@details	Detailed information about the function
@useDynLib	Indicates that compiled source code will be used for the package
@S3Method	Declares functions that go with S3 generic functions

In order for a function to be exposed to the end user, it must be listed as an export in the NAMESPACE file. Using `@export FunctionName` automatically adds `export(FunctionName)` to the NAMESPACE file. Similarly, to use a function from another package, that package must be imported and `@import PackageName` adds `import(PackageName)` to the NAMESPACE file.

When building functions that get called by generic functions, such as `coefplot.lm` or `print.anova`, the `@S3method` tag should be used. `@S3method GenericFunction Class` adds `S3method(GenericFunction,class)` to the NAMESPACE file. When using `@S3method` it is a good idea to also use `@method` with the same arguments. This is shown in the following function.

```
> #' @title print.myClass
> #' @aliases print.myClass
> #' @method print myClass
> #' @S3method print myClass
> #' @export print.myClass
> #' @param x Simple object
> #' @param ... Further arguments to be passed on
> #' @return The top 5 rows of x
> print.myClass <- function(x, ...)
+ {
+     class(x) <- "list"
```

```
+       x <- as.data.frame(x)
+       print.data.frame(head(x, 5))
+ }
```

24.4 Checking, Building and Installing

Building a package used to require going to the command prompt and using commands like R CMD check, R CMD build and R CMD INSTALL (in Windows it is Rcmd instead of R CMD), which required being in the proper directory, knowing the correct options and other bothersome time wasters. Thanks to Hadley Wickham, this has all been made much easier and can be done from within the R console.

The first step is to make sure a package is properly documented by calling document. The first argument is the path to the root folder of the package as a string. (If the current working directory is the same as the root folder, then no arguments are even needed. This is true of all the devtools functions.) This builds all the necessary .Rd files, the NAMESPACE file and the Collate field of the DESCRIPTION file.

```
> require(devtools)
> document()
```

After the package is properly documented, it is time to check it. This is done using check with the path to the package as the first argument. This will make note of any errors or warnings that would prevent CRAN from accepting the package. CRAN can be very strict, so it is essential to address all the issues.

```
> check()
```

Building the package is equally simple using the build function, which also takes the path to the package as the first argument. By default it builds a .tar.gz—a collection of all the files in the package—that still needs to be built into a binary that can be installed in R. It is portable in that it can be built on any operating system. The binary argument, if set to TRUE, will build a binary that is operating system specific. This can be problematic if compiled source code is involved.

```
> build()
> build(binary = TRUE)
```

Other functions to help with the development process are install, which rebuilds and loads the package, and load_all, which simulates the loading of the package and NAMESPACE.

Another great function, not necessarily for the development process so much as for getting other people's latest work, is install_github, which can install an R package directly from a GitHub repository. There are analogous functions for installing from BitBucket (install_bitbucket) and Git (install_git) in general.

For instance, to get the latest version of `coefplot` the following code should be run. By the time of publication this might no longer be the the the latest version.

```
> install_github(repo = "coefplot", username = "jaredlander",
+                 ref = "survival")
```

Sometimes an older version of a package on CRAN is needed, which under normal circumstances is hard to do without downloading source packages manually and building them. However, `install_version` was recently added to `devtools`, allowing a specific version of a package to be downloaded from CRAN, built and installed.

24.5   Submitting to CRAN

The best way to get a package out to the R masses is to have it on CRAN. Assuming the package passed the check using `check` from `devtools`, it is ready to be uploaded to CRAN using the new Web uploader (as opposed to using FTP) at `http://xmpalantir.wu.ac.at/cransubmit/`. The `.tar.gz` file is the one to upload. After submission, CRAN will send an email requiring confirmation that the package was indeed uploaded by the maintainer. Alternatively, the package can be uploaded by anonymous FTP to `ftp://CRAN.R-project.org/incoming/` with an email sent to Uwe Ligges at ligges@statistik.tu-dortmund.de and to cran@r-project.org. The subject line *must* be of the format `CRAN Upload: PackageName PackageVersion`. The name of the package is case sensitive and must match the name of the package in the `DESCRIPTION` file. The body of the message does not have to follow any guidelines, but should be polite and include the words "thank you" somewhere, because the CRAN team puts in an incredible amount of effort despite not getting paid.

24.6   C++ Code

Sometimes R code is just not fast enough (even when byte-compiled) for a given problem and a compiled language must be used. R's foundation in C and links to FORTRAN libraries (digging deep enough into certain functions, such as `lm`, reveals that the underpinnings are written in FORTRAN) makes incorporating those languages fairly natural. `.Fortran` is used for calling a function written in FORTRAN and `.Call` is used for calling C and C++ functions.[1] Even with those convenient functions, knowledge of either FORTRAN or C/C++ is still necessary, as is knowledge of how R objects are represented in the underlying language.

Thanks to Dirk Eddelbuettel and Romain François, integrating C++ code has become much easier using the `Rcpp` package. It handles a lot of the scaffolding necessary to make C++ functions callable from R. Not only did they make developing R packages with C++ easier, but they also made running ad hoc C++ possible.

---

1. There is also a `.C` function, although despite much debate it is generally frowned upon.

A number of tools are necessary for working with C++ code. First, a proper C++ compiler must be available. To maintain compatibility it is best to use gcc.

Linux users should already have gcc installed and should not have a problem, but they might need to install g++.

Mac users need to install Xcode and might have to manually select g++. The compiler offered on Mac generally lags behind the most recent version available, which has been known to cause some issues.

Windows users should actually have an easy time getting started, thanks to RTools developed by Brian Ripley and Duncan Murdoch. It provides all necessary development tools, including gcc and make. The proper version, depending on the installed version of R, can be downloaded from http://cran.r-project.org/bin/windows/Rtools/ and installed like any other program. It installs gcc and makes the Windows command prompt act more like a BASH terminal. If building packages from within R using devtools and RStudio (which is the best way now), then the location of gcc will be determined from the operating system's registry. If building packages from the command prompt, then the location of gcc must be put at the very beginning of the system PATH like c:\Rtools\bin;c:\Rtools\gcc-4.6.3\bin;C:\Users\Jared\ Documents\R\R-3.0.0\bin\x64.

A LaTeX distribution is needed for building package help documents and vignettes. Table 23.1 lists the primary distributions for the different operating systems.

24.6.1 sourceCpp

To start, we build a simple C++ function for adding two vectors. Doing so does not make sense from a practical point of view because R already does this natively and quickly, but it will be good for illustrative purposes. The function will have arguments for two vectors and return the element-wise sum. The // [[Rcpp::export]] tag tells Rcpp that the function should be exported for use in R.

```cpp
#include <Rcpp.h>
using namespace Rcpp;

// [[Rcpp::export]]
NumericVector vector_add(NumericVector x, NumericVector y)
{
    // declare the result vector
    NumericVector result(x.size());

    // loop through the vectors and add them element by element
    for(int i=0; i<x.size(); ++i)
    {
        result[i] = x[i] + y[i];
    }
```

```
        return(result);
}
```

This function should be saved in a `.cpp` file (for example, `vector_add.cpp`) or as a `character` variable so it can be sourced using `sourceCpp`, which will automatically compile the code and create a new R function with the same name that, when called, executes the C++ function.

```
> require(Rcpp)
> sourceCpp("vector_add.cpp")
```

Printing the function shows that it points to a temporary location where the compiled function is currently stored.

```
> vector_add

function (x, y)
.Primitive(".Call")(<pointer: 0x0000000066e81710>, x, y)
```

The function can now be called just like any other R function.

```
> vector_add(x = 1:10, y = 21:30)

 [1] 22 24 26 28 30 32 34 36 38 40

> vector_add(1, 2)

[1] 3

> vector_add(c(1, 5, 3, 1), 2:5)

[1] 3 8 7 6
```

JJ Allaire (the founder of RStudio) is responsible for `sourceCpp`, the `//` `[[Rcpp::export]]` shortcut and a lot of the magic that simplifies using C++ with R in general. Rcpp maintainer Dirk Eddelbuettel cannot stress enough how helpful Allaire's contributions have been.

Another nice feature of Rcpp is the syntactic sugar that allows C++ code to be written like R. Using sugar we can rewrite `vector_add` with just one line of code.

```
#include <Rcpp.h>
using namespace Rcpp;

// [[Rcpp::export]]
NumericVector vector_add(NumericVector x, NumericVector y)
```

```
{
    return(x + y);
}
```

The syntactic sugar allowed two `vectors` to be added just as if they were being added in R.

Because C++ is a strongly typed language, it is important that function arguments and return types be explicitly declared using the correct type. Typical types are `NumericVector`, `IntegerVector`, `LogicalVector`, `CharacterVector`, `DataFrame` and `List`.

24.6.2 Compiling Packages

While `sourceCpp` makes ad hoc C++ compilation easy, a different tactic is needed for building R packages using C++ code. The C++ code is put in a `.cpp` file inside the `src` folder. Any functions preceded by `// [[Rcpp::export]]` will be converted into end user facing R functions when the package is built using `build` from `devtools`. Any roxygen2 documentation written above an exported C++ function will be used to document the resulting R function.

The `vector_add` function should be rewritten using roxygen2 and saved in the appropriate file.

```
# include <Rcpp.h>
using namespace Rcpp;

//' @title vector_add
//' @description Add two vectors
//' @details Adding two vectors with a for loop
//' @author Jared P. Lander
//' @export vector_add
//' @aliases vector_add
//' @param x Numeric Vector
//' @param y Numeric Vector
//' @return a numeric vector resulting from adding x and y
//' @useDynLib ThisPackage
// [[Rcpp::export]]
NumericVector vector_add(NumericVector x, NumericVector y)
{
    NumericVector result(x.size());

    for(int i=0; i<x.size(); ++i)
    {
        result[i] = x[i] + y[i];
```

```
    }

    return(result);
}
```

The magic is that Rcpp compiles the code, and then creates a new `.R` file in the R folder with the corresponding R code. In this case it builds the following.

```
> # This file was generated
> # by Rcpp::compileAttributes Generator token:
> # 10BE3573-1514-4C36-9D1C-5A225CD40393
>
> #' @title vector_add
> #' @description Add two vectors
> #' @details Adding two vectors with a for loop
> #' @author Jared P. Lander
> #' @export vector_add
> #' @aliases vector_add
> #' @param x Numeric Vector
> #' @param y Numeric Vector
> #' @useDynLib RcppTest
> #' @return a numeric vector resulting from adding x and y
> vector_add <- function(x, y)
+ {
+     .Call("RcppTest_vector_add", PACKAGE = "RcppTest", x, y)
+ }
```

It is simply a wrapper function that uses `.Call` to call the compiled C++ function.

Any functions that are not preceded by `// [[Rcpp::export]]` are available to be called from within other C++ functions, but not from R, using `.Call`. Specifying a name attribute in the export statement—like `// [[Rcpp::export(name="NewName")]]`—causes the resulting R function to be called that name. Functions that do not need an R wrapper function automatically built, but need to be callable using `.Call`, should be placed in a separate `.cpp` file where `// [[Rcpp::interfaces(cpp)]]` is declared and each function that is to be user accessible is preceded by `// [[Rcpp::export]]`.

In order to expose its C++ functions, a package's NAMESPACE must contain `useDynLib(PackageName)`. This can be accomplished by putting the `@useDynLib PackageName` tag in any of the roxygen2 blocks. Further, if a package uses Rcpp the DESCRIPTION file must list Rcpp in both the LinkingTo and Depends fields. The LinkingTo field also allows easy linking to other C++ libraries such as RcppArmadillo, bigmemory and BH (Boost).

The src folder of the package must also contain Makevars and Makevars.win files to help with compilation. The following examples were automatically generated using Rcpp.package.skeleton and should be sufficient for most packages.

First the `Makevars` file:

```
## Use the R_HOME indirection to support installations of multiple
## R version
PKG_LIBS = `$(R_HOME)/bin/Rscript -e "Rcpp:::LdFlags()"`


## As an alternative, one can also add this code in a file 'configure'
##
##    PKG_LIBS=`${R_HOME}/bin/Rscript -e "Rcpp:::LdFlags()"`
##
##    sed -e "s|@PKG_LIBS@|${PKG_LIBS}|" \
##        src/Makevars.in > src/Makevars
##
## which together with the following file 'src/Makevars.in'
##
##    PKG_LIBS = @PKG_LIBS@
##
## can be used to create src/Makevars dynamically. This scheme is more
## powerful and can be expanded to also check for and link with other
## libraries.  It should be complemented by a file 'cleanup'
##
##    rm src/Makevars
##
## which removes the autogenerated file src/Makevars.
##
## Of course, autoconf can also be used to write configure files. This is
## done by a number of packages, but recommended only for more advanced
## users comfortable with autoconf and its related tools.
```

Now the `Makevars.win` file:

```
## Use the R_HOME indirection to support installations of multiple
## R version
PKG_LIBS = $(shell "${R_HOME}/bin${R_ARCH_BIN}/Rscript.exe" -e
"Rcpp:::LdFlags()")
```

This just barely scratches the surface of Rcpp, but should be enough to start a basic package that relies on C++ code. Packages containing C++ code are built the same as any other package, preferably using build in devtools.

24.7 Conclusion

Package building is a great way to make code portable between projects and to share it with other people. A package purely built with R code only requires working functions that can pass the CRAN check using check and proper help files that can be easily built by including roxygen2 documentation above functions and calling document. Building the package is as simple as using build. Packages with C++ should use Rcpp.

Appendix A

Real-Life Resources

One of the greatest aspects of R is the surrounding community, both online and in person. This includes Web resources like Twitter and Stack Overflow, meetups and textbooks.

A.1 Meetups

Meetup.com is a fantastic resource for finding like-minded people and learning experiences for just about anything including programming, statistics, video games, cupcakes and beer. They are so pervasive that as of late-July 2013, there were over 126,000 meetup groups in nearly 200 countries. Data meetups draw particularly large crowds and usually take the format of socializing, a talk for 45 to 90 minutes, and then more socializing. Meetups are not only great for learning, but also for hiring or getting hired.

R meetups are very common, although some are starting to rebrand from R meetups to statistical programming meetups. Some popular meetups take place in New York, Chicago, Boston, Amsterdam, Washington D.C., San Francisco, London, Cleveland, Singapore and Melbourne. The talks generally show cool features in R, new packages or software or just an interesting analysis performed in R. The focus is usually on programming more than statistics. Table A.1 lists a number of popular meetups but it is an incredibly short list compared to how many meetups exist for R.

Machine Learning meetups are also good for finding presentations on R, although they will not necessarily be as focused on R. They are located in many of the same cities as R meetups and draw similar speakers and audiences. These meetups tend more toward the academic than focusing on programming.

The third core meetup type is Predictive Analytics. While they may seem similar to Machine Learning meetups, they cover different material. The focus is somewhere in between that of R and Machine Learning meetups. And yes, there is significant overlap in the audiences for these meetups.

Other meetup groups that might be of interest are data science, big data and data visualization.

Table A.1   R and Related Meetups

City	Group Name	URL
New York	New York Open Statistical Programming Meetup	`http://www.meetup.com/nyhackr/`
New York	NYC Stats Programming Master Classes	`http://www.meetup.com/datascienceclasses/`
Washington, DC	Statistical Programming DC	`http://www.meetup.com/stats-prog-dc/`
Amsterdam	amst-R-dam	`http://www.meetup.com/amst-R-dam/`
Boston	Greater Boston useR Group (R Programming Language)	`http://www.meetup.com/Boston-useR/`
San Francisco	Bay Area useR Group (R Programming Language)	`http://www.meetup.com/R-Users/`
Chicago	Chicago R User Group (Chicago RUG) Data and Statistics	`http://www.meetup.com/ChicagoRUG/`
London	LondonR	`http://www.meetup.com/LondonR/`
Singapore	R User Group Singapore (RUGS)	`http://www.meetup.com/R-User-Group-SG/`
Cleveland	Greater Cleveland R Group	`http://www.meetup.com/Cleveland-useR-Group/`
Melbourne	Melbourne Users of R Network (MelbURN)	`http://www.meetup.com/MelbURN-Melbourne-Users-of-R-Network/`
Connecticut	Connecticut R Users Group	`http://www.meetup.com/Conneticut-R-Users-Group/`
New York	NYC Machine Learning Meetup	`http://www.meetup.com/NYC-Machine-Learning/`
Tel Aviv	Big Data & Data Science Israel	`http://www.meetup.com/Big-Data-Israel/`

A.2 Stack Overflow

Sometimes when confronted with a burning question that cannot be solved alone, a good place to turn for help is Stack Overflow (`http://stackoverflow.com/`). Previously the R mailing list was the best, or only, online resource for help, but that has since been superseded by Stack Overflow.

The site is a forum for asking programming questions where both questions and answers are voted on by users and people can build reputations as experts. This is a very quick way to get answers for even difficult questions.

Common search tags related to R are `r`, `statistics`, `rcpp`, `ggplot2`, `shiny` and other statistics-related terms.

Many R packages these days are hosted on GitHub, so if a bug is found and confirmed, the best way to address it is not on Stack Overflow but on the GitHub issues list for the package.

A.3   Twitter

Sometimes just a quick answer is needed that would fit in 140 characters. In this case, Twitter is a terrific resource for R questions ranging from simple package recommendations to code snippets.

To reach the widest audience, it is important to use hash tags such as `#rstats`, `#ggplot2`, `#knitr`, `#rcpp`, `#nycdatamafia` and `#statistics`.

Great people to follow are @drewconway, @mikedewar, @harlanharris, @xieyihui, @hadleywickham, @jeffreyhorner, @revodavid, @eddelbuettel, @johnmyleswhite, @Rbloggers, @statalgo, @ProbablePattern, @CJBayesian, @RLangTip, @cmastication, @nyhackr and this book's author, @jaredlander.

A.4   Conferences

There are a number of conferences where R is either the focus or receives a lot of attention. There are usually presentations about or involving R, and sometimes classes that teach something specific about R.

The main one is the appropriately named useR! conference, which is a yearly event at rotating locations around the world. The Web site is at http://www.r-project.org/conferences.html.

R in Finance is a yearly conference that takes place in Chicago and is coorganized by Dirk Eddelbuettel. It is quantitatively focused and heavy in advanced math. The Web site is at http://www.rinfinance.com/.

Other statistics conferences that are worth attending are the Joint Statistical Meetings organized by the American Statistical Association (http://www.amstat.org/meetings/jsm.cfm) and Strata New York (http://strataconf.com/strata2013/public/content/home).

Data Gotham is a very new data science conference organized by some of the leaders of the data science community like Drew Conway and Mike Dewar. The Web site is at http://www.datagotham.com/.

A.5   Web Sites

Being that R is an open-source project with a strong community, it is only appropriate that there is a large ecosystem of Web sites devoted to it. Most of them are maintained by people who love R and want to share their knowledge. Some are exclusively focused on R and some only partially.

Besides http://www.jaredlander.com/, some of our favorites are R-Bloggers (http://www.r-bloggers.com/), Zero Intelligence Agents (http://drewconway.com/zia/), R Enthusiasts (http://gallery.r-enthusiasts.com/), Rcpp Gallery (http://gallery.rcpp.org/), Revolution Analytics (http://blog.revolutionanalytics.com/), Andrew Gelman's site (http://andrewgelman.com/), John Myles White's site (http://www.johnmyleswhite.com/) and chartsnthings from *The New York Times* graphics department (http://chartsnthings.tumblr.com/).

A.6   Documents

Over the years, a number of very good documents have been written about R and made freely available.

An Introduction to R, by William N. Venables, David M. Smith and The R Development Core Team, has been around since S, the precursor of R, and can be found at `http://cran.r-project.org/doc/manuals/R-intro.pdf`.

The R Inferno is a legendary document by Patrick Burns that delves into the nuances and idiosyncrasies of the language. It is available as both a printed book and a free PDF. Its Web site is `http://www.burns-stat.com/documents/books/the-r-inferno/`.

Writing R Extensions is a comprehensive treatise on building R packages that expands greatly on Chapter 24. It is available at `http://cran.r-project.org/doc/manuals/R-exts.html`.

A.7   Books

For a serious dose of statistics knowledge, textbooks offer a huge amount of material. Some are old fashioned and obtuse, while others are modern and packed with great techniques and tricks.

Our favorite statistics book—which happens to include a good dose of R code—is *Data Analysis Using Regression and Multilevel/Hierarchical Models* by Andrew Gelman and Jennifer Hill. The first half of the book is a good general text on statistics with R used for examples. The second half of the book focuses on Bayesian models using BUGS; the next edition is rumored to use STAN.

For advanced machine learning techniques, but not R code, Hastie, Tibshirani and Friedman's landmark *The Elements of Statistical Learning: Data Mining, Inference, and Prediction* details a number of modern algorithms and models. It delves deep into the underlying math and explains how the algorithms, including the Elastic Net, work.

Other books, not necessarily textbooks, have recently came out that are focused primarily on R. *Machine Learning for Hackers* by Drew Conway and John Myles White uses R as a tool in learning some basic machine learning algorithms. *Dynamic Documents with R and knitr* by Yihui Xie is an in-depth look at `knitr` and expands greatly on Chapter 23. Integrating C++ into R, discussed in Section 24.6, receives full treatment in *Seamless R and C++ Integration with Rcpp* by Dirk Eddelbuettel.

A.8   Conclusion

Making use of R's fantastic community is an integral part of learning R. Person-to-person opportunities exist in the form of meetups and conferences. The best online resources are Stack Overflow and Twitter. And naturally there are a number of books and documents available both online and in bookstores.

Appendix B

Glossary

ACF	See autocovariance function
AIC	See Akaike Information Criterion
AICC	See Akaike Information Criterion Corrected
Akaike Information Criterion	Measure of model fit quality that penalizes model complexity
Akaike Information Criterion Corrected	Version of AIC with greater penalty for model complexity
Analysis of variance	See ANOVA
Andersen–Gill	Survival analysis for modeling time to multiple events
ANOVA	Test for comparing the means of multiple groups; the test can only detect if there is a difference between any two groups, it cannot tell which ones are different from which others
Ansari–Bradley test	Nonparametric test for the equality of variances between two groups
AR	See autoregressive
ARIMA	Like an ARMA model but it includes a parameter for the number of differences of the time series data
ARMA	See Autoregressive Moving Average
array	Object that holds data in multiple dimensions
autocorrelation	When observations in a single variable are correlated with previous observations
Autocovariance function	The correlation of a time series with lags of itself
Autoregressive	Time series model that is a linear regression of the current value of a time series against previous values
Autoregressive Moving Average	Combination of AR and MA models

average	While generally held to be the arithmetic mean, average is actually a generic term that can mean any number of measures of centrality such as the mean, median or mode
Bartlett test	Parametric test for the equality of variances between two groups
BASH	A command line processor in the same vein as DOS; mainly used on Linux and MAC OS X though there is an emulator for Windows
basis functions	Functions whose linear combination make up other functions
basis splines	Basis functions used to compose splines
Bayesian	Type of statistics where prior information is used to inform the model
Bayesian Information Criterion	Similar to AIC but with an even greater penalty for model complexity
Beamer	LaTeX document class for producing slide shows
Bernoulli Distribution	Probability distribution for modeling the success or failure of an event
Beta Distribution	Probability distribution for modeling a set of possible values on a finite interval
BIC	See Bayesian Information Criterion
Binomial Distribution	Probability distribution for modeling the number of successful independent trials with identical probabilities of success
Bioconductor	Repository of R packages for the analysis of genomic data
BitBucket	Online Git repository
Boost	Fast C++ library
Bootstrap	A process in which data are resampled repeatedly, and a statistic is calculated for each resampling to form an empirical distribution for that statistic
Boxplot	A graphical display of one variable where the middle 50% of the data are in a box, and there are lines reaching out to 1.5 times the Interquartile Range and dots representing outliers
BUGS	Probabilistic programming language specializing in Bayesian computations
byte-compilation	The process of turning human readable code into machine code that runs faster

C	A fast, low-level programming language; R is written primarily in C
C++	A fast, low-level programming language that is similar to C
Cauchy Distribution	Probability distribution for the ratio of two Normal random variables
censored data	Data with unknown information, such as the occurrence of an event after a cutoff time
character	Data type for storing text
Chi-squared Distribution	The sum of k squared standard normal distributions
chunk	Piece of R code inside a LaTeX or Markdown document
class	Type of an R object
Classification	Determining the class membership of data
Clustering	Partitioning data into groups
Coefficient	A multiplier associated with a variable in an equation; in statistics this is typically what is being estimated by a regression
Coefficient plot	A visual display of the coefficients and standard errors from a regression
Comprehensive R Archive Network	See CRAN
Confidence Interval	A range within which an estimate should fall a certain percent of time
correlation	The strength of the association between two variables
covariance	A measure of the association between two variables; the strength of the relationship is not necessarily indicated
Cox proportional hazards	Model for survival analysis where predictors have a multiplicative effect on the survival rate
CRAN	The central repository for all things R
cross-validation	A modern form of model assessment where the data are split into k discrete folds, and a model is repeatedly fitted on all but one and used to make predictions on the holdout fold
Data Gotham	Data science conference in New York
data munging	The process of cleaning, correcting, aggregating, joining and manipulating data to prepare it for analysis
Data Science	The confluence of statistics, machine learning, computer engineering, visualization and social skills
data.frame	The main data type in R, similar to a spreadsheet with tabular rows and columns

`data.table`	A high speed extension of data.frames
database	Store of data, usually in relational tables
`Date`	Data type for storing dates
DB2	Enterprise level database from IBM
Debian	Linux Distribution
decision tree	Modern technique for performing nonlinear regression or classification by iteratively splitting predictors
Degrees of freedom	For some statistic or distribution, this is the number of observations minus the number of parameters being estimated
density plot	Display showing the probability of observations falling within a sliding window along a variable of interest
deviance	A measure of error for generalized linear models
drop-in deviance	The amount by which deviance drops when adding a variable to a model; a general rule of thumb is that deviance should drop by two for each term added
DSN	Data source connection used to describe communication to a data source, often a database
dzslides	HTML5 slide show format
EDA	See Exploratory Data Analysis
Elastic Net	New algorithm that is a dynamic blending of lasso and ridge regressions, which is great for predictions and dealing with high dimensional datasets
Emacs	Text editor popular among programmers
ensemble	Method of combining multiple models to get an average prediction
Excel	The most commonly used data analysis tool in the world
expected value	Weighted mean
Exploratory Data Analysis	Visually and numerically exploring data to get a sense of it before performing rigorous analysis
Exponential Distribution	Probability distribution often used to model the amount of time until an event occurs
F-test	Statistical test often used for comparing models, as with the ANOVA
F Distribution	The ratio of two Chi-Squared Distributions, often used as the null distribution in analysis of variance
`factor`	Special data type for handling character data as an integer value with character labels; important for including categorical data in models

fitted values	Values predicted by a model, mostly used to denote predictions made on the same data used to fit the model
formula	Novel interface in R that allows specification of a model using convenient mathematical notation
FORTRAN	High-speed, low-level language; much of R is written in FORTRAN
FRED	Federal Reserve Economic Data
FTP	file transfer protocol
g++	Open source compiler for C++
GAM	See Generalized Additive Models
Gamma Distribution	Probability distribution for the time one has to wait for n events to occur
gamma regression	GLM for response data that are continuous, positive and skewed, such as auto insurance claims
Gap statistic	Measure of clustering quality, which compares the within-cluster dissimilarity for a clustering of the data with that of a bootstrapped sample of data
GARCH	See Generalized Autoregressive Conditional Heteroskedasticity
Gaussian Distribution	See Normal Distribution
gcc	Family of open-source compilers
Generalized Additive Models	Models that are formed by adding a series of smoother functions fitted on individual variables
Generalized Autoregressive Conditional Heteroskedasticity	Time series method that is more robust to extreme values of data
Generalized Linear Models	Family of regression models that model non-normal response data such as binary and count data
Geometric Distribution	Probability distribution for the number of Bernoulli trials required before the first success occurs
Git	Popular version control standard
GitHub	Online Git repository
GLM	See Generalized Linear Models
Hadoop	Framework for distributing data and computations across a grid of computers
Hartigan's Rule	Measure of clustering quality, which compares the within-cluster sum of squares for a clustering of k clusters and one with $k + 1$ clusters
heatmap	Visual display where the relationship between two variables is visualized as a mix of colors

Hierarchical Clustering	Form of clustering where each observation belongs to a cluster, which in turn belongs to a larger cluster and so on until the whole dataset is represented
histogram	Display of the counts of observations falling in discrete buckets of a variable of interest
HTML	Hypertext Markup Language; used for creating Web pages
Hypergeometric Distribution	Probability distribution for drawing k successes out of a possible N items, of which K are considered successes
hypothesis test	Test for the significance of a statistic that is being estimated
IDE	See Integrated Development Environment
indicator variables	Binary variables representing one level of a categorical variable; also called dummy variables
inference	Drawing conclusions on how predictors affect a response
integer	Data type that is only whole numbers, either positive, negative or zero
Integrated Development Environment	Software with features to make programming easier
Intel Matrix Kernel Library	Optimized matrix algebra library
interaction	The combined effect of two or more variables in a regression
intercept	Constant term in a regression; literally, the point where the best fit line passes through the y-axis; it is generalized for higher dimensions
Interquartile Range	The third quartile minus the first quartile
inverse link function	Function that transforms linear predictors to the original scale of the response data
inverse logit	Transformation needed to interpret logistic regression on the 0/1 scale; scales any number to be between 0 and 1
IQR	See Interquartile Range
Java	Low-level programming language
Joint Statistical Meetings	Conference for statisticians
JSM	See Joint Statistical Meetings
K-means	Clustering that divides the data into k discrete groups as defined by some distance measurement
K-medoids	Similar to K-means except it handles categorical data and is more robust to outliers
knitr	Modern package for interweaving R code with LaTeX or Markdown

Lasso Regression	Modern regression using an L1 penalty to perform variable selection and dimension reduction
LaTeX	High-quality typesetting program especially well suited for mathematical and scientific documents and books
`level`	A unique value in a `factor` variable
linear model	Model that is linear in the coefficients
link function	Function that transforms response data so it can be modeled with a GLM
Linux	Open source operating system
`list`	Robust data type that can hold any arbitrary data types
log	The inverse of an exponent; typically the natural log in statistics
Log-normal Distribution	Probability distribution whose log is Normally distributed
`logical`	Data type that takes on the values TRUE or FALSE
Logistic Distribution	Probability distribution used primarily for logistic regression
Logistic Regression	Regression for modeling a binary response
logit	The opposite of the inverse logit; transforms numbers between 0 and 1 to the real numbers
loop	Code that iterates through some index
MA	See Moving Average
Mac OS X	Apple's proprietary operating system
Machine Learning	Modern, computationally heavy statistics
MapReduce	Paradigm where data are split into discrete sets, computed on, and then recombined in some fashion
Markdown	Simplified formatting syntax used to produce elegant HTML documents in a simple fashion
Matlab	Expensive commercial software for mathematical programming
`matrix`	Two-dimensional data type
matrix algebra	Algebra performed on matrices, which greatly simplifies the math
maximum	Largest value in a set of data
mean	Mathematical average; typically either arithmetic (traditional average) or weighted
mean squared error	Quality measure for an estimator; the average of the squares of the differences between an estimator and the true value

median	Middle number of an ordered set of numbers; when there are an even number of numbers, the median is the mean of the middle two numbers
Meetup	A Web site that facilitates real-life social interaction for any number of interests; particularly popular in the data field
memory	Also referred to as RAM, this is where the data that R analyzes is stored while being processed; this is typically the limiting factor on the size of data that R can handle
Microsoft Access	Lightweight database from Microsoft
Microsoft SQL Server	Enterprise-level database from Microsoft
minimum	Smallest value in a set of data
Minitab	GUI based statistical package
missing data	A big problem in statistics, this is data that is not available to compute for any one of a number of reasons
MKL	See Intel Matrix Kernel Library
model complexity	Primarily how many variables are included in the model; overly complex models can be problematic
model selection	Process of fitting the optimal model
Moving Average	Time series model that is a linear regression of the current value of a time series against current and previous residuals
multicolinearity	When one column in a matrix is a linear combination of any other columns
multidimensional scaling	Projecting multiple dimensions into a smaller dimensionality
Multinomial Distribution	Probability distribution for discrete data that can take on any of k classes
Multinomial Regression	Regression for discrete response that can take on any of k classes
multiple comparisons	Doing repeated tests on multiple groups
multiple imputation	Advanced process to fill in missing data using repeated regressions
Multiple Regression	Regression with more than one predictor
MySQL	Open source database
NA	Value that indicates missing data
namespace	Convention where functions belong to specific packages; helps solve conflicts when multiple functions have the same name

natural cubic spline	Smoothing function with smooth transitions at interior breakpoints and linear behavior beyond the endpoints of the input data
Negative Binomial Distribution	Probability distribution for the number of trials required to obtain r successes; this is often used as the approximate distribution for pseudopoisson regression
nonlinear least squares	Least squares regression (squared error loss) with nonlinear parameters
nonlinear model	Model where the variables do not necessarily have a linear relationship, such as decision trees and GAMs
nonparametric model	Model where the response does not necessarily follow the regular GLM distributions such as Normal, Logistic or Poisson
Normal Distribution	The most common probability distribution that is used for a wide array of phenomenon; the familiar bell curve
NULL	A data concept that represents nothingness
null hypothesis	The assumed true value in hypothesis tests
numeric	Data type for storing numeric values
NYC Data Mafia	Informal term for the growing prevalence of data scientists in New York City
NYC Open Data	Initiative to make New York City government data transparent and available
Octave	Open-source version of Matlab
ODBC	See Open Database Connectivity
Open Database Connectivity	Industry standard for communicating data to and from a database
ordered factor	Character data where one level can be said to be greater or less than another level
overdispersion	When data show more variability than indicated by the theoretical probability distribution
p-value	The probability, if the null hypothesis were correct, of getting as extreme, or more extreme, a result
PACF	See partial autocovariance function
paired t-test	Two-sample t-test where every member of one sample is paired with a member of a second sample
PAM	See Partitioning Around Medoids
pandoc	Software for easy conversion of documents among various formats such as Markdown, HTML, LaTeX and Microsoft Word
parallel	In computational context, the running of multiple instructions simultaneously to speed computation

parallelization	The process of writing code to run in parallel
partial autocovariance function	The amount of correlation between a time series and lags of itself that is not explained by previous lags
Partioning Around Medoids	Most common algorithm for K-medoids clustering
PDF	Common document format most often opened with Adobe Acrobat Reader
Penalized Regression	Form of regression where a penalty term prevents the coefficients from growing too large
Perl	Scripting language commonly used for text parsing
Poisson Distribution	Probability Distribution for count data
Poisson Regression	GLM for response data that are counts, such as number of accidents, number of touchdowns or number of ratings for a pizzeria
POSIXct	Date-time data type
prediction	Finding the expected value of response data for given values of predictors
predictor	Data that are used as inputs into a model and explain and/or predict the response
prior	Bayesian statistics use prior information, in the form of distributions for the coefficients of predictors, to improve the model fit
Python	Scripted language that is popular for data munging
Q-Q plot	Visual means of comparing two distributions by seeing if the quantiles of the two fall on a diagonal line
quantile	Value, corresponding to a specified percentage, for a set of numbers, below which that percent of numbers falls
quartile	The 25th quantile
Quasipoisson Distribution	Distribution (actually the Negative Binomial) used for estimating count data that are overdispersed
R-Bloggers	Popular site from Tal Galili that aggregates blogs about R
R Console	Where R commands are entered and results are shown
R Core Team	Group of 20 prime contributors to R who are responsible for its maintenance and direction
R Enthusiasts	Popular R blog by Romain François
R in Finance	Conference in Chicago about using R for finance
RAM	See memory
Random Forest	Ensemble method that builds multiple decision trees, each with a random subset of predictors, and combines the results to make predictions

Rcmdr	GUI interface to R
Rcpp Gallery	Online collection of Rcpp examples
Rdata	File format for storing R objects on disk
regression	Method that analyzes the relationship between predictors and a response; the bedrock of statistics
regression tree	See decision tree
Regular Expressions	String pattern matching paradigm
regularization	Method to prevent overfitting of a model, usually by introducing a penalty term
residual sum of squares	Summation of the squared residuals
residuals	Difference between fitted values from a model and the actual response values
response	Data that are the outcome of a model and are predicted and/or explained by the predictors
Revolution R	Commercial distribution of R developed by Revolution Analytics designed to be faster and more stable and scale better
Ridge Regression	Modern regression using an L2 penalty to shrink coefficients for more stable predictions
RSS	See residual sum of squares
RStudio	Powerful and popular open-source IDE for R
RTools	Set of tools needed in Windows for integrating C++, and other compiled code, into R
S	Statistical language developed at Bell Labs that was the precursor to R
S3	Basic object type in R
S4	Advanced object type in R
s5	HTML5 slide show format
SAS	Expensive commercial scripting software for statistical analysis
scatterplot	Two-dimensional display of data where each point represents a unique combination of two variables
shapefile	Common file format for map data
shrinkage	Reducing the size of coefficients to prevent overfitting
Simple Regression	Regression with one predictor, not including the intercept
slideous	HTML5 slide show format
slidy	HTML5 slide show format

slope	Ratio of a line's rise and run; in regression this is represented by the coefficients
smoothing spline	Spline used for fitting a smooth trend to data
spline	Function f that is a linear combination of N functions (one for each unique data point) that are transformations of the variable x
SPSS	Expensive point-and-click commercial software for statistical analysis
SQL	Database language for accessing or inserting data
Stack Overflow	Online resource for programming questions
STAN	Next generation probabilistic programming language specializing in Bayesian computations
standard deviation	How far, on average, each point is from the mean
standard error	Measure of the uncertainty for a parameter estimate
Stata	Commercial scripting language for statistical analysis
stationarity	When the mean and variance of a time series are constant for the whole series
stepwise selection	Process of choosing model variables by systematically fitting different models and adding or eliminating variables at each step
Strata	Large data conference
survival analysis	Analysis of time to event, such as death or failure
SUSE	Linux Distribution
SVN	Older version control standard
Sweave	Framework for interweaving R code with LATEX; has been superceded by `knitr`
Systat	Commercial statistical package
t-statistic	Ratio where the numerator is the difference between the estimated mean and the hypothesized mean, and the denominator is the standard error of the estimated mean
t-test	Test for the value of the mean of a group or the difference between the means of two groups
t Distribution	Probability distribution used for testing a mean with a student t-test
tensor product	A way of representing transformation functions of predictors, possibly measured on different units
text editor	Program for editing code that preserves the structure of the text
TextPad	Popular text editor
time series	Data where the order and time of the data are important to its analysis

ts	Data type for storing time series data
Two Sample t-test	Test for the difference of means between two samples
Ubuntu	Linux Distribution
UltraEdit	Popular text editor
Uniform Distribution	Probability distribution where every value is equally likely to be drawn
USAID Open Government	Initiative to make U.S. Aid data transparent and available
useR!	Conference for R users
VAR	See Vector Autoregressive Model
variable	R object; can be data, functions, any object
variance	Measure of the variability, or spread, of the data
vector	A collection of data elements, all of the same type
Vector Autoregressive Model	Multivariate times series model
version control	Means of saving snapshots of code at different time periods for easy maintenance and collaboration
vim	Text editor popular among programmers
violin plot	Similar to a boxplot except that the box is curved, giving a sense of the density of the data
Visual Basic	Programming language for building macros, mostly associated with Excel
Visual Studio	IDE produced by Microsoft
Wald test	Test for comparing models
Weibull Distribution	Probability distribution for the lifetime of an object
weighted mean	Mean where each value carries a weight, allowing the numbers to have different effects on the mean
weights	Importance given to observations in data so that one observation can be valued more or less than another
Welch t-test	Test for the difference in means between two samples where the variances of each sample can be different
white noise	Essentially random data
Windows Live Writer	Desktop blog publishing application from Microsoft
Xcode	Apple's IDE
xkcd	Web comic by Randall Munroe, beloved by statisticians, physicists and mathematicians
XML	Extensible Markup Language; often used to descriptively store and transport data
xts	Advanced data type for storing time series data

List of Figures

List of Tables

General Index

Index of Functions

Index of Packages

Index of People

A

Allaire, JJ, 15, 386
Arnold, Jeffrey, 96

B

Burns, Patrick, 394

C

Chambers, John, 304
Conway, Drew, 393, 394

D

Dewar, Mike, 393

E

Eddelbuettel, Dirk, 29, 384, 386, 393, 394
Efron, Bradley, 262

F

Fisher, Ronald A., 202
Friedman, Jerome, 29, 271, 394

G

Galton, Francis, 211
Gelman, Andrew, 29, 33, 50, 85, 210, 256, 291, 293, 393, 394

Gentleman, Robert, xv
Gosset, William, 200

H

Hartigan, J.A., 340
Hastie, Trevor, 29, 271, 304, 394
Hill, Jennifer, 50, 291, 394

I

Ihaka, Ross, xv

K

Knuth, Donald, 359

L

Ligges, Uwe, 384

M

MacFarlane, John, 369
Madigan, David, 340
Murdoch, Duncan, 385

P

Pearson, Karl, 206

R

Reich, Josh, 117
Ripley, Brian, 257, 385
Romain, François, 384, 404

S

Smith, David M., 394

T

Tibshirani, Robert, 29, 271, 304, 394
Tufte, Edward, 89, 97
Tukey, John, 85

V

Vaidyanathan, Ramnath, 371
Venables, William N., 394

W

White, John Myles, 393, 394
Wickham, Hadley, 29, 85, 94, 117, 124, 129, 144, 145, 149, 155, 169, 373, 383

X

Xie, Yihui, 29, 359, 366, 371, 394

Data Index

- prêt : éco : ~~14k€~~
  ~~17k€~~ 22,5 k€

- ⓘ : - 3× derniers bulletins
  - avantages potentiels
  - → par mail
  - "CASDEN"
  - prêts à taux réduit, etc.
  - adhérir pour moi aussi

① → PEL aussi

PEL

~~1066~~ × 206
~~1038~~ × 194

~~18,284~~